THE HISTORY OF
THE NORFOLK REGIMENT

HIS MAJESTY KING EDWARD VII.
Colonel-in-Chief of The Norfolk Regiment, February 1, 1907. (*Frontispiece*)

THE HISTORY OF THE NORFOLK REGIMENT

BY

F. LORAINE PETRE, O.B.E.

AUTHOR OF "NAPOLEON'S CAMPAIGN IN POLAND," "NAPOLEON AT BAY"
ETC., ETC.

20th June, 1685, to 3rd August, 1914

The Naval & Military Press Ltd

Published by

The Naval & Military Press Ltd
Unit 10 Ridgewood Industrial Park,
Uckfield, East Sussex,
TN22 5QE England

Tel: +44 (0) 1825 749494
Fax: +44 (0) 1825 765701

www.naval-military-press.com
www.military-genealogy.com
www.militarymaproom.com

In reprinting in facsimile from the original, any imperfections are inevitably reproduced and the quality may fall short of modern type and cartographic standards.

MAPS (FULL PAGE)

	FACING PAGE
SPAIN, PORTUGAL, AND SOUTH OF FRANCE	47
AFGHANISTAN—KHYBER PASS TO KABUL	284
PARTS OF TRANSVAAL AND ORANGE FREE STATE	401

SKETCHES IN TEXT

	PAGE
BATTLE OF THE BOYNE	16
LIMERICK—SIEGES OF 1690 AND 1691	21
ATHLONE—SIEGE OF 1691	24
BATTLE OF AUGHRIM	27
SIEGE OF HAVANA	72
CAMPAIGN OF SARATOGA	87
MARTINIQUE	108
ST. LUCIA	114
GUADELOUPE	116
GRENADA	127
NORTH HOLLAND	137
ACTION OF ROLIÇA	158
BATTLE OF VIMEIRO	164
BUSACO—MOVEMENT OF 9TH FOOT	206
BATTLE OF SALAMANCA	233

	PAGE
BATTLE OF VITTORIA	247
SAN SEBASTIAN	252
WELLINGTON'S PASSAGE OF THE BIDASSOA	266
BATTLE OF THE NIVE	271
STORMING OF THE KHYBER PASS	290
BATTLE OF FEROZESHAH	316
BATTLE OF SOBRAON	322
SEBASTOPOL—ATTACK OF EYRE'S BRIGADE	335
PAARDEBERG	405

LIST OF ILLUSTRATIONS

VOL. I

1. His Majesty King Edward VII	*Frontispiece*	
2. General William Steuart	CHAPTER	II
3. Havana, 1762	,,	VI
3A. Havana, 1762 (Plan)	,,	VI
4. Earl Ligonier, K.B.	,,	VII
5. The Walpole Shakos	,,	IX
6. Sir Armine Wodehouse, Bart.	,,	IX
7. The Stuart Monument	,,	X
8. Burial of Sir John Moore	,,	XI
From a Sketch by Stanley Barwell		
9. Colonel John Patteson	,,	XI
10. Colours in Action	,,	XII
11. Batalha, 1808	,,	XIII
12. Field-Marshal Lord Clyde, G.C.B.	,,	XV
13. Sir John Cameron, K.C.B.	,,	XVI
14. Sir John McCaskill, K.C.B., K.H.	,,	XVII
15. Sir Arthur Borton, G.C.B., G.C.M.G.	,,	XVIII
16. Sir Hambleton Custance, K.C.B.	,,	XIX
From a Sketch by Stanley Barwell		
17. Brigadier-General W. E. G. L. Bulwer, C.B., V.D.	,,	XIX

18. Major-General C. Elmhirst, C.B.	CHAPTER	XX
19. The 2nd Battalion, China, 1865; Japan, 1867	,,	XX
20. The 2nd Battalion, Kabul, 1879	,,	XX
21. Volunteer Review at Holkham, 1861	,,	XXI
22. The Lord Cranworth, V.D. *From a Sketch by Stanley Barwell*	,,	XXI
23. Norwich Volunteer Officers, 1863	,,	XXI
23A. Norwich Volunteer Officers, 1863 (Key)	,,	XXI
24. Colonel James Duff	,,	XXII
25. Colonel Henry Buxton, V.D.	,,	XXII
26. Private Charles Crampion, D.C.M.	,,	XXIII
27. Bloemfontein, 1906	,,	XXIII

CONTENTS

CHAPTER		PAGE
	PREFACE	xi
	BIBLIOGRAPHY	xiii
I.	THE RAISING OF THE REGIMENT AND ITS EARLY YEARS	1
II.	THE IRISH CAMPAIGNS, 1689–1691	9
III.	BREST, THE MEDITERRANEAN, AND FLANDERS, 1691–1703	32
IV.	THE WAR OF THE SPANISH SUCCESSION IN PORTUGAL AND SPAIN, 1704–1707	47
V.	SERVICE AT HOME, MINORCA, GIBRALTAR, AND THE EXPEDITION TO BELLEISLE, 1708–1762	57
VI.	THE SIEGE OF HAVANA—FLORIDA AND HOME SERVICE, 1762–1776	70
VII.	THE AMERICAN WAR—CANADA—SARATOGA—AND HOME SERVICE, 1776–1788	83
VIII.	THE WEST INDIES, 1788–1796	103
IX.	INCREASE OF PAY—MILITIA RECRUITS—THE 2ND AND 3RD BATTALIONS. THE EXPEDITIONS TO NORTH HOLLAND AND BREMEN, 1797–1804	133
X.	THE 1ST AND 2ND BATTALIONS IN ENGLAND AND PORTUGAL—ROLIÇA AND VIMEIRO, 1804–1808	153
XI.	THE 1ST BATTALION IN THE CORUNNA AND WALCHEREN CAMPAIGNS, 1808–1809	169
XII.	THE 2ND BATTALION IN PORTUGAL—THE PURSUIT OF SOULT, 1808–1809	191
XIII.	THE 1ST BATTALION IN THE PENINSULA—BUSACO AND TORRES VEDRAS, 1809–1810. THE 2ND BATTALION AT GIBRALTAR AND BARROSA, 1809–1811	198

CHAPTER		PAGE
XIV.	THE 1ST BATTALION IN THE PENINSULA—FUENTES DE OÑORO—BADAJOZ—SALAMANCA, 1810–1812	218
XV.	THE 1ST BATTALION IN THE PENINSULA—MADRID—THE RETREAT FROM BURGOS—VITTORIA—SAN SEBASTIAN, 1812–1813	238
XVI.	THE 1ST BATTALION, 1813–1827—CROIX DES BOUQUETS—THE NIVE—BAYONNE—CANADA—THE ARMY OF OCCUPATION	265
XVII.	THE 1ST BATTALION IN INDIA—FIRST KABUL CAMPAIGN, 1827–1842	284
XVIII.	THE 1ST BATTALION, 1843–1853—FIRST SIKH WAR—SERVICE IN ENGLAND, IRELAND, AND MALTA	310
XIX.	THE 1ST BATTALION IN THE CRIMEAN WAR	331
XX.	THE 1ST AND 2ND BATTALIONS, 1856–1881—IONIAN ISLANDS—JOWAKI CAMPAIGN—SECOND AFGHAN WAR	343
XXI.	THE MILITIA AND VOLUNTEER BATTALIONS TO 1881	368
XXII.	THE 1ST BATTALION, 1881–1914, AND THE 2ND BATTALION, 1881–1900	383
XXIII.	THE 2ND BATTALION IN THE SOUTH AFRICAN WAR AND INDIA	401
	INDEX	437

PREFACE

THIS record of the history of the Norfolk Regiment during two hundred and thirty-three years, since it was first raised as Colonel Cornwall's Regiment in 1685, has been rendered more difficult to prepare by the unfortunate loss of all regimental records in the wreck of the " Ariadne " transport in 1805. The record from 1685 to 1805 has been, as far as possible, reconstructed from documents preserved in the Public Record Office in London, in the War Office, and elsewhere. Unfortunately, when the regiment was in Ireland before 1805 there is very little to go on; for the English records do not deal with details of quarters and services in Ireland in those days, and the Irish records had perished in the burning of the Four Courts in Dublin before they could be searched for this history. Information as to these periods is therefore fragmentary and only to be gleaned from muster rolls in the War Office, and a few other documents. Fortunately, these periods of Irish service were generally in times when the country was not in more than its normal state of local disturbance. The Norfolk Regiment was not there in such times as those of the Rebellion of 1798 and the French landings.

In dealing with official documents the author has generally endeavoured to avoid wearying the reader with a mere transcript of lengthy letters and orders, and has given the sense of them, except where the actual wording is of importance. The list of authorities consulted will enable anyone who wishes to read the actual document to find it without much difficulty.

Beyond these few remarks it is unnecessary to do more than leave the result to the judgment of its readers.

The history has been prepared at the request of the officers of the regiment and the thanks of the author are due to the many officers and others of the regiment who have assisted him, whether by contribution of narratives or other information, or by revising his drafts of parts relating to operations in which they took part.

Outside the regiment the author must acknowledge with grateful thanks the assistance he has received from Lieutenant-Colonel Sir Arthur Leetham and other officials of the Royal United Service Institution, and for the use of the library of the Institution. To Major Parkyn, the Librarian, he is especially grateful for much assistance, particularly in such matters as uniforms and badges, subjects in which Major Parkyn is an expert.

In conclusion, thanks are due to Brigadier-General J. E. Edmonds, C.B., C.M.G., for allowing access to the records in his charge at the Historical Section of the Committee of Imperial Defence, and to his staff for their attention in putting up the documents required.

F. L. P.

BIBLIOGRAPHY

The following is a list of the principal authorities consulted or referred to :—

(I) PRINTED BOOKS, FILES OF NEWSPAPERS, COLLECTIONS, CUTTINGS, AND MANUSCRIPTS IN THE LIBRARY OF THE ROYAL UNITED SERVICE INSTITUTION AND ELSEWHERE, EXCEPT THOSE IN THE PUBLIC RECORD OFFICE.

Authority.	*Period or Subject for which Used.*
Allenby, Sir E. : Despatches	War in Palestine, 1917–1918, 4th 5th, and 12th Battalions.
Anderson, Col. : " History of the Cheshire Regiment "	Battle of the Boyne.
Annals of Ulster	Do. do.
Baker, Lieut., 1st Norfolk Regt. : " Report on Operations in Chin Hills " (Published by Government of India)	Operations in the Chin Hills, 1892.
Beatson : " Naval and Military Memoirs of Great Britain, 1727–1783 "	Siege of Havana, etc.
Belmas : " Journal des siéges, etc., dans la Peninsule, 1807–1814 "	Siege of San Sebastian.
Berwick, Duke of : " Memoirs "	Irish War and War of Spanish Succession.
Blakeney : " A Boy in the Peninsular War "	Peninsular War.

Authority.	Period or Subject for which Used.
Boyer: "History of the Reign of Queen Anne"	1702–1714.
"British Minor Expeditions, 1746-1814" (Published by War Office)	Belleisle (1761), Helder (1799), Walcheren (1809).
Burgoyne, Lt.-Gen. J.: "A State of the Expedition from Canada"	Saratoga Campaign.
Burgoyne, Lt.-Gen. J.: Orderly Book in Saratoga Campaign	Do. do.
Cannon: "Historical Records of the 9th Foot"	General History of Regiment, 1685–1847.
Candler: "The Long Road to Baghdad"	Mesopotamia, 1914–1918, 2nd Battalion.
Carleton: "Memoirs"	War of Spanish Succession.
Chester: "Westminster Abbey Registers"	Sketch of life of Colonel Steuart.
Commons, House of: Journals	War of Spanish Succession.
Cumming, J. S.: "A Six Year Diary"	1st Afghan War.
Dalrymple, Sir J.: "Memoirs of Great Britain and Ireland"	Early History of Regiment.
Dalton, C.: (a) "English Army Lists and Commission Registers, 1661–1714," (b) "George I's Army, 1714–1727"	Periods named in titles.
Davis, Col.: "History of the 2nd Queen's Regiment"	Irish War, 1689.
De Quincy: "Histoire militaire du régne de Louis le Grand"	Campaign in Flanders, 1702-1703.
Edmonds, Brig.-Gen.: "Operations in Belgium and France" (1st Vol. Official History)	1st Battalion in 1914.

Authority.	Period or Subject for which Used.
Entick, John: "General History of the late [seven years] War"	Siege of Havana.
Fortescue, Hon. J.: "History of the British Army"	1702–1815.
"Frontier and Overseas Expeditions from India" (Published by Government of India)	Jowaki Expedition, Chin Hills, etc.
Gleichen, Brig.-Gen. Count.: "The Doings of the 15th Infantry Brigade"	Great War in France, 1914–1915, 1st Battalion.
Gomm, Sir W.: Letters and Journals	Peninsular War, Helder, Bremen, etc.
Hadden: "Journal upon General Burgoyne's Expedition"	Saratoga Campaign.
Hale, Sergeant: "Diary in the Peninsular War"	Peninsular War.
Hall: "Costumes of the British Army, 1828–1830"	Uniforms.
Hanna, Col.: "The 2nd Afghan War"	2nd Afghan War.
Hardinge, Lord, and Gough, Sir H.: Despatches	1st Sikh War.
Harvey, Sir C.: "History of the 4th Battalion Norfolk Regt."	East Norfolk Militia.
Harvey, Lt.-Col. J. R.: Manuscript History of 4th Battalion (Territorial).	Volunteers. 4th Battalion in Great War.
Hay: "The Constitutional Force"	History of Militia.
Hussey, Brig.-Gen., and Inman, Major: "The 5th Division in the Great War"	War in Belgium and France, 1914–1918, 1st Battalion.
Irwin, Hastings: Manuscript Notes on Uniform, etc. (R.U.S.I. Library)	Uniforms.

Authority.	Period or Subject for which Used.
Kaye: "History of the War in Afghanistan"	1st Afghan War.
Lamb, Sergeant: Journal	Saratoga Campaign.
Leask and McCance: "Historical Records of the Royal Scots"	Uniforms.
Le Fleming: Family Papers, published by Royal Commission on Historical Records	Siege of Londonderry.
Luard: "History of Dress of the British Soldier"	Uniforms.
Luttrell, Narcissus: "Brief Relation of State Affairs, 1678–1714"	Period referred to in title.
Macaulay, Lord: "History of England"	Irish War, etc.
Malleson, Col. J. B.: "Decisive Battles of India"	First Sikh War.
Marden, Gen. T. O.: "A Short History of the 6th Division. August, 1914 to March, 1919"	The 9th Battalion in France.
Marlborough: Despatches	Campaign in Flanders, 1702, etc.
Maurice, Col.: "Official History of the War in South Africa"	South African War, 1899–1902.
Millan, J.: "List of the Forces of the Sovereigns of Europe," etc.	Uniforms.
Military Extracts in R.U.S.I. Library.	Various periods.
Military Manuscripts referred to in the Jackson Manuscripts (R.U.S.I. Library)	Do.
Milne: "Standards and Colours of the British Army"	Colours.

Authority.	Period or Subject for which Used.
Moore, James: "The British Army in Spain"	Corunna Campaign.
Mullenaux: "Journal of the Three Months' Royal Campaign in Ireland"	Irish War.
Murray, Sir A.: Despatches	Great War in Egypt and Palestine (4th, 5th, and 12th Battalions).
Napier: "History of the Peninsular War"	Peninsular War.
Neale, Dr. Adam: "Letters from Portugal"	Corunna retreat.
Nichols, Capt. G. H. F.: "The 18th Division in the Great War"	7th Battalion in France.
Norman, Capt. C. B.: "Battle Honours of the British Army"	Battle Honours.
Oman, Sir C.: (a) "History of the Peninsular War," (b) "Wellington's Army"	Peninsular War and Uniforms.
Parliamentary History	Various Periods.
Parnell, Col. Hon. A.: "The War of the Succession in Spain"	War of Spanish Succession.
"Representation of the Clothing of His Majesty's Household, etc."	Uniforms.
Sandes, Major E. W. C.: "Kut and Captivity with the 6th Indian Division"	Mesopotamia, etc., 1914-1916, 2nd Battalion.
San Felipe: "Commentarios"	War of Spanish Succession.
Shepherd, Col.: "History of the 2nd Battalion Norfolk Regiment"	General History of 2nd Battalion.

Authority.	Period or Subject for which Used.
Stacy, Lt.-Col. S. R.: "Narrative whilst in the Brahooee Camp, etc."	1st Afghan War (Istalif).
Story, Rev. G. W.: "History of the Campaign in Ireland"	Irish War, 1689–1691.
Townshend, Major-Gen. Sir C.: "My Campaign in Mesopotamia"	Mesopotamia, 1915–1916.
Trevelyan, G. O.: "The American Revolution"	Saratoga Campaign.
Walker, Rev. G.: "Siege of Londonderry"	Siege of Londonderry.
Walton, Col. Clifford: "History of the British Standing Army, 1660–1700"	Period named in title, and uniforms.
Wellington: Despatches and Supplementary Despatches.	Peninsular War.

Newspaper Files and Extracts, etc.

"The Times"	Various periods and subjects.
"United Service Gazette"	Do. do. do.
"Broad Arrow"	Do. do. do.
"Eastern Daily Press," Norwich	Do. do. do.
"Norwich Mercury"	Do. do. do.
"London Gazette"	Do. do. do.
"The Holy Boy"	Do. do. do.

Special Manuscripts

Sir Arthur Borton's Papers	1st Afghan War, 1st Sikh War, Crimea.
Col. Hare's Diary	Mounted Infantry in Mashonaland.

Information collected by Lt. R. D. Ambrose, D.C.M.

II. Records at Public Record Office, Chancery Lane, London

(a) *War Office Papers.* (W.O.)[1]

W.O. 1. In Letters. Includes despatches from officers commanding in the field, etc. None previous to 1756.

W.O. 3. Out Letters. Commander-in-Chief. Beginning in 1767. Miscellaneous, and letters to officers commanding in the field.

W.O. 4. Out Letters. Secretary at War. Miscellaneous, and letters to officers commanding in the field.

W.O. 5. Marching Orders. All movements of troops in England. In the case of the Norfolk and some other regiments the "Letters of Service" for the raising of the regiment are in these records.

W.O. 6. Out Letters. Secretary of State. Similar to W.O. 4, but for different period.

W.O. 8. Out Letters. Ireland, 1709–1823. Contain comparatively little useful information, as they do not deal with movements of troops in Ireland, though they show movements to and from that country.

W.O. 17. Monthly returns. Showing strength and disposition of regiments, but not before 1759.

W.O. 24. Establishments. Give all sanctioned establishments and changes therein down to 1846.

W.O. 25. Casualty returns. Only fairly complete. 1809–1844.

W.O. 26. Miscellany Books. Letters to Colonels, down to 1816, on various subjects. The "Letters of Service" for many regiments are in these.

W.O. 27. Inspection Returns from 1750. Much miscellaneous information as to strengths, posts, colours, etc.

Besides these, there are at the War Office a number of location and pay lists which are often useful, and occasionally give clues to whereabouts in Ireland, etc.

[1] The figure after W.O. indicates the number of the class of papers. The particular volume or paper required can be found, according to its date, in the catalogue.

(b) *Home Office Papers* (H.O.)

S.P.Dom. Domestic State Papers. Much miscellaneous information, especially in earlier days.

Cal.S.P. Calendar of State Papers. Only completed at present down to George I. Gives abstracts of State Papers.

King William's Chest. Papers kept in sealed bag by William III. Often very useful for his reign.

Military Entry Books. Miscellaneous orders and information.

Naval Entry Books. Information of various sorts, including return of troops from Brest in 1694.

(c) *Foreign Office Papers* (F.O.)

S.P.For. Foreign State Papers. Useful for correspondence in earlier days with overseas expeditions.

(d) *Colonial Office Papers* (C.O.)

C.O. 5. (No. 574). Correspondence with West Florida.

C.O. 101. Grenada 1795.

C.O. 117. Siege of Havana—Correspondence.

C.O. 318. West Indies Military Correspondence, 1793-1795. Tobago, Martinique, St. Lucia, Guadeloupe.

HISTORY OF THE NORFOLK REGIMENT

CHAPTER I

THE RAISING OF THE REGIMENT AND ITS EARLY YEARS

THE Norfolk Regiment, originally known as Colonel Cornwall's Regiment of Foot, and at a later date as the 9th Foot, or East Norfolk Regiment, was the second of the eight infantry regiments (8th to 15th) raised by James II on the pretext of suppressing Monmouth's rebellion in 1685. Before the regiment was organized and ready for service, the unfortunate Monmouth had been defeated at Sedgemoor and executed on Tower Hill.

Sacrificing strict accuracy for convenience, we shall generally speak of the regiment, until it acquired its present title in 1881, as the 9th, even in the century during which it was generally identified, not by a number or a territorial designation, but by the name of its colonel for the time being. A few regiments, such as the Queen's or the Princess Anne of Denmark's regiment, had a personal and permanent title from the beginning, but the majority had nothing to refer to but the ever-changing personality of their colonels. The tie to a particular officer for the time being was a poor one, unless he happened to be one of outstanding celebrity, and it was only as the traditions of a regiment were gradually built up on its achievements that a solid basis of esprit de corps came into existence. The basis became still firmer in later years when the territorial connexion was introduced and consolidated. In the days when the name of the colonel designated the regiment, it was often practically a family regiment. For instance, in the case of the 9th, we find, when Colonel Cornwall commanded, that there were five officers of his family in it, and in the long colonelcy of William Steuart no less than eleven Steuarts held commissions at one time.

The first commissions of the original officers of the regiment were all dated June 19, 1685. The Letters of Service addressed to Colonel Henry Cornwall (then a captain in the Royal Horse Guards), to his lieutenant-colonel (Sir John Morgan), and the other captains of companies in the new regiment are dated from June 20 to June 23, 1685. They are in the usual form, authorizing each to raise his own company "by beat of drum or otherwise." Each company was to consist of one hundred private soldiers, three sergeants, three corporals, and two drummers. As the men were raised they were to be produced to muster "to the intent that they may enter into our pay and entertainment." When the number of each company was complete it was to march to the general rendezvous of the regiment at Gloucester, and to depute a person or persons to receive, from the Ordnance, arms for the men and halberts for the sergeants. Magistrates, justices of the peace, constables and "others our officers" were required to render assistance where required. In those days the colonel, lieutenant-colonel, and major of a regiment of foot each commanded a company, and in the case of the colonel's company the lieutenant was styled captain-lieutenant. Though he drew no more pay than any other lieutenant, he was practically captain of his company. The colonel, lieutenant-colonel, and major drew pay in their capacities as such, and, in addition, the pay of an ordinary captain in respect of their own companies. Letters of Service were therefore issued to the following: Colonel Henry Cornwall, Lieutenant-Colonel Sir John Morgan, Major James Purcell, Captains Richard Kidley, John Powell, — Cox, John Booth, Jerom Bubb, Thomas Williams, Daniel Wicherly, and Sir Francis Edwards. Thus eleven companies were provided for.

With the suppression of Monmouth's Rebellion it was decided to reduce the strength of this and other regiments. On July 16, 1685, a general order requires all companies of foot (except the Guards and the Royal Regiment) to be reduced to sixty privates, besides officers. On

July 25th, a further reduction was made to fifty privates, two sergeants, three corporals, and one drummer. In preparation for this reduction, Colonel Cornwall had been ordered (July 18th) to disband three companies, "at his choice," and return their arms, drums, etc., to store. The result of these changes was that the establishment and pay stood thus :—

STAFF AND FIELD OFFICERS

	Pay per day.
	£ s. d.
1 Colonel, as Colonel	0 12 0
1 Lt.-Colonel, as Lt.-Colonel	0 7 0
1 Major, as Major	0 5 0
1 Chaplain	0 6 8
1 Surgeon, at 4s. ; 1 Mate, 2s. 6d.	0 6 6
1 Adjutant	0 4 0
1 Quartermaster and Marshal	0 4 0
Total Staff	£2 5 2

THE COLONEL'S COMPANY

1 The Colonel, as Captain	0 8 0
1 Captain-Lieutenant	0 4 0
1 Ensign	0 3 0
2 Sergeants, at 1s. 6d. each	0 3 0
3 Corporals, at 1s. each	0 3 0
1 Drummer	0 1 0
50 Privates, at 8d. each	1 13 4
Total Colonel's Company	£2 15 4
Nine more companies at same rate	24 18 0
Total pay per day	29 18 6
Total pay per annum	10,922 12 6

[1] After this, full details of the establishment at various periods will be found in the tables in Appendix II.

The total pay of the officers acting in a double capacity was:

	Per diem.			Per annum.		
	£	s.	d.	£	s.	d.
Colonel	1	0	0	365	0	0
Lieutenant-Colonel	0	15	0	273	15	0
Major	0	13	0	237	5	2[1]

The regiment, being ready, received orders, dated July 31, 1685, to march to Hounslow Heath from Gloucester. Later orders required the first march to be on August 22nd, arrival at Hounslow Heath 28th, whence the regiment was ordered on to Kingston-on-Thames.

The King took the opportunity to review his new regiment and to endeavour to ingratiate himself with it by flattering speeches and civilities. He looked to the army which he was building up to enforce his despotic ideas of government, and in later years he complained bitterly that, notwithstanding all he had done for his English troops, they deserted him.

On August 31st, the 9th was ordered to Berwick-on-Tweed, whence they were to detach a company (to be relieved monthly) to Holy Island.

At Berwick the regiment remained till an order of March 17, 1685, required it, on relief by the Princess Anne of Denmark's regiment, to march south to St. Albans. It was followed by Sir John Haggerston's independent company of grenadiers, which was temporarily attached to it.

After receiving a batch of recruits from Shrewsbury, it proceeded to the camp at Hounslow Heath, by order of May 22nd.

This great camp had been organized by James with the double object of reviewing his army and of inspiring London with a proper respect for it. It was held in two successive parts—the first of 6,760 infantry, the second of 10,560 cavalry, dragoons, and infantry.

Orders of June 11th sent the 9th to Portsmouth for the winter.

In July, 1686, one man per company was discharged, as a contribu-

---

[1] These figures by no means represent what the officers and men actually put in their pockets. The question of payments on receipt of commissions, stoppages, and the general difficulty of getting paid at all in those days is one which is common to the whole army and has been fully dealt with by Mr. Fortescue in his "History of the British Army." It is not one to be gone into in the history of any one regiment, seeing that all were affected alike.

tion towards two companies which King James was raising for service in New England. The 9th having left Hounslow, the men discharged were sent away and not replaced. Men so discharged from regiments still at Hounslow were impressed for the new service and sent to the Tower to await shipment.

From Portsmouth the regiment went, in May, 1687, to Bramley, in Surrey, and thence to the camp at Hounslow. This time another grenadier company—that commanded by Captain Henry Villiers—was attached permanently to the regiment, which now consisted of ten ordinary and one grenadier company. The establishment of the latter differed from that of the others only in the fact that instead of having a lieutenant on 4s. and an ensign on 3s. per diem, it had two lieutenants on 4s. each.

August, 1687, saw the regiment once more marching northwards to York, whence, in the middle of September, it was sent to Kingston-upon-Hull to work, under Lord Dartmouth, at the new fortifications. Here the men were to be billeted in private houses at 8d. per man weekly for lodging. Later on room was found to be available for 300 of them at public-houses at the same rate.

In December the regiment returned to York. The nominal roll of the officers in November, 1687, was as follows:—

Captains (11).	*Lieutenants* (12).	*Ensigns* (10).
Henry Cornwall (Col.)	John Cornwall	Jonathan Driver
James Purcell (Lt.-Col.)	(Capt.-Lt.)	Edward Cornwall
James Lacy (Major)	Herbert Herring	James Wynn*
Edward Cornwall	John Atkins*	Charles Stone
John Booth	William Atkinson	Richard Etheridge*
Jerom Bubb	John Tranter	Thomas Neagh*
Thomas Williams	Edmund Barry	Mortagh Obrian
Solomon Slater*	Alban Thomas	(? O'Brian)
Cyriac Cornwall	Richard Wingfield	Harry Hastings
Richard Lech	William Tatton*	George Ord*
(? Leech)*	Richard Fitzpatrick*	Thomas Waldron*
Henry Villiers (grenadiers)*	Thomas Love*, sen. } Grenadiers Thomas Love*, jun. }	

Chaplain.	*Adjutant.*
William Burton	Charles Stone
Surgeon.	*Quartermaster.*
William Thomas	William Bissell

All of these were in the regiment in 1685, except those marked.* The latter had joined in consequence of retirements or changes to other regiments. Sir John Morgan, the Lieutenant-Colonel of 1685, left in May, 1687, to join a Welsh regiment then being raised. He was succeeded by Major James Purcell, whose place as Major was taken by Captain James Lacy. Both Purcell and Lacy being staunch Jacobites, the former certainly, and the latter probably, joined James's Irish Army after the Revolution.

As for Lieutenant Edmund Barry, who appears in the lists of 1685 and 1687, it may be noted that a Lieutenant Barry was cashiered in July, 1685, for, in particular, his "scandalous treatment of Sir Rowland Berkeley, Deputy-Lieutenant of Worcestershire." If this was the same Barry his offence must have been condoned. Charles Stone appears both as ensign and as adjutant and, no doubt, drew the combined pay of 7s. per diem. So far the regiment had been kept together and afforded an opportunity for consolidating itself and getting into working order.

From March, 1688, orders began to issue spreading its companies far and wide in small detachments. In the absence of barracks, except in the larger garrison towns, it was obviously inexpedient, if not impossible, to billet large bodies on the smaller places, or to saddle them even with smaller bodies for a long period at a time.

Between March and September the companies were distributed between Carlisle, Berwick, York, Chester, Tynemouth, Chepstow, and Scarborough; head-quarters and the larger portion being generally at Berwick or Carlisle.

On September 1st the strength of the regiment was augmented by the addition to each company of ten men, one sergeant, and one drummer, which made the company up to three sergeants, three corporals, two drummers, and sixty men at a daily pay of £3 4s. 6d., inclusive of that of officers. The grenadier company cost 1s. per diem more, owing to its having two lieutenants, instead of one and an ensign.[1] Two fresh companies were added at the same time, making thirteen, including the grenadiers.

As it became more and more probable that the approaching invasion of the Prince of Orange would be in the South of England, orders were issued to the various detachments of the regiment to march towards London, and at the time of James II's flight, in November, 1688, most of them were on the march thither, or about to start on it.

A letter of December 4, 1688, from the Secretary at War to Lieutenant-Colonel Purcell, directs him to stay at Carlisle, instead of coming to London, as he had proposed. The letter continues: "The regiment is given to Colonel Nicholas, Colonel Cornwall having laid down his commission, as have two captains and five other officers. The seven companies here are in some disorder upon this occasion, and are now quartered at Greenwich and Deptford." Cornwall had resigned on November 20th, the day after William of Orange reached London. He appears to have taken no active part against William, and some of the family elected to remain in the regiment and served the Orange cause faithfully in Ireland and elsewhere. The colonelcy of Oliver Nicholas, who had been promoted from Lieutenant-Colonel in Prince George of Denmark's Regiment, was brief. He could not make up his mind to swear fidelity to the Prince of Orange, who was not yet King, and, on December 31, 1688, John Cunningham, then Lieutenant-Colonel in Werden's Horse, became colonel of the 9th.

At the close of 1688 the scattered companies had once more been brought together at Worcester, except one still at York. On January 3, 1689, the regiment was ordered to march, in two divisions, to Warrington, Prescott, and Newton, all within easy reach of Liverpool.

Before closing this chapter some incidents may be mentioned which, though unimportant in themselves, serve to throw light on the regimental life of the period.

In March, 1687, Lieutenant-Colonel Purcell's conduct in quelling a riot in York was generally approved; but his methods were a little too

[1] At a later date the Light Company also had two lieutenants and no ensign.

drastic even for James II's Government. He is told that on such occasions he should hand over civilian prisoners to the civil authorities, instead of punishing them with the "wooden horse or other military punishments." Even Purcell thought his ensign, George Ord, had gone too far in striking a civilian on the head in the Lord Mayor's Court. The Secretary at War directed Ord to be confined during His Majesty's pleasure. He was released after about a month.

In June there is a direction to Sir Thomas Haggerston, Governor of Berwick, to hand over to the civil authorities "three robberies and deserters" of Colonel Cornwall's regiment. If he decided that they were "lusty, proper fellows, fit to serve," they might, "when the law shall pass upon them," expect His Majesty's "favour or justice."

In August, 1688, Major Lacy proposes to try by regimental court martial Ensign Wynn, who had gone away without leave, and "with great disrespect to his senior officer." The War Office ruling was that regimental courts martial were not suitable for the trial of officers. If necessary, the governor of the place, or the commander-in-chief, could suspend the offender, pending orders for a general court martial. What happened to Wynn is not recorded. Probably the case was dropped.

CHAPTER II

THE IRISH CAMPAIGNS, 1689–1691

SO far the regiment had seen no active service. It was now to receive its baptism of fire in a civil war, deeply tinged with the colour of a religious one. The struggle was to be waged between the late King James II, whose strength lay in the Roman Catholic provinces of the south and west of Ireland, and William III, whose supporters were chiefly the Protestants of the north.

In its stations in the neighbourhood of Liverpool the 9th was conveniently situated for embarkation for Ireland, and on February 3, 1689, orders were issued for its recruitment up to full strength. The company at York had rejoined it. On March 1, 1689, orders were issued for the supply of arms to the regiment up to the usual scale for regiments with thirteen companies of sixty men each, "except pikes, in lieu whereof you are to issue musquets, if the said Colonel shall desire it." This appears to be the first occasion on which it was left to colonels to exercise an option as regards pikes.

James landed at Kinsale on March 12th, and his triumphal progress to, and reception in, Dublin soon showed that, for the present, William's operations must be based on the north, and that reinforcements for the Ulster people must be despatched. It was especially necessary to save the city of Londonderry from falling into James's hands. He had been advised that he had only to show himself there with a moderate force to ensure its surrender. Its fortifications were ancient and much neglected, and though its governor, Colonel Robert Lundy, was believed to be a faithful follower of the Orange cause, it was doubtful if, without considerable support, he could hold the place against James.

It was proposed to send four battalions under the command of Major-General Percy Kirk, of Tangier fame. But only two of the four—those commanded by Colonels Cunningham (9th) and Solomon Richards (17th)—were immediately available. It was determined to send them to Londonderry in advance of the other two. Both were conveniently situated for the port of Liverpool. On March 12th Lord Shrewsbury sent a long letter of instructions to Colonel Cunningham, who, though junior to Richards, was undoubtedly placed in command of the expedition. The two regiments were to be shipped for Londonderry, "to be there employed for our service as the Governor of the said place and you shall think fit." If, on arrival near Londonderry, the place was found to be still in Protestant hands, and it was safe to land the troops, the governor was to be informed of the measures being taken to save the city, and "you are to land the said regiments and stores, and to take care that they be well quartered and disposed of in the said city, following such directions as you shall receive during your stay there from our said Governor, Lieutenant-Colonel Robert Lundy, in all things relating to our service." The landing was only to be abandoned if the risk was too great, and even then an attempt was to be made to land at Carrickfergus or Strangford before returning to Liverpool. If the landing at Londonderry was feasible, "you are to make the best defence you can against all persons that shall attempt to besiege the said city."

With these very clear instructions in his pocket Cunningham sailed from Liverpool with the two regiments on April 3, 1689. Driven back to Hoylake by contrary winds, they sailed again on the 10th, and were in Lough Foyle, in sight of Londonderry, on the 15th.

Lundy has always—perhaps rightly—been believed to be a traitor to William, though Macaulay gives him the benefit of the doubt. When, with some difficulty, Cunningham got into communication with him, Lundy, with the aid of a council from which he carefully excluded all who were for a vigorous defence, succeeded in persuading Cunningham that there were provisions only for a few days. Subsequent events showed the falsity of this, but Cunningham, accepting the statement without demur or independent inquiry, decided against landing his troops. Even when Lundy was forced by a rising of the citizens to flee in disguise Cunningham would not accept the governorship offered to him by the successful party. James's army was some miles away, and there can be no doubt that the two regiments could have landed safely.

After hanging about the mouth of Lough Foyle for a few days, Cunningham sailed back to Liverpool, pleading as his excuse that he was forced by his orders to obey Lundy.

William was naturally furious when he learnt of this, and at once dismissed Cunningham and Richards from the command of their regiments. In Richards's case the justice of the order is doubtful, as he is believed to have protested against sailing from Londonderry, and, in any case, he was clearly subordinate to Cunningham. For the latter there seems no excuse on the charge of a gross error of judgment, though there is insufficient reason to suspect his loyalty. Nevertheless, the King seems to have had suspicions, for the last notice of the unfortunate colonels is a warrant (May 24, 1689) committing them to the Gatehouse, " on suspicion of dangerous practices against the Government."

The command of the regiment was bestowed on William Steuart, then Lieutenant-Colonel of the 16th Foot.[1]

On May 2nd Major-General Kirk was instructed to see if there were any officers in the regiments lately commanded by Cunningham and Richards whom he considered unfit for service in Ireland. He was to dismiss any such and appoint others in their place.

On April 29th Kirk had been directed to go to Liverpool and make all arrangements, in communication with the Naval authorities, for sailing to Londonderry with his own (2nd), Steuart's (9th), and Sir John Hanmer's (11th) regiments. He was also to take large supplies of ammunition and food. The 17th (now commanded by Sir G. St. George) was not sent as originally intended, but was employed elsewhere.

Kirk was not expeditious enough to suit the King, and on May 13th he received a letter from Lord Shrewsbury, in very stiff terms, requiring him to sail without waiting for stores, or anything but a fair wind.

---

[1] The name is spelt Stewart, Steuart, Stuart, or Steward in the old records. He always signed himself Steuart, and the name is so engraved on the plate of his coffin in Westminster Abbey (see Chester's " Westminster Abbey Registers," p. 318). The spelling Steuart is therefore accepted as correct.

Still he only sailed on May 31st, and, encountering bad weather succeeded by calms, he was only sighted by the beleaguered garrison of Londonderry on June 15th.

On the 19th Kirk and a council of war, on board the "Swallow," decided against any attempt to force the boom which the besiegers had constructed across the River Foyle below Londonderry, and in favour of awaiting fresh troops, sufficient to enable an attack to be made by land. A despairing letter of the 26th from the sorely afflicted garrison only drew from Kirk fair promises, and a statement that he intended to try the effect of a threat against the enemy's rear from Lough Swilly.

This expedition is what is most interesting to us in the story of the relief,[1] for on July 7th Steuart was sent with the 9th into Lough Swilly, where he anchored two days later. Hearing of a large Irish "cow camp" some six miles from Rathmulton, in the south-west corner of the Lough, Steuart sent Captain Echlin ashore there, with Lieutenant Biggett, Ensign Hart, and sixty musketeers, who, during their stay, gathered in a large number of cattle.

Next day a landing was made on the Island of Inch, which is separated from the south-east shore of the Lough by a channel, dry at low water, but only passable in boats when the tide is in. Fortifications were thrown up and armed on the island facing this channel, and the Protestants of the mainland began to come across, with their cattle and belongings, at low tide. From these people ten, and eventually fifteen, companies were formed to reinforce temporarily Kirk's three regiments. By July 20th the fortifications and the troops in the island, now comprising the whole of Steuart's regiment, were strong enough to repulse such forces as attempted the passage of the channel. The distance to Londonderry was only five or six miles, and the position of Steuart's force was a constant menace to the rear of the besiegers.

On July 17th news had come that the Duke of Berwick, recalled from Enniskillen, was marching against the invaders of Lough Swilly. That evening Steuart visited Echlin's detachment at Rathmulton. He

[1] A full diary of this expedition is in the Le Fleming papers published by the Historical MSS. Commission. It is contained in a letter from one of Steuart's officers

ordered all refugees and cattle over to Inch, and reinforced the detachment. The streets of the village were barricaded, so that, when Berwick arrived next morning with 1,500 dragoons, he failed, after a long fight, to make any impression on the defenders, who claimed to have caused him a loss of 200 men. On the English side Lieutenant Cornwall was killed and an ensign wounded. The loss in men was apparently small.[1]

That night Echlin's force passed safely over to Inch. Kirk himself came to Inch on the 20th, and thence despatched two ships to Enniskillen with arms, ammunition, provisions, and ten officers (not of the 9th), but no troops.

Kirk had done nothing towards throwing provisions and arms into Londonderry, and it was only under the compulsion of a very strong order from London, and the knowledge that the garrison of Londonderry was at its last gasp, that he made up his mind to attempt the forcing of the boom across the River Foyle. With the details of this enterprise we are not concerned. It and the whole story of the siege and relief of Londonderry are beyond the scope of a regimental history. Cannon, indeed, says a detachment of the 9th was on the ships forcing the passage, but this seems very doubtful.

Meanwhile, Steuart at Inch had been very active in driving in cattle from the mainland. On July 31st, he heard of the successful forcing of the boom on the previous day, and of the raising of the siege by James's army, which was observed to be busy burning villages on the mainland. The regiment now moved into Londonderry, whence it was ordered to join Schomberg's army at Dundalk, which place was reached on September 7th.

Schomberg, with some 10,000 men, had landed at Bangor on August 12th, and reached Belfast on the 17th. After taking Carrickfergus he had met with little or no opposition to his march to Dundalk.

At Dundalk the whole army, including the 9th, entrenched itself in a low and unhealthy situation, where it suffered terrible privations. The weather was wet, the commissariat execrable and corrupt. The

---

[1] Berwick himself makes light of this repulse, saying that he had only 1,200 dragoons, and that he made no serious attempt on the village when he found it was defended by infantry.

medical service was inefficient and ill supplied with drugs. According to Story, though there was a supply of surgical appliances, there was an almost complete absence of remedies for fever and dysentery. Schomberg was not to blame for all this, and he was almost in despair at the corruption and inefficiency which he encountered in every department of the administration. Shales, the Commissary-General, was put under arrest, but he was apparently no worse than his neighbours. Corruption extended downwards to the regimental officers, and it took Schomberg a week of hard work before he could ensure the soldier's exiguous pay reaching him, instead of sticking in the captain's pocket. Harbord, the treasurer of the army, actually had a troop of horse which is solemnly recorded and shown on the establishment list as " Mr. Harbord's Troop," and pay was drawn at the same rates as for any other troop. Yet the whole personnel of it consisted only of Mr. Harbord and his clerk ! The transport was equally bad.

There can be small wonder, then, that the troops suffered heavy losses from sickness, bad food, cold, and want of shelter. From the latter cause the English troops, inexperienced in war and indolent, suffered more than the continental veterans, who took care to construct proper shelter, when the English did nothing in the way of building huts. Of the indifference of the officers there are shocking accounts.

The 9th were probably neither better nor worse than the other new regiments. A confidential report on it at this time reads, " Colonel good, but his officers not of the best."

On September 21st James's army, largely superior in numbers, appeared from the south, and for more than a fortnight endeavoured to entice Schomberg to a pitched battle outside his entrenchments. But the old marshal was wary, and, notwithstanding the grumbling and discontent in his own army, refused to be drawn into a fight, in which he would probably have been badly beaten.

James's army, too, was suffering many losses from sickness and bad feeding. It is believed that it lost in this way about 15,000 out of 40,000 men, whilst Schomberg's losses were about 6,000 out of 14,000.

James retreated on Drogheda on October 5th. It was not till a month later that Schomberg went into winter quarters, losing terribly from disease and privations in the course of the evacuation and retreat. On November 7th the 9th started the march on Newry with three other infantry regiments, and took up quarters, less bad than Dundalk but still very bad, in Greencastle and Rostrevor. These were garrisons in the front line of the army, which extended from Lough Erne in the west to Newry in the east, with head-quarters at Lisburn. In the latter part of January, 1690, Steuart organized a raiding force of 500 horse and foot, the latter from his own regiment. Having ascertained that signals of the approach of troops were made by bonfires, which gave time to the people and their cattle to hide in the mountains, he several times lighted these fires. When nothing happened suspicions were lulled, and Steuart's party had considerable success in rounding up cattle.

Beyond this there is nothing to record of the doings of the 9th till the reopening of the campaign with King William's landing at Carrickfergus on June 14, 1690, and his advance on Dublin.

On June 22nd 200 dragoons and infantry—the latter being Captain Farlow's company of the 9th—were ambushed as they advanced from Newry towards Dundalk. After a sharp fight, in which they lost twenty-two killed, they escaped; but Captain Farlow and another officer were taken prisoners.

As William advanced southwards James fell back towards Dublin, till, on the afternoon of June 30th, he was found drawn up on the southern bank of the Boyne a short way above Drogheda, in which he had a garrison of 800 men more or less protecting his right. His front was covered by the Boyne from Oldbridge to Drogheda, his left by the river above the former place, flowing from south to north before turning eastwards towards Drogheda.

At and below Oldbridge the river was passable by fords when the tide was out, but they were none too shallow. The nearest bridge was three or four miles above Oldbridge, at Slane, but practicable fords were discovered next morning about Rosnaree in the intervening stretch.

James, whose forces, Irish and French, did not exceed 26,000 men, had posted himself on the hill of Donore, which commanded a fine view of the whole field. He appears to have halted, not so much with the intention of fighting as with that of covering the march of his heavy baggage and artillery, which had been sent on to Dublin. He had only kept back twelve guns, whilst William had forty guns and four mortars. Moreover, William's army—a mixed force of English, Dutch, Danes, Irish Protestants, and French Huguenot refugees—was quite 10,000 stronger. William was determined to attack if James held fast, as he did not doubt he would do. After reconnoitring the river front, in the course of which he was slightly wounded by a round shot, the King, who has rarely if ever been accused of being a great commander, resolved

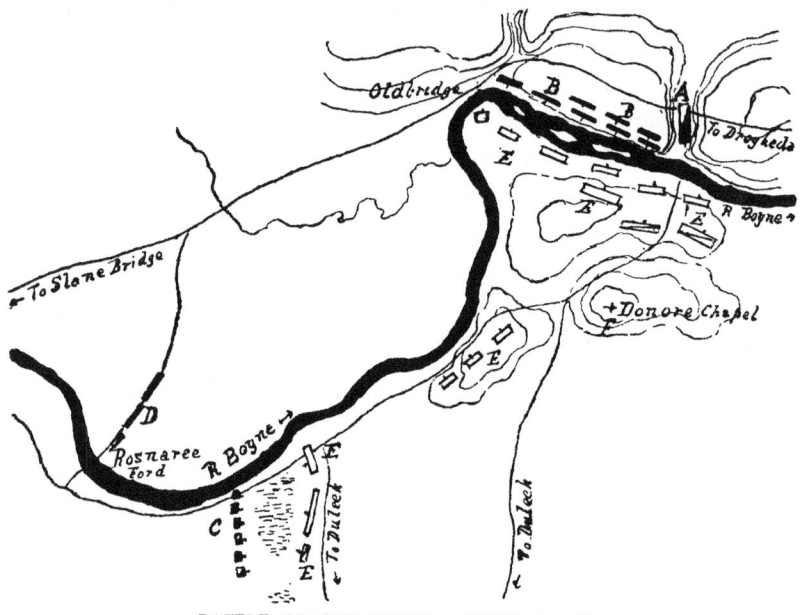

BATTLE OF THE BOYNE—ABOUT 9 A.M.

A, King William and cavalry of the left. *B*, Count Schomberg ready to pass the river. *C*, Count Mainhard Schomberg waiting for *D*, reinforcements, including **Steuart's** regiment. *E*, Irish Army of James II. *F* Head-quarters of James II.

to attack in his own way. Schomberg's plan was to send a large force round by Slane to turn James's left and seize his only line of retreat—by the road through Duleek, passing over a bog and capable of being held by a very few men against an army. James would be fixed in front by a containing force. The scheme was justified by William's large superiority of strength, but its success depended on the turning force marching in the dark, and being at and beyond Slane by daybreak.

GENERAL WILLIAM STEUART, 1652-1726.
COLONEL 1689-1715.
BY PERMISSION OF ION VILLIERS-STUART,
OF DROMANA, CAPPOQUIN, CO. WATERFORD.
FROM A PAINTING IN HIS POSSESSION.

This space reserved for Portrait—cut page out and tip on here.

GENERAL WILLIAM STEUART,
1652–1726.
COLONEL, 1689–1715.

All suggested methods, a record of which has been preserved, have been employed to find a portrait of William Steuart.

If, subsequent to the issue of this volume, a portrait should be obtained, a copy will be sent to each subscriber for insertion *at this page*.

W. H. B.

William would have none of this at first. He was bent on a frontal attack across the river and a turning movement, led by himself with the cavalry of his left wing, by a ford lower down the river between James's right and Drogheda. Later on he came partially round to Schomberg's idea and decided to send the cavalry of his right wing, supported by Trelawney's English infantry brigade, to cross at Slane and attack James's left and rear. But he was too late for the success of the manœuvre, for the turning force, under Schomberg's second son, Count Mainhard Schomberg, only started at 6 a.m. in broad daylight, and in full view of James's head-quarters at Donore. The frontal attack across the Boyne was to commence at 10 a.m., when the fords would be at their shallowest.

There seems to be little doubt that William's confidence in his English troops, especially those which had practically no experience of war, was small. He can hardly be blamed, for, in addition to their inexperience, he could not feel too sure of their loyalty to himself when they found themselves opposed to the late King, who had raised and always favoured them. It was difficult for both sides to know who would be faithful, and William had already had reason to suspect that Lundy, and even Cunningham and Richards, had betrayed him.

In his lines, as drawn out by himself at the Boyne, the only English he had in the first line for the frontal attack, on which he pinned his faith, were the Guards and Hanmer's brigade, the latter with only two English regiments (6th and 11th) in it. In the second line William placed two brigades of English behind his Dutch infantry, who formed the right of his frontal attack. These two brigades he detached some time before he intended to pass the river, and sent them to support the younger Schomberg, whose appeal for reinforcements he thus anticipated. William had evidently begun to think better of the prospects of the attack by Slane, which he had at first depreciated. Mainhard Schomberg, with the cavalry of the right wing and Trelawney's brigade, having started at 6 a.m., must have been at Slane not later than 8 a.m., two hours before the time fixed for the frontal attack. He had heard of a ford at Rosnaree, and sent part of his force across there. The cavalry, on arrival at Slane, found themselves opposed only by Sir Neil O'Neil's regiment of Irish cavalry. This was easily defeated by Schomberg's superior numbers, and the Orange general then turned leftwards towards James's line of retreat. He had already observed that James was detaching largely against him; hence his appeal for reinforcements, which William had already anticipated by ordering off the two English brigades under General Douglas.

Schomberg found his access to the Donore-Duleek road barred by a bog running southwards, and only separated by a narrow strip of good ground, beyond its southern end, from the bogs running at right angles to it in front of Duleek. There was another narrow strip between it and the river.

James, under the impression that the real battle was going to be the attack on his left and rear, had sent the whole of his French contingent, and six of his twelve guns, under Lauzun to meet it, besides other troops; so that against the frontal attack he had left only nine regiments of Irish infantry of poor quality and his Irish horse and dragoons, which were, with the French, his best troops. Mainhard Schomberg, whilst waiting for his reinforcements, had drawn up his force behind the bog in his front in alternate squadrons and battalions. When the two brigades arrived he arranged his infantry in the centre, facing the bog, his cavalry on the wings—that on the right facing the space between this bog and the farther bogs towards Duleek. Schomberg's left and Lauzun's right rested on the right bank of the Boyne. The Duleek road was behind Lauzun.

Schomberg now began his advance by moving his infantry, in line, right through the bog, instead of, as Lauzun expected, in column by the causeway crossing it. At the same time the cavalry of Schomberg's right began moving round the southern end of the bog, threatening to cut the French line of retreat to Duleek. This movement, combined with the news which now came in that William had successfully forced the river in his frontal attack, convinced Lauzun that the day was lost, and that he could do nothing but cover the retreat through Duleek. Drawing off in that direction, he was followed by Schomberg's force. As the Irish began to break up, the English cavalry were able to do a good deal of damage to the retreating enemy. Lauzun kept his French troops in good order, and was able to show such a good face in front of Duleek that William's pursuit ended, until Lauzun's retreat on Dublin enabled it to be continued on July 3rd. We have described the movement of William's detached right wing rather than his frontal attack, since it seems beyond doubt that Steuart's brigade, including the 9th, was one of the two sent by William to support Mainhard Schomberg.

Colonel Clifford Walton has very carefully worked out William's arrangement of his centre and left. The only English infantry brigades shown on the line of battle, excluding the Guards, are (1) Trelawney, (2) Bellasis, (3) Steuart, (4) Hanmer. Trelawney's had already gone towards Slane. Hanmer's we know, from the "London Gazette," was in the frontal attack. That leaves only Steuart's and Bellasis's brigades to be accounted for.

The following facts are stated in the "London Gazette" account of the battle. The strength of the originally detached right wing is given as "the right wing of the horse, two regiments of dragoons of the left wing, Trelawney's brigade of foot, and five small field pieces."

After describing the advance of the Dutch, the "Gazette" goes on : "In the meantime, the Danes came up to the left, as also the brigades of Hanmore [sic] and Mélonière to the right." There is no mention of either Bellasis's or Steuart's brigades in connexion with the frontal attack, but it is stated that His Majesty reinforced the right wing " with twelve battalions of foot and nine squadrons of horse." It seems quite clear that to get these twelve battalions William must have sent the whole of Bellasis's and Steuart's brigades.

Mulleneaux indirectly confirms the view that Steuart's brigade went to support the detached right. He states that William sent two brigades of infantry to support Trelawney's, and whilst he specially mentions Hanmer's brigade as being engaged in the frontal attack, he makes no mention of either Steuart's or Bellasis's brigades being there.

In any case, it seems clear that Steuart's regiment had very little, if any, fighting at the Boyne.[1]

The whole loss on William's side did not exceed 500 men killed and

[1] According to the "History of the Suffolk Regiment," the British regiments in the front or main attack were the 6th and 11th of Hanmer's brigade, and the

wounded ; most of it occurred in the frontal attack and the 9th does not appear to have had any casualties.

The 9th reached Dublin on July 5th with the rest of William's army, which had encountered no opposition on the march from Duleek. The city had been evacuated by James, and Captain Farlow, whose capture has been noted above, was found installed as Governor of the Castle.

On July 9th William's army, less a force detached under Douglas to attempt the capture of Athlone, marched for Limerick. Detachments occupied Waterford, Wexford, and other places, but the 9th does not appear to have played any special part in these operations. William had left the army temporarily in charge of Count Solms in consequence of bad news from England which seemed to call for his own presence there. Matters having improved by the time he reached Dublin, he returned to his Irish army on August 2nd. On the 7th that army was within seven miles of Limerick. Next day Lord Portland with a cavalry force and Steuart with the 9th were pushed forward to within artillery range of Limerick. Some Irish cavalry who issued from the place retired without fighting. The same day Douglas's detachment from before Athlone, which it had failed to take, rejoined the army, which was before Limerick on August 9th. The Irish town, on the left bank of the

---

8th, 12th, 18th, 20th, and 22nd of Bellasis's. No authority is given for this statement.

Colonel Anderson's History of the 22nd says the two brigades sent to the right were (a) 8th, 12th, 18th, (b) 20th, 22nd, and Lisburne's regiments. But these were not two brigades: they were the first and second lines of Bellasis's brigade.

These two accounts are directly contradictory, and the second is contradictory of the "Gazette," inasmuch as it accounts for only six battalions, against the twelve stated in the "Gazette."

There are two contemporary diaries quoted in the "Ulster Journal of Archæology" ("The Annals of Ulster"). One by the Rev. Dr. Davis says Portland marched at 6 a.m. with the right wing nearly to the bridge of Slane. He had twenty-four squadrons and six battalions and passed the river at two fords, where were six squadrons of the enemy, who fled, killing only one horse. When the enemy reinforcements reached the bog they had their infantry on the right, cavalry on the left. Then six more British infantry regiments arrived.

Bellingham's diary gives the strength of William's right wing as 15,000 men.

Shannon was connected by Ball's Bridge with the English town, built on King's Island in the river. This again communicated with the right bank by Thomond's Bridge, the approach to which beyond the river was defended by a bridge-head.

In face of a rather feeble resistance the enemy were cleared out of Ireton's and Cromwell's forts, which, with some bogs, covered the

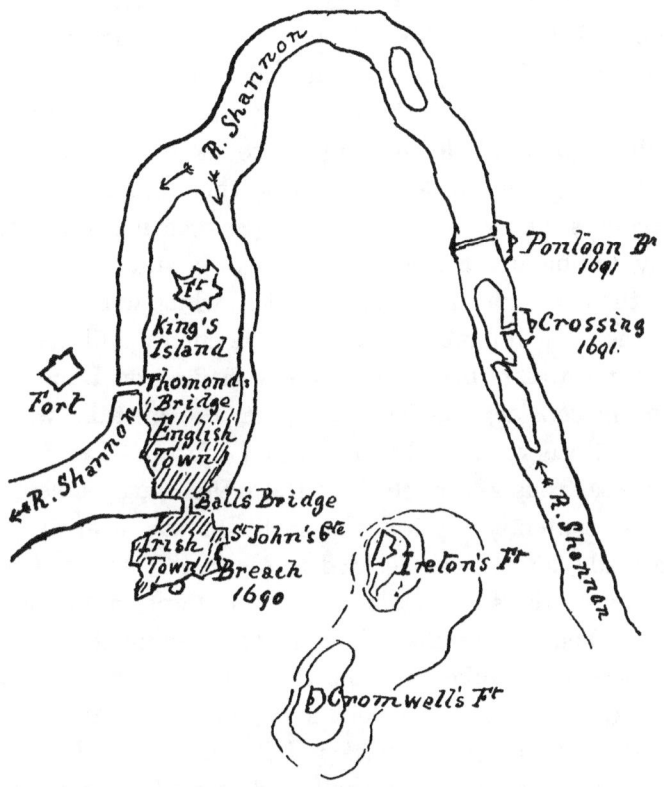

LIMERICK—SIEGES OF 1690 AND 1691

approach to the Irish town, and on the same day General Ginkel, with the 2nd, 9th, and 18th foot, and some dragoons, reconnoitred the ford of Annaghbeg, two miles above Limerick. It was found to be covered by earthworks strongly occupied; but during the night the enemy evacuated them, and Ginkel was able to leave his three infantry regiments temporarily on the right bank under the command of Kirk. The French

General Boiseleau, commanding in Limerick, with Berwick and Sarsfield under him, refused to surrender in reply to a summons. On August 11th, William's siege-train was intercepted on its march and almost destroyed by Sarsfield with his cavalry.

On the 12th, Steuart, with the 9th, Lord Meath's regiment, and four guns, was sent to take Castle Connell, four miles above Limerick. The place surrendered without resistance. Trenches had been opened against the Irish town of Limerick in the night of the 17th, and at midnight on the following night the 9th and Douglas's regiment were two of the seven battalions to take over the guard of the trenches. They were on the right, and do not appear to have realized how near the enemy was; for, being ordered to lie on their arms, most of them fell asleep without, seemingly, taking any proper precautions against surprise. The enemy, taking advantage of this very discreditable neglect, attacked and threw the two regiments into confusion, which was augmented by the Danes on their left mistaking them for the enemy and firing into them. The Danes' fire was returned, and the Irish fired on Danes and English alike, causing considerable loss. At last, the mistake was discovered and the sortie was repulsed by the united efforts of English and Danes. After this disastrous affair reliefs of the trench guards were carried out by day. By September 27th a practicable breach, near St. John's Gate, had been made, and it was decided to storm it. The attack was to be led by 500 grenadiers, amongst whom was Captain Farlow's company of the 9th. The rest of the 9th and other regiments were to support the grenadiers, who broke out from the trenches about 3.30 p.m., led by Captain Carlile of Lord Drogheda's regiment. Jumping into the dry ditch, they drove the panic-stricken Irish before them into the breach, and even into the town. They followed, but alone, for the supporting regiments did not go beyond the covered way, and employed themselves in clearing the Irish from the ditch on either side of the breach and in a futile attack on St. John's Gate.

Seeing but few English in and beyond the breach the Irish rallied and drove them out again, with heavy loss to the grenadiers and the supporting regiments. Ammunition now began to run short with the English, and after three hours' fighting, in which the Irish women fought alongside of their men, the stormers were forced to retire. The total loss of the besiegers in this ill-managed attack was about 500 (15 officers) killed, and 1,000 (44 officers) wounded. The 9th lost very heavily. Captains Lindon and Farlow were killed, and the following wounded: Brigadier Steuart, Major Cornwall, Captains Palfrey, Galbraith, Steuart, and Casseen; Lieutenants Steuart, Cornwall, and Cary, and Ensign Steuart. In consequence of this failure, and of the break-up of the weather, William decided to raise the siege. On September 30th the heavy artillery was got away with much difficulty owing to the state of the ground and the shortage of teams. The 9th and Lord Drogheda's regiment were detailed to convoy it to Tipperary, where the former received orders, on October 7th, to go into winter quarters.

From his quarters in the neighbourhood of Belturbet, Brigadier Steuart, on April 9, 1691, sent fifty musketeers of his regiment and twenty dragoons to beat up County Leitrim. Near Mohill they came upon two troops of Irish dragoons and a company of infantry. Notwithstanding their inferior numbers, the English detachment attacked, and, without any loss to themselves, dispersed the enemy, of whom they killed thirty, and took five prisoners, with most of their horses, and such baggage as they had. With the exception of constant fights with "Rapparees," otherwise bandits, who were generally hanged on capture, nothing worthy of mention seems to have happened to the 9th till the campaign reopened in the end of May, 1691. Many changes had occurred in Ireland in the winter and spring of 1690–91. Lauzun and his French troops had gone home, but St. Ruth, a French general, had been sent to command the Irish army, which had been busy recruiting, especially in cavalry.

On the English side, King William had left Ireland for good, entrusting the command there to Lieutenant-General Ginkel, a Dutchman.

On June 6th, Ginkel, marching on Ballymore, was joined by Douglas with the regiments from the north, amongst which was the 9th.

Ballymore was reached on the 7th. The place was difficult of access, owing to the lake and marshes by which it was almost surrounded. Milo Burke, the Governor, at first refused to surrender; but seeing the English were about to try a storm, he changed his mind and capitulated at discretion, with about 1,000 men and two antiquated guns. The army now marched on Athlone. After the junction of 7,000 foreigners under the Duke of Würtemberg it numbered about 18,000 men. On June 19th the enemy had been driven back into the English town of Athlone, situated on the left bank of the Shannon, and joined by a bridge to the Irish town. The construction of breaching batteries

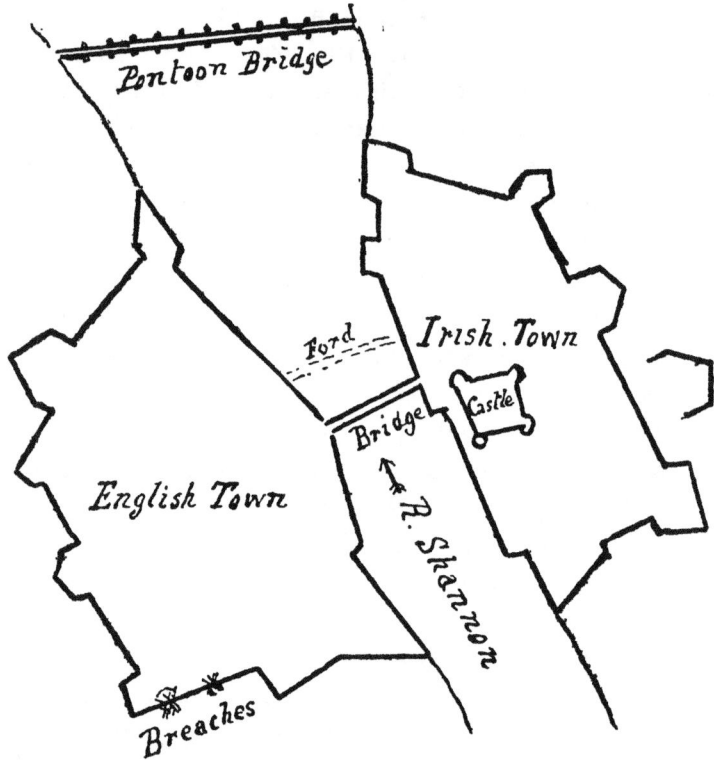

ATHLONE—SIEGE OF 1691

began at once. By the morning of the 20th a practicable breach had been made in the bastion nearest the river on the upstream side. The assault, fixed for 5 p.m., was led by 300 grenadiers, followed and supported on their left by Prince Frederick's regiment, and by the 9th on their right. Behind these followed 200 infantry with fascines and tools, and the regiments of Brewer (12th) and Nassau. The assault was completely successful, and the whole of the English town was captured with a loss on the besiegers' side of only about twenty killed and forty wounded. Unfortunately, Brigadier Steuart was so severely wounded that he had to be sent to Dublin for treatment, and was unable to lead his regiment during the rest of this campaign. Those of the enemy who escaped reached the Irish town by the bridge, the last opening of which was broken by them. The capture of the English town was but half the task, for it remained to take the Irish town across a broad and rapid river, which fortunately happened to be at its lowest in consequence of a dry season.

Entrenchments and batteries were at once thrown up in the English town along the river facing the Irish town. A vigorous bombardment destroyed the castle and made a breach in the enemy's fortifications along their side of the river. On the bridge the English carried on a bitter struggle for several days, gradually forcing their way, arch by arch, till they were brought to a standstill at the broken one.

On June 28th it was decided to attack across the river at 6 a.m. next day. Each infantry regiment was to contribute forty-three grenadiers, eighty-three privates, seven sergeants, two ensigns, five lieutenants, and three captains to the storming force, which was to be under the command of Major-General Mackay.

The men were ready at 6 a.m., but by 10 o'clock the collection of tools, boats, and other appliances was not complete. Meanwhile, deserters had carried to the Irish news of the impending attack, enabling St. Ruth to hurry reinforcements into the town from his camp beyond it. There was a good deal of throwing of grenades across the open arch of the bridge, which ended in the English fascines and a wooden gallery being burnt. The assault had to be postponed till the following day, June 30th, when it was fixed for 6 p.m., the usual hour of changing guards, when the movement of troops was least likely to arouse suspicions.

The abortive attack of June 29th had served a good purpose, in so far that St. Ruth, convinced of the impossibility of an assault across the river, withdrew his reinforcements, leaving only three indifferent Irish regiments in the Irish town. He thought he would have ample time to reinforce these, if necessary, from his camp outside.

The arrangements for the assault remained unchanged. The grenadiers were to pass the river by a ford a few yards below the bridge, which had been shown by three Danish soldiers to be only knee deep. These men, being under sentence of death, purchased their lives by this dangerous service.

Punctually at 6.6 p.m. Captain Sandys, at the head of sixty grenadiers in armour, twenty abreast, dashed into the river. The rest of the grenadiers followed, and the whole climbed the enemy's bank without difficulty.

Meanwhile planks had been thrown across the open arch of the bridge, enabling the rest of the troops to pass. At the same time a pontoon bridge was thrown across the Shannon just below the town. In less than half an hour the whole Irish town was in possession of the English. The surprise had been so complete that the loss of the stormers was only twelve killed and five officers and thirty men wounded. St. Ruth only had warning of what was happening when he found his own fortifications held against him by the victorious English, who easily beat off such detachments as he sent against them. He retired next day, with the intention of giving battle beyond Ballinasloe. He was not followed till July 10th, the interval being employed by Ginkel in making Athlone safe as a bridge-head on the Shannon. Reaching Ballinasloe on July 11th, Ginkel found St. Ruth had retired to what he considered a better position for a defensive battle at Aughrim, whither he was followed on the 12th.

The English strength is put by Story at 17,000 men, which seems a rather low estimate for the twenty-eight battalions and forty-seven squadrons shown in the order of battle. The guns numbered forty.

St. Ruth, according to Story, had 20,000 foot and 5,000 horse and dragoons. On the whole, however, it seems doubtful if his numbers were so greatly in excess of the English. He had drawn up his army on a position good for a passive but not for an active defence. His whole front was covered by a bog lying in a hollow at the foot of the gentle slope on which he stood. The small stream which issued from the bog, combined with two smaller bogs on his side of it, also gave further protection to his right, which could only be approached by the space between these bogs. On his left the only approach was by a narrow causeway, across the bog in his front, and this was swept by the fire of the small castle of Aughrim, in which he had a garrison of forty men. In the space of a few hundred yards between his front and the bog were small fields or enclosures, divided by ditches and dykes. He had opened

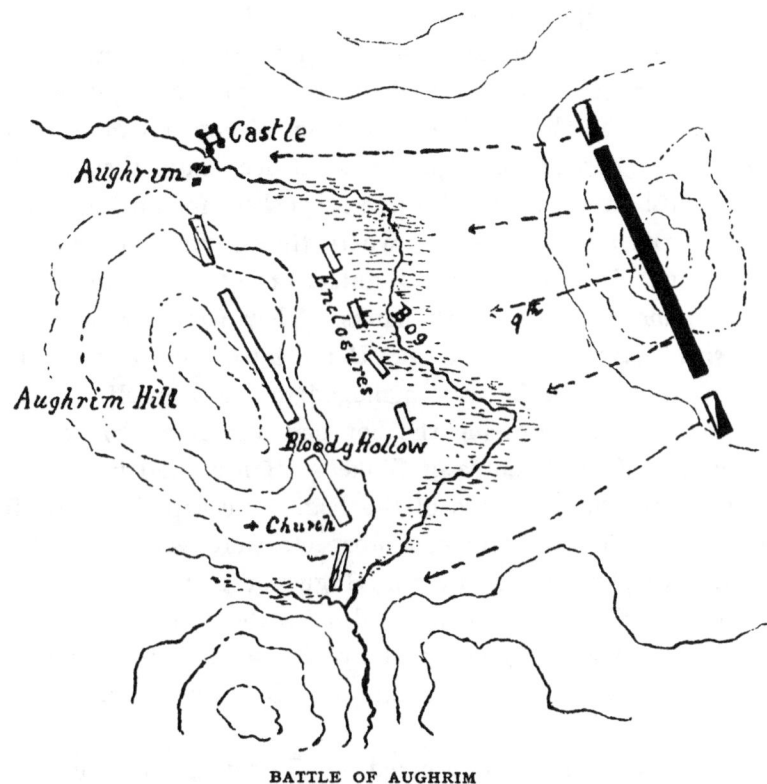

BATTLE OF AUGHRIM

lateral communications in these, and the dykes facing the bog were strongly held.

The first English attacks were by cavalry and dragoons on St. Ruth's right, which was decidedly his weakest point. They met with some success at first, but were eventually held up, and it was clear that they alone could not win the battle. About 4.30 p.m. the left of the English infantry advanced through the bog in their front. They were met by the Irish infantry, who fought bravely—much better than could have been expected after what they did at the Boyne. The battle here was more or less stationary when, about 6 p.m., Mackay with the centre sent forward the regiments of Erle (19th), Herbert (23rd), Creighton, and Brewer (12th) against the narrowest part of the bog. In support followed Ffoulkes's and the 9th. Steuart was not with them this day, being still recovering from his wounds in Dublin. The mission of this force was to get across the bog and hold on there, whilst more infantry got over on their right and followed the cavalry of the right, which was to force the pass by the castle of Aughrim. They did more than was intended. After getting through the waist-deep bog, they got out of hand and, flushed with initial success, pushed forward through the enclosures to the foot of the hill, where they found themselves overwhelmed by attacks in front, and, thanks to the lateral communications between the enclosures, on both flanks. They were forced back over the bog with heavy loss. Erle and Herbert were both taken, though the former, wounded as he was, managed to free himself. Farther to the left the infantry crossing the bog had also been driven back, so that the whole left and centre of Ginkel's infantry had been forced on to their guns on the near side of the bog. The attack on St. Ruth's right was also held up. Ginkel's prospects were very bad when the cavalry of his right, headed by the Huguenot Ruvigny, succeeded in getting through the Aughrim defile, despite the fire of the castle and of a regiment of Irish dragoons and two battalions of infantry. They were promptly followed by Kirk's (2nd) and Gustavus Hamilton's (20th) infantry.

Meanwhile the centre, reinforced by Talmash, once more pushed through the bog into the enclosures. Here they were aided by attacks by the Aughrim force on the enemy's left, and especially by a charge of Ruvigny's horse. The lateral openings were now favourable to the English.

At this juncture St. Ruth, on his way from his right to look after his threatened left, was killed by a chance round shot. No orders were forthcoming, and confusion soon began to spread in the Irish ranks. The defenders of the enclosures were forced back on to the open slope where they suffered severely from musketry fire. At the same time the attack on their right recommenced, and they were outflanked on their left. In a short time the whole Irish army melted from the field, pursued by the English cavalry and dragoons. The fall of a rainy night, and the shelter afforded to the fugitives by bogs, stopped the pursuit.

Story estimates the Irish loss at 7,000 killed, which is probably too high. There were only 450 prisoners, including twenty-six general and field officers, of which ranks eighteen or twenty more were killed.

According to official returns the English loss was 673 killed and 1,007 wounded. In those days there were pecuniary considerations which might induce returning officers to minimize losses in their companies, and the probability is that the loss in " other ranks " was higher. Of officers, seventy-three were reported killed, and 111 wounded. In the 9th, Major Cornwall and an ensign were killed, and a captain and an ensign wounded; of " other ranks " thirty-six were killed and forty-three wounded.

In so far as the Irish army defeated at Aughrim held together it drifted towards Limerick, which, like Magdeburg in 1806, was the mouse-trap in which the last remnants of James II's Irish forces were assembling. Many of the Irish infantry quietly went home. From Aughrim Ginkel marched on Galway, which surrendered without serious resistance. Such of the garrison as did not wish to go to their homes were allowed to go to Limerick. They numbered about 2,300 badly armed and worse clothed men with six guns, under the command of Lord Dillon.

Ginkel, leaving a garrison, under Sir H. Bellasis, in Galway, marched on July 28th, for Limerick. Owing to difficulties of various sorts it was only on August 25th that the second siege of Limerick could be opened. Ginkel had now been joined by Sir John Hanmer with five more regiments of foot and by his siege train.

Ireton's and Cromwell's forts were taken, practically without resistance, on August 25th. In the night of the 26th ground was broken, the English lines extending from the Shannon below the Irish town to a point on the left bank about opposite the centre of King's Island.

By August 30th the lines of circumvallation on the left bank were completed, Castle Connell had surrendered after some bombardment, and Castle Carrick, three miles below Limerick, having also been taken, the English squadron in the Shannon was able to sail up to within a mile of the place.

It soon appeared that, so long as Limerick was in free communication with the right bank of the Shannon by Thomond's Bridge, there was not much hope of a surrender. A heavy bombardment of the city was ascertained to be having little effect on the morale of the garrison, as most of the civil inhabitants had left it, and the troops were under cover in the trenches. Nor was it thought practicable to storm the English town across the branch of the river separating it from the left bank, though a practicable breach had been effected by September 9th, and had been widened by the 11th.

On September 15th it was decided to make a crossing to the right bank about two miles above Limerick, on the east side of the great loop formed by the river flowing northwards, before turning south again past the city. The spot selected was an island lying nearer the right bank than the left. The stream between it and the right bank was fordable.

The advance was led by 400 grenadiers,[1] followed by 600 workmen with the pontoons. Behind these came the 9th, four other infantry regiments, and some cavalry, with six guns, under the command of Talmash. At midnight the bridge was begun under the protection of the grenadiers, who had passed to the island in boats, and from it to the right bank by fording. The bridge was finished by daybreak, and the rest of the troops passed. There was some desultory fighting, which ended in the withdrawal of a camp, which the enemy had beyond the river. In the afternoon the expedition withdrew, leaving a guard to hold a bridge-head which had been constructed on the right bank. It was not till September 22nd that it was decided to use the bridge for passing over a large force, consisting of nearly all the cavalry, ten regiments of foot and fourteen guns.

[1] Doubtless the grenadiers of the 9th were among them in accordance with the then prevailing practice of using the grenadier companies of several regiments to form a grenadier battalion.

The 9th did not go with this force, but were left with the troops under Mackay and Talmash holding the trenches on the left bank. The regiment had no more fighting during the siege. The complete success of the force which drove the enemy on the right bank over Thomond's Bridge, and established itself there, resulted in the surrender of the place, with which we have no further concern.

With the fall of Limerick and the departure from Ireland of 12,000 Irish who elected to go to France, the Irish war was brought to a conclusion. The 9th, however, were not yet to quit the country, as they were to form part of the garrison which it was of course necessary to maintain there.

CHAPTER III

BREST, THE MEDITERRANEAN, AND FLANDERS, 1691–1703

IN the winter of 1691–92 the 9th were quartered at Fenagh, Cavan, and Killeshandra. Later they moved to Strangford and Lough Foyle, and afterwards to Co. Donegal, in which Brigadiers Steuart and Wolseley are recorded as having their quarters. On the disbandment of Lord George Hamilton's regiment, in February, 1692, all but 150 of his men, if they would volunteer, were ordered to be distributed to the 9th and other regiments in Ireland.

About this time the establishment of the regiment is given as:

Commissioned officers		43
Non-commissioned officers (including drummers)		105
Servants		69
Effective soldiers	711	780
		928

But the actual strength was much lower, as is shown by another statement accounting for the 780 effective soldiers and servants as follows:—

Effective soldiers	411
Sick men	138
Dead men	231
	780

The nominal establishment was still thirteen companies of sixty men each.

There is also a very uncomplimentary report on the regiment, not signed but apparently in the handwriting of Count Solms, which says that it *ne vaut rien*, and that everything in it was in confusion. As this report says much the same of every other English regiment in Ireland its value may perhaps be discounted as prejudiced.

In 1693 the regiment was in Dublin, and a letter of February 20, 1694, from the Lords Justices says that it was then in Dublin "intended for Flanders," but that it was not safe to despatch it until relieved by another regiment.

On March 13, 1694, Steuart writes from Dublin that he hopes to ship his regiment next day. That he succeeded is shown by a News Letter of March 19th saying that the regiment had landed at Neston the day before, and had marched into Chester in the evening, about 800 strong, under the command of Lieutenant-Colonel Hussey. It would march away in a few days to make room for the other regiments "expected over." As they had been four nights at sea, and had just been joined by 130 recruits not yet in uniform, they are described as looking "indifferent." The 130 recruits were an augmentation of ten men per company. The formal order for this augmentation is dated April 3, 1694. It provides for 130 men, twelve sergeants and twelve drummers being added to the 9th. As the Lords Justices in Ireland mention on February 20th that they had received orders to "increase the company" of the regiment, it would appear that informal orders had been issued before that date.

Though the regiment was described as "intended for Flanders" it was destined for a different service. As the marching orders for the early part of 1694 are missing from the Public Records Office, it is not possible to say exactly where the regiment was quartered and how it marched to Portsmouth. The matter is not of great importance, since the 9th must have marched fairly straight for the south to join the secret expedition in which it was to take part. What their destination actually was, was not divulged till they were at sea.

It was not till May 30, 1694 that the fleets destined for the Mediterranean and Brest sailed from Spithead. On June 5th Lord Berkeley received orders at sea from Admiral Russell to proceed with his portion of the fleet to Brest, and land there the troops commanded by General Talmash,[1] in such manner as might be decided by a Council of War to be held on board. Great endeavours had been made in England to keep secret the true destination of the expedition, which it was generally known was about to sail. Few knew whether it was for the Mediterranean, for Dunkîrk, for Cherbourg, or where, until Marlborough, then out of favour, managed to discover its true objective, which he at once communicated to James II, who naturally passed it on to his friend and ally Louis XIV. It was known in England that the French fleet had left Brest, and that the defences of the place were slight and the garrison weak. Everything pointed to the probability of success in a landing as planned. But Marlborough had given the whole thing away, and the French utilized the period of nearly a month between their acquisition of positive news of the destination of the expedition and its arrival. Vauban was sent to repair and improve the fortifications of Brest, and reinforcements of troops were sent to the place.

On June 6th the fleet made Ushant, and on the 7th anchored in Camaret Bay, south of the entrance to Brest. Talmash's reconnaissance in a yacht the same evening having failed to discover any trenches or batteries, it was decided to attempt a landing. It was to be covered by Lord Carmarthen with seven frigates bombarding the Camaret Fort, so as to prevent its interference. As soon as the bombardment began Talmash was to land his troops from boats. Lord Cutts was to lead the landing party with nine companies of grenadiers, amongst them being the grenadier company of the 9th, supported by Lieutenant-Colonel Venner with the 24th, and Lieutenant-Colonel Hussey with the 9th[2]—the rest of the troops to follow.

When the leading troops approached the shore they were disagreeably surprised to find formidable defences, in the shape of three batteries on their right and two on their left connected by a triple line of trenches filled with troops, with more batteries behind them. It is said there

---

[1] These were a mixed battalion of Foot Guards, the 6th, 9th, 13th, 19th, and 24th Foot, besides the regiments of Cutts, Collier, Rowe, and Coote—ten battalions in all.

[2] Brigadier Steuart was in Flanders with another brigade.

was some hesitation amongst the landing party in face of such defences, and, according to the account given by Captain Greene of Talmash's staff, even "Salamander" Cutts was not so eager as usual to dash his head against them. Talmash was determined to carry through an enterprise which he is said to have suggested himself, but which it should now have been apparent to him was impossible of execution in the altered circumstances. His order to land was at first only carried out by an ensign and nine grenadiers. Talmash himself landed, and when 150 grenadiers were ashore sallied out from a rock behind which he had taken temporary shelter. Most of the grenadiers were killed or wounded by the enemy's fire, and Talmash himself was wounded in the thigh. Nevertheless, when another 200 had landed he led them forward, only to be repulsed with heavy loss. Meanwhile, there had been much confusion and heavy loss in the boats attempting to land the other troops. Some were sunk, others grounded and could not be got off.

Talmash was now got off with much difficulty, and Lord Macclesfield, who succeeded to the command, seeing the hopelessness of the attempt, gave orders to withdraw. The loss in killed, drowned, and wounded on shore and in the boats had been very heavy, and, as the boats began to get away, French cavalry, which had been hovering in the background, descended and cut off those who had not succeeded in embarking.

According to a statement recorded by Lord Berkeley a few days later, he had on board his fleet the following soldier casualties :—

Killed and missing	467
Wounded	107
	574

How the "missing" could be on board is not clear, and it is certain that the total loss was very much heavier than this : it is believed to have been about 1,100 killed, wounded and missing. It is not possible to give the loss of the 9th separately. Of course, according to the prevailing practice, their grenadier company would be with the grenadiers landing first.

Talmash died of his wound shortly after landing in England.

On June 21st Cutts reports that all the troops under his command had been landed at St. Helens in the Isle of Wight. On June 23rd, Lord Macclesfield is ordered to go with his ten battalions in Lord Berkeley's fleet to operate further against the French coasts. Lord Berkeley reports, on the 26th, that he had landed part of the troops on the fleet, but the 9th is not among the regiments named, and appears to have sailed again with the fleet. An attempt was first made on Dieppe, but failed owing to bad weather, which compelled a return to Dungeness without landing troops. On July 13th, Dieppe was bombarded, and on the 16th Havre received the same attention, but no troops were landed.

Cherbourg was then visited, but, beyond alarming the French, nothing was done, as the fleet encountered heavy seas which compelled its return to St. Helens on July 26th. On August 9th, the fleet was in the Downs, and after that an attempt was made on Dunkirk, which came to nothing. Thus the unfortunate 9th was kept on board the fleet for about four months, watching bombardments and doing nothing save suffer the discomforts of bad weather and confinement in close quarters aboard ship.

Early in October, 1694, the regiment was landed piecemeal, chiefly at Chatham and other places at the mouth of the Thames. After a rest of three or four days the several companies were concentrated at Marlborough, whence two companies were marched to Bristol, and the rest, in single company detachments, to Bridgewater, Taunton, and other places in Somersetshire. On December 6th, eight companies had been collected at Bristol, and on the 19th the whole regiment was ordered to Wiltshire and Hampshire. Two companies each were allotted to Winchester and Southampton, three to Salisbury, and the remaining six to various places. It is unnecessary to trace the movements of each company. When a regiment, in the absence of barracks, had to be billeted on small towns and villages, it obviously could not be kept for long in one place. Consequently, we find frequent, often weekly, orders from the War Office, moving individual companies from one small place to another, or ordering them to extend themselves over several villages.

Life in a regiment, under such circumstances of constant movement, must have been almost intolerable in peace time. The men's billets were often very bad, being no better than a straw bed in a barn. Moreover, the system must have had disastrous effects on discipline, training, and esprit de corps.

The regiment was now destined for another short turn of active service abroad. At the end of 1694 orders were sent to Portsmouth for the collection of transport for 2,000 men, and on March 12, 1695, Steuart received orders for embarkation of these troops, which were to be under his command and comprised his own regiment and those of the Marquis Puizar,[1] Colonel Brudenell (Marines), and Colonel Coote (late Lord Lisburne's). A warrant, dated February 7, 1695, had directed the supply to the 9th of arms to replace those lost at Brest. Sailing on March 18, 1695, the force reached Cadiz on April 18th. Steuart's orders were to place himself under the orders of Admiral Russell, commanding the fleet in the Mediterranean.

After touching at Alicant, the fleet reached Barcelona on May 18th, and put to sea again two days later. There was an idea of an attack on Toulon, which was abandoned at the instance of the Savoy Government, and an expedition to reconnoitre Marseilles was thwarted by a storm, which drove the fleet fifty leagues southwards on June 2nd. It was employed in covering the movement of the Turkey convoy. The ships were mostly in very bad condition when Russell was again off Barcelona on July 19th. He was still hankering after Toulon and Marseilles, when he was requested to back the Spanish Viceroy's proposed expedition to retake Palamos by land.

On August 9th, he landed Steuart with the English and Nassau with the Dutch troops, about 4,000 in all, at Blanes, to join in the attack on Palamos. They encamped about half way to Palamos, on which they advanced next day.

Strong French forces were discovered in order of battle on the neighbouring hills. The English were kept under arms all that day and the ensuing night, suffering much from the neglect of the Spanish authorities to furnish them with supplies. They entrenched them-

---

[1] Commanding temporarily the 24th, *vice* Venner, dismissed.

selves in front of the place, constantly threatened, though not actually attacked, by the French. The fleet subjected Palamos to a heavy bombardment from the sea, which almost destroyed the town. Russell now advised the Spaniards that they had no chance of retaking Palamos, seeing that they and his force together scarcely equalled the strength of the French. He accordingly again embarked his troops and started for the coast of Provence, but the fleet was dispersed by heavy weather, and it was not till the end of September that it was again at Cadiz.

Sir George Rooke was, soon after this, ordered to take over the Mediterranean command, and Russell, leaving a squadron at Cadiz, sailed for England with the rest of the fleet and the troops. The 9th landed on November 17, 1695, and was ordered to various places in Surrey and Kent, extending from Reigate to Camberwell and Eltham. In December it was sent to Leicester and other places in the Midlands, whence it moved in February, 1696, to Reading, Newbury, Maidenhead, etc., which, owing to various contradictory orders *en route*, it only reached about the middle of March. In May it was ordered to Bristol, Wells, etc., but its destination was altered on the way to Exeter, Dartmouth, and other places in Devonshire.

There had been trouble at Reading, for we find on May 28, 1696, a complaint from the Mayor that the officers of the 9th, instead of paying for their quarters in cash, had drawn bills for the amount on the Secretary at War. This was hardly astonishing in view of the extreme difficulty in those days of getting pay and subsistence allowances. On this complaint the Secretary ordered that the regiment was only to be paid sufficient to see them over their march to the west, the bills being met from the balance due.

In connexion with the stay at Reading, an order of June 27, 1696, may be mentioned. It points out that no prisoner for debt (if under forty years of age) can be discharged during the present war with France, unless he agrees to enlist, or finds a substitute to do so. The colonel is accordingly authorized by the Secretary at War to enlist Thomas Ganior, in lieu of Samuel Doan, a prisoner for debt in Reading Jail, thus enabling the latter to be discharged under the recent Act of Parliament.

In Devonshire the regiment, with the usual local moves, remained till June, 1697, when it was ordered to arrive at Blackheath on July 1st. In less than a month it was moved to Windsor, Kingston-on-Thames, Uxbridge, and other neighbouring places, and in August it was ordered to undertake the usual duties at Windsor during the visit of the Prince and Princess of Denmark. October saw it once more on the way to Devonshire, six companies being posted at Exeter. In November eleven companies out of the thirteen were at Plymouth. In February, 1698, the whole regiment was ordered to concentrate at Bideford for embarkation for Cork or Waterford.

It is unfortunately impossible now to discover the stations at which the regiment was posted during this term of service in Ireland. The regimental records might have shown them, but these were all lost up to the year 1805 in the wreck of the " Ariadne " transport near Calais in that year. The actual posting of troops in Ireland appears to have been left to the discretion of the authorities at Dublin. Search among the records of that Government in the seventeenth and eighteenth centuries is no longer possible, owing to their destruction with the Four Courts, Dublin, in which they were kept. All that we have to depend on for records of service in Ireland are casual entries in inspection reports, monthly returns, pay sheets, and the like preserved at the Public Records Office or the War Office in London. But these even are only available from about 1760 onwards, and are rather fragmentary. Such information as can be gleaned from them will be given in its proper place, but nothing can be said about the regiment's stations in Ireland previous to their date.

Fortunately the matter is of comparatively small importance, since the periods during which the regiment was in Ireland between 1691 and 1805 were not times of special disturbance, and it is unlikely that its sojourn there was eventful. It was not in Ireland at the time of the Rebellion of 1798 or of the French landing.

On the renewal of peace by the Treaty of Ryswick in 1697 William III had to reduce his army in accordance with what he could get from the House of Commons for it. The establishment of the army in Ireland was fixed at two regiments of horse, three of dragoons, and twenty-one battalions of foot, of which the 9th was one. The Irish establishment was proportionately much higher than that of England, where the infantry consisted of only five battalions. In the King's constant struggle with Parliament over the maintenance of a standing army it was generally convenient to quarter regiments in Ireland, where they were less under the observation of the English Parliament. The total strength of the Irish establishment, to be maintained at the expense of Irish funds, was limited by Parliament to 12,000 men, that of England to 7,000. With this limited establishment William was forced to resort to what Mr. Fortescue describes as the "wasteful and extravagant system" of preserving the skeleton of a larger force to provide against the possibility of a fresh war. A lien on the services of large numbers of officers was maintained by the grant of half pay. "It was," says Mr. Fortescue, "a current jest of the time that the English army was an army of officers."[1]

On November 28, 1698, an order fixed the pay, in Ireland, of the 9th and other infantry regiments as follows, compared with English rates:—

	English pay per annum.			Irish pay per annum.		
	£	s.	d.	£	s.	d.
Colonel, as Colonel	219	0	0	201	12	0
Lt.-Colonel, as Lt.-Col.	127	15	0	117	12	0
Major, as Major	91	5	0	67	4	0
Chaplain	121	13	4	112	0	0
Adjutant	67	4	0	67	4	0 [2]
Quartermaster	67	4	0			
Captain	146	0	0	134	8	0
Lieutenant	73	0	0	67	4	0
Ensign or 2nd Lieutenant	54	15	0	50	8	0
Sergeant	27	7	6	25	4	0
Corporal	18	5	0	16	16	0
Drummer	18	5	0	16	16	0
Private	12	3	4	8	8	0

[1] "History of the British Army," I, p. 389. The reader will doubtless call to mind the efforts of Germany since the Great War in this direction.

[2] One officer.

On March 20, 1699, the establishment paid at the above rates for infantry battalions in Ireland was reduced from thirteen to eleven companies, each of two sergeants, two corporals, one drummer and thirty-six privates, besides commissioned officers. With this establishment there was a proportion of one commissioned officer to every eleven privates.

The establishment was reduced in 1700 to ten companies, each of two sergeants, one drummer, three corporals, and thirty-six privates.

By the spring of 1701 it was becoming clear that Europe was threatened with a new war over the question of the Spanish Succession. As this is the history of a regiment and not of Europe, we can only indicate very briefly the political events which led to the war. Its cause was the ambition of Louis XIV, which led him to accept for his grandson, Philip of Anjou, the succession to the imbecile King Charles II of Spain—a succession which was also claimed by the Emperor Leopold for his grandson, the Archduke Charles. Louis's claim threatened, by the union under one family of France and Spain, to upset the whole European balance of power in favour of France. An alliance was therefore concluded in August, 1701, between England, Holland, and the Emperor, pledging the signatories to support the claim of the Archduke and to wrest Italy and Flanders from the French, unless an amicable settlement could be made within a limited period. William III and the Dutch had not recognized the French claimant, and a settlement was not in the least likely with Louis, who had now thoroughly exasperated William and the English by his recognition, as King of England, of the eldest son of James II, on the death of the latter. He had already practically come to blows with the Dutch by capturing some 15,000 of their best troops, who were, under former treaties, in garrison in certain towns in Spanish Flanders. This had induced William to send a British force to Holland to be ready for emergencies. All his difficulties with Parliament were solved by Louis's mistake in recognizing the Pretender, and he could rely on it now for ample supplies of troops and money.

The orders for the despatch of troops to Holland are dated May 14, 1701. They directed the embarkation of eleven out of the twenty-one battalions of the army in Ireland.[1] The 9th embarked at Cork on June 15th and reached Spithead. Here, however, Steuart received orders, dated June 11th, to land his regiment and await further orders. The reason was that William had decided to substitute for the 9th the 1st battalion of the First Guards.[2] On July 3rd orders were issued for four companies to go to Windsor on duty, during the visit of the Prince and Princess of Denmark, and next day for six companies to march to the Tower of London. On July 15th, two new companies, which had been added to bring the regiment up to a total of twelve, were directed to join the six at the Tower. The strength of the companies (order of June 2, 1701) was, two sergeants, three corporals, two drummers and fifty-nine privates in each. In January, 1702, the regiment was still partly at Windsor and partly at the Tower. On February 6th the four companies in the Windsor neighbourhood were ordered to the Tower. On the previous day the Lord High Admiral had been ordered to provide, in the Thames, transport for the regiment to Holland, its strength being stated at approximately 700 men.[3] On February 9th, the regiment was ordered to embark next day. It had hardly arrived in Holland when William III died, on March 8, 1702. War with France was not declared until May 4th.

The chief command in the Low Countries had been given to Marlborough, but he had not yet joined the army. The Earl of Athlone, whom we formerly knew in Ireland as Ginkel, was at the head of some 25,000 men posted south-east of Nimeguen, covering the siege of Kaiserwerth on the Lower Rhine against the French army, some 60,000 strong, under Boufflers, about Xanten and Uedem. On June 10th Boufflers made a dash to cut Athlone from Nimeguen and take that place. Athlone was only just in time to escape disaster by hurrying to Nimeguen, which Boufflers found himself unable to take.

[1] 1st, 8th, 9th, 10th, 13th, 15th, 16th, 17th, 18th, 23rd, and 24th Foot.
[2] Fortescue, " History of British Army," I, p. 399 *n*.
[3] By orders dated March 12, 1702, a thirteenth company was added to this regiment, and some others, in Holland ; but the actual addition appears to have been delayed, for, in August, 1703, Marlborough reports that this regiment had only twelve companies in Holland and that a thirteenth should be added before it went to Portugal

It seems probable that the 9th was not in this affair, as the bulletin of Marlborough's army for July 10th shows that it, with another battalion and four regiments of horse, all under General Lumley, had only joined him on the previous day. It was only on July 2nd that Marlborough was able to get to Nimeguen, where he at once endeavoured to impart a more active spirit to the operations. With 60,000 men, of whom 12,000 were British, he moved to Ober Hasselt, on the right bank of the Lower Meuse, where he had the French army some five or six miles from him on the same side of the river.

It took him till the 26th to overcome the opposition of the Dutch deputies to his crossing the river. He then marched rapidly south to Hamont. The direction of his march alarmed Boufflers for his communications with the Spanish Netherlands. Starting soon after Marlborough, he hastened up the right bank of the Meuse, which he crossed at Venloo, a fortress then held by the French, and reached Peer and Bray, south of Hamont, as Marlborough reached the latter place. Bouffler's troops were exhausted and dispirited by hard marching; Marlborough's, which had had a longer time and a shorter march, were fresh and confident. Had Marlborough's hand not been stayed by his Dutch watchdogs, he might have destroyed Boufflers. As it was, the Frenchman escaped to his lines at Diest. It was at this period that the British infantry was brigaded under Generals Withers, Hamilton, and Stanley. The 9th were in the brigade of Withers.

Marlborough now proposed to besiege Venloo, when Boufflers, taking heart of grace, moved north to cut off a large convoy on its way by Hamont to join Marlborough. The latter promptly gathered in his convoy and threw his army across Bouffler's line of retreat to the Demer. Again the French general was saved by the obstructive timidity of the Dutch deputies and the insubordination of the Dutch General Opdam. He slipped away in the night, with nothing worse than some damage to his rearguard, inflicted by Marlborough's cavalry. The 9th had been in all these manœuvres, but there was little or no fighting, and there is nothing to be recorded regarding them.

Marlborough now proceeded to the siege of Venloo, Stevenswaert, Maseyk, and Ruremonde, the fall of which gave him possession of the whole line of the Meuse up to Maestricht, which place he already held. These operations were carried out by thirty-two battalions and thirty-six squadrons detached for the purpose. They were covered by the rest of the army, of which the 9th was part, posted facing south-west against Boufflers, who made no attempt to relieve his fortresses.

Boufflers, having now detached Tallard to Cologne and Bonn to meet an expected movement of Marlborough to the Rhine, took post at Tongres with much weakened forces, hoping to cover both his lines on his left rear and Liège on his right. This was too near Maestricht for Marlborough's liking, and he decided to move Boufflers on. The latter, fearing for the safety of Liège, moved towards that fortress, intending to occupy it with his army. Arriving near it on October 12th, he was astounded to find Marlborough drawn up ready to meet him with superior forces. Again he escaped, thanks to the interference of the Dutch, and Marlborough was left in front of the fortress. The unfortified town at once yielded and was occupied by three English and three Dutch battalions.

The citadel and the Chartreuse remained to be taken. The former, fortified and holding a garrison of eight battalions, required to be attacked in regular form. It was not till October 19th that the siege artillery from the recently captured fortresses lower down the river was got up by boat and disembarked. The bombardment began next day, when the trenches were begun. By the 23rd Coehorn, the famous Dutch engineer in charge of the siege operations, decided that the breach was ready for an assault from the trenches, which were now close up to the counterscarp. Between 4 and 5 p.m. 1,000 English grenadiers, amongst them the grenadiers of the 9th, led the stormers forward. Forcing their way across the covered way, they dropped into the shallow dry ditch. According to the French account,[1] their first attack on the right-hand breach was beaten off. They were then replaced by a fresh lot of grenadiers, supported by ten battalions, who not only effected a lodgment in the breach, which was all that Coehorn contemplated, but pushed on, as Cutts had already done at Venloo, and took the whole place sword in hand. The 9th played a prominent part in this storm,

[1] Quincy.

as is shown by the fact that it was to a lieutenant in that regiment, whose name we have been unable to discover, that the governor, M. de Violaine, delivered his sword in the breach. Quincy ascribes the success of the attack to treachery on the part of the English, in renewing the attack during a cessation of hostilities, which had been agreed to after the failure of the first assault. This charge is not mentioned by Berwick, and it is extremely unlikely that the English would have agreed to a parley under such circumstances. The story may be treated as an attempt to gloss over the failure of the defence. The Chartreuse Fort then surrendered after a short bombardment.

After this the army went into winter quarters and Marlborough returned to England.

In the middle of March, 1703, Marlborough again joined his army, and, finding it impossible to get sanction to his more ambitious projects, went off to besiege Bonn, leaving Overkirk in command of the covering army about Tongres, and taking with him the Prussians, Hessians, and Hanoverians.

Wither's brigade, including the 9th, was left with the covering army under Overkirk. When Marshal Villeroi attempted, in Marlborough's absence, to seize Maestricht, Overkirk fortunately got information in time to enable him to reach it first. Villeroi found him in such a strong position, with his left flanked by the guns of the fortress, that, after some threats and manœuvres, he again returned to Tongres.

Marlborough, having taken Bonn, was back again at Maestricht by May 20th. His real design was to take Antwerp. After forcing Villeroi towards his lines, and keeping him in uncertainty whether the danger was to Antwerp or Huy, Marlborough, on June 26th, suddenly marched for the Demer *en route* for Antwerp. Villeroi at once marched in the same direction by Diest.

Meanwhile Coehorn had mismanaged affairs nearer Antwerp, and Opdam, who had been left isolated at Bergen-op-Zoom, was badly surprised by Boufflers before Marlborough could reach him. This upset Marlborough's plans and he returned with his whole army to the Meuse.

In a despatch of August 8th, he enumerates the regiments he proposes to send to Portugal, viz. those of Portmore, Stanhope, Steuart (9th), and Sir M. Bridges. He said he would send them to Breda and Bois le Duc to be ready for embarkation at Willemstad on the Scheldt on August 20th. He describes the regiments as "all four old regiments, and I think very good ones." He mentions that Steuart's was one of the strongest regiments he had, and adds that it should have a company added, as it and Portmore's (2nd) were only twelve companies against thirteen in the other two regiments.

The fleet on which they were to sail, under Sir George Rooke, only arrived at the end of October. The Archduke Charles, the Allies' candidate for the throne of Spain, was to sail with it, and he only arrived at the Hague on November 2nd. Owing to various delays, it was not till early in January that Charles, with the fleet, on which was the 9th, arrived in England and went to Windsor to be received with royal honours by Queen Anne.

The warrant for the extra company recommended by Marlborough for the 9th had been issued on August 25, 1703, though its constitution had been ordered so far back as March 12, 1702.[1]

---

[1] Cf. *ante*, p. 42.

SPAIN, PORTUGAL, AND SOUTH OF FRANCE

CHAPTER IV.

THE WAR OF THE SPANISH SUCCESSION IN PORTUGAL AND SPAIN, 1704–1707

WE have now to turn to operations in the Iberian Peninsula, where Portugal had been drawn into the alliance against France and Spain. Under the treaty 7,000 troops had to be sent to Portugal, and it was decided to take the Royal Dragoons and six regiments[1] of British foot from the Lowlands. The Archduke Charles was also to go and push his claims to the Spanish crown in person.

In January, 1704, Admiral Sir George Rooke was waiting at Spithead for the arrival of the troops from Holland. On the 31st he was ordered to sail as soon as he had got transport for 6,000 troops. If any had still not arrived then, he was to leave a convoy to bring them after him. On February 7th he was at St. Helens. On the 8th there is an order to the officers of Ordnance to supply 582 muskets in lieu of pikes to three regiments of foot, of which the 9th was one—that is 194 to each regiment. Rooke was at Spithead on February 10th, and it was only on the 13th that he reached Plymouth with about 400 sail, warships and transports. It took him till February 29th to reach Lisbon, where his troops and the Archduke were safely put ashore.

Most of the English and Dutch troops were encamped in an unhealthy spot near Lisbon, where they suffered severely from sickness in the period up till May, 1704, when the allied army was ready for operations.

The Portuguese army was in a wretched condition, the fortresses

---

[1] 2nd, 9th, 11th, 13th, 17th, and 33rd Foot.

were dilapidated, and everything in the way of supplies was wanting. Mainhard Schomberg (now Duke of Leinster), commanding the English troops, and Fagel, the Dutch general, were on bad terms, and, with the exception of the Marquis Das Minas, there was no Portuguese commander of any worth. Schomberg, with 4,200 English, joined Las Galveas, an old man of between eighty and ninety commanding the Portuguese in the Alemtejo Province, south of the Tagus, whilst Fagel and his Dutch joined Das Minas in Beira. Altogether there were about 9,000 English and Portuguese in Alemtejo and 12,000 Dutch and Portuguese in Beira. Of these the 4,200 English and 2,000 Dutch were the only troops of any real value. The Portuguese were mere militia.

Against the allies Berwick, now a general of Louis XIV, commanded 28,000 good troops.

With the progress of the ensuing campaign we need not concern ourselves; for the interest of it, for the 9th, centres in the small fortress of Castello de Vide, where they had been sent to stiffen the rest of the garrison, consisting of two Portuguese battalions. They saw none of the early part of the campaign, and it was not till June 21st that Berwick was able to despatch d'Asfeld, his lieutenant and a good engineer, to aid the Spanish General Villadarias besieging Castello de Vide. The town was poorly fortified, but the citadel was strong, and might easily have been held for some time by an energetic defence, which the 9th would doubtless have made had they been alone. But the rest of the garrison of about 900 men consisted of two wretched Portuguese battalions, and the commander of the whole garrison was a Portuguese. Steuart was not in this campaign, and the 9th was commanded by Lieutenant-Colonel Hussey. The siege was begun, according to San Felipe's account, by the establishment of a battery of nine guns in a bad position, where, with their light metal, they did no harm to the defences. Then twelve guns, mostly field, were placed in a better position on a small height; but they too were not heavy enough to make a breach. In Berwick's words, the Spanish artillery had only begun "to scratch the walls" when, on June 25th, the cowardly Portuguese governor began to open negotiations for surrender, sending as envoys a Portuguese colonel and Colonel Hussey. The reply was that the garrison must surrender as prisoners of war. Thereupon the Englishman, according to Berwick's account, " swore and stormed " that he would never consent. The Portuguese governor, however, was easily frightened by threats of the usual horrors consequent on the storming of a place, and cajoled with promises that he and the officers should retain their arms and property, and that there should be no pillage. He consented to the terms, and the French and Spaniards were admitted to the town. Hussey, still intent on fighting, was for retiring to the citadel with his regiment, but found that, during his absence negotiating, the treacherous governor had managed to throw the regiment's powder into a well. Hussey was now powerless and had no choice but to surrender. The same undeserved fate had already overtaken Stanhope's regiment under similar circumstances at Portalegre.

After its capture the regiment was sent off on a long march through Spain to France. It was said that the Duc d'Anjou ordered this in the hopes that most of them would desert on the way.[1] Meanwhile the victory of Blenheim had given the English numerous prisoners. On September 29, 1704, Marlborough writes to Harley that the French have agreed to exchange the battalions taken in Portugal against a like number of the Blenheim prisoners. The English were to be embarked at Bordeaux, where we hear of the 9th, in November, 1704, waiting for transports.[2] They appear to have gone direct back from Bordeaux to Portugal.

When the 9th got back to Portugal, Schomberg had been replaced by the Earl of Galway, the Ruvigny of the battle of Aughrim. Great events had occurred during its absence from Portugal, of which that which most concerned the Peninsula was the capture of Gibraltar by Rooke and the Prince of Darmstadt. Encouraged by the various successes of the Allies elsewhere it was determined to renew the campaign in Portugal. For the spring campaign of 1705 there were available 2,700 English and five guns under Galway, 2,300 Dutch under Fagel, and 12,000 Portuguese under Corsana, all of whom were by no means in agreement about plans. The difficulty was supposed to be solved by each of the three generals commanding in turn for a week at a time.

---

[1] N. Luttrell's Diary, August 5, 1704.   [2] *Ibid.*, November 21, 1704.

On the other side, de Tessé, who had succeeded Berwick on the latter's recall, having failed to retake Gibraltar, proposed to cover Estremadura with his Spanish army.

Though Galway said the intention of the Allies was to take Alcantara and march by that route on Madrid, very little was done. Valencia de Alcantara[1] was taken early in May, Albuquerque on May 20th, and Salvaterra on the 21st. The 9th appear to have been at these sieges, or some of them, but are not specially mentioned; indeed, there was very little fighting. After a feeble threat against Badajoz the Allies retired to quarters till the heats of summer were over.

On July 12, 1705, the 9th received a draft of 227 men from Hill's (11th) regiment. In the autumn, when operations recommenced, Das Minas was generalissimo, with Galway, Fagel, and Corsana still commanding in turns in the field. On September 30, 1705, the army was concentrated on the River Caya, between Elvas and Badajoz, ready to besiege the latter. With this siege of Badajoz we need not concern ourselves, as the 9th had no fighting in it. After various manœuvres by de Tessé and the Allies, the siege was raised and the besiegers retreated on the Portuguese frontier.

In the spring of 1706 Berwick, now a Marshal of France, was again in command of the enemy in Spain, and was sent to the Portuguese frontier with a small force, which was all that could be spared in this direction, looking to the necessity for action in Catalonia and Valencia to save Madrid from the clutches of Peterborough, with whose remarkable campaign of 1705-1706 we need not deal.

Das Minas had 19,000 men, of whom 200 cavalry and 2,000 infantry were English and 2,000 Dutch. The 9th were among the English and marched throughout with Galway.

However interesting they may be as military history, the events of the next year may from the point of view of a regiment be summed up very briefly.

Alcantara was besieged by the Allies in April, and the 9th were largely instrumental in repulsing an attempt to recover the Convent of St. Francis, which had been stormed by two other regiments on April 10th.

[1] Not to be confused with Alcantara on the Tagus.

This and other fortresses having capitulated without further serious resistance, the advance of the Allies on Madrid was almost unopposed. That capital was occupied at the end of June, but the French were now reinforced, and, after some endeavours to stay their advance, Galway found himself compelled to abandon Madrid and to retire in the direction of Valencia, in which province the winter of 1706–1707 was passed in quarters. Berwick's manœuvres with very superior forces had resulted in the severance of the Anglo-Portuguese army's communications with Portugal. When it had left Madrid it had been joined by the forces of the Archduke Charles from Saragossa, but even then totalled only about 14,000 men of several nationalities—certainly not equal in military value to half the 26,000 good troops under Berwick.

In the early weeks of 1707 Galway had decided to march round the head waters of the Tagus, and then down its right bank on Madrid; but, owing to the movement away from him of Charles, he was deprived of 10,000 Catalonian regulars.

It was first desirable for him to destroy the French magazines on the Murcian frontier, and to replenish his own supplies, which were very short, from them. He hoped that Berwick would fall back from Villena to await the Duc d'Orleans, now on his way with 8,000 French troops from Navarre. Galway and Das Minas, with 15,500 mixed troops, advanced from Elda on Yecla, where they seized Berwick's chief magazines, the French commander falling back on Montealegre. To that place and Caudete Galway followed, again capturing magazines and inducing Berwick to retire to Chinchilla. The allies then returned to Villena to besiege a small castle held by 150 French and 150 Murcians. The place put up a good defence and had not been taken when, on April 22nd, Galway was warned that Berwick was marching with his whole force on Almanza, and would very shortly be reinforced by the Duc d'Orleans's fresh troops.

Hurrying off at once, Galway and Das Minas were at Caudete on the 24th, where they boldly, if not rashly, decided to attack Berwick before his reinforcements arrived. On the morning of the 25th they marched for Almanza in four columns. Their heterogeneous force consisted of about 4,500 horse and 11,000 infantry. There were 4,800

English, 1,480 Dutch, 1,100 French Huguenots, and 250 Germans, the remainder being Portuguese levies of poor quality. Berwick had 25,400, of whom a large proportion were cavalry. The French numbered 11,900, the rest being Spaniards. Hearing of the allied advance he sent his baggage into the town and, as they began to come in sight, arranged his army for battle in two lines in front of Almanza. His infantry was in the centre, the Spanish horse on the right, and the French horse on the left. His right rested on rising ground, on which he had a battery; his left was on a height above the Valencia road. In front of his centre was a ravine which disappeared as his right was reached.

It was noon when the heads of the allied columns debouched on the plain, about a mile from Berwick's position. The troops, after halting and resting, were drawn up in two lines, with the bulk of the infantry in the first line. The post of honour on the right wing being claimed by Das Minas, the Portuguese cavalry was posted there, interspersed with infantry to compensate for their inferior numbers. The same arrangement was made with the left wing, where Galway was in person. Here, in addition to the English, were some Portuguese cavalry on the extreme left of the second line. The 9th and 36th foot were immediately on the right of these squadrons.

About 3 p.m. Galway and Carpenter attacked Berwick's right with only three squadrons of Carpenter's dragoons, under a heavy fire from the battery on the height. At first they were overpowered by superior forces, but the tables were turned by the fire of the infantry of Wade's brigade.[1] An attempt to take the hostile battery with dragoons failed, as the enemy withdrew his guns in time. Carpenter, being joined by Killigrew's five squadrons, then drove back the Spanish cavalry on their second line. At the same time Erle, with the English, Dutch, and Huguenots of the first line of the left centre, drove the French and Spanish infantry back and, supported by Shrimpton with the second line, almost forced them into Almanza. Now was the time for the Portuguese on the right to attack and keep the enemy's left from supporting his centre.

---

[1] The brigades (British infantry) at Almanza were : 1st, Macartney—Guards, 28th, 35th, and Macartney's. 2nd, Hill—6th, 9th, Lord Mark Kerr's. 3rd, Wade—17th, 33rd, and five squadrons. 4th, Buller—2nd, Breton's, Nassau's, Caulfield's.

They did nothing, and d'Avaray, with parts of Berwick's French infantry, was able to fall on the right flank of the British infantry, which was compelled to stop its advance and fight for very existence against attacks in front, on right flank, and even in rear.

At the same time Berwick sent forward his French cavalry of the first line of the left against the Portuguese, who, with the exception of a few squadrons commanded by Das Minas himself, fled at once from the field. Their infantry also fled after a feeble resistance. Deserted by most of his men, Das Minas passed over to the left, where Galway had been temporarily disabled by a sabre cut over the eye. With his four Portuguese squadrons on the extreme left, Das Minas joined in the fight carried on by the first line of the allies with fair success so far. Now, however, Berwick, was able to send nine battalions from the second line of his centre against Wade's brigade and the 9th and 36th Foot, which had been called up to its assistance. More cavalry was also sent by Berwick against the allied left, which, overwhelmed by numbers, was forced to retreat, losing very heavily in killed, wounded, and prisoners. To facilitate this retreat gallant charges were made, under Galway's orders, by Harvey's horse and the Huguenots, led by Carpenter, on the infantry attacking the flank of Wade's brigade and the 9th and 36th. Thanks to these Galway was able to send away six guns and some stores and baggage to Valencia. He himself, with some 3,500 men, including the remains of the 9th, who were all that remained of the left wing, then retreated unmolested on Onteniente, twenty-two miles east.

In the allied centre only about 2,000 men—the remnants of five English,[1] three Portuguese, three Huguenot, and two Dutch regiments—succeeded in reaching the hills near Caudete, pursued by d'Asfeld with the enemy's cavalry. There they took up a strong position, but next morning, being surrounded by the enemy and without food or ammunition, they were compelled to surrender as prisoners of war.

What remained of the 9th got away with Galway. How well they had fought against desperate odds is shown by their casualty list. The officers casualty list is as follows :—

[1] Portmore's (2nd), Hill's (11th), Gorge's (35th), Macartney's, and Breton's. The last two were disbanded later so are not numbered.

Killed: Captains John Campbell, James White, Alexander Wallis or Wallace, Robert Phillips, and Joseph Gregory.

Prisoners: Captains Parsy (? Dansey), —Steuart, Thomas Hills, — Charlton, Thomas Hussey, David Bell, John Johnston, James Steuart; Lieutenants Mark Kerr, Thomas Constable, John Ash; Ensigns William Adams, — Smith, James Steuart, James Montgomery, John Irwin.

All the prisoners were wounded except Lieutenant Ash and Ensign Irwin.[1]

On April 26th Galway marched to Alcira, a fortified place not far from the coast. Here he stayed a few days, and then left Lieutenant-Colonel Steuart[2] with 800 foot, chiefly Dutch and English, including the remnants of his own regiment, to hold the place. On May 5th d'Asfeld, who had been left by Berwick to deal with the sieges of Valencian strongholds, despatched the Spanish General Mahoni (otherwise Mahony) with 3,000 men to take Alcira. Steuart held out bravely till, finding himself short of provisions, with no present hope of relief, he surrendered on honourable terms, which provided for him and his garrison being sent back to Galway's army in Catalonia. Unfortunately it was not stipulated that they were to be sent by the shortest route—an omission of which Berwick took a mean advantage by sending them round on a three months' tramp through Aragon. Berwick excuses his conduct also by saying that, as some officers and men had escaped after the capitulation and joined the *miqueletes* in the Valencian

---

[1] This is the list as given by Dalton. Another MS. list at the R.U.S.I. (authority not stated) shows the following:—*Officers killed:* Captains Campbell, Wallace, White, Phillips, Gregory; Lieutenants Wilcocks and Steuart; Ensign Carey. *Officers wounded and prisoners:* Captains Dansey, Steuart, Hill, Carleton; Lieutenants Hussey, Bell, Johnston, W. Steuart, Carr, Constable; Ensign Adams. It is added that Lieutenant Ash was the only unwounded officer and he was a prisoner. Boyer's "Annals of Queen Anne" gives:—*Killed:* Captains Campbell, Wallace, White, Phillips, Gregory; Lieutenants Wilcocks, Robert Steuart, senr., Robert Steuart, junr.; Ensigns Casey (killed at Villena) and Bussière. *Prisoners:* Captains Dansey, William Steuart, Hill, Carleton; Lieutenants Hussey, Bell, Johnston, Jas. Steuart, Carr, Constable, Ash; Ensigns Adams, Smith, Jas. Steuart, Montgomery, Erwine—all wounded except Ash.

[2] Nephew of the colonel. He had succeeded Hussey as Lieutenant-Colonel. His uncle in his will cut him off with a shilling for alleged ingratitude.

hills, he would really have been justified in detaining the whole force as prisoners.

After suffering great privations on their long march this small force, including the late garrison of Xativa, marched into Galway's camp at Tarrega, twenty miles east of Lerida, on September 16, 1707, with flags flying and drums beating. Galway had gathered in about 2,000 of the stragglers or escaped British prisoners of Almanza, and from these he constituted five battalions, with which he resuscitated five of the oldest regiments which had been taken or practically destroyed at Almanza. They were Portmore's (2nd),[1] Southwell's (6th), Steuart's (9th), Hill's (11th), and Blood's (17th). The 9th was made up to 386 rank and file; at Almanza it had been practically destroyed, not taken whole, as it had been, through no fault of its own, at Castello de Vide. It had lost, killed, or captured about twenty out of its twenty-six officers, of whom only one, or perhaps two, were unwounded. An unknown number of other ranks had suffered a similar fate. The new regiment can have contained very few elements of the old, but Steuart on his return from Alcira again took command of it.

Galway had now again got together an army of 14,600 men, of whom 3,100 were English, 1,400 Dutch, 200 French Huguenots, and the rest Portuguese and Spaniards. He was now defending Catalonia on the river front of the Segre, holding Lerida with a garrison of 1,800 regulars, including three British regiments, and 800 *miqueletes*. As Orleans advanced on August 23rd, Galway's cavalry retired to Iqualada leaving the French to invest Lerida, which made a desperate defence till October 29th.

On that day Galway advanced from Tarrega to Las Borjas, on the left bank of the Segre, whilst Orleans retired to the right bank, blew up his bridges, and withdrew the troops investing Lerida on the left bank only. Galway, finding it impossible to relieve Lerida after advancing to the Segre, retired again to Las Borjas, though he managed to get into communication with Prince Henry in Lerida. That place at last surrendered, when only 600 men were left fit for duty. Having obtained

[1] The number was reduced to four by breaking up Portmore's for the time being.

the honours of war, the remnants of the garrison joined Galway, who then retired into winter quarters at Reuss and Tarragona.

In these operations of the autumn of 1707 the reconstructed 9th appears to have played no special part, though it was doubtless present at them. Its career in Spain was for the present over, for it was one of the regiments sent home in the winter of 1707–1708. All that went home was a mere skeleton.

Orders were issued on September 15, 1707, for recruiting Steuart's regiment up to full strength, to rendezvous at Hereford in anticipation of the return of the nucleus of the regiment from Spain. From December 24, 1707, its establishment was fixed at thirteen companies of three sergeants, three corporals, two drummers and fifty-six men each, besides the usual staff of officers.

Exactly when the remnant of the regiment left Galway's force and sailed for England is not ascertainable. It probably arrived home early in 1708.

CHAPTER V

SERVICE AT HOME, MINORCA, GIBRALTAR, AND THE EXPEDITION TO BELLEISLE, 1708–1762

FROM the date of its return from Spain after Almanza the regiment's history for a full half century is blank in the matter of active service, or at least of fighting. Not that the period was one of peace, but it so happened that, when there was war, and the regiment was out of Great Britain or Ireland, it was at Minorca or Gibraltar, neither of which was attacked. Beyond changes in establishment, commissions, promotions, and the ordinary routine of a regiment on peace service there was nothing to record officially, and owing to the unfortunate loss of the regimental records in the wreck of the "Ariadne" in 1805 we are deprived of any regimental record of its life.

In March, 1708, we find recruits for the regiment being ordered from Hereford and London to Winchester, evidently in anticipation of its arrival from Spain. As there is a hiatus in the records of marching orders in the earlier part of 1708 it is not possible to say exactly where the regiment marched on landing from Spain, but it appears to have gone first to Winchester and then to have moved on to Worcester and Hereford (three companies). There is a further order for recruiting it to full strength on September 15, 1708; rendezvous at Worcester and Hereford. On November 22, 1708, and again on December 6th, we find recruits being marched from London to join the regiment at Worcester.

On January 22, 1709, the three companies at Hereford are ordered to join the rest of the regiment at Worcester. This was followed, on February 12th, by an order for the whole regiment to march to

Portsmouth, which, ten days later, was changed to one ordering four companies to Stockport and the rest to Manchester. On April 24, 1709, Steuart was ordered to reduce his regiment from a strength of thirteen companies, each of three sergeants, three corporals, two drummers and fifty-six privates, to twelve companies of two sergeants, three corporals, two drummers and fifty men. He was to send thirteen sergeants and seventy-eight men (i.e. one sergeant and six men from each company) to Brigadier Wynn's regiment, and one complete company (at the reduced strength) to Brigadier Evans's. The complete company was to be the 13th or junior company, and its officers were to be the junior captain, lieutenant, and ensign. These officers were to be reinstated in the 9th, if they so desired, on the occurrence of vacancies in their respective ranks. In June, 1709, the regiment was concentrated at Chester for transfer to Ireland. It is on record that, on September 26, 1709, thirty sergeants, corporals, drummers and privates " lately arrived from Flanders " and belonging to Steuart's regiment were sent after it by Holyhead. On February 1, 1710, Captain Carleton, three sergeants, three corporals, one drummer, and thirty privates are similarly sent after it. From these entries, combined with the fact that the orders for concentration at Chester deal with only ten companies, it looks as if a considerable draft had been lent to other regiments in Flanders, and the remains of it were now being returned. That such a practice prevailed is confirmed by an entry in 1711 showing the regimental establishment as 724, including officers, but noting that, as the eight regiments then remaining in Ireland had had to contribute drafts to fill up the four ordered to Spain, they were 1,000 under strength, 125 per regiment on the average.

For reasons already stated[1] it is not possible to say where the regiment was stationed in Ireland between 1709 and 1718.

On June 5, 1718, the regiment was reduced, as a consequence of the Peace of Utrecht, by two companies, so that its establishment stood at ten companies, each with two sergeants, two corporals, one drummer and thirty-eight privates. The rates of pay are given as follows :—

[1] P. 39. *supra*.

| | Per diem. |
	£ s. d.
Colonel, as Colonel	0 12 0
Lt.-Col., as Lt.-Col.	0 7 0
Major, as Major	0 4 0
Chaplain	0 6 8
Surgeon and Mate	0 6 6
Adjutant and Quartermaster	0 4 0
Captain	0 8 0
Lieutenant	0 4 0
Ensign	0 3 0
Sergeant	0 1 6
Corporals and Drummers	0 1 0
Privates	0 0 6

From this it would appear that the major and the private were the only ones who were on the lower Irish pay. One regiment (Selwyn's) in Ireland was kept at a higher strength and pay, and this was laid down as the standard to which regiments ordered to the West Indies were to be raised. In it the major got 5s. and the private 8d. per day.[1]

In 1714 the precedence of certain regiments was fixed. The 9th, as on previous occasions, was placed ninth in the list of line regiments, commencing with the 1st Royals. There had never been any variation in this matter, as none of the regiments of earlier raising were disbanded.

In 1715, after the accession of George I, Steuart, who had now commanded the regiment since 1689, appears to have come under suspicion of leanings towards the cause of the Stuarts. Whether the suspicion was justified or not—and it is difficult to believe that one who had for so long strenuously opposed the Jacobite cause would now turn round—he sold his commission as colonel of the 9th to Colonel James Campbell, Lieutenant-Colonel of the Scots Greys, and retired from military service. He was certainly one of the most notable of the

[1] By an order dated March 12, 1754 (W.O. 8, vol. 4), the following additions " clear of all deductions " were sanctioned in Ireland: Captains, 6d. per diem; subalterns, 2d.; privates, 1d.

regiment's colonels. In direct command of his own regiment and later as brigadier, major-general, lieutenant-general, and general, he had served William III and Anne with great fidelity and distinction.[1]

Campbell was only with the 9th till February, 1717, when, on his transfer to the colonelcy of the Scots Greys, he was succeeded as colonel of the 9th by the Hon. Charles (afterwards Lord) Cathcart, who, retiring a year later, gave place to Colonel James Otway in January, 1718.

In July, 1718, the regiment was transferred from Ireland to the Mediterranean, and was sent to Minorca, where it was destined to serve for many years. It embarked on May 8, 1718, but did not reach Gibraltar till July 12th. It was only on the latter date that Ireland was relieved of the charges of the regiment. It was peace time in 1718, and for service in Minorca the establishment was fixed at twelve companies, each with two sergeants, two corporals, two drummers, and thirty-seven privates, except the grenadier company, which had forty-five privates. An order of May 20, 1718, says that, on arrival in Minorca, James Otway's regiment is to be completed by a draft from that of Major-General Whetham, which it was relieving, as follows : " The two youngest companies entire, consisting of seventy-four privates, four sergeants, four corporals, four drummers, the two youngest captains, two youngest lieutenants, two youngest ensigns. Also a quartermaster and twenty-eight men with all arms and accoutrements, etc." As the N.C.O.'s and men were drawn by lot, it resulted in some of very long service abroad being drawn. Later on these were returned to their own regiment and replaced by men of shorter service.

Colonel Otway, dying in 1725, was succeeded on December 25th in the colonelcy of the 9th by Brigadier Richard Kane, who had been appointed Lieutenant-Governor and Commander-in-Chief of Minorca on its cession to England in 1713. He was an officer of high reputation on account of his excellent administrative work in the island, and his improve-

[1] A full and interesting account of his services is given in Dalton's " Army of George I," vol. I, p. 71. He was, in February, 1712, appointed Commander-in-Chief of the Army in Ireland. The date of his commission as brigadier-general has not been traced. His later commissions were : major-general, June 1, 1696 ; lieutenant-general, February 11, 1703 ; general, January 31, 1710. A short account of him is given in Appendix I.

ments there, especially his construction of a good road right across the island.[1] The regimental establishment remained unchanged till December 25, 1729, when it was fixed at ten companies, each of three sergeants, three corporals, two drummers, and fifty privates. The number of grenadiers was now again the same as that of the privates in the other companies.

The establishment remained unchanged till Brigadier Kane's death in 1737. He was succeeded by Colonel Hargrave, who was transferred to the 7th Fusiliers in 1739. To him succeeded Brigadier-General George Reade, on August 28, 1739. In June, 1739, the number of men in each company was raised to sixty, in anticipation of war with Spain, and on August 12th, a week after the declaration of war, it was raised to seventy. The total establishment was now 815, including officers. The garrison of Minorca, which had so far been four battalions, was now raised to five. War continued, in one form or another, till the Peace of Aix-la-Chapelle in October, 1748, and the establishment of the 9th remained unaltered, though it was not called on to serve in the field.

In 1746 the regiment was moved from Minorca to Gibraltar, to replace two other regiments sent to America. There it remained, still undisturbed by the storm of war raging elsewhere, till 1749. In that year Brigadier-General Reade was transferred to the colonelcy of the 9th Dragoons, and was succeeded by Sir C. A. Powlett, on November 1, 1749. The regiment was put on the Irish establishment from December 25, 1749. They were still at Gibraltar, but were under orders for Ireland. The Irish stations of the regiment from 1749 to 1755 are not ascertainable.

On January 26, 1751, Sir C. Powlett, having been transferred, was succeeded in the colonelcy by the Hon. J. Waldegrave. On July 1, 1751, was issued a "Regulation for the colours, clothing, etc., of the marching regiments of foot," of which the following provisions must be noted :—

(1) No colonel was to put his arms, crest, device, or livery on any part of the appointments of the regiment under his command. No alterations outside this warrant were to be made without Royal authority.

---

[1] He was also well known as the author of a book giving the history of William III's Irish and continental campaigns, besides other matters such as formations for attack, etc. See also Appendix I.

(2) *Colours.*—The King's, or first, colour of any regiment to be the Great Union throughout.

The second colour to be the colour of the facing of the regiment, with the Union in the upper canton. (Exception was made in the case of regiments with red or white facings, but this did not concern the 9th.)

In the centre of each colour is to be painted, or embroidered in gold Roman characters the number of the rank of the regiment, within a wreath of roses and thistles on the same stalk, except those regiments which are allowed to wear any Royal devices or ancient badges, on whose colours the rank of the regiment is to be painted towards the upper corner. (This exception is important, inasmuch as the 9th is not recognized as coming within it, and there is no mention of the famous " Britannia " badge.)

The size of the colours and the length of the pike to be the same as those of the Royal Regiment of Foot Guards. The cords and tassels of all colours to be of crimson and gold mixed.

(3) *Drummers' Clothing.*—After providing for the drummers of all the Royal Regiments, which did not include the 9th, the warrant goes on to say that the drummers of all the other regiments are to be clothed with the colours of the facings of their regiments, lined, faced, and lapelled on the breast with red, and laced in such manner as the colonel shall think fit, for distinction' sake; the lace, however, being of the colours of that on the soldiers' coats.

(4) *Grenadiers' Caps.*—The front of the grenadiers' caps to be the same colour as the facings of the regiment, with the King's cypher embroidered, and crown over it ; the little flaps to be red, with the White Horse and motto over it " Nec aspera terrent " ; the back part of the cap to be red ; the turn up to be the colour of the front, with the number of the regiment in the middle part behind.

(5) *Drums.*—The front or fore part of the drums to be painted with the colour of the facings of the regiment, with the King's cypher and crown, and the number of the regiment under it.

(6) *Bells of Arms.*—To be painted in the same manner.

Then follow the special regulations for the Royal Regiments and the six old corps, which do not concern the 9th.

Finally, there is a schedule of the facings of marching regiments in which the entry against the 9th is—

Colour of the Facings.—Yellow. *Rank and title of Regiment.*—9th Regiment. *Distinctions in the same Colour.*—Blank. *Name of present Colonel.*—Colonel Waldegrave.[1]

Besides being a definite attempt to fix regulations on the subjects dealt with, this warrant is of the greatest importance as a distinct official recognition of a new and fixed title for the regiment, which hitherto had been officially known generally by the name of its colonel for the time being, a practice which sometimes involved a change of title every few years, sometimes even, as in 1688–89, three changes in a few months. Henceforward, till it acquired also a territorial title, it was officially known as the "9th Regiment of Foot," though in practice it took some years before the habit of occasionally alluding to it in official correspondence by the name of its colonel was entirely abandoned. It now had a number to which to attach its traditions and its honours. It was not till thirty-one years later (August, 1781) that it became the "9th or East Norfolk Regiment of Foot." By that time the title of "the 9th" had been so thoroughly adopted that many years afterwards we find Sir William Gomm affectionately speaking of it as "The old 9th." When, finally, a century later, it became, as it now is, the "Norfolk Regiment" it is probable that, as generally happened, officers and men were loth to give up the title of the "9th Foot," and occasionally incurred an official rebuke for speaking of "The 9th" instead of the "Norfolk Regiment." One thing is certain, that till 1781 there was no official recognition of the connexion between the 9th Foot and the County of Norfolk. Till then, if the regiment was specially connected with any particular county, it was so with Gloucester, where it was originally raised. It is a curious fact, recorded by Sergeant Hale, that, even so late as August, 1807, he and 170 others volunteered from the North Gloucestershire Militia for service in "His Majesty's 9th or 'Britannia' Regiment of Foot."

In 1755 the 9th, with seven other regiments, having been ordered from Ireland to England, was transferred to the English establishment

---

[1] For a full account of uniforms, badges and colours see Appendices III and IV.

from March 12th. Its establishment was fixed, as from December 25, 1754, at ten companies, each having three sergeants, three corporals, two drummers, and seventy privates—the allowances for servants, widows, etc., as usual. In this year Colonel Waldegrave was transferred, and Sir Joseph Yorke became colonel on March 18, 1755.

From October, 1755, the establishment was further augmented by the addition of two strong companies, each with four sergeants, four corporals, two drummers, and one hundred privates. The officers of these companies were not increased above the ordinary strength of one captain, one lieutenant, and one ensign.[1]

The regiment, landing at Bristol in March, 1755, was distributed—five companies to Bristol, four to Exeter, and one to Tiverton.

Orders of October 28 and November 1, 1755, directed the move of the regiment from Exeter and Bristol to Carlisle, where it would receive orders for their further march into Scotland. A detachment of sick, who had been left behind in Ireland, was sent after them to Glasgow in 1756.

They had been inspected at Bristol on October 18, 1755, by Lieutenant-General Sir J. Mordaunt, who described them as being of an unsoldierlike appearance, being nearly all recruits in so far as he saw them. He was therefore unable to say whether they were fit for service as a regiment. He saw about 600 men, as 207 were on board the fleet, from which it appears that they were going by sea.

From Scotland they again went to Ireland in the spring of 1757; the Irish stations are not to be found.

On return from Ireland in February, 1759, the regiment was sent from Bideford to Oakhampton, Tavistock, Dartmouth, Falmouth, Launceston, and Penrhyn, and the four companies at Falmouth were directed to take over, from three companies of Lord George Bentinck's regiment, the duty of guarding the French prisoners at Falmouth and Penrhyn.

On March 6th one company from Oakhampton and one from

[1] An order of January 21, 1756, however, directs Colonel Yorke to turn over to the 57th the two additional companies of his regiment with eight sergeants, eight corporals, four drummers, and forty men.

Launceston were sent to take over the guard of French prisoners at Bideford from Lieutenant-General Wolfe's regiment.

In June the regiment was concentrated at Plymouth, where it remained till June, 1760. From June 25, 1759, the establishment of the regiment was fixed at nine companies, each of four sergeants, four corporals, two drummers, and one hundred men. The grenadier company had two fifers in addition to the drummers. Total, 1,034, including officers. Orders of June 7, 1760, directed its march to Chatham Lines, where it was encamped till, on October 13th, it was ordered to be moved into Chatham Barracks.

An order of January 24, 1761, addressed to Major-General Hodgson, empowers him to move the 9th and four other regiments, which were to be under his command for an expedition abroad, to places suitable for embarkation; but the regiment was left at Chatham till March 5th, when it received orders to march to Hilsea Barracks, near Portsmouth, to arrive on the 16th and 17th in two divisions.

The secret expedition for which troops and transports had been collected about the time of George II's death, in October, 1760, had had to be abandoned, and it was now decided to utilize the means then prepared for the capture of Belleisle, a French island lying off Quiberon Bay in the Bay of Biscay.

The escort of the expedition consisted of eight line-of-battle ships besides frigates, and the commander of the troops was on board the "Valiant" (74 guns). The troops numbered about 10,000 men, and consisted of a detachment of the 16th Light Dragoons and the 9th, 19th, 21st, 30th, 67th, 76th, 85th, 90th, 97th, and 98th Foot, or parts of them. The 9th, commanded by Lieutenant-Colonel R. Phillips, were 800 strong. The fleet, with a fair wind, sailed from Spithead on March 29th, and arrived off Belleisle on April 7th. The same day, whilst the flat-bottomed boats for landing the troops were being got ready, General Hodgson, in command of the troops, and Commodore Keppel sailed round the island to reconnoitre. It was not a promising looking object to attack, for the few gaps in the wall of cliffs were fortified, and at Palais, the citadel of the island fortress, the works had only recently been strengthened. There seemed a possibility of landing at the south-eastern end of the island, near the village of Lomaria. Early in the morning of April 8th the fort there and the shore batteries were silenced by fire from the fleet, and troops were put ashore, led, as usual, by the grenadiers from the different regiments of infantry. But the cliffs, which had been scarped at the bottom, were too steep for the troops to reach the enemy in any considerable force. Several attempts were made without success, but sixty grenadiers of the 67th succeeded in scrambling unobserved to the top of the cliff from a neighbouring bay where they had landed. There, however, they were overwhelmed by superior numbers and all but twenty either captured or killed. The attempt was abandoned after some 400 men had been killed, wounded, or captured. A simultaneous attempt to create a diversion by landing the regiments of Grey and Stuart at Sauzon was abandoned without being pressed home, as the enemy were ready and the weather was beginning to break. Bad weather set in on the evening of the 8th, and, besides scattering the fleet and damaging many of the flat-bottomed boats, prevented further attempts till the 22nd. A reinforcement of four battalions[1] was despatched from England as soon as this failure was known.

The garrison of the island was very weak compared to the invaders. It was commanded by the Chevalier de St. Croix, and, including officers, artillery, engineers, and coastguards, did not exceed 2,500 regular troops. There were 4,000 local militia, but these were probably of very small value, and were not called up at first.

It was not till April 22nd that the weather would allow of fresh landing operations. It was calculated that, if attacks were made at several points simultaneously, the probability was that the weak garrison, unable to defend the cliffs everywhere, would be surprised at some place which had been left unguarded, in the belief that it was unassailable. That is precisely what happened when the various attacks and feints were started at 5 p.m. on April 22nd. A party of Beauclerk's regiment, under Captain Patterson, landing at a point near Lomaria, supposed to be invulnerable, succeeded in scrambling up the cliffs, and was able to beat off an attack by some 300 men who were sent against them. The rest of the regiment, and a detachment of marines, following Captain

[1] 3rd, 36th, 75th, 85th (2nd Battalion).

Patterson, advanced against the enemy, who were compelled to retire with the loss of three field pieces and some wounded prisoners. Once the circle of the cliffs was broken through the whole of the expeditionary troops landed without difficulty, and the enemy, including the militia, retired before them to Palais.

Hodgson now advanced with his whole force against Palais, in front of which St. Croix had his garrison and the 4,000 local militia. The siege artillery was much delayed in landing by continued bad weather, and the enemy took advantage of the delay to construct six new redoubts barring the approaches to the town. At the end of April, trenches were opened and, on May 3rd, a vigorous sortie was made by the garrison against the British left. In it Brigadier-General Crawford and his two aides-de-camp were captured, a good many men were killed and wounded on both sides, and the besiegers' left works were damaged, though not seriously. As the approaches progressed it was found absolutely necessary to capture the defenders' six new redoubts. They were assaulted on May 13th, beginning with the one on the British left, and all were taken in succession by a detachment of Loudon's regiment, reinforced by Colvill's and some marines. The storming party penetrated into the town, and the garrison were driven into the citadel, where St. Croix continued his active defence. There were several sorties which did no great harm. By May 25th, however, the siege works had been carried so far forward, and the bombardment had been so severe, that the fire of the defence visibly slackened. On June 7th the breach in the citadel was declared practicable, and the place was summoned, in contemplation of an assault. St. Croix, who had held out for nearly two months, now saw that, with the British fleet barring the approach of any relieving force, his position was hopeless. He decided to capitulate, and, in consideration of his gallant defence, he was accorded the honours of war, his troops and himself to be landed at Nantes and other places on the neighbouring coast.

As in other sieges of the eighteenth century, it is difficult to disentangle the exact part played by the 9th Regiment as a whole. The practice was to form a separate battalion or battalions of grenadiers by taking the grenadier companies of the infantry regiments present and forming them into a special corps, which was at the disposal of the commander-in-chief for assaults and other such services. The system was good from the commander's point of view, as it gave him a picked force for desperate work. From the regimental point of view it was bad, for the grenadier company was temporarily lost to the regiment and absorbed in the grenadier battalion to which it was attached. The losses of the grenadier company in officers are generally ascertainable, as in their case names and the regiments to which they belonged are given in the casualty lists of the grenadier battalion. But it is not so with other ranks.

That the 9th were seriously engaged is shown by a return of May 31, 1761, which states that since the last monthly return Major Thomas and Lieutenants Surman and Ryder were prisoners of war, and twenty-two men were dead. We may be sure that the grenadier company, at any rate, was in all assaults, including the first attempt at landing when Cannon, without quoting his authority, says that "the Ninth leapt on the beach in the face of the enemy's entrenchments, and rushed up the steep acclivity to storm the works, but were unable to gain the summit without ladders." Amongst the "Military Extracts" at the R.U.S.I. is one which shows the casualties of Whitmore's (9th) regiment on April 8th as killed, two sergeants and nine rank and file; wounded, three rank and file; prisoners, three officers (Lieutenant-Colonel Thomas wounded, Lieutenants Surman and Ryder), one sergeant, and forty rank and file.

The total British loss up to the capitulation was: Killed, thirteen officers and 271 other ranks; wounded, twenty-one officers and 477 other ranks.[1]

[1] According to the MS. notes quoted above the losses were:

Officers	4 killed,	1	wounded,	15	prisoners	=	20
Sergeants	10 ,,	1	,,	4	,,	=	15
Drummers	4 ,,	1	,,	1	,,	=	6
Privates	76 ,,	72	,,	245	,,	=	393
Total -	94	75		265		=	434

The figures in the text are from "British Minor Expeditions," and are perhaps the more reliable, though doubt is thrown on them by the omission of prisoners. These were of course recovered on the French surrender.

The 9th remained in garrison in Belleisle till the beginning of 1762, when they embarked with General Hodgson for England. From December 25, 1761, the establishment was fixed at nine companies, each of four sergeants, four corporals, two drummers, two fifers (for the grenadiers), and one hundred men. A second surgeon's mate was allowed. Total, 1,034, including officers.

On January 9th there is an order to the governor of Portsmouth to distribute the nine companies of the 9th, on arrival, four companies to Chichester, four between Petersfield and Havant, and one to Arundel. From a letter from Hodgson to the Secretary at War it appears that the fleet, having been scattered by a gale, still had four transports missing on January 16th.

The regiment was being completed for a fresh foreign service, as is shown by a new order to the governor of Portsmouth to send for such officers as he might choose to receive drafts for the 9th and march them to its head-quarters at Chichester. On the same date, the Earl of Albemarle, who was to command another foreign expedition, is authorized to march the 9th and the regiments of Lord F. Cavendish, Keppel, and the Duke of Richmond by such routes and to such places as he might find convenient for embarkation.

CHAPTER VI

THE SIEGE OF HAVANA—FLORIDA AND HOME SERVICE, 1762-1776

THE expedition which Lord Albemarle was to command was directed against the Spanish possessions in Cuba. It had been contemplated as it became clear that Spain was going to declare war and join France. When war was actually declared on January 18, 1762, all was practically ready for movement.

The secret instructions to Albemarle are dated February 18, 1762. He was to go to Portsmouth and embark the 22nd, 34th, 56th, and 72nd, as well as two companies of Protestant prisoners, apparently French, who had taken service under Major Freron with the English. He would also find the necessary supply of artillery, engineers, etc. In the West Indies he would pick up what remained of Monckton's expedition to Martinique; also the 69th, 76th, 90th, and 98th sent from Belleisle. He was further to receive 4,000 men from General Amherst from North America. His whole force to be used in Cuba was, however, not to exceed 14,000 men. As a matter of fact, Monckton's force was greatly reduced: the 4,000 men from America did not turn up, and Albemarle could not even reach his limit. He sailed from Spithead on March 5th, and, after a good passage, the fleet, which was commanded by Sir G. Pocock, reached Barbados on April 20th. There Albemarle found that Monckton's shortage of supplies had prevented his coming to Barbados, so there was nothing for it but for Albemarle to go to Martinique. There he found what he describes as "the remains of a very fine army greatly diminished, since the reduction of the island, by sickness." He was also disappointed in the corps of negro free labourers which he expected to find. This deficiency had to be supplied by buying slaves when he could not hire free negroes ; for the climate of the West Indies was not one in which the white soldier could be expected to do much of the work of digging trenches and erecting batteries. The 4,000 troops from North America had not arrived. Time was passing, and, unless the expedition hurried up, it would find itself before Havana only when the hurricane season would add enormously to its difficulties, and might be fatal to the fleet on which so much depended. Accordingly, to save time, Sir George Pocock, sailing from Martinique on May 6th, took the fleet through the difficult Bahama passage and arrived off the north coast of Cuba, a few miles east of Havana, on June 6th. Part of the fleet was sent to bottle up the Spanish ships in Havana Harbour, and next day the army was landed without opposition beyond the fire of two small forts, about three miles apart, between which the landing was made. A few shots from the ships sufficed to drive out the garrisons of negroes and peasants, who took refuge in the woods.

After leaving ten battalions to garrison the Leeward Islands, Albemarle had with him for the siege of Havana four infantry brigades (sixteen battalions) in the second of which, under Brigadier-General H. Walsh, were the battalion companies of the 9th.

The light companies of the regiments from England, among them the 9th, and two battalions of grenadiers formed from the grenadier companies of all the regiments, formed a separate *corps d'élite* under Colonel Carleton. Including artillery and engineers, the whole force was just over 10,000 strong. The American and Jamaican contingents did not arrive till the end of July, and then only added about 2,000—far less than the losses, chiefly from sickness, in the interval.

The 9th mustering 977 of all ranks, and the 34th with 976, were by far the strongest regiments of the force. The next after them were the 72nd (686), 77th (605), and 22nd (602).

On June 8th the troops marched for Havana. On the River Coximar they encountered a force of some 6,000, chiefly militia, strongly posted. These were driven back on the fortress without much difficulty, and Colonel Howe, with two battalions of grenadiers, reconnoitred nearly up

72 HISTORY OF THE NORFOLK REGIMENT

to Fort Moro, the principal defence on the eastern side of the entrance of Havana Harbour.

On the 9th the army encamped in the woods between their landing-place and the eastern side of the harbour. To keep open his communications with the landing-place, and to collect supplies in the surrounding country, Albemarle left a force under General Elliott. A useful part of it consisted of one hundred men who were formed into dragoons, or

SIEGE OF HAVANA
A British batteries. B " Twelve Apostles " battery. C "Shepherd's" battery.
D Sunken ships. E Breach.

we might say mounted infantry, under Captain Suttie of the 9th, to which presumably the bulk of the men belonged. Mounted on horses found in the neighbourhood, they were found very useful during the siege, both as patrols and in rounding up cattle for the commissariat.

The harbour, which is a very fine one, is entered by a passage some 200 yards in breadth and half a mile long, the mouth of which was commanded by Fort El Moro on the east and Fort Punta on the west.

HAVANA, 1762.
From a contemporary painting at Quidenham. (*Ch. VI*)

From the Moro Fort, along the east side of the harbour, extends a ridge called the Cavaños, on which there was a fort known to our men as the Spanish redoubt. This ridge overlooked the town, which lay on the west side of the harbour and had a fortified enceinte. In any attack from the east this ridge, and the Moro Fort at the end of it, clearly had to be taken first. When they had fallen the western defences could hardly hold out long. The Moro stood on a high rock at the western end of the Cavaños. It was roughly triangular in form, the landward side having two demi-bastions at the ends towards the sea and harbour, and a curtain with a redan in the centre. It had forty guns. On the harbour beach, about opposite the centre of the town, there was a battery called the " Divina Pastora " which in the despatches appears as " The Shepherd's Battery." Another battery called the " Twelve Apostles " was on the beach near the Moro. The approaches to these key positions were very difficult, being through dense forest to within a few hundred yards of the glacis of Fort Moro. Moreover, the ground was extremely unfavourable for siege operations, as the layer of soil overlying the rock was too thin to allow of trenches being sunk. The parapets had to be largely built up with earth scraped together from the neighbourhood, supplemented by fascines and gabions. The Spanish garrison of Havana consisted of about 4,600 regular troops and 9,000 sailors from the fleet, which had been driven in by the British, and had effectually prevented its own exit by the sinking of ships in the entrance. There were also 14,000 militia and " people of colour " whose military value was insignificant.

On June 10th the ridge and the Moro were reconnoitred and invested by Brigadier Carleton with the light infantry and grenadiers, including those of the 9th. Next day Carleton succeeded in storming the Spanish redoubt with little loss. This capture enabled the establishment of a howitzer battery to drive the Spanish ships, which were being dismantled, farther up the harbour. On the 13th, when this battery was begun, Colonel Howe, with 300 light infantry and 800 marines from the fleet, were landed and entrenched themselves at Chorera, some miles west of the harbour mouth. This was intended to divert the enemy's attention from the main attack on the east and the Moro, and to serve as a base for the possible attack on the town and the Punta Fort from the west.

The attack on the Moro was pushed steadily forward in the face of enormous difficulties of ground, and still more of climate. The latter soon began to play havoc with the troops. At first the weather was so dry that much delay was caused by the fascines and other dry materials for the parapets being set alight by the enemy's fire. The first and main battery had been built within 250 yards of the Moro, and this was eventually completely destroyed by fire. It had been placed so near the Moro in consequence of an under-estimate of the powers of resistance of that fort, which it was hoped would be very quickly knocked to pieces. At its best the climate of Havana was trying to British troops. When the rain came, it became still more fatal to men unaccustomed to a hot, damp climate, and deprived of proper shelter against tropical downpours. Returns up to July 17th show 4,863 sick, against 5,553 fit for duty, out of the whole army. The 9th were not quite as badly off as some regiments, for on that date they had 612 fit for duty against 242 sick. Many, even of those who were not actually in hospital, were weakened and incapable of great exertions.

Lord Albemarle's despatches enclose an excellent diary of the siege by his chief engineer, Mackellar, but we must resist the temptation to describe fully the details of trench and battery construction which he gives.[1]

The thick woods and undergrowth interfered with the use of guns till the clear space in front of the fort was reached, and when fire was first opened, on June 18th, only howitzers and mortars could be employed.

On the 29th the enemy landed 1,000 men from the harbour against both ends of the British position on the Cavaños ridge. They were beaten off with a loss of 200 killed, against the trifling loss of only ten men on the British side.

On July 1st it was possible to use twelve guns, nine mortars, and twenty-six " royals "[2] against the fort, and these were aided by H.M.S.

---

[1] Beatson's long diary of the siege contains the whole of this diary, but gives a good deal of information which is not in the original diary. The whole is in inverted commas, and only comparison with the original will show the additions by Beatson.

[2] Small (5.5 inch) mortars.

"Cambridge" and H.M.S. "Dragon" bombarding from the sea. A good deal of damage was done to the defences, but the two ships were so severely battered that they had to draw off after losing many men. Fires among the combustible trench materials, on July 3rd, destroyed the work of many days. As already mentioned, the approaches, owing to the thin covering of soil on the rock, had mostly to be raised, and amongst other materials employed were a quantity of bales of cotton which Albemarle was able to purchase from the Jamaican fleet. He was beginning to find a shortage of powder by July 17th, and the North American troops had not yet arrived. They only began to put in an appearance on the 27th. There had been difficulties in collecting them, and when they did sail, they were not more than about 2,200 instead of the 4,000 expected. This includes the force from Jamaica. The first division of them was delayed by ships running ashore in the Bahama Straits, and the second division, which only arrived on August 2nd, lost 300 men taken on five transports cut out from the fleet by French men-of-war.

By July 20th the British approaches had reached the covered way of the Moro. In front of them was a dry ditch seventy feet deep, the lower forty feet being cut in the solid rock. The only passage across it was along the top of a thickness of rock left at the seaward end to prevent the ditch being flanked by the fire of ships. The passage was so narrow that it was impossible to raise defences on it. On the other hand, enemy ships in the harbour could sweep the whole ditch up to this traverse of rock.

Nevertheless, miners were sent across the rock to make a mine under the seaward bastion, and at the same time shafts were sunk outside the covered way, farther to the left, with the object of blowing the counterscarp into the ditch and so filling it up in part. On the 22nd the enemy made a desperate attempt from the harbour to drive the British from the Cavaños ridge. Had it succeeded the siege must almost certainly have been raised. Indeed, it seems doubtful if even that would have been the end of the disaster. The force, landed from boats, numbered about 1,500 men, who attacked at daybreak. The first attack was held up by thirty men of the 90th and some sappers till reinforcements enabled them to drive the enemy down the hill towards the beach. The engineer's diary says that about 150 of them were "drownded." This attack was on the Shepherd's Battery. Another attack was delivered near the glacis of the Moro Fort, but this was beaten off easily. A third attack was launched against the Spanish redoubt in the centre. Here, however, the enemy, finding the British ready, retreated to their boats without pressing the attack home. The enemy's loss in these attacks was about 400 killed or drowned, besides numerous wounded whom they succeeded in carrying off. This was the most serious affair in the siege, and in the then state of the besiegers, suffering from sickness and the enervating effects of the climate, it was a question whether the attack could be repulsed.

According to Cannon the grenadier and light companies of the 9th took part in the repulse of this attack. The fact is not mentioned either in the despatches or by Beatson, and Cannon quotes no authority. Nevertheless, his statement is highly probable, as the grenadier company of the 9th was one of the constituents of the grenadier battalion.

On July 30th enemy boats and floating batteries from the harbour attempted to drive away the workers in the ditch, but were driven off by the covering party. At 2 p.m. on that day the mines were fired. Those intended to blow in the counterscarp were not fully effective in filling up the ditch; but that under the salient of the right bastion, by the rock traverse, brought down part of both faces and left a narrow but practicable breach. Though it was only wide enough for a file at a time, the storming party dashed gallantly across the rock traverse and up the breach, at the top of which the enemy met them, but were carried away by the impetuosity of the attack. They were surprised and did not move till the British were already in the breach. The whole fort was carried with the trifling loss on the British side of three officers and thirty-nine killed or wounded. The Spanish loss, including those killed and wounded in the assault, or as they attempted to get away in boats, was about 700. Among the killed was the gallant commander of the fort, Don Luis de Velasco, a naval captain. He was mortally wounded defending his colours, and, at his own request, was sent into Havana to die. The second in command, the Marquis de Gonzales, was also killed.

When the enemy had been driven from the ramparts of the fort a party of the garrison took refuge in the lighthouse. Thinking the whole affair was over, Lieutenant C. Forbes, the leader of the stormers, Lieutenant Holland of the 90th, and Lieutenant Nugent of the 9th were congratulating one another on their success when the defenders of the lighthouse fired on them, killing both Nugent and Holland. Forbes, exasperated at the death of his friends, at once stormed the lighthouse and put the whole garrison to the sword.

This incident shows clearly that some of the 9th took part in the assault on the Moro. It is extremely difficult to ascertain exactly the part played in this siege by the regiment as a whole, or rather by the "battalion" companies, as the remainder, after deducting the grenadier and light companies, were called. The system of separating the flank companies for the constitution of separate battalions has already been explained in dealing with the Belleisle expedition. In the case of Havana we also know that the 9th contributed what may be called a "mounted infantry" company. In the case of the assault on the Moro we know that Lieutenant Nugent was killed, and his name is shown in the casualty list of the grenadiers, but it does not appear amongst the casualties of the rest of the regiment. Beatson gives details of the storming party as follows :—

Royals	113
Marksmen	145
90th	60
35th	181
Sappers	151
Total	650

Of these two lieutenants and twelve rank and file were killed ; one lieutenant, four sergeants, twenty-three rank and file wounded.

It would appear that the contribution of the 9th came under the head of "marksmen."

With the fall of the Moro the fate of Havana was sealed. A heavy fire was kept up from the captured fort and the Cavaños on the town and the Punta Fort, and preparations were made for opening an attack on the west, to which side Albemarle moved his head-quarters on August 6th. On the 10th a summons to surrender was refused by the governor.

Next morning, however, the fire of forty-three guns and eight mortars soon silenced Fort Punta, and shortly afterwards the north bastion of the enceinte. At 2 p.m. white flags were displayed, and negotiations for a capitulation commenced. The honours of war were granted in consideration of the gallant defence. Albemarle was not in a position to insist on harsh terms, for, as he says in his despatch of August 21st, " The army was so very sickly and that sickness increasing daily." So terrible had been the mortality and the disablement from disease, that he reports that the 17th and 77th Foot, between them, had not twenty men fit for service, and had to be sent to America to recover. They had numbered in all 1,140 at the landing. Later on, in October, he says the army had buried 3,000 men, mostly the victims of disease, and that he had not 700 men fit for duty. His position was dangerous, for the governors of other parts of Cuba had refused to submit in accordance with the capitulation of Havana. He estimates that a garrison of 6,000 was required for the island. The whole of his first despatch announcing the fall of the fortress breathes the spirit of thankfulness that he had got it at all, and shows how uncertain he had felt of success, with his army exhausted as it was. The capture was of immense importance, as the place was the heart of the Spanish power in the West Indies. The booty, too, was great, including as it did nine or ten large warships and great stores of tobacco and other valuables not belonging to private persons.

As for the 9th, a return of August 13th shows its losses up to that date as follows :—

Officers : killed—Ensign Wood ; died of disease—Lieutenant-Colonel Thomas, Captain Suttie, Lieutenant Surman.

Other ranks : killed—nineteen ; wounded—thirty-one ; missing—one sergeant and ten men ; died of disease—two sergeants, two drummers, twenty-four men ; died of wounds—five men.

As Lieutenant Nugent's name does not appear, these returns evidently do not include the flank companies.

Even after the surrender of Havana enabled the unhappy army to find better shelter from the weather its health improved scarcely at all. Nevertheless, it had to be kept in this pest-house to guard its conquest till the peace of 1763. Under that peace, signed at Paris on February 10, 1763, Cuba was returned to Spain, who surrendered her possessions in Florida, with Fort St. Augustine and the Bay of Pensacola, to Great Britain.

On Albemarle's return to England the Cuban command had passed to his brother, General Keppel, to whom orders were addressed by Lord Egremont, on April 18, 1763, saying that Whitmore's (9th) and Charles Otway's[1] (35th) regiments were to take possession of Florida, and that a reliable officer should be sent at once to make arrangements there with the Spanish authorities.

On July 8, 1763, Keppel reports from Havana that all his troops had embarked on the 6th, that the transports began moving out of harbour on the 7th, and that they would all be away by the 10th.

Meanwhile, Albemarle had, on October 19, 1762, reported that he had sent a captain and two subalterns from each of his depleted regiments to recruit in North America, where he believed plenty of recruits would be found.

From Havana the 9th were sent to Fort St. Augustine on the Atlantic coast of the Peninsula of East Florida. In this they were more fortunate than some of the regiments, which, after suffering so terribly from fever and other tropical diseases, found themselves stationed either at unhealthy places in West Florida, or in healthy stations farther North, where the severity of the winter was almost as fatal to the enfeebled wrecks of the siege. St. Augustine had the merit of being generally healthy and having a mild climate in winter, which was beneficial to fever-stricken men. It was not always healthy, for in October, 1766, Major-General Gage (Commander-in-Chief in North America) reports to the Secretary at War that it had lately been infected with a bad fever which had carried off Lieutenant Sharpe and several men of the 9th. In this station the regiment was kept for six years. Of their life there we have no records, beyond a few small references in the

[1] Not to be confused with James Otway, who was colonel of the 9th and died in 1725.

correspondence of General Gage with the Home Government. The province was peaceable and quiet, and life at St. Augustine cannot have been anything but monotonous for most of the regiment. They did not even have the excitement of the constant squabbles which occurred in West Florida as to the respective limits of civil and military authority.

In March, 1764, the regiment is shown as having six companies at St. Augustine, and one each at Fort Apalache, the Island of New Providence, and the Island of Bermuda. These detachments were reduced next year to three sergeants and forty-four men in all.

When the regiment reached Florida, in August, 1763, its present state shows sixteen commissioned officers, sixteen sergeants, nine drummers, and 234 rank and file. As it had landed in Havana nearly 1,000 strong, and its losses in action up to the capitulation had only been twenty killed and five died of wounds, this statement shows the havoc played by disease.

That there were some amenities, at any rate in the early days of the occupation of St. Augustine, is shown by a request by Major Ogilvie for an allowance to recoup his expenses in returning the hospitalities of the Spanish garrison before they left, and entertaining visitors to the colony. He also had to pay £40 a year for a house at first. There is an estimate submitted to General Gage about this time for building quarters for the officers.

From March, 1763, the establishment of the regiment was reduced to nine companies, each of two sergeants, two corporals, one drummer, and forty-seven men. At the end of the following July the regiment was still 106 men short of this sanctioned establishment, and it was not till December, 1767, that it was within seventeen of full strength. In July, 1765, it had nine officers absent on leave.

On December 21, 1765, General Gage writes to the Secretary at War that on the death of General Bouquet he had appointed Lieutenant-Colonel Taylor of the 9th to the command of the Southern District. This involved Colonel Taylor, but not his regiment, in the quarrels as to jurisdiction between the military at Pensacola in West Florida and Governor Johnstone. The latter appears, from his correspondence with

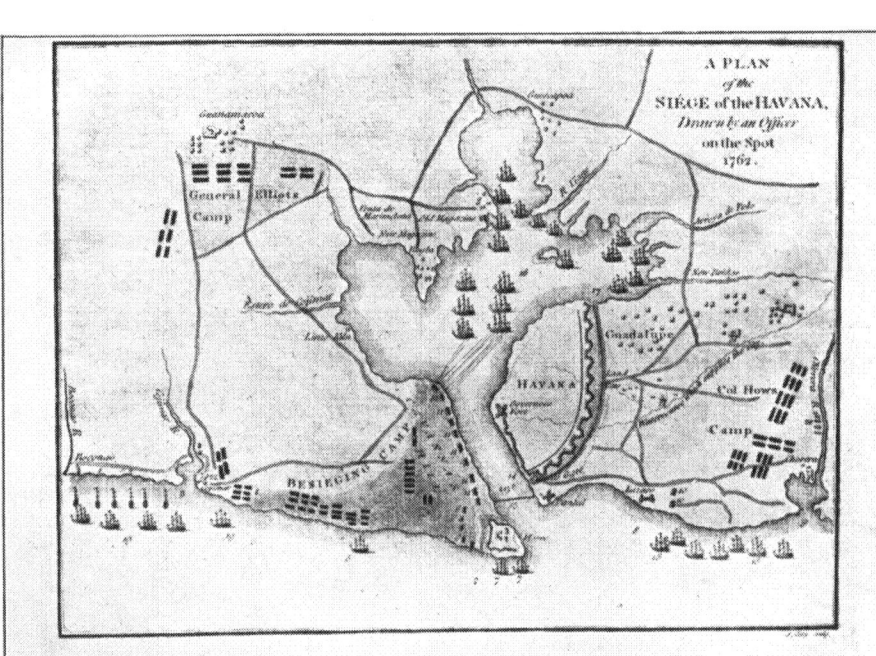

1. Place where the troops landed June 7. 2. March of the army after landing. 3. The Dragon against Coximar. 4. Where the army first encamped. 5. Where the cannon, &c. were landed. 6. Batteries against the Moro. 7. The Dragon, Cambridge, and Marlborough, against the Moro. 8. The bombs against the Punta. 9. Belleisle against Chorea fort. 10. Batteries against the Punta. 11. Batteries on the Cavanina hills. 12. Howitzers against the shipping. 13. Three Spanish men of war sunk. 14. One company's ship overset. 15. The chain and boom. 16. Spanish admiral and fleet. 17. Two ships on the stocks. 18. Admiral Pocock, with the men of war and transports. 19. Commodore Keppel, with ditto. 20. Camp at the water mills. 21. Fortified houses. 22. Head-quarters.

the Colonial Office, to have been a most verbose and quarrelsome person. He fell out with his lieutenant-governor, his chief justice, and nearly every other official.

In June, 1766, we find General Gage complaining of a batch of recruits arrived from England for the 9th under Captain Peyton. He says they were so sickly that he had great difficulty in getting medical attendance sufficient for them. This was shortly before the epidemic of fever at St. Augustine above mentioned.

On February 2, 1769, a letter to Ireland orders the 9th to be taken on the Irish establishment from December 25, 1768, though it had not arrived there, or even left Florida. On May 10, 1769, General Gage acknowledged orders of February 18th directing him to reduce the regiment to the Irish establishment, or even lower, if he thought expedient, and to send it to Ireland. He promises to do so and to distribute to other regiments in America any reduced men who would volunteer for further service in that country. He had been instructed that the Irish establishment was not to exceed nine companies, each of two sergeants, two corporals, one drummer, and twenty-eight men. As for volunteers transferred to other regiments in America, each man was to have a bonus of one and a half guineas, and the regiment to which he went was to pay £5 to the 9th to replace him.

The regiment landed in Ireland on January 5, 10, and 20, 1770, and on the 31st an order was issued augmenting its establishment by nine sergeants, nine corporals, nine drummers, two fifers, 117 privates, and nine "contingent" men. It was placed on the Irish establishment from January 11th. In the summer of 1771 General Whitmore died and was succeeded, on August 8th, by Viscount Ligonier as colonel.

For the period of Irish service 1770 to 1776 we are able to find some rather scanty information as to stations. The pay lists show that the regiment was in Limerick in January, 1772, and in March it had moved to Dublin. There it was inspected, on July 15th, by Lieutenant-General Dilkes, who was not favourably impressed by it, going so far as to say, " This regiment is really a very bad one. Notwithstanding, they fired and marched well. By the plan laid down by the colonel it must certainly improve." He complained of the officers' appearance and saluting as "indifferent," and of the short stature of the second and third ranks.

When he inspected them on May 18, 1773, again in the Phœnix Park, Dublin, he found the regiment "very much mended since the last review, and I doubt not it will be better against the next, as most of the old men are discharged." On both occasions he noted that they had "a band of musick." By July, 1773, the regiment was at Waterford, where they were inspected, on May 26, 1774, by Lieutenant-General Lord Blayney, who remarked that they were "of good appearance, saluted well, uniforms correct." January, 1775, saw them at Dungannon, and in July of the same year they were back in Dublin, where they still were in January, 1776, and up to April, when the pay list shows them "at sea."

CHAPTER VII

THE AMERICAN WAR—CANADA—SARATOGA—AND HOME SERVICE, 1776-1788

THE 9th were ordered to be in readiness to sail from Ireland to Quebec in April, 1776, to form part of the army endeavouring to suppress the revolt of the American colonies. It was to consist of twelve companies, of which two were to remain behind for purposes of recruiting, each company to have fifty-six effective rank and file. To assist recruiting, enlistments were to be for three years only, or the period of the war, whichever were shorter. The strength of the regiment at embarkation was one lieutenant-colonel, one major, seven captains, ten lieutenants, six ensigns, adjutant, quartermaster, surgeon's mate, thirty sergeants, twenty-two drummers and fifers, and 462 rank and file, corporals included. There had been sixty-six desertions since the order to go on service. The regiment sailed from Cork on April 8, 1776. During the voyage three men, of whom only one was saved against his will, jumped overboard for trifling reasons. The coast of Newfoundland was sighted on the 18th. Sergeant Lamb of the 9th, to whose published diary we are indebted, gives many details of the voyage up the St. Lawrence which we need not transcribe. Quebec was reached on April 29th.

The military position at this time in Canada was this. The Americans, under Allen and Arnold, had taken the frontier fortress of Ticonderoga, between Lakes George and Champlain, in the summer of 1775 and obtained control of Lake Champlain. Allen, attempting an attack on Montreal, was defeated and taken. Arnold, now in sole command, projected the invasion and conquest of Canada, whilst Sir Guy Carleton, the British governor of the province, was planning the recovery of the lake and Ticonderoga. Both sides endeavoured to enlist the Indians in this domestic quarrel—a policy which, looking to the savagery of the proposed allies, was regrettable. Montgomery, an American brigadier, now at the head of 6,000 men, passing Lake Champlain laid siege to St. John's, a fort on the Sorel, north of Lake Champlain. Carleton's attempt to relieve it having failed, the fort capitulated. Montgomery then, advancing to the St. Lawrence, severed the river communications between Montreal and Quebec. Having captured the former, he pushed down the river, though it was November and the difficulties were great, on Quebec. Before the Canadian capital Montgomery joined Arnold, who, in the face of appalling difficulties and hardships, had brought 1,000 men direct from New York through the wilderness. The siege, which commenced on December 1st, is outside our province. An assault on the city was beaten off and Montgomery was killed. Carleton being reinforced by the arrival of the 29th Regiment, assumed the offensive and drove the besiegers off with the loss of their artillery and stores. They retreated to Three Rivers.

With the reinforcements received from England, amongst them the 9th, Carleton, at the beginning of June, 1776, advanced to Three Rivers, which he found abandoned by the Americans, who had fallen back to Sorel at the south-western end of St. Peter's Lake. Moving in boats up the St. Lawrence, the 9th was disembarked on June 5th, near Three Rivers, which place it reached next day.

At 3 a.m. on the 8th the Americans from Sorel attacked Three Rivers with 2,000 men. The attempted surprise failed, and the enemy was easily beaten off with considerable loss to themselves and very few British casualties. The American General Tomson, commanding the reinforcements for Arnold which had made this attempt, was taken. On the 9th the regiment again embarked and sailed for Sorel, where, owing to difficulties of navigation, they only landed on the 14th, two hours after the Americans had evacuated it to march southwards. Carleton and Burgoyne followed them in three columns.

The unfortunate American force, now greatly outnumbered, faced with great difficulties in dragging their boats up the rapids, and decimated by small-pox, hurried south as fast as they could. St. John's was abandoned, after being set on fire. There, on June 18th, the British found twenty-two guns and the burnt remains of all the larger American boats, which could not be dragged up the neighbouring rapids. On the 26th the pursuit stopped for want of boats, in the building of which the next three months were spent. The enemy had fallen back to Crown Point, at the south end of Lake Champlain, and to Ticonderoga, at the northern entrance to Lake George. By the end of September a considerable fleet was ready, the largest ship carrying eighteen twelve-pounders. October 11th to 13th saw a miniature naval battle, in which the Americans were so badly worsted that they abandoned Crown Point, after firing it, and retired to Ticonderoga. The British army now occupied Crown Point ; it was about 12,000 strong. Here the campaign ended for the year, and the British force went northwards into winter quarters. The 9th spent the winter in the Isle Jésus, near Montreal.

During this winter New York was captured by Sir William Howe, and he was now established there with a force quite inadequate for what he was expected to do.

The plan of campaign for 1777 was elaborated by the Secretary of State for the Colonies, Lord George Germaine, better remembered, in connexion with the battle of Minden, as Lord George Sackville. Seeing that he was entirely ignorant of local conditions in America, that he worked at a desk 3,000 miles away, and that he certainly was not the soldier he chose to believe himself, it was hardly to be expected that his plan would be valuable or practicable. He required a triple advance from great distances against the American forces, supposed to be somewhere about Albany on the Hudson. Sir William Howe was to push up the Hudson from New York, a force from Canada under General Burgoyne (whose appointment was meant as a snub for Germaine's enemy Sir Guy Carleton) was to move southwards by Ticonderoga to the Hudson about Saratoga, and thence on Albany. Yet another small force, also from Canada, was to descend the Mohawk after capturing Fort Stanwix. The American army of course would be so kind as to remain quietly till it was crushed by these three converging forces ! The scheme was worthy of the Austrian Aulic Council of 1796–1797

Notwithstanding his instructions, Burgoyne was eventually left in ignorance of the fact that Howe had gone off on an expedition to Pennsylvania.

We are only concerned with Burgoyne's force, which, when he started from the St. Lawrence in June, 1777, consisted of the following troops :—

British

(1) The battalion companies, that is, the companies other than the right flank company of grenadiers and the left of light infantry, of the 9th, 20th, 21st, 24th, 47th, 53rd, and 62nd Foot.

(2) Ten companies each of grenadiers and light infantry, drawn from these seven regiments, with the corresponding companies of the 29th, 31st, and 34th.

German

Five regiments of infantry, a company of artillery, and about forty Jägers, to whom were added the same number of picked marksmen selected from the British infantry. This latter small body was known as the " Rangers."

To these were added 250 British artillerymen, some 250 Canadians, and a variable body of Indians never, according to Burgoyne, exceeding 500. The whole force was between 7,000 and 8,000 combatants, besides workmen, artificers, etc.

The artillery, guns, howitzers, and a few mortars of various calibres, numbered forty-two pieces. In the order of battle the 9th, as the senior regiment, was on the extreme right in Brigadier-General Hamilton's brigade, the other regiments in it being the 53rd and 47th. The other British brigade, under Brigadier-General Powel, consisted of the 20th, 21st, and 62nd. On their left were the German brigades of Goll and Specht. Later, when Powel returned to Ticonderoga with the 53rd, the whole right wing became one brigade under Hamilton.

This little army assembled early in June at the northern entrance to Lake Champlain, through which it was conveyed by the fleet constructed in 1776 without incident to Crown Point, where it disembarked on June 27th.

CAMPAIGN OF SARATOGA

At Ticonderoga the remains of the American invading force of 1776, about 3,000 in number, under the command of General St. Clair, were entrenched, partly at Ticonderoga itself and partly at Mount Independence on the opposite (eastern) side of the entrance to Lake George. Far behind this force, on the Hudson north of Albany, was an American force of 10,000 or 12,000 men.

The whole force being assembled and landed, Burgoyne, on June 30th, sent forward the light troops and the 24th under Brigadier-General

Simon Fraser, Lieutenant-Colonel of the 24th, by the west bank of the channel between Lakes Champlain and George, and some of the Germans by the east bank, towards Ticonderoga and Mount Independence respectively. The rest of the force followed, and the advanced guards occupied posts on either bank within three miles of the American force, the ships being anchored across the channel out of range of the enemy's guns.

At the north end of the land which separates South River from Lake George was a height called Sugar Loaf Hill which commanded all the works both of Ticonderoga and Mount Independence. St. Clair had not occupied it, since he considered it impossible to get artillery on to it. He was mistaken; for the energy of the British artillery, under General Phillips, overcame the difficulties of the ascent. By the evening of July 5th, it was clear to all that a powerful battery on the top would be ready next day to fire on the American works.

St. Clair, recognizing that his position was no longer tenable, started his retreat in the night. The forts were promptly occupied next morning by the British, and Fraser pushed forward in pursuit. The great bridge connecting the two wings of the American defences and the boom in front of it were successfully broken so as to enable the pursuit to continue by water, up South River, as well as by land.

The American retreat was by the east bank, and by 3 p.m. on the 6th Burgoyne arrived by water at South Bay, where he captured or destroyed without difficulty the whole of the American craft, which were unable to escape from the cul-de-sac. At Ticonderoga and Mount Independence the 62nd and a German regiment were left in garrison,[1] thus reducing the force for the farther advance by 900 men.

In South Bay the 9th, 20th, and 21st were disembarked, in hopes of cutting off the retreating enemy, who, however, effected their escape without fighting. That evening Fraser, leading the pursuit by land, came up. Next morning he pushed on, followed, when he came up, by Riedesel, the German commander. He found the enemy making a stand in a strong position. Without waiting for Riedesel, Fraser at

[1] The 62nd were relieved on August 10th by the 53rd, and were sent to the front.

once attacked and was engaged in a desperate fight with his grenadiers and light infantry, amongst them the flank companies of the 9th, against double their numbers of Americans. When Riedesel with his Germans came up he turned the American right and compelled them to retreat again. The losses of the British alone in this action, besides those of the Germans, were seventeen officers and 109 other ranks killed or wounded. They would have been less but for the treachery of an American regiment, which advanced with arms reversed, as if to surrender, and then suddenly fired a volley into the grenadiers. Of the 9th, Captain Stapylton and Lieutenant Rowe were wounded, the former mortally. As the enemy were reported to be still retreating the battalion companies of the 9th were detached towards Fort St. Anne to observe them. Lieutenant-Colonel Hill, commanding the 9th, reporting that the enemy had been reinforced, the two other regiments (21st and 47th) of Powel's brigade were ordered up in support, and as the sound of heavy firing reached Burgoyne he also ordered up the 20th. None of these, however, arrived before the action was over.

What followed for the 9th is thus described in Burgoyne's letter of July 17th to the Colonial Secretary:—

"A violent storm of rain, which lasted the whole day, prevented the troops from getting to Fort Anne so soon as was intended; but the delay gave the 9th Regiment an opportunity of distinguishing themselves by standing and repulsing an attack of six times their number. The enemy finding the position not to be forced in front, endeavoured to turn it; and from the superiority of their numbers that inconvenience was to be apprehended; and Lt.-Col. Hill found it necessary to change his position in the height of action; so critical an order was executed by the regiment with the utmost steadiness and bravery. The enemy, after an attack of three hours, were totally repulsed and fled towards Fort Edward, setting fire to Fort Anne, but leaving a saw-mill and a blockhouse in good repair, which were afterwards possessed by the King's troops. The 9th Regiment acquired, during their expedition, about 30 prisoners, some stores and baggage, and colours of the 2nd Hampshire Regiment."

A somewhat fuller account of this action is given by Sergeant Lamb in his journal. He says that the 9th, after capturing some American boats in Wood Creek, were within a quarter of a mile of Fort Anne when a pretended deserter managed to convey news to the strong garrison of the fort of the weakness of the British. He also told Lieutenant-Colonel Hill that the garrison of the fort was 1,000 men, and that they were in great consternation. Hill had barely sent off news of his situation to Burgoyne, now nearly ten miles behind, when he was attacked by superior forces which the American editor of Lieutenant Hadden's journal says were by no means six-fold of Hill's force. Lamb gives the numbers present of the 9th as only about 190 men.

The woods were very thick, but it was soon ascertained that the British were being outflanked. To avoid this, Hill had to retire up a hill in his rear. There the ammunition was nearly exhausted, and firing had perforce to cease. Just at this moment an Indian war-whoop was heard, which so alarmed the Americans that they retired to Fort Anne. The whoop really emanated only from Captain Money of the 9th, then acting on the staff, who had been sent up by Burgoyne with a party of Indians to relieve Colonel Hill. The Indians refusing to go on, Captain Money proceeded alone and resorted to this device.

The American editor above mentioned says the Americans had also exhausted their ammunition, and that this was the real cause of their withdrawal, since they did not know the English were in the same case.

The losses of the 9th in this sharp and very creditable affair were eleven killed, nineteen wounded, and the following officers: killed, Lieutenant Westrop; wounded, Lieutenant and Adjutant Fielding and Lieutenants Staveley and Murray. Captain Montgomery was wounded just as the regiment changed its ground, and his wound was being dressed by Surgeon Shelley. Being left behind by the movement of the regiment, both fell into the enemy's hands.

The enemy were now reported to have been reinforced at Fort Edward, and the British, who were busy clearing roads, were posted with the Germans on the left towards Castleton River—Fraser in the centre, and the British right about Skenesborough. The 9th, after the affair of Fort Anne, had fallen back to the extreme right of this line.

Burgoyne, who held that his instructions to march on Albany were imperative, had now to arrange for the passage of the strip of forest, some eighteen miles wide, which separated the southern end of Lake George from the Hudson, and was part of the watershed between the systems of that river and the St. Lawrence. Burgoyne held Fort George and the command of the lake.

The country in this strip was densely wooded, and what tracks there were had been diligently broken up or obstructed by the enemy. The work of reopening them, and of reconstructing the bridges over numerous streams and causeways over the swamps, was a heavy task for the little army. Of all these difficulties Germaine, working at his desk in London, had taken no account when framing his plan of campaign. His maps could not show them, and he had no personal knowledge of the country or its conditions. The supply of Canadian workmen and artificers to aid the soldiers in this work was disappointingly short, and consequently the combatants, in addition to their proper work, were exhausted by labours which should have been performed chiefly by civilians.

Moreover, when the British force should get over the Hudson it would be practically cut off from communication with Canada. Therefore it was necessary to collect thirty days' supplies, and the transport for them, before advancing. So great were the difficulties of all sorts that Burgoyne was induced to attempt a surprise of the enemy's stores at Bennington, thirty miles south-east of Fort Edward. The latter he had reached with difficulty on July 30th. With the details of this expedition we need not deal, since it was almost entirely carried out by German and provincial troops. The only British engaged were a few of Fraser's Rangers. Sergeant Lamb shows Lieutenant Wright and Ensign Baron de Solms of the 9th as wounded in it; but, if he is correct, it is not clear in what capacity they were there. It suffices to say that the expedition was a miserable failure. Colonel Baum's advanced guard of 500 men, only 300 of whom were regulars, was almost destroyed, and himself captured before he could be rescued by Breymann with the main body. The latter was surrounded by the Americans and nearly all captured or killed. Four guns were lost.

This was on August 14th, and at the same time Burgoyne threw a bridge of rafts across the Hudson above Saratoga, to which place he pushed an advanced guard. The raft bridge being carried away by a freshet, one of boats was then thrown nearer Saratoga, the main body being still on the left bank.[1]

It was not till September 13th that Burgoyne, disappointed of the supplies hoped for from the Bennington expedition, could collect sufficient stores from the rear, complete his bridge, and begin to pass his troops over to the right bank, an operation which occupied September 13th and 14th. The heights and plain of Saratoga were then occupied, the enemy being at Stillwater, some twelve miles south, under the command of General Gates.

Half that distance was covered by the British on the 15th, but owing to broken bridges it was not till the 17th that they could arrive at their next camp, at Sword's Farm, about four miles short of the position in which Gates was busy fortifying himself. The British portion of the force now consisted of the battalion companies of the 9th, 20th, 21st, 24th, and 62nd Foot ; six companies of the 47th, ten companies each of grenadiers and light infantry, 300 artillerymen, about 150 recruits, and fifty marksmen under Captain Fraser. Including the Germans, the whole force numbered about 6,000, of whom not more than 5,000 were effective. The artillery comprised thirty-five guns and howitzers and six mortars. On September 19th Burgoyne moved to the attack of the enemy's entrenched position on Bemmis Heights. Fraser,

[1] An entry in General Burgoyne's order book, dated August 24, 1777, shows that Private George Hundertmark of the 9th Regiment, was found guilty of quitting his post as sentry and of desertion. He was sentenced to death by a courtmartial and was duly executed by a party of his own regiment on August 26th. That of course was quite right, but another entry of September 12th throws a curious light on the treatment of officers at that time. An officer (name or corps not mentioned) quitted his post (one of great importance) to attend to private business. On his expressing sorrow for his misconduct he was released from arrest without being tried. In passing this order Burgoyne said he could only justify it by " the confidence that the officers of this army in general do not want an example of punishment to impress upon their minds a knowledge of the great principle of their profession, a consciousness of their respective stations, and a regard to personal honour, and he forgives and will forget the fault in question, convinced that it is impossible that it should happen twice."

with Breymann's Germans in support, was sent to the right so as to turn the head of a ravine running across the line of advance; Riedesel, with the rest of the Germans, moved near the river till they had passed the mouth of the ravine. Then they turned to the right towards Freeman's Farm. The centre column moved by the road across the ravine, and then also turned towards Freeman's Farm. Line was formed with the centre near the farm. At first it was formed of the 9th, 21st, 62nd, and 20th, in that order from right to left. As the line approached the farm the 9th fell behind as reserve. The artillery was with the left column, in whose line of march the country was not obstructed by the thick woods through which the other columns had advanced. Between 2 and 3 p.m. the advanced guard of the centre encountered superior forces of the enemy and had to fall back on the main body.

Gates had at first moved out his troops in force to attempt a turning movement round the British right, but encountering Fraser's troops, among whom were the flank companies of the 9th, he had a sharp fight with them, and moved to his right against the British centre. The woods were so thick that his movement was not observed at first by the British. The brunt of the fighting here, which lasted from about 3 p.m. till after sunset, fell upon the 20th, 21st, and 62nd, who were opposed by an enemy constantly reinforced. Including the 9th, in reserve, the British centre counted only about 1,100 men. The fight put up by them against overwhelming odds was truly magnificent. The losses on both sides were heavy, and the British officers suffered especially from snipers posted in trees to pick them off. Eleven were killed and seventeen wounded. Among the latter were Major Forbes, Captain Swetenham, and Lieutenant Price of the 9th, a fact which belies Cannon's statement that the regiment on this day, being in reserve, suffered no loss. The other three regiments lost 350 killed and wounded out of 800.

Meanwhile Fraser and Breymann were not inactive in making sallies, but, holding as they did a strong height, they were not permanently moved off it.

General Phillips, with the artillery and Riedesel's Germans on the left, brought welcome aid to the hard-pressed centre, and as darkness fell on the field the enemy were finally repulsed, with a loss which Burgoyne estimates at 500 killed and 1,500 wounded. No pursuit being possible, the British force lay that night on their arms.

On the 20th they took up a position within cannon shot of the enemy's entrenchments. Their centre was covered by a fortified line, bending back on the right, behind which a horseshoe work was erected and occupied by Breymann's Germans. Behind the left, near the river, three redoubts were built, and a bridge of boats was thrown across the Hudson nearly opposite the British left. The magazines, hospitals, and head-quarters were between the three redoubts and the river. Some of the supplies were in boats on the river. On the 21st Burgoyne's hopes were raised by a message from Sir H. Clinton promising to bring relief by an attack (which he duly carried out) on the Americans lower down the Hudson. Through no fault of his it was too late to save Burgoyne.

The latter remained in his new fortified position, inactive save for work on entrenchments. His troops had gained nothing, save glory, from the battle of the 19th. Gates was too strongly fortified to justify an attack, and the only real hope was that he might himself attack. On October 3rd provisions in the British camp were running low and rations had to be reduced ; by the 7th it was clear that the present state of inactivity could not continue without starvation. On that day Burgoyne, still intent on forcing his way to Albany, started on an attempt to turn Gates's weaker left wing. The enemy replied by an attack, with very superior forces, on the British left, which promptly stopped Burgoyne's turning movement.

The weight of the enemy's first attack fell on the British grenadiers and on Riedesel's Germans on their right. At the same time his great superiority of numbers enabled Gates to start a second turning movement round the British right, which necessitated the forming of a second line with the light infantry and the 24th, to cover a retreat to the camp from which Burgoyne had started.

Presently his left gave way before renewed attacks, and was only saved by the 24th and the light infantry moving across to its assistance.

With great difficulty and heavy loss of men, and of six guns, the camp was reached in good order. Fraser was mortally wounded by one of the numerous marksmen of the enemy—men who, like the Boers of our own time, had lived by their skill with the rifle. The existence of these, and their great power of fighting in woods, where they were often posted as snipers in trees, was one of the many difficulties which Germaine had failed to recognize in his plan of campaign. No sooner was the camp reached than the Americans continued their attack on it with great fury, under a heavy fire of grape and musketry. The attack was first against the British right centre, where the works defended by Lord Balcarres were finally held. On the extreme right, almost in rear of Lord Balcarres, however, Breymann's Germans were driven out of the horseshoe work. The general himself was killed and his opponent (Arnold) was wounded. Only the fall of night put an end to this disastrous action, which left the British in a most precarious position, with the enemy in front and on their right flank. Every regiment of the now greatly reduced force had been tested to the utmost. The British loss in officers alone was six killed and nineteen wounded. The 9th in this action seems to have been held back as a last reserve, for it had no officer casualties. The whole British fighting strength by this evening cannot have exceeded 4,000 effectives. During the night the British fell back to the heights crowned by the three redoubts above the hospital, where they stood with their backs to the river, still in a most precarious position. They were not attacked on the 8th, but as intelligence was received that the enemy was again seeking to turn their right and cut them off from Saratoga, there was no hope except in retiring to that place as quickly as possible. Though the retreat was conducted within musket-shot of the enemy during the night of October 8th–9th it was completed without loss. Owing, however, to heavy rain, and difficulties in protecting the baggage and stores, it was evening on the 9th when the army was safe across the Fishkill stream. So trying had the march been, in dreadful weather, that the men were exhausted and unfit to do anything to shelter themselves from the pitiless rain and cold. Some 500 or 600 of the enemy were already entrenching themselves on the Saratoga heights, but retired to the east bank of the Hudson as the British appeared, and joined other enemy forces already gathered there to oppose any attempt to cross. It was soon found impossible to keep the stores on the river, as the boats were often sunk by hostile fire, so they had to be landed under fire from across the river. Attempts to work at repairs of the bridge by which Burgoyne had crossed from Fort Edward on the way to Stillwater also failed, as the Canadian guard abandoned the workmen, and the 47th Regiment had to be recalled to aid in the defence of the Fishkill line against the advancing enemy.

Gates, constantly reinforced, now had about 16,000 men, and his immense numerical superiority enabled him easily to form a semicircle round the British on the right bank, and still to provide a considerable force on the left bank to watch the fords and prevent any crossing.

Burgoyne fortified himself in this position, most of his British troops being in a large work on the hill west of Saratoga and north of the Fishkill. Here were the American Volunteers, the 24th, the 21st, and the grenadiers, with the 9th acting as a central reserve against any attack on this position. The 20th and 47th, on the right of the great work, connected it with the Germans of Riedesel, posted along a ridge, with their backs to the river, to which they were perilously near.

The night of October 13th found the British force still standing ready, hoping against hope for relief from Sir H. Clinton, or for an attack by the enemy, and suffering day and night from his artillery and infantry fire, especially from the rifles of the snipers in the trees. A stocktaking of the provisions revealed the fact that there was enough only for three days more. The force had been reduced to 3,500 men, of whom not 2,000 were British fit for duty; many of the Canadians and all the Indians had deserted; 460 sick and wounded had had to be left behind in hospital when the force marched for Saratoga on the 8th.

In this desperate situation Burgoyne, with the concurrence of a council of all his principal officers, opened negotiations for a capitulation. He had first proposed retiring by Fort Edward and Fort George, but learnt that the road was barred by an American force. He had long ago known that Ticonderoga had been in great part retaken by the enemy, and most of four companies of the 53rd captured. What forces

EDWARD, FIRST EARL LIGONIER, K.B.
Colonel, 1771–1782.
"It was probably due to his efforts that the crest of Britannia was restored to the Regiment."
(*Ch. VII*)

Reproduced by permission of the National Portrait Gallery.

remained there were blockaded and helpless. The terms granted, after the usual haggling, were extraordinarily good, considering the hopeless position of the British force.

Burgoyne was able to say that he had saved the remains of his army for England, since Gates had agreed that they should be marched to Boston and embarked for England, on condition that they should not again serve in the war in North America—a condition which clearly did not bar their employment to set free other troops in England, the Mediterranean, or even the West Indies, to serve in North America. Burgoyne had of course said that his army would die rather than submit to worse terms, but he was really helpless, and a more experienced soldier than Gates would have insisted on unconditional surrender. All the same, the Convention having been executed, it would have been carried out honourably by men like Gates or Washington. But when the politicians of the Congress got hold of it they proceeded to evade its execution on one pretext or another, and thereby certainly did not add to their own repute for good faith. The numbers who surrendered at Saratoga were—

British troops	2240
German troops	1700
Canadians, Provincials, Boatmen, etc.	480
	4420

But these numbers included many sick and wounded in camp. Less than 3,500 soldiers fit for duty laid down their arms. Besides these the Americans had the 460 sick and wounded left in hospital when Burgoyne made his last march to Saratoga.

Burgoyne was presently allowed to return to England on parole; but his troops were detained under circumstances of hardship and ill-usage which were often very bad. They were moved first to the neighbourhood of Boston, and then, in the summer of 1778, to Rutland County, some fifty miles south, where they were confined in a large pen and given nails and planks with which to erect some shelter for themselves. Needless to say the result was very insufficient for protection from the inclemency of the weather. Food, too, was mainly rice and salt pork, and not too much of that. Only the officers were allowed to lodge in neighbouring farms. Burgoyne, in January, 1778, before he went home, had (whilst admitting that some of the incidents which had occurred were due to indiscretions of his troops, perhaps excusable under the circumstances) issued an order as follows : " The Lieutenant-General makes known to the troops that he is using every possible means to bring to justice the Provincial Officer who wounded two men of the 9th Regiment on Thursday last." Another order, in February, 1778, mentions that " a soldier of the 9th Regiment has been dangerously stabbed this evening by a man of the Provincial guard."[1]

Remonstrances against the violation of the Convention were ignored or treated as " insolent."[2]

Endeavours, which aroused the indignation of George Washington, were constantly made to seduce the British soldiers from their allegiance and induce them to join the American Army. A report in October, 1778, shows that the Americans were sending recruiting parties to enlist deserters from the " Convention " troops.

Entirely disregarding the Convention of Saratoga the American authorities exchanged some of Burgoyne's officers as if they had been prisoners of war. Otherwise the unfortunate " Convention troops," as they were called, were held in captivity for years.

The end of it appears to be that they were made the subject of ordinary exchanges against American prisoners, and were sent home in batches during 1781.

A list of officer-prisoners exchanged after October 25, 1780, shows of the 9th Major Forbes, Captain Sheldon, Lieutenants Fife, Prince, McNeill, Murray, Hoy ; Ensigns Fielding, Waddle, and Spencer.

A later list, ratified September 3, 1781, gives Captains Maclean, Lieutenants Vincent and Kemmis ; Ensigns Piercy, Gwyn, Dean, and Leslie.

A list of promotions proposed by Sir H. Clinton on April 30, 1781

---

[1] For above see Lamb, p. 208 ; and Hadden, pp. 339, 341.

[2] Lamb, p. 209. It was about this time that Lamb succeeded in escaping to New York.

seems to indicate that the regiment was free again by that date. It landed again in England at various dates in 1781.

Meanwhile the two companies left behind in Ireland for recruiting purposes had been sent to England ; for on October 31, 1780, the Colonel, Lord Ligonier, is directed to enlarge the quarters of the company of the 9th at Stoke Newington so as to include Hackney. In January, 1781, it is recorded that a composite battalion of four additional companies, belonging respectively to the 8th, 9th, 20th, and 47th, embarked at Portsmouth under the command of Major-General Medows for the East Indies. The last three of these regiments were " Convention Troops." The composite battalion was commanded by Major Douglas of the 47th. It landed in India on June 24, 1781, and was from that date chargeable to the East India Company. A letter from the War Office to General Medows, dated November 10, 1781, says : " The Secretary of State will signify His Majesty's pleasure to Sir Eyre Coote concerning the detachments of the 8th, 9th, 20th, and 47th Regiments of which you propose to draught the private men into the 98th and 100th Regiments and send the officers to Great Britain." A month previously (October 7th), in a list of promotions recommended and approved, we find, under the heading " 9th Regiment," that Lieutenant James Fraser of the 98th was promoted to be lieutenant in one of the additional companies. Evidently, therefore, the 9th company was to go to the 98th.

The officers returned to England in April, 1783, and the N.C.O.'s subsequently. The men were drafted to the 98th early in 1783, as evidenced by a letter, dated Bombay, April 23, 1783, from Colonel Norman Macleod to the Secretary at War.

It would not have been surprising had the regiment lost its colours at the surrender of Saratoga, but they were saved by the care of Lieutenant-Colonel Hill, who ripped them from their poles and concealed them in his personal baggage, which, under the Convention, was not liable to search. There he preserved them till his return to England in 1781, when they were presented to the King and Colonel Hill was rewarded by being promoted to the rank of Colonel in the Army on May 16, 1781. The American editor of Hadden's journal claims Hill's concealment of the colours as a breach of the Convention, partially justifying the refusal to ratify. However this may be, the concealment was of course not known to the Congress at the time, so can hardly be pleaded as an excuse.

On August 31, 1782 the first serious attempt to territorialize the infantry regiments of the army was made by a letter addressed to their colonels. It is worth quoting in full :—

"LONDON, *August* 31, 1782.

"SIR,

"His Majesty having been pleased to order that the regiment of Foot which you command shall take the county name of "9th or East Norfolk Regiment"[1] and be looked upon as attached to that division of the county, I am to acquaint you it is His Majesty's further pleasure that you shall in all things conform to that idea, and endeavour by all means in your power to cultivate and improve that connexion, so as to create a mutual attachment between the county and the regiment which may at all times be useful towards recruiting the regiment ; but as the completing of the several regiments, now generally so deficient, is in the present crisis of the most important national concern, you will on this occasion use the utmost possible exertion for that purpose, by prescribing the greatest diligence to your officers and recruiting parties, and by every suitable attention to the gentlemen and considerable inhabitants, and as nothing can so much tend to conciliate their affections as an orderly and polite behaviour towards them, and an observance of the strictest discipline in all your quarters, you will give the most positive orders on that head ; and you will immediately make such a disposition of your recruiting parties as may best answer that end.

"I am, etc.,

"(Sgd.) H. S. CONWAY.

"To Major General
    Lord Saye & Sele,
        Colonel of the 9th or East Norfolk Regiment of Foot."

[1] It may be mentioned that the 54th Foot was given the title of " 54th or West Norfolk Regiment." It is now the Dorsetshire Regiment. Its old colours still hang in Norwich Cathedral.

Unfortunately the War Office appears by no means to have played its part in carrying out these excellent instructions ; for we find recruiting parties for the East Norfolk Regiment being sent to Lancashire, Ireland and other places very remote from its own county, whilst, on the other hand, in 1803 a second battalion was raised for the North Lancashire Regiment from men raised under the Additional Force Act in Norfolk. When the 2nd battalion of the 9th was constituted for the second time in 1803 its head-quarters were established, not in its own county of Norfolk, but at Sherborne in Dorsetshire. As for the territorial name, there can be no doubt that, after knowing their regiment for thirty years as the " 9th Foot," officers and men, amongst themselves, if not officially, continued to describe it in the old way. In official despatches the regiment continued to appear as the 9th. Even in 1881, when the territorial title was positively insisted on by the authorities, it will be remembered what difficulties were encountered in every regiment whose traditions had been associated with a number, and how often officers were snubbed by inspecting generals or the War Office for continuing to describe their regiment by its old number.

On its return to England the regiment was quartered at Norwich, a fact which may have led to its being selected as the regiment to be attached to the county of Norfolk. In giving territorial titles in 1782, selections of regiments appear to have been made in a rather haphazard manner. The 47th, according to a story, was to have been the Lanarkshire Regiment, as it was raised in that county. Some clerk wrote " Lancashire " instead of " Lanarkshire," and the error was pointed out to the revising officer. He inquired if Lancashire had been given a regiment, and on hearing it had not left the 47th as Lancashire.[1] The 9th being at the time at Norwich, it was quite natural that it should be assigned to Norfolk, though it had had no previous special connexion with the county, and had never even been quartered in it. If any importance had been attached to the county in which it was raised the regiment should have been given to Gloucestershire.

On April 15, 1782, a company was ordered from Norwich to Watford,

[1] Major Purdon's " Historical Sketch of the 47th (Lancashire) Regiment," p. 85 *n*.

"intended for the King's duty," and on June 20th it was sent to Windsor.

On April 4, 1783, four companies were ordered from Norwich to Yarmouth, Lowestoft, Pakefield, and Gorleston. On June 2nd we find an order for a sergeant and seven men to go from Yarmouth to Southwold, there to assist the Revenue Officers in the prevention of "owling and smuggling," a duty in which the company at Lowestoft was also employed in its own neighbourhood. The party at Southwold was sent later to Lowestoft to assist the company there in these probably very unpopular duties. In September the detached companies rejoined the regiment at Norwich, and on the 22nd of that month the 9th was ordered to march a week later for Berwick and Tweedmouth, to arrive there on November 1, 1783. It was there to await orders from the General Commanding in North Britain for its farther movement into Scotland.

In 1785 the regiment again went to Ireland, where they were reviewed, on July 28, 1786, at Dublin by Major-General C. O'Hara, whose general remarks said: "The general appearance of this regiment is smart and soldierlike, with great attention, both in officers and men; but from the inferior size of many men in the rear rank it is at present, upon the whole, not very fit for active service."

On May 10, 1787 the regiment, being still at Dublin, was reviewed by Major-General J. Paterson, who, after noting its good appearance, added, "This regiment is particularly well disciplined in the field."

Later in this year the head-quarters of the regiment were at Clogheen in Co. Tipperary, and by July at Cork, where apparently it completed this tour of Irish service.

CHAPTER VIII

THE WEST INDIES. 1788–1796.

IN 1788 the regiment was sent abroad again—this time to the West Indies. In June, 1788, it was quartered at Brimstone Hill in the Island of St. Christopher's, or St. Kitts, with one company detached as garrison for the island of Nevis. Here it remained peaceably till the spring of 1793, when it again commenced active service in consequence of the outbreak of war with the Revolutionary Government of France. Operations were now about to commence against the French West Indian islands, the first of which to be attacked was the little island of Tobago north-east of Trinidad. On this expedition only the two flank companies of the regiment were employed.

Major-General Cuyler, at Barbados, had orders to sail to the capture of the island of Tobago. Admiral Laforey, who was to convoy the expedition with his squadron, had brought from St. Kitts the two flank companies of the 9th, commanded by Major Baillie. In addition to these, Cuyler embarked, on April 11, 1793, with a detachment of artillery and nine companies of the 4th battalion of the 60th. Sailing on the 12th, the little force arrived in Great Courland Bay on the 14th at 1 p.m. All the troops, and twenty-five marines from the "Trusty," were disembarked by 3 p.m., and advanced at once to within sight of the enemy's fort above the town of Scarborough. A summons was sent to the French commander, M. de Monteil of the French 32nd of the Line, and was duly refused.

Cuyler now found that the work was stronger than he had been led to expect, and that he had not the means for a regular siege. He resolved, therefore, to attempt an assault the same night.

Forming at 1 a.m., the troops, less the artillery left behind, started half an hour later on their two mile march. Their numbers were too small to allow of any deliberate division of the attack. They arrived before Scarborough undiscovered, but there the garrison of the fort were alarmed by some shots fired by French inhabitants from a house, to which no reply was made, as the men had been ordered only to use the bayonet. The negro guide leading the grenadiers had played them false and bolted, which caused delay and separation, unavoidable in the darkness. The light infantry and part of the grenadiers were fortunate enough to arrive at the weakest side of the fort, where all should have been, but the rest of the troops wandered towards the "barrier."[1] There they began an attack which fortunately drew away the attention of the garrison before the light infantry and grenadiers began theirs. The flank companies of the 9th now very gallantly rushed at the fort and got into it. Thereupon the garrison surrendered as prisoners of war. General Cuyler gives high praise to officers and men for their conduct, especially to Major Gordon of the 60th and Major Baillie of the 9th. The former, it is stated, had left the command of his own regiment and solicited that of the flank companies, which Baillie should have had. In this affair the 9th had none killed, but Lieutenant Stopford, one drummer, and three men were wounded. Their strength on landing was one major, four lieutenants, four sergeants, three drummers, and eighty-five rank and file. The total force was 394 rank and file, besides officers.

The French prisoners were sixty-eight of the 31st Regiment, ten gunners, about seventeen officers, and, according to Monteil's account, about eighty National Guards. From Tobago the flank companies of the 9th returned to Barbados.

In the following June an expedition was organized for the capture of Martinique, which had been represented by French Royalists of the island as ripe for revolt against the Republican authorities. Major-General Bruce, commanding this expedition, took with him the battalion companies of the 21st and the flank companies of the 9th and seven other

[1] This term is used without explanation in Cuyler's despatch, from which this account is taken. It is in C.O. 318.11.

battalions. He landed at Case de Navire, north-west of Fort Royal, with about 1,100 men, which was a good margin over the 800 he had been assured would suffice, with local aid, to overcome all opposition. He soon found that he had been misled, that the Royalist support promised was worth very little, and that a much larger British force than he could dispose of was required. He therefore wisely re-embarked his little force, besides such Royalists as had so far committed themselves as to be in danger if left behind, and returned to Barbados, whence the flank companies of the 9th were sent back to the regiment at St. Kitts.

It had meanwhile been decided in London to make a serious attempt to destroy the French West India trade by the capture of their possessions in the Leeward and Windward Islands. The officer selected to command the expedition was Lieutenant-General Sir Charles Grey, who was formally appointed Commander-in-Chief in the West Indies on September 2nd, and received instructions to proceed to Barbados with the fleet commanded by Sir John Jervis, his coadjutor on the Naval side. With them were to go the troops being sent out from Great Britain. At Barbados, Grey would take over the troops collected in the islands by Generals Bruce and Prescott.

His objectives were the three islands of Martinique, Guadeloupe, and St. Lucia, which he was left to deal with in the order he thought best. He was furnished with very full instructions as to proclamations to be issued to the French anti-Republicans in those islands, and as to his conduct if he succeeded in their capture. At that time there were in the Leeward Islands nine line battalions of the low average rank-and-file strength of 330. The 9th and four other battalions were completed by drafts from the other four to a strength of 600 rank and file each.

From Ireland five regiments were to go with Grey and Jervis, who at last sailed from Portsmouth on November 26th. When they reached Barbados on January 6, 1794, Grey found the Irish detachment not yet arrived, and General Whyte, who was in command at Barbados, was by no means ready with his preparations; two battalions had been sent away to Leeward, and even the flank companies were not all collected.

Grey utilized the time of waiting by specially training the officers of his light infantry companies. As usual in those days, the flank companies of regiments were detached for service in battalions of Grenadiers and light infantry. There were as yet no separate battalions of light infantry in the British Army. Grey's training was more or less of an attempt to create them at the expense of his infantry regiments.

By the end of January he found himself in command of about 7,000 men, with whom he resolved to attempt the capture of Martinique. He was aware that Rochambeau, the French commander in that island, could oppose him with at least equal numbers, though many of them would be negroes and mulattoes of inferior military value.

The infantry were brigaded thus:

First Brigade—Sir C. Gordon : 13th, 39th, 43rd.
Second Brigade—Thomas Dundas : 56th, 63rd, 64th.
Third Brigade—John Whyte : 6th, 9th, 58th, 70th.

Grenadier Battalions, under Colonel Campbell (of the 9th) :
First Battalion—Grenadier companies of 6th, 8th, 12th, 17th, 22nd, 23rd, 31st, 41st.
Second Battalion—Grenadier companies of 9th, 33rd, 34th, 38th, 40th, 44th, 55th, 66th.
Third Battalion—Grenadier companies of 15th, 21st, 39th, 43rd, 56th, 60th, 64th, 70th.

Light Infantry Battalions, under Colonel Myers :
1st Battalion—Light companies of 6th, 8th, 9th, 12th, 17th, 22nd, 23rd, 31st, 68th.
2nd Battalion—Light companies of 15th, 31st, 34th, 35th, 38th, 40th, 41st, 44th, 55th.
3rd Battalion—Light companies of 21st, 39th, 43rd, 56th, 58th, 60th, 64th, 65th

There were also fifty Light Dragoons, detached from five regiments, besides artillery, engineers, and sailors.[1]

Sailing from Barbados on February 3, 1794, this force was off the southern end of Martinique on the 5th. The island is mountainous throughout, some forty miles in extreme length, from south-east to north-west, and about twenty miles across in its widest part. With very few decent roads or tracks, almost every march in the island imposed great difficulties and hardships on the troops. Near the south-west corner the coast is cut into by the bay of Fort Royal, now known as Port de France, which makes a fine harbour, well sheltered from the trade winds, and having on its northern side the town of Fort Royal, with its two chief forts, Fort St. Louis on a promontory in the bay, and Fort Bourbon some way up the hills at the back of the town. Towards the north-west end of the island, lying almost under the shadow of the Mt. Pelée volcano, which was destined to destroy it a century later, is the town of St. Pierre, the principal commercial centre of the island. On the opposite side of the island, in about the same latitude, are the bay and town of La Trinité.

[1] This statement does not quite agree with that given by Mr. Fortescue ("History of British Army," vol. IV, p. 354), which seems to be incorrect. In the first place, it shows the grenadier company of the 56th both in the 1st and the 3rd battalions. As in the case of the 1st battalion it makes nine companies against eight in the 2nd and 3rd, it is probably wrongly entered here.

The light company of the 9th is not entered at all; yet it was certainly in the force, and can be identified, as having been in the 1st battalion by the statement of casualties attached to Sir C. Grey's Martinique despatch of March 16, 1794 (C.O. 318.13). In this, against the 1st battalion of light infantry, is shown as wounded Lieutenant Stopford of the 9th.

The battalion companies of the 9th are not shown at all. But, in the above-mentioned despatch casualties are shown, in General Whyte's 3rd brigade, against the 9th and 70th. There are, in addition, casualties shown in the artillery, engineers, three battalions each of grenadiers and light infantry, and the 1st and 2nd infantry brigades. It is clear, therefore, that the battalion companies of the 9th were in the 3rd brigade. The distribution of the regiment, therefore, was—

Battalion companies, in the 3rd infantry brigade.

Grenadier company, in the 2nd battalion of grenadiers.

Light company, in the 1st battalion of light infantry.

As regards regiments other than the 9th, Fortescue's list has been followed, without any admission of its correctness.

108 HISTORY OF THE NORFOLK REGIMENT

The Republican governor and commander of Martinique, Rochambeau, had a reputation for competence, and commanded a considerable regular force, supplemented by large numbers of negroes and mulattoes

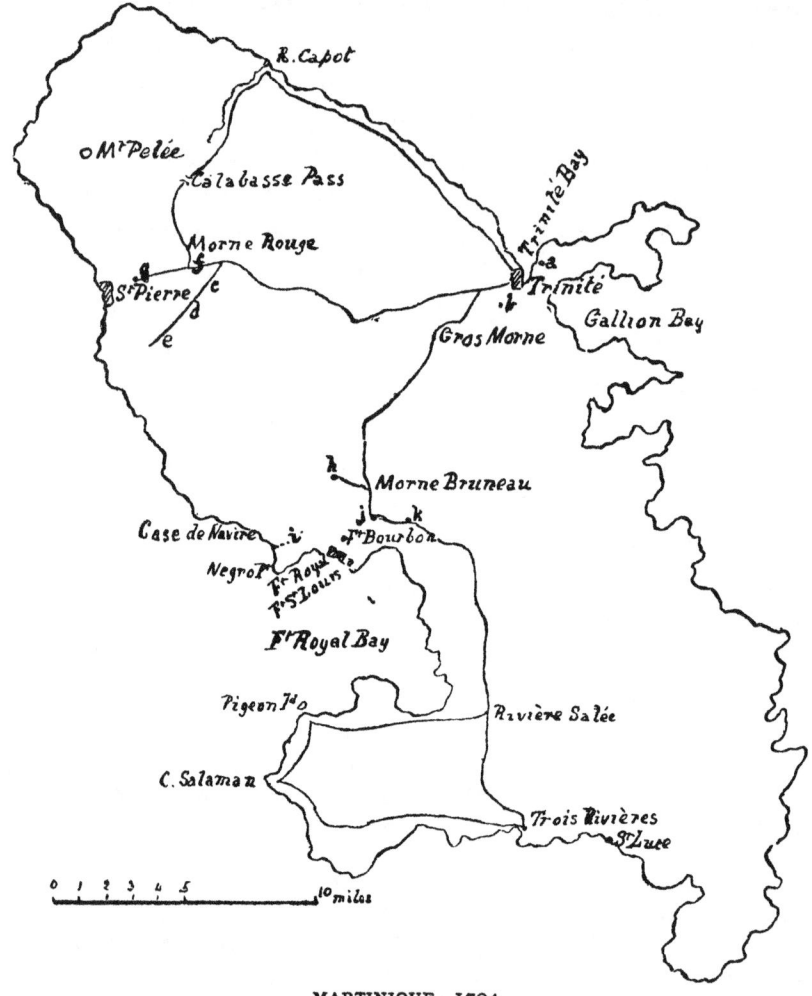

MARTINIQUE, 1794

a, Fort abandoned by Bellegarde after his defeat on February 6th by 1st Light Infantry. *b*, Morne le Brun—Bellegarde defeated by 1st Light Infantry on February 6th. *c*, Campbell with three companies Light Infantry on February 15th. *d*, Poste au Piu taken by Campbell, February 16th. *e*, Redoute Coloniale. *f*, Dundas on February 16th. *g*, Redoubt taken morning of February 17th. *h*, Lemâitre, taken by Campbell with Light Infantry on February 11th. *i*, Positions of La Coste and Gentilly. *j*, Sourier heights and batteries. *k*, Fort Mathilde. Craddock with three companies Light Infantry on February 8th.

obedient to the orders of the popular mulatto leader Bellegarde. The sympathies of the negroes especially had been enlisted by the grant of liberty and citizenship by the French Republic, privileges which they had not, and could not hope for, under the old form of government.

Had Rochambeau concentrated his forces it is extremely doubtful if Sir C. Grey's force would have sufficed; but the defenders were scattered all over the island in small detachments, in forts and batteries distributed haphazard in all sorts of out-of-the-way places. It was on this dispersion of the French forces that Grey reckoned for success. He decided to land in three places, having in each a force sufficient to overcome local opposition, and to destroy one by one the scattered defences in the neighbourhood, so that eventually, all three could unite for the conquest of the capital and the enemy's main force.

One landing, near La Trinité, was entrusted to Major-General Dundas with his second brigade, the 1st battalion of light infantry, and the 2nd battalion of grenadiers, with Colonel Campbell of the 9th as commander of the grenadiers. Thus both flank companies of the 9th were with Dundas's force. The battalion companies were with the force which Sir C. Grey kept under his own control. Dundas landed, on February 5th and 6th in Galion Bay, south of La Trinité, and on the latter date Colonel Campbell, with Lieutenant-Colonel Coote and the 1st battalion light infantry, carried Morne le Brun under a heavy fire, whilst other troops attacked Fort Bellegarde at La Trinité. During the night Bellegarde evacuated this fort and retired south-westwards to Gros Morne with his mulatto garrison, after setting fire to La Trinité. A detachment of British sailors succeeded in saving most of the town. The troops now advanced against Gros Morne, which was taken by midnight, Bellegarde again retreating to Morne Bruneau. At Gros Morne, Dundas was in possession of the communication between the north and south of the island, and he left the 64th to hold it.

On the 9th Bellegarde evacuated Morne Bruneau as the British advanced, and on the same day Fort Mathilde, covering a good landing place two miles on Dundas's left, in the north-east corner of Fort Royal Bay, was taken. From Morne Bruneau Dundas looked down on the harbour of Fort Royal.

On the 10th Campbell was detached, with five companies of grenadiers, to seize Colon, which he did that night. That same night, Lieutenant-Colonel Craddock, who had been left in charge of Fort Mathilde, was vigorously attacked by Bellegarde. Putting himself at the head of the grenadiers of the 9th, who were with him, Craddock charged the enemy with the bayonet and completely repulsed him.

On the 11th Campbell was reinforced by Coote with four companies of light infantry. Leaving a light company at Colon, Campbell and his grenadiers and light infantry, including those of the 9th, occupied the strong post of Lemâitre.

Meanwhile Sir C. Grey had landed on the south coast on February 6th. With him was Whyte's brigade, containing the battalion companies of the 9th. The operations by which the south side of Fort Royal Bay was cleared and the entrance opened to the British fleet need not be described, as what little fighting there was did not fall to the lot of the 9th.

A third landing was made by Sir Charles Gordon at Case de Navire, north-west of the capital, on which he advanced. As none of the 9th were with him, his operations require no description.

Grey, passing round the eastern end of Fort Royal Bay, was in communication with Dundas, at Morne Bruneau on February 14th. On the same day Dundas moved back with the 2nd battalion of grenadiers (in which were the grenadiers of the 9th), and the light companies of the 33rd, 40th, and 65th, to Gros Morne and La Trinité. Thence he detached Campbell with three light companies to Montigné, before which he was on the morning of the 16th. Dundas himself proceeded to the heights of Calebasse, which he reached by the north-east coast and the mouth of the River Capot. The march, over bad tracks high up on the shoulder of Mt. Pelée, was of extreme difficulty. Dundas's objective was St. Pierre, and from Calebasse on the morning of the 16th he saw Campbell heavily engaged with 500 or 600 of the enemy at Porte au Pin, half a mile short of Montigné. He at once sent his advanced guard of sixty-three men, under Captain Ramsay, against Campbell's opponents, who were silenced by his fire.

Ramsay, reinforced by the 2nd battalion of grenadiers (amongst them those of the 9th), occupied Montigné. Posting his force on Morne Rouge, Dundas then went to see after Campbell. That officer was attacked at 9.30 a.m., and the enemy had got within twenty yards of the 40th light company when Campbell, gallantly heading its charge with the bayonet, met his death in the moment of victory. Dundas now observed large bodies of the enemy forming, under the Redoute Coloniale, against Ramsay's position on Morne Rouge. Hastening there, he was attacked by 500 or 600 of the enemy. After about twenty minutes they retired to the redoubt, which they abandoned that night, leaving two guns behind.

At daybreak on the 17th two columns advanced on St. Pierre—the right to Lejeune, and the left to the Colonial Redoubt.

Next morning a letter was received from the commandant of St. Pierre, who, however, could not be found when an answer was sent with a flag of truce. His absence is perhaps to be accounted for by the fact that Colonel Symes, despatched by sea by Sir C. Grey, with three light companies and a detachment of the 58th, had landed to the north of the town and was already in possession of it. Colonel Myers, from Sir C. Gordon's force, had also marched up from La Coste with five companies of grenadiers and five of light infantry, and was already facing St. Pierre on the south side.

With St. Pierre in his possession, Grey still had to take Fort Royal, with its two forts of St. Louis (on a promontory projecting from the town) and Bourbon in the hills above it. In the first place it was necessary to capture the Sourier heights, on which Bellegarde stood with a strong force of blacks and mulattoes. Grey decided to attack at 1 a.m. on the 19th. The attack was to be with the bayonet only, and on such occasions Grey's practice was to send his men forward with the flints removed from their muskets, so as to prevent firing.

But at noon on the 18th Bellegarde destroyed his own hopes by attacking Grey's left, near the landing-place, with part of his troops descending the heights. Prescott, hurrying up reinforcements to this point, checked and charged the enemy. Meanwhile Grey, observing that Bellegarde had left his fortified camp only weakly held, sent from his right the 3rd battalion of grenadiers, supported by the 1st and 2nd battalions of light infantry, the company of the 9th being in the 1st battalion. Attacking the camp on its left, these troops captured it and Bellegarde's guns there with small loss, thus saving the necessity for the hazardous attack proposed for the 19th February.

On the night of the 28th, to quote Grey's account, Bellegarde and Pelocque, his second in command, " finding their situation too perilous, outside their forts and exposed to our attacks, surrendered—the two former being sent to Boston on condition of never carrying arms against His Majesty's forces, and their followers (300) as prisoners of war on board H.M.'s ships."

By the date of Grey's first despatch (March 16th) he had erected the batteries of his second parallel against Fort Bourbon, and expected to open fire from them on the 20th at a range of 400 or 500 yards.

The despatch gives the highest praise to all the troops and their commanders. Of Lieutenant-Colonel Campbell of the 9th Sir C. Grey writes: " In him the service lost a most excellent officer and a valuable man, justly regretted both by the army and navy."[1]

The total loss, so far, had been two officers, six sergeants, and sixty-three men killed; nine officers, six sergeants, one drummer, and 177 men wounded, and three men missing. The loss of the 9th was Colonel Campbell killed and one man wounded; but this does not include losses of men in the flank companies, which cannot be separated from the losses of the battalions to which they belonged. We know Lieutenant Stopford of the 9th was wounded in the 1st light infantry.

In a private letter of the same date Sir C. Grey urges the necessity for more troops, and describes the great strength of Fort Bourbon. He also asks for more medicines. We do not in these days look upon the West Indies as specially unhealthy; but at the end of the eighteenth century they had a very evil reputation as the " white man's grave." It was calculated that a battalion employed there required complete renewal every two years. Yellow fever was rife and other diseases very prevalent. With the evil effects of a plentiful supply of local rum, the improvident ways of the British soldier, and his exposure on service, without any proper shelter against sun and rain, it is not difficult to

[1] This officer was Campbell of Blythswood, an officer of the 9th.

understand this evil repute. One of the great difficulties in recruiting for the army at this time was the fear of the West Indies. It was this which necessitated engaging men with limitations exempting them from service outside of Europe.

On March 25th Grey was able to report the fall of the capital and Fort Bourbon, sooner than he had hoped for.

Measures had been concerted with Sir J. Jervis for a combined attack by the army and navy on the town and Fort St. Louis. The batteries of the 2nd parallel against Fort Bourbon were ready to open on the evening of the 19th, and they kept up a heavy fire all that night and next morning, till the fleet was in position. At the same time, the batteries at Morne Tortenson from the west, and Carrière Point from the east, fired heavily on Fort Royal and Fort St. Louis.

The forces intended to be used on the 20th were as follows :—

Naval.—H.M.S. " Asia " (64 guns) and H.M.S. " Zebra " (16 guns), with a force of seamen in flat boats.

Land.—1st grenadier battalion and 3rd Light Infantry, at La Coste, on Gordon's front ; 3rd grenadiers and 1st Light Infantry, from Prescott's camp on the Sourier heights.

Of the 9th only the light company was engaged as a constituent of the 1st light infantry.

Fort St. Louis was carried by escalade by the seamen under Captain Faulkner, R.N., whilst Lieutenant-Colonel Symes, with the force from Gordon's side, broke into the town from the west and, hoisting the British colours, renamed the place " Fort Edward," after Prince Edward, Duke of York, who had recently joined Grey.

Rochambeau surrendered Fort Bourbon on the 23rd. The British losses in storming Fort Royal had been trifling, none of them in the 9th.

Grey now announced his intention of proceeding against St. Lucia. Though he complained that his men were very short of proper clothing, he found himself well provided with ammunition from the captured arsenal.

No time was lost in starting for the conquest of St. Lucia. On March 30th the following troops embarked with Grey, and sailed next day :—

H.R.H. Prince Edward—3 battalions of grenadiers (including a company of the 9th).

Major-General Dundas—3 battalions of light infantry (including a company of the 9th).

ST. LUCIA

Col. Sir Charles Gordon—6th, 9th and 43rd foot (battalion companies), detachments of Engineers and the artillery with some light ordnance.

The rest of Grey's force was left in Martinique for the present.

St. Lucia was reached on April 1st, and a landing was effected with little resistance and no loss, by:

(1) Major-General Dundas with the 3rd light infantry at Anse du

Cap, and the 2nd light infantry at Anse du Choc. These two battalions were to join in taking the enemy's batteries in reverse, and occupy a position for the purpose of investing the works of Morne Fortuné.

(2) Prince Edward, landing at Marigot des Roseaux with the 1st and 3rd grenadiers, was to join Dundas in the investment.

(3) Colonel Coote, with the 1st light infantry, only landed at 7 p.m. at Anse de la Tocque. Thence, after capturing a four-gun battery, he completed the investment of the Fort of Morne Fortuné on that side. The light company of the 9th was in this force. Sir Charles Gordon, with the 2nd grenadiers (in which was the company of the 9th) and the 6th, 9th, and 43rd battalion companies, was left in reserve on board ship in Cul-de-Sac Bay. Thus, the light company was the only part of the 9th landed or engaged on this occasion.

At 7 p.m. on the 2nd Coote, with four light companies, stormed a redoubt and two batteries. He clearly surprised them, as he inflicted on the enemy the only loss that was incurred on either side. Next day Ricard, the French commandant, capitulated on the same conditions as Rochambeau, and his garrison laid down their arms. As they only numbered 125 regulars of the Regiment d'Aunis, resistance was clearly hopeless against Grey's overwhelming superiority. St. Lucia was captured absolutely without loss on the British side, and the French loss was only the two officers and thirty men killed in Coote's attack.

Grey, returning to Martinique, left Sir C. Gordon as Governor of St. Lucia, with a garrison consisting of the battalion companies of the 6th and 9th Foot.[1]

With Martinique and St. Lucia in his possession, Sir C. Grey still had to deal with Guadeloupe, the most northerly of the three French islands to windward. His task, owing to his losses, mainly from sickness amongst his troops, and the necessity for leaving garrisons to guard his conquests, became more and more difficult as it progressed.

Though Grey only left St. Lucia on April 4th, he had shipped his

[1] There can be no possible doubt as to this, as the statement is repeated in Grey's next despatch. Cannon speaks of the 9th returning to Martinique and going to Guadeloupe, which is wrong, except as regards the flank companies.

116 HISTORY OF THE NORFOLK REGIMENT

stores and supplies at Martinique, and was ready to sail again for Guadeloupe on the 8th. After his detachment of the 6th and 9th, his force consisted only of the 43rd, and the battalions of grenadiers and light infantry, with which the flank companies of the 9th still were.

Guadeloupe consists of two distinct islands though they are only separated from one another by an arm of the sea—the Rivière Salée, averaging 300 yards in breadth. The western and larger island is as mountainous and rugged as Guadeloupe, and the Soufrière volcano in

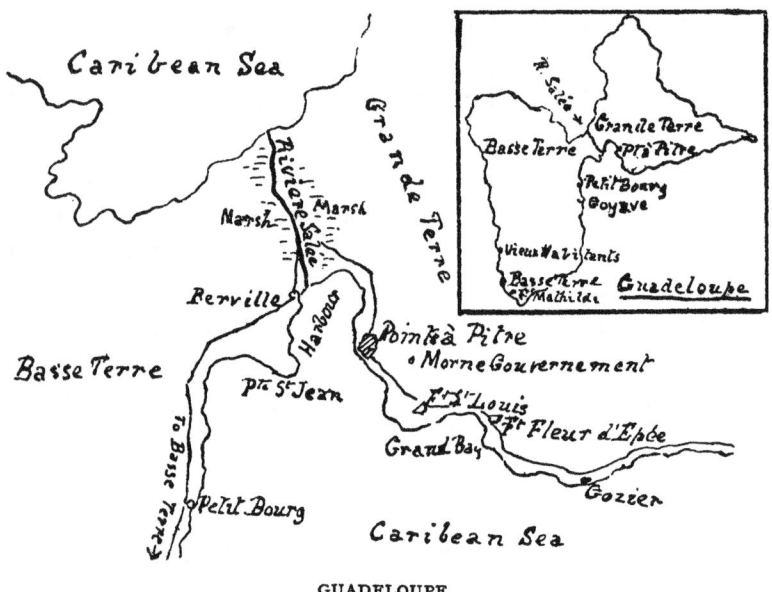

GUADELOUPE

the south rises to 4,900 feet. The eastern island is comparatively flat, never rising to a greater height than 450 feet. A strip of land, some three miles long and about the same breadth, juts out from Basse Terre, the western island, to the Rivière Salée, across which Grande Terre, the eastern island, begins. The part of the islands which is of most interest in connexion with Grey's expedition is the western portion of Grande Terre, and the connecting isthmus.

Grey landed in Grand Bay, south of Pointe à Pître, the capital of Grande Terre, in the early morning of April 11th, under a fire from Fort

Fleur d'Épée, and another fort which he calls Fort Gozier.[1] He had with him only part of the 1st and 2nd grenadier battalions, one company of the 43rd and 500 sailors and marines. The rest had been delayed by wind and current, and arrived later. The landing was protected by Lord Garlies on the "Winchester," laying her close under the forts and silencing their batteries.

At 5 a.m. Fort Fleur d'Épée was stormed. It was of considerable strength, on a hill with a battery on the slope below it; but it was commanded by another fort on Morne Mascot, the capture of which would render it untenable. Prince Edward, with the 1st and 2nd grenadiers (including the grenadiers of the 9th) and one hundred men of the naval battalion, attacked the fort at Morne Mascot, whilst Dundas, with the 1st and 2nd light infantry (including the light company of the 9th) and one hundred men of the naval battalion, attacked the gorge of Fleur d'Épée and cut its communications with Fort St. Louis to the west and Pointe à Pître. At the same time Colonel Symes, with the 3rd grenadiers and 3rd light infantry, co-operated with Dundas by the coast road. The storm was a very gallant affair, carried out entirely with the bayonet, according to Grey's almost invariable practice in such cases. The sailors climbed into the fort by the embrasures, whilst the soldiers attacked and burst open the gates. Inside the fort the enemy still fought bravely till, at last, they were broken and fled as best they might to Pointe à Pître.

The losses of the British army (besides thirteen sailors) were fifteen killed, forty-five wounded, and two missing. No officer of the 9th figures in the casualty list, but, as usual, it is impossible to separate its losses in men from the total losses of the grenadier and light infantry battalions to which its flank companies were attached. The enemy lost sixty killed, fifty-five wounded, and about one hundred prisoners. With the fall of Fleur d'Épée, Grey was master of Pointe à Pître, and the whole of Grande Terre was speedily in his possession.

[1] Grey's despatch says he landed in Gozier Bay, which, from the map, does not seem to exist. Mr. Fortescue ("History of British Army," vol. IV, part I, p. 363) shows that the landing was probably in Grand Bay, but does not mention Fort Gozier, which was probably Fort Morne Mascot, an outwork north of Fleur d'Épée.

Leaving garrisons in Grande Terre, Grey again embarked the rest of his troops on April 14th. On the 15th Grey, with Prince Edward, the 1st and 2nd grenadiers, and the 1st light infantry, landed at Petit Bourg, on the east coast of Basse Terre, and marched south by the coast road towards the town of Basse Terre, on the south-west coast of the island, capturing as he went such coast batteries as he found.

On April 17th Dundas landed with the 3rd grenadiers and 2nd and 3rd light infantry at Vieux Habitants, seven miles north-west of Basse Terre, with little opposition and no loss. He marched south to meet Grey on the 18th. On the way he took several batteries and posts. Meanwhile Grey's force, with which were both flank companies of the 9th, reached St. Mary's on the 15th, and on the 16th, after finding the enemy's post at Trou Chain abandoned, halted before dark near Trois Rivières, above the enemy's two redoubts and strong post at Palmiste, in front of Basse Terre.

Grey arranged to attack the redoubt at Grande Anse and the battery d'Arnet; but the former was evacuated at 8 p.m. on the 17th, and the latter was stormed by Colonel Coote with the 1st light infantry (including the company of the 9th), without loss, in the night of the 18th–19th. At midnight on the 19th Grey advanced from Trois Rivières and Grande Anse with the 1st light infantry and the 1st and 2nd grenadiers (including the company of the 9th), and stormed the port of Palmiste, with all its batteries. In possession of this, he commanded Fort St. Charles and the town of Basse Terre.

On the morning of the 21st he was in communication with Dundas. Collot, the Republican Governor of Guadeloupe, now finding himself surrounded in Basse Terre, though he had a considerable force there, capitulated on terms similar to those allowed at Martinique and St. Lucia. He had made a very poor defence of the island entrusted to his charge; for, one way or another, he could lay hands on 6,000 men, of whom 4,000 had been armed. Yet the conquest of Guadeloupe had been effected by Grey with less than 3,000 men, with a total loss of eighty-six killed, wounded, and missing. Of these, only two killed, four wounded, and five missing are accounted for in the Basse Terre operations.

Collot's garrison in Fort St. Charles alone, at its surrender, was fifty-five regulars of the Guadeloupe Regiment, the 14th French of the line, and eight hundred and eighteen National Guards, etc.

When he wrote his despatch of April 12th from which the above account is mostly taken, Grey reported that he had left Dundas in Guadeloupe, but had reduced his garrison by the flank companies of the regiments in the West Indies, which he had sent back to the stations of the battalions to which they belonged. That meant that the grenadier and light companies of the 9th were sent to rejoin the battalion companies in St. Lucia.

Grey had reported that with the capture of Guadeloupe his operations must end. The remains of his force were only sufficient to garrison his conquests, the unhealthy season was approaching, and his troops were worn out by their exertions in a most trying climate, and generally in very difficult country. He again reverts to this subject in a letter of May 6th.

St. Lucia seems to have been less unhealthy than some of the other islands, for, on June 18, 1794, Sir C. Gordon, the governor, writes to Dundas that in the two regiments (6th and 9th) of his garrison he had lost no officer, and only a few men from disease. In this letter he also mentions that he had sent back the flank companies of both regiments to help Sir C. Grey to recover Guadeloupe, and that there were sixty rank and file in each of them. If he had the whole of his two regiments, he says, he would have about 800 men, and that was only about half the garrison really necessary for the island.

Sir C. Grey had left Guadeloupe to return to Martinique on April 13th. He and Jervis were both anxious to get home for a change, and to concert measures for a further campaign. He was also busy over the distribution of prize money.

Whilst Grey was at Guadeloupe on May 31st Dundas was taken ill and died three days later of yellow fever, after Grey and Jervis had left for St. Kitts. There he heard that Grande Terre had been lost to a French fleet and troops. He could only leave Jervis to shut in the French whilst he collected all available troops, including the flank companies of the 9th from St. Lucia.

With the troops so collected Grey landed at Gozier on the 19th without opposition, and began batteries against Fleur d'Épée.[1] A detachment of grenadiers and sailors, on the 22nd, surprised an enemy post at St. Anne's, seven miles east of Gozier, bayoneted 400 of them, and destroyed their guns. Only one man was wounded on the British side.

The enemy held a strong position between Gozier and Fleur d'Épée which was taken in reverse by a wide detour round its left in the night with six companies commanded by Colonel Fisher of the 9th. Yet another position between Grey and Morne Mascot was surrounded by Colonel Symes. The enemy was driven headlong past Morne Mascot into Fleur d'Épée. The same afternoon the French, having collected a motley force of every shade of colour, counter-attacked Symes in great force. They had plenty of ammunition, and the fire was so severe that the grenadiers lay down, a procedure which would be a matter of course now, but in 1794 was considered unusual. As the enemy approached, the grenadiers sprang to their feet, fired a deadly volley, and charged with the bayonet, driving the enemy back in wild confusion.

On the 29th Victor Hugues, the Republican mulatto commanding the French expedition, had succeeded in collecting another 1,500 men of many colours whom he launched at Symes's position. Once more the unconquerable grenadiers drove them back, with even greater slaughter than on the 27th. In all this desperate fighting the flank companies of the 9th took their share.

The unhealthy season was now advancing, and Grey could not afford to waste time. At daybreak on July 2nd Symes was sent to storm Pointe à Pître. He had with him the 1st grenadiers, the 1st and 2nd light infantry, and the 1st battalion of seamen. The light company of the 9th was with the 1st light infantry, but the grenadier company was not present, as its battalion was the 2nd. They remained with

---

[1] In command of the landing party of grenadiers and light infantry was Brigadier-General Symes. The light infantry were led by Lieutenant-Colonel Gomm of the 55th, father of Field-Marshal Sir W. M. Gomm, who owed to his father's death in the West Indies his first commission, at the age of ten, in the 9th. He joined the regiment when he was fifteen.

Grey at Morne Mascot watching Fleur d'Épée, which he meant to attack if Symes succeeded.

As so often happens, the guides, whether by mistake or treachery, took the wrong road in the darkness, and brought the British troops right on the enemy outposts. It had been proposed to attack the works above the town at Morne Gouvernement, but, the alarm being given, Symes decided to attack the town itself. Unfortunately he came upon the most difficult part of it, where it was almost unscalable. There was great confusion, and the men began to load and fire their muskets, which was quite contrary to Grey's practice in night attacks, and led to their firing accidentally on one another. Their numbers were reduced by illness, and despite their heroic efforts they were finally driven out of the town, without even destroying the magazines, which were their objective.

Symes himself was wounded,[1] and Lieutenant-Colonel Gomm, leading the light infantry, was killed. Many other officers were killed or wounded. The rearguard in the retreat was formed by the grenadiers. The total losses, which were undoubtedly heavy, are not known.

The failure of the attack on Pointe à Pitre compelled the abandonment of the projected attack on Fleur d'Épée. The 2nd grenadiers, with whom were the company of the 9th, had to be used to cover Symes's retreat.

The troops were now so exhausted by their exertions, and by exposure to the rainy season, that Grey felt forced to fall back on Gozier, whence he despatched the 2nd light infantry by sea to Petit Bourg. From Petit Bourg they moved eastwards to the low ground at Berville, on the isthmus west of the Rivière Salée, and entrenched themselves. Here it was intended that they should prevent incursions from Grand Terre into Basse Terre. Grey now found himself compelled, by the weakness and bad condition of his force, to abandon further attempts on Grande Terre for the present, till he could get reinforcements from home. He strengthened the garrison of Berville up to forty-eight companies. With the rest of his force he embarked for Martinique on

[1] He died of his wounds at St. Kitts on July 19th.

July 4th. The grenadier and light companies of the 6th and 9th were returned to their regiments at St Lucia.[1]

The total loss in Guadeloupe, between June 11th and July 3rd, is given by Grey as 111 killed, 330 wounded, and fifty-six missing. No officer of the 9th appears among the casualties, and, as usual, it is impossible to identify the losses in men in particular companies of the grenadier and light infantry battalions.

In a private letter of the 9th July, to Mr. Nepean, Sir C. Grey writes of Colonel Symes and the disastrous failure at Pointe à Pître as follows : " I fear his [Symes's] mind is not at ease—not that he has any occasion ; for no man could do more at the head of a corps than he did. . . . Between ourselves they [the men] were so completely worn down that they would not advance when ordered. It is a serious fact. The light infantry refused to make the least exertion, therefore I suppose they could not." He gives a lamentable account of the ravages of the climate, not only among the troops but in his own " family," of which he says there remained only one black servant. All the rest, including his sons, had died or been invalided.

Of the subsequent fate of Guadeloupe we need not write, as the 9th had now said adieu to this island. On September 10, 1794, Grey states that the whole of his forces in the three conquered islands was reduced, in rank and file fit for duty, to 872 in Martinique, 470 in Guadeloupe, and 478 in St. Lucia. The corresponding figures on July 17th had been 893, 1,357, and 558.

The service of the regiment in the deadly climate of the West Indies was, however, far from ended. With the return of the flank companies from Guadeloupe to St. Lucia the whole regiment, or what remained of it, was together in the last-named island. The three French islands had been conquered, but they now had to be defended against Victor Hugues and his crew, who had already got back Grande Terre, and were soon to complete the recapture of Basse Terre. Ruffians though they were, they were by no means wanting in ability or enterprise, and they at once set to work to stir up revolt, not only in Guadeloupe, St.

---

[1] Grey clearly states in his despatch of July 8, 1794, that he had returned the four flank companies of the 6th and 9th, borrowed from St. Lucia, to their regiments.

Lucia, and Martinique, but also in the islands which were already in England's possession in 1793. For this purpose they had ready instruments, not only in the French planters and other settlers, white and brown, in the three islands, but also in the negroes, free or slaves, whom they could attract by promises of liberty and French citizenship, not to speak of the attractions of plunder or revenge. They found little difficulty, with small craft, in evading the English cruisers and carrying arms and officers to the other islands. St. Lucia was the first of the islands to be affected. On September 9, 1794, Sir C. Grey wrote home reporting that the negroes in the island had risen, and enclosed a copy of Major Baillie's letter giving an account of what had happened. Baillie had succeeded temporarily to the governorship of St. Lucia when Sir C. Gordon was tried by Court Martial, and sent home, for peculations as governor. It will be remembered that Baillie was in command of the light companies of the 9th at Tobago when it was taken.[1] His letter states that he had sent after the rebels part of the 9th and 6th with some local militia, who had found the enemy drawn up in a strong position and in considerable force. The fire which the British encountered was so well directed and heavy that they were unable to charge till they had mastered it. Then they went in and dispersed the rebels at the point of the bayonet. In this fight Captain Houston and Lieutenant Rennie, both of the 9th, were wounded, and the command devolved on Lieutenant Armstrong of the 6th, who reported on the action. Besides these officer casualties the loss was one man of the 6th killed, one of the 9th, and three of the militia wounded.

The strength of the garrison of St. Lucia (6th and 9th) was reported by Grey on September 10th to be 478 rank and file fit for duty: by November 24, 1794, this figure was reduced to 346. The strength of the 9th on September 1st had been fifteen officers, twenty-three sergeants, ten drummers and fifers, with 258 rank and file fit for duty, one hundred sick, and seventeen on command—423 of all ranks.

On January 31, 1795, Sir J. Vaughan, who had succeeded Sir C.

[1] From October 1, 1794, Baillie was promoted to Lieutenant-Colonel in the 58th, his vacancy as major in the 9th being taken, by purchase, by Brevet-Major F. Maitland of the 60th.

Grey as commander-in-chief, reports that the St. Lucia rebels had beaten off Captain Malcolm's Black Rangers, with a loss of two officers and twelve men. He now sent to command in St. Lucia Lieutenant-Colonel Steuart of the 68th, with the flank companies of his own regiment to strengthen the 6th and 9th, both of which were lamentably weak. Steuart quickly drove the rebels into the hills in the interior, but was unable to pursue them, and had no success with an offer of pardon on surrender made to them.

By April he had been reinforced by the 31st and 61st from England, but both regiments consisted mainly of boys and unseasoned men, who, for the moment, were not of much use in that climate. Even with them, he was not able to cut the rebels from the interior.

His next operations were directed against Vieuxfort in the extreme south of the island.[1] Leaving the rest of his garrison at Fort Charlotte (Morne Fortuné), he sailed, with the whole of the 61st, the flank companies of the 9th and 68th, and Malcolm's Black Rangers.[2] Landing near Vieuxfort on April 15th, with altogether about 1,000 men, he sent Malcolm's men, supported by the flank companies of the 9th and the light company of the 68th, to dislodge the enemy from a hill. "They effected this order," he writes to Vaughan, "with much spirit and drove the enemy before them with great execution." The 9th lost in this fight two men killed and six wounded. Next day Vieuxfort was occupied, and Steuart then marched by the coast road, via Laborie, to Choiseul, whence, on the 19th, he turned inland to march due north on Soufriére, the enemy's chief stronghold in this part of the island. On the 20th he heard that the enemy was advancing, and presently considerable numbers were seen in front and on his right. He sent the flank companies of the 9th and Malcolm to turn the enemy's left, whilst the 61st and the flank companies of the 68th attacked in front. Before the frontal advance had got half-way on its journey firing was heard from the right, and Steuart withdrew his frontal attack to go to the assistance of his right. Before it arrived the enemy's attack had been

---

[1] See map at p. 114.
[2] The 9th and 68th were weakened at this time, as will appear later, by having to contribute 150 men to help against the rebellion in Grenada.

beaten off, though not without considerable loss. Malcolm was so badly wounded that he had to be sent back. In the 9th Captain Nesbitt was wounded in the leg (which had to be amputated), two men were killed, and fourteen wounded.

On the 21st the enemy was found in position across the road to Soufriére ,and was cannonaded ; but it was too late to attack that day. When the attack was begun on the 22nd the enemy was occupying a strong position on both sides of the road, across which an earthwork had been built. His right flank rested on a high hill, his left on a lower one crowned by a breastwork and protected in front by a marsh.

About noon Steuart sent Malcolm's Rangers to try and turn the rebel right. The flank companies of the 9th, the light company of the 61st, and the grenadiers of the 68th moved round the marsh to attack the enemy's left flank. His guns Steuart could not move, so he planted them on the road, and placed a company of the 61st to protect them. Seeing this company, the enemy opened fire on it. This would have done no harm, provided the turning columns had not prematurely disclosed their whereabouts, and had remained hidden by the woods. But Malcolm's Rangers getting excited by the fusillade, began also to fire, and the contagion of this bad example rapidly spread, so that very soon the whole of Steuart's men, white and black, were blazing away the precious ammunition which it was so hard to replenish in that difficult country and disclosing Steuart's outflanking operations.

The commander of the rebels was clearly a soldier. Realizing the advantages of breaking the British centre and isolating the two flanking columns, he sent heavy columns down the road towards the guns. This motley crew behaved far better than could be expected, and made two vigorous attacks before they were driven back by the British on the road, who followed them up to the parapet across it. There the rebels rallied and drove back the attacking British with heavy loss.

After seven hours of fighting, when his ammunition was exhausted, and his men without food, which they had thrown away rather than carry it in the terrible heat, Steuart reluctantly retreated to Choiseul in the night. The enemy had suffered too, and, besides that, were not the class of troops likely to follow up an advantage ; so Steuart got away without being destroyed. His casualties had been terribly heavy. One officer (of the 68th) was killed and nine officers wounded; of other ranks there were twenty-nine killed, 127 wounded, and five missing. The heaviest fighting was on the road, and the 9th, away to the right, only lost three men killed.

Steuart was not strong enough to leave a garrison in the south, except at Vieuxfort, where he left 200 men, most of them negroes, and himself sailed back to the north and took post at Morne Fortuné, in Fort Charlotte. Even this, he said, he would probably have to evacuate unless the fleet could prevent the arrival of small craft with enemy reinforcements from Guadeloupe and elsewhere.

Sir J. Vaughan's correspondence in early June contains a letter to the Secretary of State in which he complains of the large number of field officers absent from their regiments on leave, and specially mentions Colonel Fisher of the 9th as one of them. He remarks that the service must suffer from their "neglect of duty." The fact shows how extremely unpopular and irksome service in the West Indies then was.

Steuart was left unmolested at Morne Fortuné during the early part of the rainy season, the enemy knowing well how his force would be weakened by death and disease. On June 6th they recommenced operations by taking Vigie, on the promontory on the north side of Castries Bay, and Pigeon Island. Their numbers in St. Lucia at this time were reckoned by Vaughan at about 6,000 of all sorts.

With the loss of these two positions Steuart felt himself compelled to evacuate St. Lucia. On June 19th he successfully embarked all his garrison, except a few sick who were too bad to be moved. The whole white garrison was represented, in rank and file, by 575 fit and 625 sick, all that remained of three whole regiments and part of the 9th. Baillie was now Lieutenant-Colonel of the 9th, the strength of which at the evacuation was only 105 fit and eighty sick, of all ranks. This of course does not include the men sent to Grenada in March to assist against the rebels in that island.

The scene now changes to Grenada, an island in English possession before the commencement of this war, but with many French white or mulatto planters. Like most of the neighbouring islands Grenada was mountainous and thickly wooded, and the settlements and plantations were chiefly near the coast. The island, oval in shape, is about twenty miles from north to south, and about half that breadth. The principal towns were the capital, St. George's, Goyave on the west or leeward coast, and Grenville, with St. Andrew's or Fort Royal a little south of it, on the east or windward coast.

On the afternoon of March 2, 1795, the lieutenant-governor, Mr. Ninian Home, was absent from St. George's on the east coast, quite unsuspicious of impending trouble.

GRENADA

That night the negroes rose under the leadership of a brutal mulatto named Fédon, who owned a plantation at Belvedere near Goyave. At that place Mr. Home, on his way back to St. George's, and forty-three other white men were captured, and Fédon compelled Home to write a letter to Mr. Mackenzie, the senior member of Council, threatening death to all the prisoners if the rebels were attacked. That threat was carried out later, all but three of the forty-four prisoners being brutally massacred.

Mackenzie now stepped into Home's office, by virtue of his position as president. Under the Constitution of the colony he also acted as commander-in-chief if the senior military officer was below the rank of brigadier-general. It was only on March 28th that Mackenzie sent his full report to Vaughan and the Secretary of State. He stated that the insurrection was of the " French Free Coloured People." Martial law had been at once proclaimed, and help called for from the commander-in-chief, the governors of other islands, and even from the Spanish governor of Trinidad, who had generously sent his small contribution of forty men.

The garrison of the island was only 190 regulars at Richmond Hill, 280 militia at St. George's, and a few at St. Andrew's and St. Patrick's. Mackenzie sent Captain Gurdon of the 58th, with 150 men (forty of them regulars) to pick up the militia at St. Andrew's and St. Patrick's and attack the rebels at Mont Ste. Catherine. The militia being safe on board ship and refusing to move, Gurdon found the rebel position too strong for his force, and returned to St. George's after a slight skirmish.

Sir J. Vaughan's reply to Mackenzie's appeal was the despatch of 150 men under Brigadier-General Lindsay. They were drawn mostly from the 9th and 68th at St. Lucia, as is stated in Vaughan's despatch of March 15th. These detachments were commanded by Colonel Schaw of the 68th. Lindsay acted promptly. Marching on March 15th, with all but the Spaniards and 200 of the weaker men left at St. George's and Richmond Hill, he was before the rebels' position on the 17th. He found it very formidable, being in three tiers up the steep slope of a very high wooded hill, and defended by four guns.

Lindsay successfully stormed the lower tier, but heavy rain prevented his going farther. A later report mentions that Captain Sandieman of the 9th was wounded in this affair. Five days later the unfortunate Lindsay, delirious from fever, took his own life. Colonel Schaw, left in command, considered the capture of the position beyond the powers of his little force.

Mackenzie was now again acting as commander-in-chief in the island,[1] and his amateur military ideas appear to have been based on two

[1] He yielded the position to Lindsay as a brigadier-general, but, on his death, resumed it till Nicolls' arrival.

principles—to divide up his forces, and to make converging attacks on positions from different directions, no matter what difficulties there might be in the way of concerted action. He sent Gurdon, with a hundred regulars and some militia, to Grenville, where Gurdon thought it unsafe to stay, so took post on Observatory Hill, five miles off. The enemy had a fortified post on Pilot Hill, outside Grenville. Mackenzie also had a post holding the captured portion of the enemy's position at Belvedere. Picton, from Barbados, had sent the 25th and 29th, on their arrival from home, direct to Grenada under Colonel Campbell. Campbell landed near Goyave, though Mackenzie had sent him a message to land at three places. Mackenzie still insisted on a converging attack from the directions of Goyave, St. George's, and Grenville, which latter place, as already mentioned, was commanded by the rebels on Pilot Hill. The consequence was that Campbell found himself with about 450 men, of whom nearly two-thirds were recruits just out from England (the rest being the detachment of the 9th and 150 seamen, volunteers from H.M.S. "Resource"), in front of a very strong position, occupied by about double his numbers of desperate rebels who could hope for no mercy if beaten. They were just preparing to massacre the unfortunate lieutenant-governor and his companions. Campbell, driven against his better judgment by Mackenzie, attacked. He could not refuse to obey the orders of his commander-in-chief, though the latter was a civilian. Mackenzie had sent off 300 men, under Major Mallory of the 29th, by sea to Grenville, and 250, under Major Wright of the 25th, to support Gurdon at Observatory Hill. Neither of these forces was at hand when Mackenzie forced Campbell to attack the Belvedere position alone. The lowest position was still held by the British and formed the starting point. The enemy, before the attack of the British, retreated from the second to the highest position, which was defended by abattis and a slope greasy from the rain, where it was not absolutely a precipice. The attack was beaten off, and Campbell had to retreat, after losing thirty-two killed and sixty-six wounded. Of the 9th Captain Stopford, one sergeant, and four men were killed, and two sergeants and eight men wounded.

    Brigadier-General Nicolls was now sent to take command in Grenada, and Mackenzie, who appears to have at last realized that military matters were beyond him, retired to his civil duties.

Nicolls landed on April 16th, and at once prepared to attack Pilot Hill, which was evacuated by the rebels, who retired to the mountains on May 5th. Their numbers, swelled by negro recruits, were now reckoned at 10,000. Nicolls had abandoned Goyave, when he started for Pilot Hill, and now only held the most important landing-places in the island. The rebels were scattered in the hills and there was no immediate danger from them. Nicolls, realizing that to pursue them actively would mean very heavy losses from sickness at that season, decided to confine himself to burning their plantations and cutting off their supplies. In this work he used chiefly black troops, to whom the climate was less destructive than to Europeans. There were, nevertheless, occasional skirmishes with the brigands, in one of which, in June, Nicolls reports to the commander-in-chief that Lieutenant Darling of the 9th and four men were slightly wounded. Writing on August 2nd, he says he hears a rumour that the detachment of the 9th was to be taken from him. This he regrets " as they have, for their numbers, turned out more duty men than any regiment here, and are besides perfectly well acquainted with the kind of warfare we are engaged in."

In a statement of the garrisons in the various islands on July 7, 1795, the strength of the 9th is given as follows :—

In Grenada—two officers and 177 rank and file fit for duty.

In Martinique—six officers and 213 others, including 114 sick.

The commander-in-chief, now General Leigh, reports on October 2nd that he has already sent the rest of the 9th from Martinique to Grenada, where they were sent to Richmond Hill Barracks, above St. George's.

The revolt was still going on spasmodically. On October 18th, Nicolls reports that Schaw had left Goyave after Fédon had stormed a hill commanding it. There were none of the 9th there. At this time the French Government were proposing to put a stop to the barbarity with which Fédon and others of his stamp had been carrying on the war, and he was ordered to Guadeloupe to answer for his conduct. He thereupon set the French Government at defiance. In the beginning of

January, 1796, matters were reported to be much as usual in Grenada. There had been rebel demonstrations against Pilot Hill, which was the only outpost in the island now held by the British. All the rest of the troops were at and about St. George's, and there were none of the 9th at Pilot Hill, which had to be evacuated towards the end of February.

There was then nothing left in British possession but St. George's. Nicolls now received reinforcements of the 7th Light Dragoons, the 3rd (Buffs), 8th, 63rd, and 88th. When the enemy, growing bolder after their capture of Pilot Hill, occupied a hill commanding Hospital Hill above St. George's, Nicolls promptly attacked them with all of the garrison he could spare, and occupied the hill. What part, if any, the 9th played in this is not certain. On March 22nd Nicolls felt himself strong enough, with his recently arrived reinforcements, to resume the offensive, and set out to retake Port Royal (St. Andrew's). The 9th accompanied him; but, though he says that at one time he ordered up half of them " to assist if necessary," it is clear they were not actually engaged. No losses are shown against the regiment, though all the other regiments (3rd, 8th, 29th, 63rd, and 88th) figure on the casualty lists. Port Royal being taken on March 27th, the rebels were followed to their last stronghold, in the centre of the island, which was stormed. They were utterly broken, terms of surrender being accorded only to a few regular French troops. Fédon escaped for the moment and committed a few more atrocities, but it was surmised that he had been drowned when trying to escape in a canoe which was found capsized off the coast with Fédon's compass nailed in the bottom of it. The 9th took no part in these final operations after the recapture of Port Royal.

The rest of their service in Grenada was peaceable at Richmond Hill, and presently they were sent home, after a very trying eight years' service in the West Indies. They had been joined by volunteers from the 6th, when that regiment was sent home, and similarly, when the 9th was bound for England in the summer of 1796, many of its hardier men, perhaps those who were safer and happier out of England than in it, volunteered to go on serving in the West Indies in the 27th. It was but the wreck of the regiment that arrived in Norwich in September, 1796. Its first monthly return (for October, 1796) at that station shows as present with the colours, fifteen officers, ten sergeants, fourteen drummers, and only eighty-nine effective men! By December 1st the number of men had risen to 205, but the regiment was still 807 rank and file short of its sanctioned establishment.

At Norwich the regiment remained till the end of 1797. In January, 1798, it moved to Colchester; in February and March it was at Bury St. Edmunds. In April and May head-quarters were at Sudbury (Suffolk) with eight companies, the other two being at Ipswich in May. In June the detached companies were at Clacton and Colchester, and in that month the eight companies, with head-quarters, went to Stowmarket. In July, headquarters with nine companies were at Yarmouth, where they remained till the end of the year, with one company at Needham. In January, 1799, the regiment went to Amherst Barracks in Guernsey, whence it returned to Newport, Isle of Wight, in June. In July it was at the Tower of London, whence, owing to the difficulty of receiving there the large number of recruits volunteering from the Militia, it was moved at the end of the month to Romford. On September 1st it was in camp at Barham Downs, preparatory to going on active service in North Holland.

CHAPTER IX

INCREASE OF PAY—MILITIA RECRUITS—THE 2ND AND 3RD BATTALIONS. THE EXPEDITIONS TO NORTH HOLLAND AND BREMEN. 1797–1804

THE years after 1797 were of great importance to the regiment, in common with the rest of the army. In the first place, on May 25, 1797, the pay of the army was raised. Hitherto the infantry private had received 6d. a day and 2¼d. more as commutation of certain allowances abolished. He was now to have 7s. a week (1s. a day), from which the stoppages were to be:—

	s.	d.
For messing, not more than	4	0
Necessaries	1	6

leaving him 1s. 6d. per week, or a trifle over 2½d. a day. The pay of officers was fixed as follows per diem:—

	£	s.	d.
Colonel (plus 6d. per company of his regiment in lieu of the pay of a "warrant man")	1	2	7
Lt.-Colonel	0	15	0
Major	0	14	1
Captain	0	9	5
Lieutenant	0	5	8
2nd Lieutenant or Ensign	0	4	8
Paymaster	0	15	0
Adjutant	0	8	0

	£	s.	d.
Quartermaster	0	5	8
Surgeon	0	9	5
Assistant Surgeon	0	4	6
Sergeant-Major or Quartermaster-Sergeant	0	2	0¾
Paymaster-Sergeant	0	1	6¾
Sergeant	0	1	6¾
Corporal	0	1	2¼
Drummer or Fifer	0	1	1¾
Private	0	1	0

Chaplains, as regimental officers, had disappeared in 1796. The following now appear who were not formerly shown on the regimental establishments: Paymaster, sergeant-major, quartermaster-sergeant, and paymaster-sergeant.

By 1797 great difficulty was being found in obtaining recruits for the regular army from the ordinary sources. Mr. Fortescue attributes this partly to mismanagement, and still more to the rapid development of English manufactures, due to the cessation of continental competition. Many expedients had been tried and failed, including the enlistment of boys under eighteen in the 9th and some other regiments. The eyes of the authorities were turned towards the Militia as a promising nursery for recruits. In the beginning of 1798 an Act was passed which allowed 10,000 men of the Supplementary Militia, constituted in the previous year, to enlist in the regular army. A further limitation to the numbers provided that such enlistments should not in any county exceed twenty per cent of the Supplementary Militia raised in that area. The places of men so enlisting were not to be filled by ballot. The Supplementary Militia were to be incorporated in the regular Militia.

The experiment was, generally speaking, a failure, as no special inducements to volunteer were held out, and there was no exemption for the volunteers from serving in dreaded parts of the world, especially the West Indies. Norfolk was the most notable exception, and the volunteers for enlistment from that county were numerous. So pleased were the authorities with the way in which the Supplementary Militia had come forward in the case of the 9th that we find a letter, dated June 25, 1798, from the Adjutant-General to Major Sandieman, then commanding the regiment, in which it is stated that all but thirteen of the recruits received from the Supplementary Militia had re-enlisted in the 9th. They are to be told that the commander-in-chief highly appreciates their spirit in thus responding to the call, and, as a mark of his appreciation, orders that each of these recruits is to have an additional bounty of three guineas, which, with what he had already received, would raise the bounty to ten guineas, the largest allowed for the recruiting service.

A previous order of April 14th directed commanding officers concerned to form, from the private men and Supplementary Militia recruits, two or more companies each of one captain, two lieutenants, one ensign four sergeants, two drummers, and eighty men. The officers remaining after the formation of these companies were to be detached into the counties allotted for recruiting the regiment, in order that they might raise as many more men as possible. In this work half-pay officers and officers on leave from regiments abroad were to assist, as well as in training the parts of the Supplementary Militia still to be called out previous to being formed into new battalions. Leave was given to raise as many recruits as could be obtained from the Supplementary Militia. The disappointment of the hopes then entertained, except as regards the 9th, is acknowledged in a letter from the Adjutant-General to Sir Charles Grey, dated June 8, 1798.

In 1799 another Act offered a bounty of ten guineas to men from the Supplementary Militia volunteering for the regular army, service to be in Europe only for five years, or for the period of the war and six months after. In July and August, 1799, nearly 3,000 men from the Militia units volunteered for service in the 9th. The regiment being then at the Tower of London, Lieutenant-Colonel de Bernière was informed on July 19th, that he would probably have to be moved to a more convenient place for receiving recruits, especially as 300 were expected by the river next day. Obviously, these large numbers could not be accommodated in a single battalion, so the 9th was now increased to a three-battalion regiment, in August, 1799.

The Colonel of the regiment, Lieutenant-General Bertie, commanded the 1st battalion; Major-General Robert Manners (from Major in the 3rd Foot Guards) became colonel-commandant of the 2nd battalion; and Colonel G. Fisher, then Lieutenant-colonel of the 1st battalion, was promoted to colonel-commandant of the 3rd battalion. The lieutenant-colonels were Henry de Bernière, Gideon Shairpe, John Sandieman, Robert Montgomery, John Crewe and Richard Bingham. Six majors were also appointed, and the total staff of officers was 157. The establishment of each battalion was fixed as follows: One colonel (or colonel-commandant in the 2nd and 3rd battalions) and captain; one lieutenant-colonel and captain; one major and captain; eight captains; one captain-lieutenant; twenty-three lieutenants; nine ensigns; one paymaster; one adjutant; one quartermaster; one surgeon; one assistant surgeon; one sergeant-major; one quartermaster-sergeant; one paymaster-sergeant; forty-four sergeants; forty-four corporals; twenty-two drummers; two fifers; 836 privates. Each battalion had eleven companies.

In 1799, also, the following order was issued by the Adjutant-General, dated July 30, 1799:—

"I have received His Royal Highness the Commander-in-Chief's directions to signify to you that His Majesty has been pleased to confirm to the 9th Regiment of Foot the distinction and privilege of wearing the figure of Britannia as a badge of the regiment."[1]

We have stated the movements of the 1st battalion from its return from the West Indies to its arrival at Barham Downs camp on the eve of proceeding on active service. The 2nd and 3rd battalions appear to have been assembled direct at Barham Downs.

When the 1st and 2nd embarked for North Holland, in the middle of September, 1799, the 3rd was moved to Ashford, and thence, in October, to Canterbury. In December it was at Bishop Stortford on its way to Norwich, where it remained till the return of the other two battalions from Holland united the whole regiment at its county town.

A treaty between England and Russia, dated June 22, 1799, provided for the joint invasion by the two Powers of the Batavian Republic,

---

[1] For a fuller account of this badge, see Appendix III.

COLOURS OF THE WEST NORFOLK MILITIA, *circ.* 1800-1855, and SHAKOS WORN BY EARLS OF ORFORD.
George, 1730-91; Horatio, 1782-1860; Frederick, 1822-76; and Robert Horace, b. 1854
(*Ch. IX*)

which had been set up under the French Republic. Russia was to furnish 17,000 men, to be paid by England, who would provide 30,000 more. With the discussions in the British Cabinet and the strategical considerations which led to the Helder being selected as the neighbour-

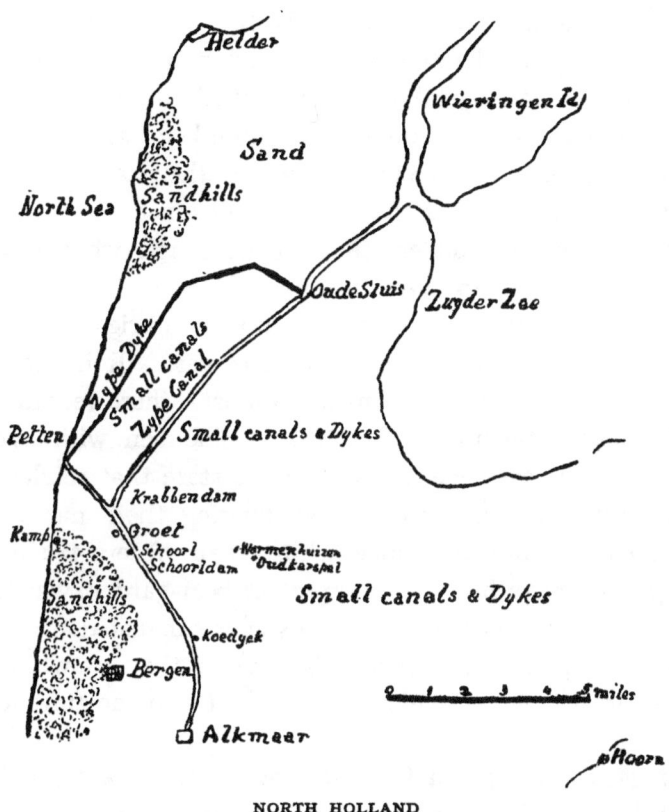

NORTH HOLLAND

hood for the landing we are not concerned.[1] Nor need we describe in detail the landing or the first operations, for it was not till a later date that the 9th appears on the scene. Sir Ralph Abercromby, with about 10,000 men, sailed for the Helder on August 13th, but a succession of storms delayed the landing till the 27th, when it was made on the west coast of North Holland, south of the Helder. It was rather feebly

[1] They are summarized in Mr. Fortescue's "History of the British Army," vol. IV, part II, pp. 642–650.

opposed by the Dutch General Daendals, whose strength was about equal to Abercromby's.

Orders for an attack on the Helder fortifications were issued, but the fortress was abandoned by the Dutch garrison of 2,000 men.

By August 30th the whole Dutch fleet had surrendered, at the Helder and in the Zuyder Zee, to the British under Admiral Mitchell.

The experiment of landing an advanced guard of only four brigades, and a reserve of two battalions, was certainly a dangerous one, seeing that the Dutch army alone equalled it in numbers, without counting the French, who would shortly be up. However, the troops were of the best, especially the Guards, and the British remained unmolested in the neighbourhood of the Helder till September 1st, when difficulties of supply compelled them to move forward.

They had just been reinforced by two more brigades counting just over 5,000 effectives, but very short of officers. Reinforcements had been collecting at Barham Downs all August, where recruits had been coming in, most of them from the Militia. The men, with an enlistment bounty of ten guineas each, arrived in the state that might have been expected—most of them drunk and flinging their money away on extravagant modes of conveyance, whilst their officers trudged on foot. The camp appears to have been a perfect bear-garden, which was only got into decent order as the men's funds were exhausted.[1]

The recruits had been good militiamen; they were now regulars sadly in want of training, which there was little or no time for them to get.

Amongst the troops on Barham Downs were the 1st and 2nd battalions of the 9th. There is no reason to suppose they were either better or worse conducted than other line regiments. The 3rd was also there, but was not to go; it was commanded by Colonel Fisher, the officer about whose absence from his regiment in the West Indies we saw Sir J. Vaughan writing in 1795. He was also a guardian of young Gomm under his father's will. He had, at Gomm's earnest request, allowed the boy (he was not yet fifteen) to join the regiment when it was detailed for the Helder Expedition. He joined the 1st battalion on August 13,

[1] See Fortescue, vol. IV, part II, p. 658.

1799, his first commission as ensign (aged under ten years), was dated 1794, and that of lieutenant (under eleven) 1795.[1] The regiment was in the 9th brigade, consisting of its 1st and 2nd battalions and the 56th, and commanded by Brigadier Manners of the 2/9th. It sailed on September 13th, and landed on the 16th at the Helder, each of the two battalions having about 800 rank and file. By this time some 7,000 Russians had arrived and been placed on the right of the position occupied by the British after beating off an attack by 1,400 Dutch under Daendels and 7,000 French under Brune on September 10th. Brune, left in peace after this defeat, had been busily entrenching his army. On the 18th it was posted thus: The extreme left was at Kamp, below the northern boundary of the sandhills which cover the west coast in varying breadth to that point, whence there is a gap in them as far north as Petten, where they again commence. These sandhills constitute a difficult country, rising very steeply from the sea, and attaining a height, in places, of 150 feet. From Kamp the inland border of them runs south-eastwards past Groet and Schoorl. The greatest breadth of the sandhills is just north of Bergen, where it is nearly three miles from their eastern boundary to the seashore. Besides occupying the strongest positions in the hills, Brune's French troops had strongly fortified posts at Kamp, Groet, and Schoorl. They also occupied Bergen, which was fortified. A fortified post at Schoorldam barred the road along the Zype Canal, and another held Warmenhuizen, nearly three miles north by east of it. Brune's right was across the main road leading south from the Helder to Alkmaar, at Oudkarspel. He had not protected his right flank, as he might have done, by inundating the country east of Oudkarspel. The whole country below the sandhills was a network of small canals, "many of which could not be passed without wading through, being too wide to leap, and at the same time very deep."[2]

[1] The letters of Field-Marshal Sir W. Gomm were published in 1881, and are a most fruitful source of information about the regiment in his early days. Fortunately for himself, but unfortunately for the historian of the regiment, he was at an early age taken permanently on to the staff and could no longer continue to write such full details of the 9th's doings. He always, however, retained his affection for it.

[2] Gomm's letters, p. 37.

This network was crossed by larger canals, of which the chief was that of the Zype, and by great dykes built to keep out the sea, and at the same time serving to carry roads.

The whole British and allied army, which was now about double the enemy's strength, was commanded by the Duke of York. His qualifications as a general in the field certainly did not warrant his selection, but it was necessary to have someone of royal rank whom the Russians would obey as a matter of course. Moreover, he had done excellent service at the War Office in reorganizing the army, which gave him a claim to active employment.

The attack which was now to be made, with the object of crushing Brune and forcing a way to Amsterdam, was designed as follows :

The Russians, under General Hermann, were to lead the right in an attack on the French left in the sandhills as far south as Bergen. To support them the 9th brigade and the 7th Light Dragoons were told off. In this country of defiles separated from one another by the difficult country of the canals, it was only possible to move by the roads in detached columns, and to attack frontally. The next column, to the left of the Russians, comprised the brigades of D'Oyley and Burrard, all Guards, the 8th (line) brigade, and two squadrons of the 11th Light Dragoons. These were to move on Schoorldam and Warmenhuizen, and, after taking these places, to assist the right column. Beyond them two more brigades had Oudkarspel for their objective, whilst still farther east Abercromby with three brigades, the reserve, and two battalions, comprising the light companies and grenadiers of the line regiments, was to make a very wide turning movement, by Hoorn, round the enemy's right, and then to march south on Purmerend.

The British right is, of course, the part of the battle which interests us chiefly, though the flank companies of the 9th were with Abercromby. The attack was fixed for daybreak, but part of the Russians took it into their heads to start at 2 a.m., in the pitch dark, along the coast. Instead of recalling them when he heard of the movement half an hour later, Hermann sent the rest of his men forward in support. For some time the superior numbers of the Russians carried them forward through the French advanced posts. But the Russian troops of that day were an undisciplined crowd with officers of the poorest quality. At Eylau, eight years later, the men were better, but the officers much the same.

There were wild scenes on the Russian front. In the darkness, which still prevailed, the columns lost their sense of direction and fired freely into one another, as did their artillery when it came up. Then the men got completely out of hand and dispersed in search of loot and drink. Nevertheless, they somehow or other managed to get possession of Groete and Schoorl, and even got for a short time into Bergen. Thence the French, now rallied, very soon drove them with heavy loss, after almost surrounding them. Hermann was taken prisoner, and Essen, his second in command, did his best to rally and reform the disordered troops. He also sent in haste for the 9th brigade to help in restoring the battle. It can hardly have been light even when the Russians were turned out of Bergen. Dundas, with the Guards column, meanwhile, had stormed Warmenhuizen and moved on Schoorldam about 6 a.m. There, however, he was held up by a broken bridge till 9 a.m. It was just after the capture of Schoorldam that the Duke of York received Essen's appeal for help. The advance of the 9th brigade was at once ordered.

The Russians were now in a hopeless state, looting the captured villages, and a large proportion of them scattered about drunk and laden with plunder.

For what happened with Manners's brigade we cannot do better than quote Gomm's diary, which, for a boy of sixteen, must be admitted to be a very remarkable production, bearing on its face the mark of truth, simple and unexaggerated. He writes:

"*September* 18*th*, 1799.—At ten o'clock at night the two battalions of the 9th marched, according to orders, towards the villages of Schorel [Schoorl] and Schoreldam [Schoorldam], where the French had intrenched themselves, and arrived at the post occupied by the Russians, close to the village above named, about two o'clock in the morning of the 19th, after a march of fourteen miles. Here we halted.

"*September* 19th.—At daybreak, about 3 a.m.,[1] the Russians began the attack upon the village of Schorel, and, after a pretty obstinate resistance, drove the enemy from thence. The two battalions of the 9th advanced gradually in the rear of the Russians, joined by the 56th Regiment, under the command of Major-General Manners, being the brigade destined to the reserve of the Russians that day. About 6 a.m., the 9th and 56th Regiments mounted the sandhills behind the village of Schorel, in order to drive from thence any enemy that might remain in that part. Having met with none, we descended from the hills, and everything seemed again perfectly quiet. We marched through the village of Schorel, and marched on to the plain, where the enemy opened a very heavy fire of musketry and grape upon us. The Russians were now gone off in different directions, and consequently the brigade, consisting of the two battalions of the 9th and the 56th Regiments, was at this time engaged alone—the two battalions of the 9th being each about 600 men,[2] and the 56th Regiment about the same number. For about two hours the heaviest fire of musketry possible was kept up on both sides, the British advancing by degrees, but not very regularly; the plain being intersected every twenty yards nearly with small canals, many of which could not be passed without wading through, being too wide to leap, and at the same time very deep. At length the British advanced with the bayonet. The enemy were unwilling to stand the charge, and retreated very precipitately through Schoreldam, which they were obliged to evacuate, the English still advancing, but in the greatest disorder; for being very much fatigued by the night's march, and still more so by the former part of the action, most of the troops were scarcely able to walk. We were therefore ordered not to advance any farther, but to form in the plain between Schorel and Schoreldam, where the action had commenced.

"We remained here about half an hour, when we received

[1] Of course it must, on September 19th, have been pitch dark at 3 a.m. The sun rises about 5.45.

[2] It will be remembered that the flank companies were with Abercromby.

intelligence that the enemy were at that time in the very same part of the sandhills behind Schorel where we had been searching for them before we entered into the action on the plain, so that they could never have been driven completely from the sandhills, but must have been in some part of them even at the time we were searching for them.[1] Upon this intelligence, we were obliged to march against them immediately, notwithstanding our fatigue, to prevent being cut off, for they were getting in our rear. We got up the hills as quickly as possible, and the enemy immediately opened a fire upon us from all sides. The enemy's riflemen had got into the woods about Schorel, and by that means fired upon our officers and men on the hills, without being themselves seen or exposed. The Russians were now returned to our assistance, but our numbers were even then far inferior to those of the enemy, who were now stronger than ever. Had our numbers been known, it is generally believed that we should have been made prisoners, but we were so dispersed about the hills that it was impossible for the enemy to judge of our strength. For about two hours and a half, an unceasing fire of musketry was kept up. The enemy had several pieces of cannon upon the hills, with which they played upon us during the whole time. By this time it was nearly one o'clock. Great numbers of our men began to want ammunition. We were ordered to descend from the hills and rally once more, determining to make another vigorous attempt to drive the enemy from the woods and hills. H.R.H. Prince William of Gloucester had now joined us with the 1st battalion of the 35th Regiment.[2] A battalion of the Guards also arrived[3] and advanced upon the sandhills. The 2nd battalion of the 9th, the 1st battalion of the 35th, and the 56th Regiments, after having formed a continued line, began a vigorous fire upon the enemy in the woods, and in a short time drove them along the hills and the woods. The Guards lost great numbers upon the hills.

---

[1] Concealment was quite simple, for small bodies, in the scrub and the hollows between the hills.

[2] Fetched from the Helder, where it had been left in garrison.

[3] From Dundas's column on the left at Schoorldam.

Small parties of the Russians were still with us upon the hills. The firing continued till four o'clock, great slaughter being made on both sides. The enemy had now been able to make a stand for the space of two hours. Nearly the whole of our ammunition was now exhausted, and, numbers of our troops being absolutely useless from the excessive fatigues of the day, at about 4.30 p.m. a general retreat was made. While we were retiring a body of the enemy's hussars came up with the rear of the 9th Regiment (for we happened to be hindmost of those who retreated on that side). They cut down and took prisoners a few stragglers, but advanced no farther, being unwilling to encounter our dragoons. The whole of the army took up their former position as soon as possible. Part of the 9th returned to their quarters at Grotskerk the same night. The remainder went only as far as Petten that night. Both our battalions lost nearly the same number in killed and prisoners, our whole loss consisting of about 370 men, or perhaps more."

Whilst the course of events on the British right had led to its retirement to the position held before the battle, Pulteney's attack on the redoubt at Oudkarspel had been held up for many hours. An attempt to turn the position had been foiled by the difficulty of the canals, and it was only when the Dutch attempted a counter-attack that the British were able to defeat them and take the redoubt with its sixteen guns. The Dutch retired in disorder towards Koedyck. Pulteney advanced a short way and then bivouacked till 11 p.m., when he was recalled to his position before the battle. He destroyed the captured guns at Oudkarspel.

As for Abercromby's detached left wing, with which were the flank companies of the 9th, it captured Hoorn at 2 a.m., with its Dutch garrison, who were mostly, sentries included, sleeping in fancied security. There Abercromby remained, totally inactive, till, at 4 p.m., he also received orders to return to his starting-point—a difficult matter, and the cause of loss owing to the heavy rain and consequent swampy condition of the road. The 55th were left at Hoorn.

The battle had produced absolutely no results save a heavy loss on

SIR ARMINE WODEHOUSE, BART.
Colonel of the East Norfolk Militia, 1758. (*Ch. IX*)

both sides. The total British killed was six officers and 127 men; wounded, forty-four officers and 397 men; missing, inclusive of the 1/35th, which appears to have been taken whole, 840. Of these, the two battalions of the 9th accounted for the following :—

1st Battalion : Lt. Woodford and Quartermaster Holles, killed; Lts. Grant, Rothwell, and Smith (prisoner), ten sergeants, one drummer, 203 rank and file killed, wounded or missing.

2nd Battalion : Capt. Balfour, one sergeant, and six men killed; Lt.-Colonel Crew, Ensigns French (prisoner) and Butler (missing), four sergeants, forty-six men wounded; one sergeant and ninety-seven men missing.

Lieutenant Gomm was very slightly wounded, only enough to give him a headache and not to necessitate his going off duty. He says he slept for thirty-six hours after the battle. He adds that " the 9th and 56th have received all the thanks from H.R.H. the Commander-in-Chief due to their distinguished activity and exertions that day."

On September 24th, 3,000 or 4,000 more Russians arrived. The French and Dutch had made no attempt to follow up what, on the whole, must be admitted to have been their successful action on the 19th. They had themselves probably suffered nearly as heavy losses as their opponents.

The British commander, in consultation with Abercromby and Dundas, had now decided on a fresh attack for September 29th. This time, the attack on the French left was to be made in overwhelming force. Brune, had been improving his defences, and the inundation of the country east of Oudkarspel and Alkmaar was to render his right almost unassailable. He had also received French reinforcements, bringing his strength up to about 25,000 men. On the 29th there was so severe a gale from the south-west that the attack had to be abandoned, as it was impossible to advance against the driving sand by the seashore. The attack was deferred till October 2nd. Against the northern and eastern sides of the sandhills were sent the right column of about 8,000 British infantry and 750 cavalry; the second, of 8,000 Russian infantry and 200 cossacks, under Essen, supported it, and its left flank was guarded by 4,500 British infantry and one hundred cavalry, part of whom would also keep it in connexion with Abercromby on the right, and part would turn the French defences in the sandhills. The column of the left consisted of three British brigades (of which Manners's 9th was one), two battalions of Russians, and a couple of squadrons, in all about 5,000 men. The function of this last force was to watch the whole tract as far as the Zuyder Zee, and, if opportunity offered, to attack the enemy's right. In the end no such opportunity did offer, and the two battalions of the 9th never came into action at all. Under the circumstances we need not describe the battle in detail. The fighting was very severe, and in some cases by no means too well managed on the British side, especially in the case of Macdonald's reserve. Nevertheless, the extreme right got forward as far as Egmont aan Zee, whilst Groet, Schoorl, and Schoorldam were taken, and the communication severed between the French left near the sea and their comrades in Bergen. The French on this side were commanded by Vandamme, whom Napoleon afterwards described as a "mighty man of war," afraid neither of God nor the devil. His defence was such as might have been expected. When the battle ended, the British line extended from Egmont to Oudkarspel. The losses had been heavy and the troops were at the end of their tether, but a distinct victory had been gained. Pulteney's left column, in which was Manners's brigade, had efficiently carried out its part, in keeping the enemy troops tied to the direction of Oudkarspel. It had had no fighting, though constantly expecting it.

The victory was somewhat Pyrrhic, for the losses had amounted to over 2,000 British and Russians. The two battalions of the 9th were destined to see no more fighting in this expedition, for the British advance was practically ended. On October 6th, there was a severe action on the right, developing out of Abercromby's endeavour to drive in the French advanced posts. It ended none too favourably for Abercromby, and the British and Russian forces were now again withdrawn to the Zype position, from which they had started on September 19th.

Negotiations were now opened by Brune, which ended in a Convention, of October 18th, under which hostilities ceased at once. The British and Russians were to evacuate Holland by November 30th, and to return 8,000 French and Dutch prisoners from England, irrespective of exchanges of those taken in the late campaign. The British army was almost at the end of its supplies, and, had it been six years earlier, Brune would probably have gone to the guillotine for allowing such easy terms.

On their return from Holland the 9th, all three battalions, were quartered at Norwich, and in the summer of 1800 on Bagshot Heath. Thence, being again ordered on foreign service, they marched to Southampton. This time they formed a brigade to themselves, again under the command of Major-General Manners. The new expedition's first objective was the capture of Ferrol, on the north-western coast of Spain, and the infliction of other damage upon that country, especially by the destruction of naval arsenals at Vigo and Cadiz.

On August 1, 1800, Lieutenant Gomm's diary records that he embarked at Southampton, on board the " Brailsford," with part of the 9th. The rest of the three battalions embarked at the same time on other transports. Besides this brigade were those under Major-General Coote and Major-General Lord Cavan, as well as the Royals, and the 27th, under Major-General Morshead. All told, the expedition, including artillery, was to consist of about 13,000 men, assembling in the first instance at Quiberon Bay, where the supposition among the junior officers was that it was intended to land. The expedition was under the command of Lieutenant-General Sir James Pulteney.

The fleet arrived off Belleisle on August 16th, sailed again on the 22nd, and was off Ferrol on the 25th. In this neighbourhood the troops were landed, without opposition beyond the fire of a small Spanish fort, which was soon silenced. They then advanced on Ferrol, about six miles up the bay. There were slight skirmishes that night and next morning. The 9th took no part in them, beyond following closely in reserve to the 52nd and 79th. The troops were now in sight of Ferrol but it was impossible for them to attack the town, or for the fleet to enter the harbour, without first capturing Fort Philip, which commanded the former and the entrance to the latter. It was however held to be impossible to get the requisite artillery into position in that hilly country, and the attempt on Ferrol was abandoned, the troops again embarking on the 26th. The responsible task of covering the embarkation was entrusted to the 1st battalion of the 9th, who, however, were not attacked in their position on the hills.

Gomm, in a letter, expresses a good deal of contempt for the Spanish defenders of Ferrol, and remarks that " the French would have made it much warmer work for us."

Sailing again on the 27th, the expeditionary fleet reached Vigo Bay with what Gomm calls appropriately " Sir James Pulteney's Floating Army." In Vigo Bay they remained till on September 6th a heavy gale drove some ships ashore and nearly wrecked the whole. From Vigo they sailed to Tetuan Bay, where they were joined by a part of Sir Ralph Abercromby's army from Minorca, and by more of them as they sailed through the Straits of Gibraltar, *en route* for Cadiz. Abercromby had arrived at Gibraltar on September 11th with about 10,000 men, and, on October 4th the whole force of over 20,000 men was off Cadiz. It appeared that the Spaniards were as ready to meet an attack, which they had long expected, as they were ever likely to be, and moreover, they had plague in the town. Nevertheless, on the 7th, 3,000 men were actually in the flat boats ready to land on the north shore of Cadiz Bay when Abercromby, being informed that supports could not be landed for several hours, cancelled the orders, and sailed again for Tetuan, which was reached on the 12th. On the 31st they crossed over to Gibraltar. Crossing once more to Tetuan, they sailed again on November 5th for Lisbon, off which they were on the 12th, but, owing to a gale, could only anchor in the harbour on the 14th. Gomm states that there was much sickness on the fleet at this time, some regiments accounting for 200 or 300 sick. The 9th were fortunate, and Gomm is able to say, " I don't believe we have twelve men sick in the whole three battalions. In our ship we have not one." Before this Manners had given over command of the brigade to Colonel Fisher of the 3rd battalion. The troops were landed when accommodation for them was available.

On November 20th the 9th was once more on board ship, but only sailed on the 29th for home. On the way they encountered very bad weather; the " Brailsford " sprang a leak and was in great danger. At last, Portsmouth was reached on December 21, 1800, and the regiment disembarked. As soon as the ships had been fumigated the three battalions were again sent off to Jersey, where the 1st battalion was quartered in Granville Barracks, and the 2nd and 3rd in St. Heliers. The long confinement on board ship had now begun to tell upon the men's health, and Gomm records that the 1st battalion had scarcely 200 effective men left out of an initial strength of 700. The 2nd and 3rd battalions were very sickly, though not quite so bad as the 1st—this at a time when a French attack was thought probable.

In March, 1801, Gomm was sent with a recruiting party to Liverpool where, on April 1st, he remarks, " I was unsuccessful, in common with nearly the whole army, in raising men." He was at this time acting as A.D.C. to General Benson, commanding the north-western district. In June, 1801, the three battalions embarked for Portsmouth. On landing there the 1st battalion marched to Fairlight Camp, near Hastings; the 2nd and 3rd were quartered respectively in Silver Hill and Riding Street Barracks, Hastings. Thence the 3rd battalion moved to Shorncliffe. The 1st and 2nd, on the breaking up of the camp at Fairlight Hill, went first to Bexhill and afterwards to Battle Barracks.

In 1802, on the signing of the Peace of Amiens, the usual reductions in the army commenced, without considering the probability of a renewal of the war with France. The 3rd battalion of the 9th was the first to be disbanded, in May, 1802. The men enlisted from the Militia for limited service, that is, service not out of Europe, were allowed to volunteer for unlimited service in the 1st battalion.[1] Those limited service men who did not so volunteer, including those of the 1st as well as the 3rd battalion, were drafted into the 2nd, which was itself disbanded in December, 1802. The 2nd battalion was destined to be twice reconstituted; but the 3rd disappears for good, since the present 3rd battalion cannot be held to be a reincarnation of that of 1799–1802. For the present the regiment consisted only of the 1st battalion, which in September, 1802, was at Chatham Barracks. In November it was partly (658 rank and file) at Plymouth and partly (288 rank and file) at Chatham. In December there were five companies at each of those stations, and by

[1] The regiment would have gone to Egypt with Sir R. Abercromby in the end of 1800 but for the fact that it contained a very large number of limited service men, whose terms of enlistment forbade their being sent out of Europe.

January 1, 1803, the whole battalion, over 1,000 strong, was at Plymouth, where they still had thirteen officers, thirteen sergeants, and eight or nine drummers out recruiting on the 1st June.

On September 25, 1803, the battalion embarked for Ireland.

Landing at Kinsale, it marched via Cork to Kilkenny, where it was reviewed by Lord Cathcart, the commander-in-chief.

The only other incident recorded in Gomm's diary at Kilkenny is that two sentries were fired on, and one wounded, by some ruffian who, of course, was not discovered. During this service in Ireland the light company was attached to the 2nd light battalion of the line at Limerick.

In January, 1804, the battalion marched to Kilbeggan, Moate, and Clara in Co. Westmeath. Gomm remarks: "The country is quiet now; invasion by the French, or rather an attempt at invasion, expected daily."

In March the battalion was transferred to Dublin, where it was kept busy with an inspection by the commander-in-chief every three weeks or so, not to speak of route marches of ten miles out and home. On June 15, 1804, General Bertie was appointed to the colonelcy of the 77th, and was succeeded as colonel of the 9th by Lieutenant-General Peter Hunter from the 15th Foot. Here we lose, temporarily, the advantage of Gomm's diary. He was now a captain, and applied to be allowed to join the Military College at High Wycombe, where he was, on his twenty-first birthday, November 10, 1805. In May, 1805, about eighty volunteers from the Militia in Ireland joined the battalion. In August, 1805, the 1st battalion marched to the Curragh, whence, in September, it proceeded to Clonmel. On October 3rd a new colonel was appointed in Major-General Robert Brownrigg, who succeeded Lieutenant-General Hunter, deceased. Brownrigg was then Adjutant-General.

In the beginning of November the battalion, again ordered on foreign service, and now rejoined by the light company, embarked at Cork, on November 10th, on a very unfortunate voyage. The headquarters of the battalion, with Lieutenant-Colonel de Bernière, the staff, and part of the men, were on board the transport "Ariadne." Bad weather was encountered in the Straits of Dover, and whilst the other two transports, carrying the rest of the regiment, succeeded in getting shelter in the Downs, the "Ariadne" was driven on the French coast near Calais. The colonel, staff, and 262 men were saved as prisoners of war, and sent to Valenciennes; but the records, plate, etc.,[1] of the regiment were lost with the vessel. Captain Gomm had got leave to rejoin the 1st battalion, and was lucky enough to get on board the "Isis," one of the two transports which had been driven into the Downs. On December 22nd the "Isis" sailed with a fair wind, and anchored in the mouth of the River Weser, two miles below Lehe, on Christmas Day, with the other transport, the "Harriet."

After some adventures, due to dragging anchors in a snow blizzard, the battalion, less the portion lost on the "Ariadne," was landed at Lehe by January 7, 1806. The regiment had left Ireland about 1,000 strong; now there were only about 600, owing chiefly to the loss of the "Ariadne." Gomm's own company had been on the "Ariadne." The European situation was now extremely bad for England, though Trafalgar had fixed her supremacy at sea. Napoleon's victory at Austerlitz had caused Pitt to say that it was time to roll up the map of Europe, and there remained but another eighteen months before the Emperor reached the pinnacle of his ascendancy at Tilsit, after the great victories of Jena and Friedland, the latter of which almost obliterated the remembrance of the partial check at Eylau.

The expedition to the Weser and Elbe consisted of about 14,500 British and 12,000 Germans under Lord Cathcart, who was to advance into and recover Hanover. The expedition had been arranged before the news of Ulm. Part of the troops had landed in the Elbe at Cuxhaven, and the last of the reinforcements, including the 1/9th, were sent to the Weser.

It might have been expected that the colours of the 9th would have been lost in the "Ariadne." How they were saved is explained in the following extract from Gomm's letter to his sister of January 7, 1806:—

"We have saved the colours by a singular good fortune. It is always customary to lodge them on board the head-quarter ship,

[1] The only piece of plate saved was a snuffbox which an officer put in his pocket and which is still in possession of the 1st battalion.

and the 'Harriet' happening to be so at Falmouth, on account of Colonel de Bernière having left the regiment for a few days, they were brought from the 'Ariadne,' and have remained on board our vessel ever since."

The landing of the 9th had been effected some four miles from Lehe, and the march to that place, over roads rendered almost impassable by the thawing of the snow, had been most trying. What was experienced there showed what the rest of the country was likely to be for movements. Presently came the news of Austerlitz, and of Prussia's treacherous acceptance of Napoleon's offer of the occupation of Hanover. There was nothing for it but to withdraw the expeditionary force, and to leave Prussia to reap the fruits of her treachery, which she did at Jena in October, 1806.

On February 8, 1806, the 1/9th arrived off Yarmouth, as the wind had interfered with their intended landing in the Downs. They were kept on board for some time, waiting for orders from London before they landed. Captain Gomm soon after returned to his Staff College studies at High Wycombe; thence he proceeded, on the staff, to the Copenhagen expedition of 1807, in which the 9th took no part.

Major Molle, the senior officer, now reorganized what remained of the battalion after its losses by the wreck of the "Ariadne." Command of it was taken by Colonel John Stuart from the 52nd Regiment on December 26, 1806, Colonel de Bernière being a prisoner in France.

CHAPTER X

THE 1st AND 2nd BATTALIONS IN ENGLAND AND PORTUGAL —ROLIÇA, AND VIMEIRO. 1804–1808

FROM Yarmouth the 1st battalion went to Shorncliffe, where we will leave them for the moment whilst we briefly sketch the movements of

THE 2ND BATTALION FROM 1804 TO 1808

This battalion, as already noted, had been disbanded on the conclusion of the Peace of Amiens in 1802, soon after the disbandment of the 3rd battalion.

In October, 1804, after the resumption of war with France in 1803, orders were issued for the reconstitution of a second battalion. Major Crawford of the 1st battalion, with staff and non-commissioned officers selected from that battalion, was sent over from Ireland to Sherborne in Dorsetshire to raise the new 2nd battalion,[1] the establishment of which was fixed as follows: Ten companies; one lieutenant-colonel, two majors, ten captains, twelve lieutenants, eight ensigns, one adjutant, one quartermaster, one surgeon, two assistant-surgeons, one sergeant-major, one armourer-sergeant, forty sergeants, forty corporals, twenty drummers, two fifers, 760 privates. On October 28th the battalion was organized, and the badge of Britannia assumed. Recruiting was carried out in Dorsetshire, and a number of men were raised under the Additional

[1] The warrant for raising the battalion, dated October 1, 1804, was addressed to General Hunter as Colonel of the 9th. He being in command in Canada, it was passed to Colonel de Bernière of the 1st battalion, who deputed Major Crawford with sixteen sergeants, sixteen corporals, and eight drummers, to raise the new battalion. Also Quartermaster George Fraser as paymaster, Lieutenant H. Godwin as adjutant, and Quartermaster-Sergeant Durt as quartermaster.

Force Act. In July, 1805, sixty rank and file with non-commissioned officers were sent to the 1st battalion in Dublin. In May recruiting, except for unlimited service, had been stopped on the repeal of the Additional Force Act.

In June, 1806, the new 2nd battalion was still weak when it was marched from Sherborne to Tamworth, where it received its colours from the colonel of the regiment, Major-General Brownrigg. On October 31st, the battalion arrived at Ashby-de-la-Zouch from Tamworth.

On December 7, 1806, the 2nd battalion moved to Burton-on-Trent, after sending recruiting parties into Lancashire and the north of Ireland, as well as Norfolk. At Burton it remained till June, 1807, when it marched to Chelmsford, arriving there on July 3rd. At Chelmsford it received 494 volunteers from the Militia of Leicester (134), West Kent (148), 2nd Somerset (134), West Norfolk (58), East Norfolk (20). Hitherto, the battalion had been at a very low effective strength. It had only fifty-nine rank and file with the colours in 1805 and 248 on May 1st, 1807.

It was now recruiting up to full strength. By December 1, 1807, there were 780 rank and file present. On September 21st it marched to Shorncliffe, and on the 25th, the day of its arrival there, orders were issued raising the establishment of ten companies to the following strength: One lieutenant-colonel, two majors, ten captains, twenty-two lieutenants, eight ensigns, one paymaster, one adjutant, one quartermaster, one surgeon, two assistant-surgeons, one sergeant-major, one quartermaster-sergeant, one armourer-sergeant, fifty sergeants, fifty corporals, twenty drummers, two fifers, 950 privates.

On October 1st command of the battalion was assumed by Lieutenant-Colonel Cameron, an officer destined to render most distinguished service with this, and later with the 1st battalion. He at once published a code of orders and regulations as standing orders of the battalion.

Of all the colonels of the regiment (Sir J. Cameron was appointed to the office in 1833), none is so much identified with the regiment as he. He commanded the 2nd battalion, as lieutenant-colonel, from 1807 till 1808, when he took command of the 1st till 1821. Throughout the greater part of the Peninsular War he not only commanded, but personally led, the regiment; for he was a most gallant soldier, so much so that, according to Colin Campbell, he was known by the men as "The Devil," and they were always ready to follow him anywhere. He was a strict disciplinarian. When Colin Campbell irregularly slipped out of hospital to command his company at the passage of the Bidassoa in 1813 he was duly had up and lectured by Cameron, who told him it was only his conduct when he was wounded at San Sebastian which saved him. Cameron, strict though he was, was certainly glad of the excuse to pass over an irregularity which must have appealed to his own gallant spirit. The state of efficiency to which he raised the regiment was made apparent at San Sebastian, the Nive, and elsewhere. A sketch of his life and services is given in Appendix I.

On May 24, 1808, the 2nd battalion marched to Canterbury, whence on June 9th, it sent a draft of 100 rank and file, with non-commissioned officers, to the 1st battalion in Ireland.

On July 17th the battalion marched to Ramsgate, where it embarked for Portugal, and landed on August 19th, in rear of and covered by the British position on the heights of Vimeiro. It was just in time to take part in the battle of the 21st, which will be described presently. A detachment of three officers and sixty-three other ranks was left, as a sort of depot company, at Canterbury.

The 1st Battalion 1806 to 1808

We left the 1st battalion at Shorncliffe in the beginning of 1806.[1]

[1] From 1807 to 1814 we have the benefit of the "Journal" of James Hale, a private, and afterwards sergeant, in the 1st battalion. This little book, published at Cirencester in 1826, is very difficult to obtain. It is not to be found in the London Library, the R.U.S.I., or even in the British Museum. The author is indebted for the loan of a copy to Sir C. Oman, the historian of the Peninsular War.

Hale enlisted in the 3rd Royal North Gloucestershire Regiment of Militia in 1803. In August, 1807, he, with 170 others from the same regiment, volunteered, on a bounty of ten guineas, for seven years' service in the 9th, with a liability to extension for a further period not exceeding three years if required. Being physically qualified for that service, he was put in the light company, with which he served throughout, whilst his brother, a bigger man who joined the regiment later, was in the grenadier company. Hale's "Journal," he says, was written up at

In December of that year it embarked at Dover for Ireland " the house of bondage " as Gomm calls that " distressful " country. It landed in Cork in January, 1808, and marched to Fermoy, where it received 359 recruits from the North Gloucester, Devon, Lancashire, and Berkshire Militia. Here also a new grenadier company was organized to replace the one lost in the " Ariadne." When Captain Gomm again rejoined in April, 1808, the battalion was at Mallow, after having been at Cashel with detachments in the neighbourhood. There he heard of Sir John Moore's expedition to Sweden with a force which was afterwards used in the Peninsula. Fortunately for us, he failed in his endeavour to get a job on it. By June 1st the regiment had been warned of its approaching departure for Portugal.

The battalion marched to Cork on July 29, 1808, under the command of Lieutenant-Colonel John Stuart, with a rank and file strength of 833.[2] They did not, however, sail till July 12th. They formed part of Sir Arthur Wellesley's corps from Ireland. The whole of this corps numbered 8,123 infantry, 394 cavalry (only 180 of whom had horses), and 226 artillerymen. Arriving off the coast of Portugal on July 26th, the corps began its disembarkation in Mondego Bay on August 1st, though there was a heavy surf at the time. The last of the troops had just landed on the 5th, when General Spencer, with a second force from the south of Spain, appeared in the offing. He brought 4,503 infantry and 245 artillerymen, so that Wellesley's total British force, for the few remaining days before he would be superseded by Burrard and Dalrymple, amounted to 12,626 infantry, 394 cavalry, and 471 artillerymen, just over 13,500 combatants, after adding the staff. Horses locally obtained enabled

the time, till he was wounded at the storming of San Sebastian. After that he continues it on the strength of what he heard from his brother until the latter also was wounded at the battle of the Nive. In August, 1814, James Hale was admitted an out-pensioner of Chelsea Hospital on 9d. per day, and his brother on 1s. a day. In the preface to his "Journal" (which is only 130 small pages) Hale says it is exactly as he recorded it on the spot, save for corrections in spelling, etc.

[2] This is from the regimental record. On the other hand the private diary of an officer of the 5th Foot shows the strength of the 9th on August 17, 1808, as 1,026 men, thirty-nine women and five children. Rations 1,048¼. The fighting strength, on the then sanctioned establishment, if officers and N.C.O's were at full strength, would with 823 rank and file (i.e. all below sergeants) be about 930 all ranks.

him to mount another sixty of his handful of cavalry and to horse some of his guns. But he could only equip his own three batteries, and was compelled to leave behind the two brought by Spencer, as well as nearly 150 dismounted dragoons.

The strategical reasons which led to the disembarkation being made in Mondego Bay do not concern us. It was effected, with some difficulty from the surf, by the troops from Ireland between August 1st and 5th, and by General Spencer's troops on the 7th and 8th. By the evening of the 8th the little army was ready to take the field, for in the intervening days Sir A. Wellesley had been busy arranging his commissariat and transport. He had already been promised by the Junta the services of Bernardino Freire's 5,000 Portuguese troops for the contemplated advance on Lisbon. Junot, the French general commanding in Portugal, had about 26,000 men at his disposal, though Wellington's information indicated only 18,000. But his forces were scattered, and Junot himself was not the man to deal with a really difficult situation. He was in constant dread of an insurrection in Lisbon, which deterred him from uniting all his forces to march against Wellesley, of whose landing he was aware. He had Loison with 7,000 or 8,000 men in the neighbourhood of Estremoz, near Elvas on the Portuguese eastern frontier, 2,500 more in garrison at Elvas and Almeida, 1,000 each in Santarem and Peniche, a few hundreds at Abrantes, and a brigade under General Thomières at Alcobaça. The rest of the army was at Lisbon and the neighbourhood, on both sides of the Tagus.

On August 3rd Junot had sent orders to Loison to march by Portalegre and Abrantes to join Delaborde, who, with 3,000 infantry and 500 or 600 cavalry, had left Lisbon on the 6th in the direction of Leiria. Junot himself remained in Lisbon to overawe the inhabitants with the rest of his troops there.

Wellesley's force was divided into six brigades—three of them with three, and three with only two, battalions each. The 1/9th was allotted to General Hill's 1st brigade, the other two battalions being the 5th and 38th.

The general had decided to march on Lisbon by the road near the coast, in touch with the fleet, rather than by the inland road to Santarem and thence down the right bank of the Tagus. The first day's march through heavy sand,[1] though only twelve miles in length, was very trying to men out of condition through a long sojourn on board ship. Freire's Portuguese were left behind at Leiria, for their general was clearly not going to be a useful assistant to Wellesley, and his troops were but untrained levies, likely to hamper rather than aid the British. A few cavalry, of which he was so short, and light troops were all that

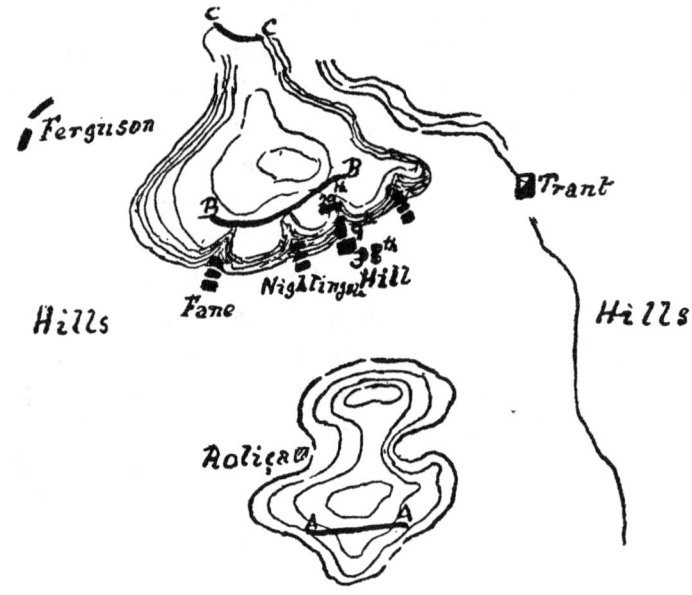

ACTION OF ROLIÇA
A First position of French.   B Second position attacked by British.   C Rally of French

the English commander insisted on taking out of the 5,000 Portuguese—in all about 2,000 men, under Colonel Trant, a British officer in the Portuguese service.

From Leiria the British commander reached Alcobaça on August 14th, where he found Thomières's brigade had been till the day before, and also that Delaborde with a small force was somewhere about Obidos and Roliça, across the road he was following. Delaborde's force was

[1] "A great part of the road was very sandy, sometimes sinking nearly ankle deep in sand."—Hale.

only about 5,000 men—five battalions of infantry, a regiment of chasseurs à cheval, and five guns. He had fallen back on Roliça, leaving a rearguard at Obidos, and sending six companies of Swiss to garrison Peniche on the coast. That left him with only 4,350 men.

Wellesley reached Caldas on August 15th. Four companies of his advanced guard, driving in the French outposts, rashly pursued them till they came upon Delaborde's rearguard at Obidos, by whom they were attacked. They were only rescued by the arrival of Spencer's brigade.

On the 15th Delaborde was in a position at Roliça which he deemed good for a defensive action. The road from Obidos to Lisbon, after passing the former, runs through a sandy, open plain with steep hills on either side. The eastern and western hills are connected beyond the village of Roliça by hills running from east to west, thus forming a sort of cul-de-sac, from which the road only escaped by partly mounting the transverse ridge and passing through a gorge. In front, to the north of the transverse ridge, is the village of Roliça,[1] situated on the slope of an isolated hill about a mile in front of the mouth of the gorge through which the road passes the transverse ridge.

Delaborde had posted his force on the hill of Roliça. He did so with the deliberate intention of falling back, after forcing the enemy to deploy, and making his real defence on the slopes of the ridge behind him. His position at Roliça was obviously open to envelopment, and Wellesley advanced against it with both wings well in front of his centre; for he had at least three times the French force, and could afford the

[1] The name of this village is correctly entered in the Army List, among the battle honours of the 9th, but has always appeared on the colours as Roleia. The origin of this inaccuracy is thus described in the "History of the British Army," vol. VI, p. 207 *n* : "This is the true name of this unfortunate village which has suffered much at the pens of the ignorant. In the collected edition of Wellington's despatches it is correctly spelt. Napier gives it as Roriça, which is intelligible, for the liquids ' l ' and ' r ' are known to be subject to phonetic interchange ; and War Office clerks at once reproduced it in the ' Gazette ' as Borica. In the next despatch, however, of August 17th, Wellesley used the form Roliça, whereupon the same clerks converted it in the ' Gazette ' into Roleia ; and as Roleia the action has remained commemorated on the regimental colours ever since. It is high time such an absurdity were corrected."

luxury of a double enveloping movement. Trant, with three battalions of Portuguese and fifty horse, was on the extreme right, moving along the western side of the valley round Delaborde's left, whilst the brigades of Ferguson and Bowes, commanded by the former, went on to the eastern hills to envelope the French right. The rest of the army moved forward in two lines against Roliça. Hill's brigade, with the 5th, 1/9th and 38th, formed the right of the first line, whilst its left touched the right of Nightingale's brigade, of which the 29th was the right hand regiment.

Delaborde was well prepared for this movement. Waiting till the last minute, when the jaws of the pincers were almost closing on his flanks, he slipped rapidly away to his intended position on the transverse ridge behind. He had succeeded in compelling his enemy to rearrange his troops for a fresh attack and wasting several hours of his time.

The new attack was precisely similar to the first, though the country was different. Trant again went round to the right and Ferguson to the left, whilst from Roliça hill two of Wellesley's batteries opened fire on the French position. Of the three brigades forming the first line of the centre, Hill's and Nightingale's formed on the right, Fane's on the left, of the road. The British commander would have waited for his frontal attack on the French position till the two turning movements had begun to take effect, but his scheme was thwarted by part of his centre pushing forward prematurely. Once it was in action there was nothing for it but to send up the rest.

Wellesley's despatch is a little confusing at first in its description as "passes" of what were really four ravines cutting into the face of the hill on which the French were drawn up above the woods which partly covered the lower slopes. Each of these ravines was used by part of the British centre as an approach to the French position. That on the extreme right served for the light companies of Hill's brigade, supported by the 5th of the same brigade. Into the next, towards the left, went the 29th of Nightingale's brigade, with the 9th of Hill's in support. Similarly the other two ravines were used by the regiments to the left.

The ravine into which the 9th found themselves following the 29th was in places so narrow that there was only room for three men abreast.

THE STUART MONUMENT.
In Canterbury Cathedral. (*Ch. X*)

Of this part of the action Sergeant Hale says : "We found great difficulty in some places in ascending, being obliged to pull ourselves up by some bushes or tufts of grass; at the same time they [the French] continued pouring musket shot on us very sharply." Lieutenant-Colonel Lake of the 29th, a very ardent officer, was the first to start the attack on the French. Leading his regiment, right in front, he reached the head of the ravine, where he encountered four companies of Swiss, most of whom deserted the French. The right wing of the 29th having issued from the ravine began to re-form on the slope above its head. Before they could complete this, they were suddenly charged by French troops in the rear. These were men who, as Lake passed up the ravine out of sight, had been left on the slopes behind him; in fact, he and his right wing had partly penetrated the French.

These French, in danger of being completely severed from their comrades above, now came together and charged Lake, who was himself killed, whilst six of his officers and about thirty men were captured by the exultant French. The rest of the right wing rushed back down the slope into a wood, where it re-formed on the uninjured left wing and all advanced up the hill with the 9th following in support. Hale's account of this is as follows :—

"The 29th regiment being about a quarter of a mile on our left, and having some little better road than our regiment, they ascended the heights a few minutes before us; upon which the enemy immediately attacked them with a much superior force, and caused them to fall back with the loss of their colours and about three hundred men; but as soon as we made our appearance on the top of the heights, it was a great relief to them; and the first thing our colonel thought most proper to do was to show them the point of the bayonet, which we immediately did; and much to their shame and disgrace we drove them off the heights in a few minutes; at the same time the remains of the 29th regiment gave them another grand charge, by which they re-took their colours and some prisoners. But, unfortunately, in this attack, Lieutenant-Colonel Stuart, who commanded the 9th Regiment, was killed, and also the colonel of the 29th Regiment. The enemy fell back a little distance, and then turned and attacked us again; but was received most gallantly and soon repulsed. They afterwards made several attacks upon our regiment and the 29th, before any other regiment came up to our assistance, but without effect, as they found true Englishmen every time; and it is certain that the 9th and 29th regiments were exposed to nearly all the French army for some time; but when some other regiments came up we obliged them to retreat."

Delaborde had only four battalions on the hill now, for, aware of Ferguson's turning movement, he had sent away four companies to check it. With these four battalions he made a most gallant resistance, charging each detachment of the British as it got out of its ravine and was beginning to get a hold on the slope. Thrice he repulsed British assaults, and it was only after two hours of desperate fighting that the assailants got a good footing on the crest at several points. Ferguson was now beginning to threaten Delaborde's right rear. He should have done so earlier, but had lost his way.

Delaborde, seeing he could hold no longer, began his retreat by alternate pairs of battalions. Two held up the pursuing British, who had got somewhat disordered, whilst the other two doubled to the rear and prepared to receive their comrades. His single regiment of cavalry, which the Portuguese cavalry dared not face, also assisted by charging the pursuers. In this way he had retired about a mile when his men, clubbed in a narrow pass, lost three guns and some prisoners. Here the retreat became somewhat disorderly as far as Cazal da Sprega, where Wellesley called off the pursuit.

Delaborde's loss was 600 men and three guns. That of the British was not much less, being 479 killed, wounded, and prisoners: 190 of these were in the 29th, whilst the 9th lost Lieutenant-Colonel John Stuart and four men killed; Major George Molle, Captain S. Sankey, Ensign S. Nicholls, and forty-nine rank and file wounded; twelve men missing.

Of the fighting on this day on the front of the 9th and 29th,[1] Sir

---

[1] Though the 9th and 29th had served together before, notably in Grenada, Roliça is perhaps the beginning of the intimacy between the two which is noted in Appendix IX.

Arthur Wellesley's despatch of August 17, 1808, says: " These passes were all difficult of access, and some of them were well defended by the enemy, particularly that which was attacked by the 29th and 9th Regiments. These regiments attacked with the utmost impetuosity, and reached the enemy before those whose attacks were to be made on their flanks "—high praise from a commander who never allowed himself to be swayed by sentiment. Gomm wrote: " The 9th have behaved in the most gallant manner. I fear we have lost our invaluable colonel."

On the 18th Wellesley received a welcome reinforcement by the arrival off Peniche[1] of General Acland's brigade from Harwich. It would add about 1,500 men to his force. General Anstruther's brigade, which was close behind, would add another 2,700; in all 4,200. Of Acland's brigade, 1,332 landed on the 19th a little north of Porto Novo at the mouth of the Maceira, twelve miles south of Roliça; the rest did not land till late on the 21st. They were only two and a half companies of the 20th, so Acland's brigade at Vimeiro numbered 1,332. Anstruther's brigade (2/9th, 43rd, 52nd, and 97th) landed at Porto Novo on the 20th. To cover this operation Wellesley took up his position on the heights of Vimeiro.

It was only on August 15th that Junot at last made up his mind to leave Lisbon in charge of a garrison of 6,500 men and the Russian squadron in the river, and to join with Loison in a decisive battle with the British. The two forces joined at Cercal on the evening of the 17th. Whilst Wellesley was covering the disembarkation of Acland's brigade, Junot and Loison reached Torres Vedras on the 18th, where they heard of Delaborde's defeat at Roliça, and were joined by him on the 19th. On the 20th Junot, who had hitherto been in doubt whether Wellesley would hold to the coast road or would march on Lisbon by Torres Vedras, Montechique, and the inland road, decided to attack the British in their position above Vimeiro.[2] He was ignorant of the arrival of Anstruther's

[1] No landing there was possible as the fort was still held by a strong French garrison.

[2] This, according to Mr. Fortescue, is the correct spelling. The name appears on the regimental colours as Vimiera, a corruption which is less flagrant than that of Roleia for Roliça. Modern maps show it as Vimeiro.

brigade to reinforce Wellesley, and of course that Acland's also was nearing the same point by sea.

Sir C. Oman has worked out the strength of Junot's army present at the battle of Vimeiro at 8,305 infantry (including the reserve of grenadiers), 1,951 cavalry, 700 artillerymen, engineers, etc., and twenty-three guns. The total is 13,056, against Wellesley's estimate of 14,000.[1]

The British army covering the disembarkations stood on the heights

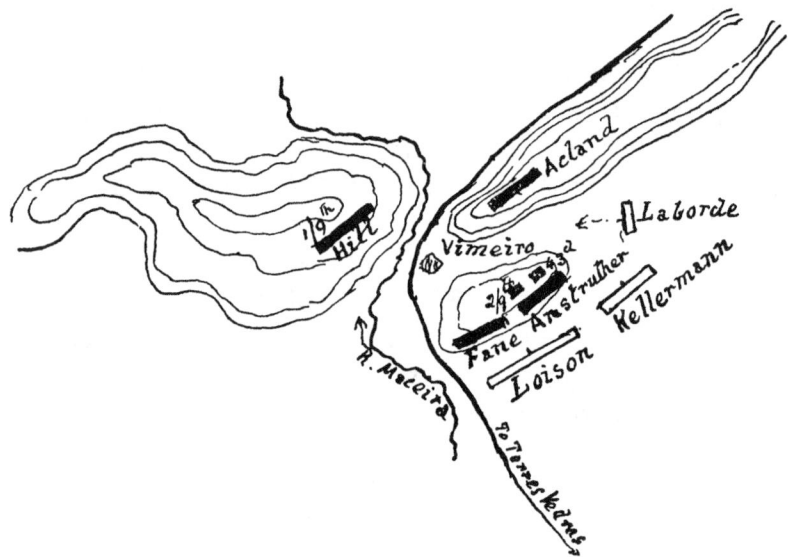

BATTLE OF VIMEIRO. BRITISH CENTRE AND RIGHT

of Vimeiro, in a strong position with its back to the sea, about three miles off. It numbered nearly 19,000, including Trant's 2,000 Portuguese.

The heights of Vimeiro run north-east and south-west, a distinct ridge about three miles in length, cut through towards its southern end by the valley of the Maceira. The south-west end reached back nearly to the seashore on the left bank of the Maceira. The steepest part facing the enemy was the southern, though the northern part was strong. Its least strong part was the extreme north, where it sinks to the plain towards Lourinha.

In front of the gap east of and above the village of Vimeiro was an

[1] "History of the Peninsular War," vol. I., p. 246.

isolated hill bearing somewhat the same relation to the British main line as the hill of Roliça did to the position which Delaborde took up after leaving Roliça on August 17th. For the battle of August 21st, Wellesley posted on this hill Fane's brigade and Anstruther's, which latter had landed on the previous day, and included the 2nd battalion of the 9th, 633 strong. On the extreme right, on the highest part of the ridge south of the Maceira, was Hill's brigade, including the 1/9th. On Hill's left, along the heights south-west of the Maceira gorge, were the brigades of Catlin Crauford and Nightingale in front down the slope, and those of Acland, Bowes, and Ferguson behind on the crest. Trant's Portuguese were in support of Ferguson, and the 500 British and Portuguese cavalry were also behind him in the low ground of the Maceira valley. Of Wellesley's eighteen guns, six were with Anstruther in the advanced position, eight on Hill's left, south of the Maceira valley, and four in reserve.

Just before the battle Sir A. Wellesley found himself superseded in the command of his army by Sir Henry Burrard, who had arrived off the mouth of the Maceira. Fortunately for Wellesley and the British army, Burrard very feebly decided to remain on board till next day, and Wellesley was left in executive command for the 21st.

At daybreak of the 21st, the approach of the French having been detected soon after midnight, all the British and Portuguese were under arms. But it was nearly 9 a.m. when Junot, who had halted to rest and feed his men after their night march, began to put in an appearance. His plan was to attack Wellesley's centre in front, and turn his left flank, where the ridge was weakest. He decided to attempt nothing against the threatening heights south of the Maceira gorge. Consequently, when the French deployed their left rested on the north bank of the Maceira and the south-western hill had no enemy in front of it.

Wellesley had expected to be attacked on both sides of the Maceira, but as Junot deployed in front of the hill on which were Anstruther's and Fane's brigades it could be seen that he was sending part of his force away northwards, evidently to turn the British left. Sir A. Wellesley instantly realized the design, and the necessary counter-measures were ordered. The brigades on the south-western ridge were moved across the Maceira, behind the ridge beyond it, Acland's remaining as a connecting link between them and the two on the advanced hill. At the same time it acted as a reserve to those of Ferguson, Nightingale, and Bowes on the left. Hill's brigade alone remained on the ridge on the left bank of the Maceira, and it was moved leftwards till it stood facing the Maceira, nearly at right angles to the position formerly held by Nightingale. The 1/9th was destined to be no more than a spectator of the action in the centre about Vimeiro. Sergeant Hale, who was in it, says: "Our whole brigade, which formed the reserve under the command of General Hill, was not brought into action." He gives practically no details of the battle, but describes the indignation at the pursuit being stopped. "As Sir Arthur Wellesley," he writes, "was riding up and down in front of our brigade, the men loudly called out to him from one end of the line to the other, saying, 'Let us advance! Let us advance! the enemy is in great confusion!' But his answer was 'I have nothing to do with it. I have no command.'" It is hardly likely that Wellesley would have replied thus.

The second battalion, however, was to be more in the fighting, for it was in reserve to the rest of Anstruther's brigade, which, with Fane's, was left to bear the brunt of Junot's attack on the hill in front of Vimeiro.

Junot's detachment to his right had at first consisted only of a cavalry regiment and Brennier's brigade, which had fought so well at Roliça; but, as he saw Wellesley's movement to his left, he despatched, in support of Brennier, Solignac's brigade of Loison's division.

The French force drawn out against the hill held by Anstruther and Fane, who had seven battalions between them, consisted of a first line of four and a quarter battalions, of the brigades of Charlot and Thomières, and seven guns, with a reserve of four battalions of grenadiers under Kellermann, besides the cavalry and reserve artillery. Anstruther's brigade, on the right of the English defence, had the 52nd and 97th in front line, with the 43rd and 2/9th behind them in column as reserve. On Fane's front most of the 60th and 95th riflemen were in front at the foot of the hill as skirmishers, with some of their companies and the 50th behind. The slope was covered with vines and brushwood.

As the French skirmishers drove in the riflemen, the English battalions, after a salvo from the six guns, fell in line on the heads of the enemy columns, whilst the 52nd attacked their left flank. It was the same on both Anstruther's and Fane's fronts. The French were driven down the hill hotly pursued, and the first attack was defeated.

Again the French attacked with two battalions of grenadiers in front line, and the remains of the brigades just defeated, which were rallied and sent in support. The result was the same. Then Junot, with his two remaining battalions of grenadiers, tried to turn Fane's left. Kellermann himself headed this attack, which made for the space between the back of the hill and the north-eastern ridge. To meet this attack Anstruther sent the 43rd, of his reserve, against Kellermann's left flank, whilst Acland, who was now acting as reserve to the British left, sent four companies against his right, and fired upon the French with two field guns. There was fierce and confused fighting, even in Vimeiro village, in which the 43rd lost heavily; but in the end Kellermann's grenadiers were forced to retreat. The 2/9th had lost their chance of doing what the 43rd did owing to their position on the right making them the battalion farthest from Kellermann's attack.

With this repulse the battle in the British centre ended, except for the cavalry charge of the 20th Light Dragoons on the retreating French. Little need be said about what happened on the left. Briefly, Brennier, coming upon a ravine, thought it impossible to get his guns over there, so moved still farther round to find a better passage. Solignac, however, crossed where Brennier had refused to, the result being that these two brigades were widely separated. First Solignac, and then Brennier coming to his assistance, were utterly defeated by Ferguson's and Nightingale's brigades. These attacks on the British left only began when the fight near Vimeiro was practically over. The French were now retreating in much disorder, and, had Wellesley continued in command, would probably have been completely ruined. But Burrard now interfered and forbade pursuit, as he wished to await the arrival of Sir John Moore's division, and thought enough had been done for the day. The British losses at Vimeiro were four officers and 131 other ranks killed, thirty-seven officers and 497 men wounded, and two officers and forty-nine men missing. The 2/9th lost on this day four men killed,

Lieutenant Taylor, one sergeant, and sixteen men wounded.[1] There were no casualties in the 1st battalion. The French losses were much heavier, not less than 1,800, including 300 or 400 unwounded prisoners, and thirteen out of their twenty-three guns.

Next day Burrard, who had done irreparable damage in his short period of command by stopping the pursuit, was superseded in turn by Sir H. Dalrymple. The new commander was no better than his predecessor, and also wanted to wait for Sir John Moore, who, as a matter of fact did not complete his landing till August 30th.

The negotiations which ended in the Convention of Cintra began on August 22nd and ended in the evacuation of Portugal by the French—Junot, with over 25,000 men, being sent back by sea to France in British ships, with no restriction on their fighting again. All this is no matter for a regimental history.

The 1st battalion, commanded from August 23rd by Lieutenant-Colonel Cameron *vice* Stuart, killed at Roliça, was sent to Quelus, eight or ten miles north-west of Lisbon; the 2nd, under Major David Campbell, to the castle of Belem in the suburbs of the city.

---

[1] At Vimeiro, Lieutenant Colin Campbell (whose real name was Colin Macliver) was for the first time under ffre. He was appointed ensign in the 2/9th on May 26th, 1808, when he was under sixteen. He was transferred to the 1st battalion soon afterwards, and back to the 2nd after Walcheren. He finally rejoined the 1st in 1812. For a further account of him see Appendix I.

CHAPTER XI

THE 1st BATTALION IN THE CORUNNA AND WALCHEREN CAMPAIGNS, 1808–1809

ON October 6, 1808, the command of the British Army in Portugal passed from the incompetent hands of Sir H. Dalrymple into those of Sir John Moore, probably, after Sir A. Wellesley, the best of the British generals of the day. The latter, who had reached England two days earlier, highly approved the appointment.

Though the British Government had long been meditating an invasion of Spain, and had even authorized Dalrymple to cross the frontier, Sir John Moore found that practically nothing had been done in preparation for the new enterprise. The whole army, save Hope with two brigades sent to try and stop the Portuguese siege of Elvas, was about Lisbon doing nothing. Dalrymple had even neglected to reconnoitre the various roads to the Spanish frontier, or to organize the transport necessary.

Of the total force at his disposal in Portugal, Moore left behind to guard Lisbon, Elvas, and Almeida about 9,000 men, amongst them being the second battalion of the 9th. The strength of the army with which he marched on Salamanca was somewhat over 20,000 men. He was to be joined in Spain by reinforcements from England under Sir David Baird, raising the total to over 33,000.

Moore had decided to march for Salamanca by the following routes :—

(1) Beresford, in command of his own and Fane's brigades, by Coimbra, Celorico, and Almeida. His own brigade was composed of the 1/9th, 2/43rd, and 2/52nd Regiments.

(2) Fraser, with Craufurd's, Bentinck's, and Hill's brigades, one battery, and two odd battalions, by Abrantes and Guarda.

(3) Paget, with the brigades of Alten and Anstruther, starting from Elvas, by Alcantara and Coria on Ciudad Rodrigo.

(4) Owing to information about these roads, which turned out to be incorrect, Moore believed that they were impracticable for the mass of his artillery, which he accordingly sent, escorted by his two cavalry regiments and four battalions of infantry all under the command of Hope, by a most circuitous road. This road, which passed by Elvas, Talavera and Arevalo, measured about 380 miles from Lisbon to Salamanca, against 250 by the Coimbra route. By it went six out of Moore's seven batteries.

Meanwhile Sir David Baird with the reinforcements had arrived at Corunna on October 13th, but was held up on board ship there for nearly a fortnight, thanks to Spanish obstruction.

The march of Moore's three left columns was only obstructed by the difficulties of supply and the rains, before the setting in of which he had in vain endeavoured to get clear of the mountains of the Portuguese frontier. Hope's column was still far away when Moore's first troops began to arrive at Salamanca on November 13th. The three columns were there complete by the 23rd. There Moore had about 15,000 infantry and one battery. Hope's column was then near the Escorial. At this time Baird had only got as far as Astorga from Corunna, with his main body and three batteries. His three cavalry regiments, which had arrived very late from England, were between Lugo and Astorga. A few battalions were still not up from Galicia. Hale says that the reception of the British in many of the Spanish villages was bad; but it was otherwise in Salamanca, and the men were anxious to have a little money to spend. They were five months in arrears of pay. "As our commanding officer would not advance any money, we passed the word to Sir John Moore, upon which our request was immediately granted; and an order was given that every man should be paid all his demands, except ten shillings, which sum should be kept in hand in order to purchase such articles as, in a little time, we might stand in need of."

With his army thus dispersed Moore knew that there were no

Spanish troops between him and the great army with which Napoleon was marching to recover possession of Spain, from which, as far north as the Ebro, his brother and his lieutenants had been ejected. He had also to avenge the disasters of Dupont at Baylen and Junot in Portugal. Milhaud's dragoons were already near Valladolid and Lefebvre's corps at Carrion. A French advance to Zamora on one side, or to Avila on the other, might cut off Baird or Hope. Without the latter's cavalry and guns Moore could not take the offensive, or fight at all. He could not know that Napoleon was intent on the recapture of Madrid, but he did know that, if the Emperor advanced westwards instead of southwards, there was nothing for it but for Baird to return at once to Corunna, and for himself and Hope to fall back at their utmost speed on Lisbon. He was not aware that the Emperor was entirely ignorant of the existence of a British force on the right flank of his march to Madrid. On the other hand, Moore did know of the many defeats, ending with Tudela, suffered by the Spaniards, and he despaired of rousing them to any energetic support of himself. By November 28th he had decided to retreat, and Baird had actually started on his way back to Corunna when he was stopped by counter-orders. Moore had thought better of it, and Hope was on his way to Salamanca, which he reached on December 3rd, without being attacked. He brought the welcome news that the French were moving southwards, and showed no symptom of marching on Salamanca. Captain Gomm had actually ridden into Valladolid and spent some hours there at a time when every fugitive inhabitant whom he met assured him the French were in occupation of the town.

On December 5th Moore sent orders to recall Baird, for he had decided on an attempt to cut the French communications. He had, too, received letters informing him that a Spanish force was still in existence, under the Marquis de la Romana, in Leon, and was available to aid him. A mission from the Junta at Madrid had in vain besought him to march to the rescue of that capital, for he had better information than they, and knew that Napoleon was at the gates of Madrid, which he reoccupied on December 4th.

When Sir J. Moore started on his adventure against Napoleon's communications he had about 25,000 men, including Baird's force, when it should join him. He hoped to be joined by La Romana, who said he had 20,000 men, though their military value was another matter.

On December 11th General Edward Paget's reserve, with Beresford's brigade, in which was the 1/9th, marched to Toro, where they had been preceded by Baird's three cavalry regiments (7th, 10th, and 15th Hussars under Lord Paget). The strength of the 1/9th on October 15th had been 945 rank and file. Its effective strength was now probably not over 650.[1]

Next day Hope marched on Tordesillas to the right (east) of Beresford's brigade, with his right flank covered by Charles Steuart with Moore's two cavalry regiments. The latter came in contact, at Rueda, with a French cavalry detachment, which they surprised, and either killed or captured nearly the whole of it. This affair seems to have given the French at Valladolid their first news of the whereabouts of Moore's army, which they believed to be retreating on Portugal. On the 13th there fell into Sir J. Moore's hands an intercepted despatch from Berthier to Junot, which showed him that Soult, with two infantry divisions and four regiments of cavalry, was towards Saldaña, seventy or eighty miles north of Valladolid, and was to seize the Province of Leon, which he could easily do as the English were off back to Portugal. Junot was marching on Burgos with the 8th corps and Napoleon himself was in Madrid. Moore had intended to march on Burgos, but with the knowledge now acquired it was clear that, if he continued, he would be marching right into the jaws of the pincers which might be formed by Junot in front, with Soult closing on his left rear, and troops from Madrid on his right. Madrid being submissive, Napoleon could easily send a strong detachment to the north.

On the other hand, it appeared that Soult was, for the present, isolated, and might, if he did not retreat at once, be cut off by Moore's superior force. The latter at once changed direction: Baird was ordered to Benavente, whilst Moore himself moved on Toro.

On the 14th cavalry skirmishes on Moore's right flank warned

[1] It was only 607 a week later. There had been much sickness, especially in the army from Portugal, which accounted for the majority of the 4,000 sick early in December.

Franceschi at Valladolid of his northward move, and that place was at once evacuated. On the 15th Moore crossed the Douro at Toro and Zamora, the latter being the crossing-place of the 1/9th with Beresford's brigade. The cavalry on the right raided Valladolid and had several skirmishes with French cavalry.

Still pushing northward, Moore's force reached Mayorga on December 20th. The weather was bitterly cold, as it had been even before Salamanca was left, and the march was already a trying one, though the hard ground facilitated progress. At Mayorga, Baird's force joined up, and the whole army was now concentrated.

Of Romana's Spanish army, from which assistance was expected, very poor accounts came in, and that general himself said he dared not march across Soult's front to join the English to the south of him till they, threatening the French left, should open the way for him. However, Moore's combined force—about double Soult's in strength—was more than sufficient to deal with the Duke of Dalmatia unsupported.

The British army was now redistributed into four divisions under Baird, Hope, Fraser, and E. Paget, with the two light brigades of Alten and R. Craufurd. The five cavalry regiments, in two brigades, were under Lord Paget. Fraser's division consisted of the brigades of Fane and Beresford, and the constituents of the latter were now the 1/6th, 1/9th, 2/23rd, and 2/43rd.

Soult, meanwhile, whether he had, like Bernadotte in 1807, received no duplicate of Berthier's intercepted despatch, or whether he was alarmed by the English raid on Valladolid, had made no advance on Leon. He was still at Saldaña, with his cavalry out as far as Sahagun, where it was within nine miles of the outposts of the English. At Sahagun, the French cavalry were brilliantly surprised and defeated by Lord Paget's cavalry. Soult was thoroughly alarmed, and it was fortunate for him that he had not, by the proposed advance into Leon, run his head into the noose which was prepared for him.

The cavalry affair was on December 20th, on the 21st the British infantry were at Sahagun in the evening. Moore's intention was, after resting and closing up his troops on the 22nd, to attack Soult on the

23rd, though he had now lost the great advantage of being, as he had hoped, on the French left rear.

The French cavalry who escaped from Paget at Sahagun had brought no tidings to Soult of Moore's main body, which they had not seen ; but the Marshal inferred, from the strength of the cavalry attack, that it was not far off, and at once concentrated on Carrion and sent to Palencia and Burgos for reinforcements. He got only Lorge's dragoon division and Delaborde's infantry, which were diverted to him as they were marching from Burgos to Madrid. They only reached him, however, well on in the morning of the 23rd.

Moore's orders for the advance against Soult at Carrion prescribed a rest till the evening of the 23rd, and then a night march so as to fall on Soult, if he were still there, at daybreak on the 24th. But this march was never completed, for grave news had reached Moore just in time to enable him to stop his troops, which were already on the march.

In the first place, Romana's promised assistance had now dwindled down to an offer to advance with 8,000 or 10,000 men. He was at Mansilla, on Moore's left rear, on the 23rd. He could not possibly have taken part in the projected battle of the morrow.

The really bad news, long expected by Moore, was that Napoleon was marching north-westward from Madrid with overwhelming forces, aiming, through Benavente, at Moore's destruction, or at least at driving him on to the sea.

The British general at once saw that there was nothing left but to retreat to the north-west corner of Spain, and, if followed, to endeavour to embark his army at Vigo or Corunna. Great was the disappointment of the infantry as they marched over frozen snowy roads, cheered by the hope of meeting the French in a few hours, when they were suddenly ordered to retrace their steps to Sahagun. Hale describes the disappointment of the troops at the counter-orders reaching them just as they were looking forward to a fight. "Now what a contrast was here," he says: "no honour had we gained, and the enemy about three to one ; all that we could do was to turn our backs on them, and get away in the best manner we could."

Romana was requested to retire to Astorga, where Moore thought that, with his assistance, the defence of Galicia might be organized. On the 24th Hope's and Fraser's divisions—the latter including Beresford's brigade with the 1/9th—started for Benavente by Mayorga and Valderas. Baird's division was sent farther north by Valencia de Don Juan, and on the 25th Sahagun was evacuated by the rear-guard of the reserve, the two light brigades, and the cavalry. Naturally the bulk of the army did not in the least understand the peril of the situation, or that their leader was doing the only thing possible to save them from destruction. They were spoiling for a fight, and retreat before an enemy whose strength and position they did not realize was bound to produce disappointment, grumbling, and discontent in, at any rate, the lower ranks. The officers, even some of the subordinate generals, cannot escape blame for the grumbling and indiscipline, which were heightened by their outspoken criticism and blame of the commander-in-chief's action in retreating without fighting, except where it was necessary to cover the retreat. It is not for us to describe the rear-guard actions in which the reserve and Lord Paget's cavalry so constantly covered themselves with glory. Of the whole army they were the least blameworthy for the excesses and indiscipline which were so bad during all the latter part of the march to Corunna. They were constantly fighting, and it was almost always the case with all the troops that indiscipline tended to disappear with even the prospect of a fight.

On the 24th the frost which had so far prevailed broke, and the roads, churned up by the passage of men, horses, guns, and vehicles, became mere strips of quagmire, whilst the snow which still covered the face of the country was turning into slush under the action of the thaw. On the 26th Baird's column with difficulty passed the River Esla at Valencia de Don Juan. The river was fast rising with the melting of the snow and the pouring rain. Fraser's and Hope's brigades passed the Esla lower down, by the bridge at Castro Gonzalo.

The whole countryside was fleeing in panic before the news of the French advance, and the Spanish drivers of the British transport were deserting their charges, redoubling the already serious difficulties of transport. What with their anger at their apparent desertion by the

Spaniards, and the terrible weather and roads, the temper of the British soldiers grew worse, and they began plundering and drinking in the villages through which they passed. There had already been excesses at Mayorga, Valderas, and Benavente, and they were to be worse later.

Moore publicly blamed the officers for this, and said plainly that it was for himself only to judge when he should fight and when he should **not**. But his general orders were powerless to stem the tide of indiscipline, drunkenness, and licence which was running so strongly.

On the 26th there was a cavalry rear-guard action, covering the destruction of the bridge at Castro Gonzalo, which was so well built that it was only with great difficulty that it was blown up after the British cavalry had passed.

Though the French were held up on the Esla, at Valencia and Castro Gonzalo, Franceschi, with Soult's cavalry, had broken through Romana's rear-guard, higher up at Mansilla, and again at the passage of the Carueño farther west.

At Benavente, Moore had to halt for a day to pick up his ammunition and stores, which had had to make a detour on account of flooded rivers.

On December 27th Hope and Fraser again started for Astorga, where they were joined by Baird's column arriving by the direct road from Sahagun. Fraser's division, leading the retreat, had reached Astorga on the 29th, when Hope's was only at Baneza. At Astorga, Moore had at one time contemplated a stand to defend the entrance to the mountains of Galicia. Romana's ragged army also was now in Astorga, useless for action, and serving rather as an incitement to indiscipline amongst the English. Romana urged on Moore the necessity for fighting here with the united armies, if his own could be reckoned anything better than a mob. But Moore saw that he would be playing Napoleon's game by offering him a chance of fighting, and perhaps destroying, the British. It would be far better to draw him on in pursuit, even to Corunna or Vigo. Therefore, notwithstanding the increased discontent and indiscipline in his own army caused by his decision, he insisted on continuing his retreat. He had hoped that Romana would leave the road to Corunna open to him and retreat northwards to Asturias. He

Braid formerly worn by the drummers of the Regiment in memory.

CORUNNA, JANUARY 16, 1809.

The 1st Battalion furnished the escort, with drums, and sounded "Last Post" at the unveiling of the memorial to Sir John Moore, at Sandgate, November 19, 1909. (*Ch. XI*)

had requested him to do so, but the Spaniard replied that the snow prevented him; hence his unwelcome presence at Astorga.

The excesses at Astorga had been the worst so far. "From that moment it seems that discipline in many battalions ceased altogether," says Mr. Fortescue.[1] What the condition of the 9th was, as compared with other regiments, we are unable to say. Gomm's diaries and letters are silent on this point and give no details of the regiment in the retreat. Hale says very little about his own regiment, as distinguished from others. As there is no particular reason for supposing the regiment was either better or worse than its neighbours, it is perhaps as well that the veil of mystery which shrouds its doings should remain untorn.

On December 30th Fraser, Hope, and Baird started on their march to Villafranca by the northern road through the pass of Manzanal, whilst Romana, less his guns sent by the better but longer road with the British, marched by the southern. The rear-guard followed on the 31st, after destroying all the remaining stores, ammunition, etc., at Astorga. Alten's and Craufurd's light brigades (3,000 or 4,000 men) were sent by Moore by the southern road to embark at Vigo, which they did, unmolested on the way, on January 12, 1809.

At Astorga, Napoleon's personal conduct of the pursuit ceased. Recognizing that Moore had escaped the snare which the Emperor had set for him, and that the probability of any great success was small, Napoleon, after his usual custom, left the job to be finished by his marshals, whilst he himself returned to Madrid, whither he had been called by news of Austria's arming for a new war.

Soult now had 20,000 infantry and 4,000 cavalry for his pursuit of Moore, whilst Ney, with another 16,000 men, was left at Astorga, ready to bring help if required.

At Bembibre, less than half the distance from Astorga to Villafranca, the first halt after entering the Galician mountains, in fearful conditions of freezing rain and bottomless roads, there was another terrible orgy amongst the British troops. The cellars, in which was collected the wine produced in the surrounding country, were broken into, and the streets and houses were littered with drunken soldiers, many of whom

[1] History of the British Army, vol. VI., p. 359.

were too far gone to be driven forward, even on the morrow, when the main body again marched for Villafranca, protected by the gallantry of the rear-guard of the reserve and the cavalry. At Villafranca again there were the same disorders, since the men would not even wait for the orderly distribution of large quantities of food which had been collected there but could not be moved up to Astorga for want of transport.

Crime of this sort was not altogether absent even in the rear-guard, as is shown by the case of three men whose execution, for plundering and ill-treating the villagers, was only interrupted by the arrival of the French cavalry at Cacabellos. Here again there was a sharp rear-guard action of all arms.

At Herrerias, on January 4, 1809, Moore, to whom many had recommended the retreat of the whole army on Vigo and its embarkation there, received reports of the state of the roads and ports which decided him to adhere to Corunna as his place of embarkation, except for the two light brigades already on their way to Vigo. Orders were sent to bring the transports round from Vigo to Corunna, and to stop Fraser and Hope, who, after passing Lugo, had been directed towards Vigo. The march on Lugo was resumed and the main body of the army reached it unmolested. The rear-guard was, as usual, pressed by the pursuing French cavalry, who, on January 5th alone, picked up over 900 prisoners mostly stragglers or men too drunk to move. When the rear-guard reached Lugo, in the morning of January 6th, Fraser's division, in which was the 1/9th, had passed a full day's march beyond it on the road to Vigo in ignorance of Moore's decision to embark at Corunna. Orders had been sent to Fraser by a drunken trooper, who had lost them, and the consequence was the brigade had to counter-march and got back to Lugo worn out, whilst the troops who remained there had had two days' rest.

The difficulties of the troops continued, and the horrors of the retreat were much augmented by the sight of the sufferings of women and children, who, under the pernicious practice of those days, had been allowed to accompany their husbands and fathers. The march from Villafranca to Lugo was the worst part of the whole retreat. Here is what is said of it by Adam Neale,[1] himself an eye-witness:

"All that had hitherto been suffered by our troops was but a prelude to this time of horrors. It had still been attempted to carry forward our sick and wounded; here the beasts which dragged them failed, and they were left in their wagons to perish among the snow. As we looked round on gaining the highest point of these slippery precipices, and observed the rear of the army winding along the narrow road, we could see the whole track marked out by our own wretched people, who lay expiring from fatigue and the severity of the cold, while their uniforms reddened in spots the white surface of the ground. Our men had now become quite mad with despair, excessive fatigue, and the consciousness of disgrace, in thus flying before an enemy whom they despised, excited in them a spirit which was quite mutinous. A few hours' pause was all they asked, an opportunity of confronting the foe, and the certainty of making the pursuers atone for all the miseries that they had suffered. Not allowed to fight, they cast themselves down to perish by the wayside, giving utterance to feelings of shame, anger, and grief. But too frequently, their dying groans were mingled with imprecations upon the general who chose rather to let them die like beasts than to take their chance on the field of battle. That no degree of horror might be wanting, this unfortunate army was accompanied by many women and children, of whom some were frozen to death on the abandoned baggage wagons, some died of fatigue and cold, while their infants were seen vainly sucking at their clay-cold breasts."

The cavalry and reserve still continued to turn at intervals and check Soult's pursuing horsemen.

At Lugo provisions had been found in store and the army caught up Leith's brigade of Hope's division, which had never reached Astorga after its circuitous march by the Escorial, and had been sent on, to march comparatively at leisure, when the retreat was ordered. Some

[1] Letters from Spain and Portugal. Neale was a doctor serving at this time with the army.

rest for the exhausted men of the rest of the army was absolutely necessary, and an endeavour must be made to restore order and discipline to some extent. Accordingly, the army was drawn up in a strong position about three miles in front of Lugo, where the rear-guard joined it on January 6th. It now numbered about 19,000 men[1] and forty guns. That day Soult's cavalry appeared, and some infantry, but did nothing. If the retreat had exhausted the British, the pursuit had tried the French too, and they had had considerable losses from hardship, and left many stragglers along the road behind them. One division had not yet left Villafranca.

On the 7th Soult was up in force, and found the British position unpleasantly strong. A feint against its right, covered by the river Minho, was not pressed against the Guards brigade. On the British left, which was the least strong part of the line, was Leith's comparatively fresh brigade, which, when attacked by two French infantry regiments, charged with the bayonet and drove them back down the hill with considerable loss.[2] The effects of the prospect of a fight had been marvellous in restoring order and spirit among Moore's troops, and on this day the French were decidedly in inferior strength, pending the arrival of Heudelet. Fraser's division was the most fatigued of the British, thanks to its unfortunate march towards Vigo.

On the 8th the British still stood ready to receive the attack of Soult, who could now put into line about 18,000 men, still 1,000 short of his opponent. He hesitated to attack, and the two armies watched

---

[1] Sir C. Oman thus reckons the losses and gains since Benavente:

Losses: Two light brigades sent to Vigo	3,500
Dismounted cavalry sent on to Corunna	1,000
Sick, too ill to be moved, left at Astorga and Villafrança	500
Losses by the way, Astorga to Lugo	2,000
	7,000
Less Leith's brigade joined at Lugo	1,800
Net loss (approximate)	5,200

[2] According to Oman, 300 men. Fortescue suggests a loss of 100 on each side as more probable.

each other all day, doing nothing. That night Moore, who was once more running short of food, left his camp-fires burning, and started to retreat again. But in a terrible storm many of his troops failed to strike the road, and next morning had hardly got beyond Lugo. Of the start from Lugo, Hale says : " About six o'clock in the evening we had some very comfortable fires, and we all placed ourselves round them as comfortable as our situation would allow ; but at that time we were in a miserable dirty condition, not having our clothes off for about six weeks." By 10 o'clock the exhaustion of the night march compelled another halt some ten miles beyond Lugo. Fortunately, the bridge over the Minho, a couple of miles short of the halting-place, which extended along the road, was blown up after all had passed. Late in the evening of the 9th the retreat was resumed in atrocious weather, which resulted in more losses in straggling, and a return in most corps of the old indiscipline.

On the morning of the 10th all was changed when, like Xenophon's soldiers of the *Anabasis*, the British at Betanzos could feast their eyes on the sight of the sea, and enjoy a climate and surroundings which were the very reverse of the desolate mountains and the terrible storms through which they had passed only a few hours earlier. Of the arrival at Betanzos, Hale says :

"When we assembled all hands, our regiment did not exceed sixty men ; neither did any regiment in the brigade exceed that number ; however, the whole brigade could not muster two hundred and fifty men. It consisted of the 9th, 23rd, 43rd, and 52nd Regiments of Foot. . . . During this miserable retreat from Lugo to this place, we lost between three and four hundred men of our regiment, merely with fatigue and hunger, who fell into the hands of the enemy ; and it is certain that some few individuals were seen to breathe their last on the roadside. There is one thing more that I cannot help mentioning, which was a most melancholy scene : that was, an English woman, one of our soldier's wives, lying dead on the roadside, with a young child sucking at the breast, and, to all appearance, likely to survive if taken care of."

The French had been left behind, and it was possible to take a much-needed rest on the 10th. On the night of the 11th Moore's main body was in Corunna, the reserve still just on the British side of the Mero River, the bridge over which had been destroyed. There had been some fighting during the day and, as usual, many stragglers had fallen into the enemy's hands.

At Corunna, Moore met with a fresh disappointment, for unfavourable winds had detained at Vigo the transports which he hoped to find awaiting his wearied troops at Corunna. He had still to fight a battle to cover his embarkation. He at once began to improve the landward defences of the fortress, at the expense of those to seaward, where he was of course safe. Stores and arms were plentiful in Corunna, and with them Moore's army was soon in a state very different from what it had been a few days earlier. What he did not want he destroyed, or prepared to destroy.

On the 13th the transports were still not in, and after withdrawing his reserve from its advanced position at El Burgo, Moore had posted his army in the position outside Corunna where he meant to offer the battle which the ignorance of his men had blamed him for not fighting long before.

Two of the lower bridges on the Mero had been destroyed by the British, but the French had found one higher up, by which Franceschi had passed with his cavalry. On the evening of the 13th infantry had crossed by the repaired bridge near El Burgo, but only in the afternoon of the 14th could the French artillery pass.

That same evening the transports from Vigo at last sailed into the harbour, and Moore at once began embarking sick men, dismounted cavalry, spare guns and horses, and everything he did not want for the expected battle, for which he only retained twelve guns and their teams.

Moore's dispositions for the battle which he might have to fight to cover his embarkation were made on the 14th. The heights of Penasquedo, the nearest to the River Mero, were too extensive for his numbers, so he decided to defend Monte Mero, a height having the estuary of El Burgo on its left, but being weaker on its eastern side, where it sank down before rising again to the heights of San Christobal.

From right to left the front line on the outer slope of Monte Mero was held by the divisions of Bentinck, Manningham, Leith, and Hill, with Catlin Craufurd's behind the left on the northern slope, concealed from view, and the Guards behind the right. Light troops were out towards the heights of Palavea, the eastern part of those of Penasquedo. To reinforce his right, which was liable to be turned, Moore placed the division of Paget at the village of Oza, more than a mile in rear. For still further security, as a last reserve, he held Fraser's division, in which was Beresford's brigade, comprising the 1/9th, on the forward slope of the heights of Santa Margarita. On January 15th there was a fight between Moore's advanced troops and some of Soult's army, which ended in the retirement of the former to their main line.

Of the battle of the 16th, we shall give but a brief outline, as it never became necessary to call in the active assistance of Fraser's division, and the 9th remained ready to help, but inactive spectators of the fight raging more than a mile in front of them. Says Hale:

"In consequence of the garrison being so much out of repair, we were put to work the following morning, repairing ramparts and batteries; and having a belly-full of good victuals and drink, we continued our work as well as our strength would allow, until about the middle of the day, when we were alarmed by a sharp firing of musketry between our outposts and the enemy. . . . In a few minutes we were all ready for action except the sick. . . . We marched out of the town about two miles where a sharp engagement . . . continued till it was dark. . . . However, it did not fall to our lot to partake of this action, neither did any of our brigade fall in with them; nevertheless we were within call during the whole time, expecting to be summoned up every minute."

The British force was slightly superior in numbers to that of Soult, being about 15,000 infantry against 12,000. The French delayed their attack till after 2 p.m., which left little time in the short winter afternoon.

As was to be expected, that attack took the form of a frontal action, combined with an attempt to turn Moore's right by a heavy attack on Bentinck's and Manningham's divisions. For a time the attack on Elvina was succeeding, but was finally driven off with the arrival of the Guards on Bentinck's left. Two of Paget's regiments, coming up on the French left, completed their repulse and sent them back to the heights of Penasquedo, whence they had started. The French attempt against Leith's and Hill's divisions on the British left was equally unsuccessful. The fighting, which for reasons given above we refrain from describing in full, had been very severe, Elvina was at times in possession of the French, who advanced even beyond it. When darkness fell the whole French line had been driven back on to the Penasquedo and Palavea heights, the English had maintained their position, and in places, especially on the right, had advanced beyond it. The losses on both sides were about equal—somewhere about 900 on each side killed, wounded, and prisoners, the last-named being mostly French. Neither Catlin Craufurd's division of the left reserve nor Fraser's of the right was called up or fired a shot during the day.

But the British suffered an irreparable loss in their commander, Sir John Moore, who only a few minutes after Baird had been wounded was struck on the left breast and shoulder by a round shot and thrown from his horse by it. His case from the first was clearly hopeless, though he bore himself with undaunted courage in the fearful suffering caused by being carried off the field in a blanket. As his agonizing journey towards Corunna progressed he stopped his bearers at intervals to enable him to view the progress of his last battle. Like Wolfe at Quebec, he was dying in the very moment of victory. That night he died, as he had lived, a true British soldier and gentleman.

Moore and Baird both being wounded, the command of the army devolved on Sir John Hope, who finally decided to embark at once, rather than to attack Soult or await a second battle. At 9 p.m. the troops retired from Monte Mero, all but the piquets left to keep the camp-fires burning and deceive the French. All night the embarkation continued, and at daybreak the piquets also were withdrawn, and Soult was able to see that the position of the day before was empty. He advanced to the heights of Santa Margarita just at the moment when a few random shots hurried on the completion of the funeral of Sir John Moore. The honour of laying to rest the mortal remains of their commander fell to the 1/9th, who were detailed to form the extreme rear-guard covering the embarkation.

COLONEL JOHN PATTESON, 1755–1833.
Lieutenant-Colonel, Norwich Volunteers, 1803. (*Ch. XI*)

Before daybreak of the 17th the grave was dug, in the central bastion of the Corunna landward defences, by a fatigue party of the 9th. The body was born to the grave by four officers, and the short service was read by a chaplain, Mr. Symonds. Hard by the grave was that of General Anstruther, who had died of dysentery a few days before. No description of the short and interrupted ceremony is needed, for every one has read one of the best known of short English poems—" The Burial of Sir John Moore," the author of which was Charles Wolfe.[1] Soult, moved by an honourable feeling of respect for his late enemy, ordered the erection of a monument to Sir John Moore on the spot where he fell.

All through the 17th the embarkation continued, interrupted to some extent by Soult's guns from the heights south of the harbour. By evening all were on board except Beresford's brigade, which only embarked on the 18th. The honour of being the very last, even of this brigade, to leave the coast of Spain was enjoyed by the 9th. " The last fragment of rear-guard withdrawn from the heights," writes Gomm, " consisted of my own company of the 9th regiment, the regiment which had just

' Buried him darkly at dead of night
With his martial cloak around him.'

We were thus the last British remnants (I believe I was the last English fighting man) embarking." Hale says twenty men of his and twenty of another company stayed with Beresford and his staff to bring off a number of English wounded who had been left in the town.

A south-westerly gale carried the remains of the army home in a very few days. During this terrible retreat the battalion lost one officer (Ensign Davis) and 148 men by death on the road, or by capture when compelled to lag behind by exhaustion.

[1] The authorship was much disputed, but has been finally proved to be Wolfe's. He wrote the poem in 1816, a year before he took orders. Byron disclaimed, with regret, the credit for an ode of which he expressed the highest opinion. For notes concerning the commemoration of this sad event in the uniform, see Appendix. The description in the poem is of course inaccurate in describing the time of burial as " dead of night."

Before returning to the doings of the 2nd battalion it will be convenient to finish up the history of the 1st during 1809.

Landing at Portsmouth and Plymouth on its return to England from Corunna, the 1st battalion marched to Canterbury, arriving there on February 9th. Hale says when his party reached Portsmouth, " in our present dirty ragged condition, we were not fit to march through a clean Christian country," and it was intended to send them by sea to Dover as being close to Canterbury. Bad weather prevented this, and meanwhile the men cleaned themselves up and patched their uniforms after a fashion. So successful were they that he says that at Farnham " the people came flocking round us with pots of beer saying, ' Drink, soldiers ! for several parties have marched through this town but not one appeared so clean and soldierlike as this party.' " At Canterbury they received about 300 recruits, two-thirds from the Militia and the rest from the 2nd battalion. From Canterbury the battalion marched on July 17th to Deal, under orders to join the unfortunate Walcheren expedition. Hale tells how, the night before, two men misbehaved and were tried, before the march began, by drumhead court martial, and sentenced to 200 lashes. In order to prevent the severity of the punishment being an excuse for the men not going on the expedition, the colonel reduced the lashes to 100, and ordered the men to be marched with the baggage as prisoners.[1]

The object of this expedition was, in the first place, to nip in the bud Napoleon's attempts to strike at England's commercial prosperity through his possession of Antwerp and the mouth of the Scheldt, and secondly, to afford some relief to Austria, by detaining in Holland troops which the Emperor might otherwise have used against her. It will be remembered that, when he abandoned his personal conduct of the pursuit of Sir John Moore at Astorga in December, 1808, he had received disturbing news of Austria's preparations, which required his return to Paris.

To the command of the projected expedition the Earl of Chatham was appointed on July 16th. The troops allotted to him numbered about 39,000 rank and file, divided thus :—

[1] For examples of sentences passed by courts martial about that date, see Appendix VII.

Cavalry	3,015
Artillery	3,032
Infantry	33,096
	39,143

The infantry was all British, except two German light battalions, and the cavalry was also British, except two German light dragoon regiments.

The 1/9th was reckoned at 932 rank and file.

There were sixteen companies of field artillery, with ninety-six guns, and one troop of horse artillery with six guns.

The 1/9th was brigaded on this occasion with the 38th and 42nd, under Major-General Montresor, and formed part of the 2nd division, commanded by Lieutenant-General the Marquis of Huntley.

There is not much to be said about this most disastrous expedition, in which few regiments had any opportunity of distinguishing themselves, and the 9th had none.

The 2nd division, under the escort of a squadron commanded by Captain Owen, R.N., anchored off Cadzand on the afternoon of July 29th. Why no landing was attempted is uncertain, but the fact remains that it was not, though the tide was favourable at 3 a.m. on the 30th.

In the meanwhile the main body of the army had got ashore on the north-east side of the island of Walcheren, which lies between the eastern and western mouths of the Scheldt. Very little resistance was encountered as the English pressed southwards across Walcheren, through Middleburg, towards Flushing, the extreme southern point of the island, where the fortress was held by the French General (Mounet) with about 3,000 men, who were reinforced later from the Cadzand side across the West Scheldt. On August 1st the enemy's troops, after a short action, were forced into Flushing and the place was invested.

East of Walcheren, still between the two branches of the Scheldt, lie the smaller island of North Beveland and the much larger one of South Beveland. They are separated from Walcheren by a channel, and from one another by a second channel.

North Beveland was unoccupied, and in South Beveland the enemy's general (Bruce) withdrew on July 30th to Fort Bath in the extreme south-east of the island, the point where the two branches of the Scheldt divide.

On August 1st Sir John Hope with the reserve landed on the north-east side of South Beveland, captured Goes, the principal town, from which the garrison retired without fighting, and by the morning of August 3rd held the whole island, except Fort Bath itself, which was occupied by General Bruce with 600 Dutch troops. He, too, attempted no resistance and retired to Bergen-op-Zoom. The guns in the fort were spiked, thanks, according to French accounts, to Admiral Misiessy, who landed some seamen for the purpose, whilst he with his ships retired to a safe position in the Scheldt close to Antwerp. With the surrender of Fort Rammekens on the afternoon of the 3rd the whole island was in Hope's possession. On the 5th Fort Bath was bombarded by French gunboats from the Antwerp direction, which were beaten off with the aid of the fort's guns, which had been unspiked by a private in the Guards. This might have been avoided if Hope's demand for reinforcements had been complied with; but it was not till the 9th that Lord Chatham sent him the 2nd division and the light troops under Lord Rosslyn, who superseded Hope in the command in South Beveland. It was only on August 10th that the 1/9th landed on South Beveland and went into cantonments at Heinkensart and St. Heerenrook.

On August 14th Mounet at Flushing surrendered, after a very destructive bombardment. The prisoners taken with him numbered 4,379.

The whole of the islands of Schouven and Duixeland, on the right bank of the East Scheldt, had also submitted to Lord Rosslyn at the same time as Flushing fell. So far the French had given little trouble to the expedition. Napoleon's hands were full in Spain, as well as in Austria, but he had now begun to organize the defence of Holland and Antwerp, and by August 15th Bernadotte, now in command there,[1] had 15,000 men and twenty-four guns ready to take the field.

---

[1] He had been deprived of his corps and sent home in disgrace for his conduct at Wagram, which met with Napoleon's disapproval.

But the British had a far more dangerous enemy than the French in the pestilential climate of the Dutch islands.

> "The island [Walcheren], being so flat, and nearly level with the sea, is little better than a swamp; the ditches are filled with putrid vegetable and animal matter, the quantity of pure water very limited. The inhabitants are sickly and infirm. The sickly season begins about the middle of August, and continues till the frost stops the exhalations from the earth; the dry hot weather causing the greatest amount of sickness. Nearly one-third of the population is attacked with fever every sickly season, in spite of the greatest attention to cleanliness, both in buildings and person.
>
> "The fever first showed amongst the troops in South Beveland who had not the opposition of an enemy to keep their minds and bodies in healthy action. But, on the fall of Flushing, it broke out amongst the troops in Walcheren.
>
> "At first the disease appeared as a low fever, but subsequently took a form similar to jail fever. It spread with unexampled rapidity."[1]

Under this dreadful scourge the British sick increased with terrible rapidity, and deaths were numerous.

One regiment—the 81st—had 656 men fit for duty at the landing, 468 on September 7th, and only forty on September 29th. On September 19th, there were sick 224 officers and 9,627 men.

Something might have been done if Lord Chatham had boldly marched on Antwerp, but he was not the man to act boldly, and, in the conditions existing, it was finally decided, with the concurrence of the Home Government, to abandon the expedition, but to leave a garrison in Walcheren. Even this had to be withdrawn on November 1st.

The 9th, fortunately, were not among the garrison left at Walcheren. They landed again in England on September 15th, after being aground for a week on the Dutch coast, and returned to their old quarters at Canterbury. A very large proportion of this, as of other regiments, was suffering from "Walcheren" fever or its results.

[1] Report of John Webb, Inspector of Hospitals.

In this terrible expedition the actual numbers embarked in July were 1,738 officers and 37,481 other ranks. The dead numbered sixty-seven officers (seven killed in action) and 4,108 others (ninety-nine killed in action).

There landed in England 1,671 officers and 33,373 others, of whom 217 officers and 11,296 others were sick.[1] Of the sick, a very large proportion were probably broken down for life, if they did not die of the fever. To again quote John Webb's report: "Men who have suffered from this fever have their constitutions so shattered that their physical power will for the future be materially diminished." Hale says, after the regiment's arrival in Canterbury, " In a short time our hospital was crowded with sick; every day the number of the sick increased with the ague and fever, for in about one month nearly half our regiment was on the sick list, by which a great many were summoned to their last homes. Several times three or four in a day were carried to the burial ground; and there were but few in the regiment who escaped having the ague either sooner or later." The regiment suffered for many months from the after effects of "Walcheren" fever. It had not suffered so severely as others at South Beveland, no doubt owing to its only being on the island from August 10th to September 4th, on which day it embarked, though it did not sail till the 14th. But the seeds of disease had been sown in the twenty-five days ashore and they developed later at Canterbury. The 1/9th was the first of the Walcheren regiments to be again sent on foreign service.

---

[1] These figures are exclusive of the 59th Regiment, whose return was not received.

CHAPTER XII

THE 2ND BATTALION IN PORTUGAL—THE PURSUIT OF SOULT. 1808–1809

WE left the 2nd battalion forming part of the garrison of Portugal when Moore's advance on Salamanca began in November, 1808. On January 6, 1809, they were at Santarem, on the right bank of the Tagus a few miles above Lisbon, together with the 3/27th, a detachment of the 5/60th,[1] another of artillery, and two troops of the 14th Light Dragoons, all under Major-General Mackenzie. They were at Coimbra when, on May 7, 1809, Lieutenant-Colonel G. Molle joined and took over command of the battalion.

The command in Portugal had been taken over by Sir John Cradock on December 14, 1808, on his arrival from England, and he was led to believe that a British force to occupy Cadiz would be welcomed by the Spanish authorities. With Cadiz as a fortified base, British operations in the south of Spain might be feasible, but not without it. Accordingly he despatched General Mackenzie thither by sea, with the 2/9th, 3/27th, 2/31st, 1/30th, and two companies of artillery, in all 4,271 of all ranks. When Mackenzie arrived off Cadiz on February 5th, he found that the supposed situation had altered, and he was told that the Spaniards objected to the landing of British troops. He was kept hanging about there, listening to and refusing various proposals by the Spaniards, till March 5th, when General Sherbrooke, with four battalions and two batteries from England, had arrived. He then, as well as Sherbrooke, received orders from Cradock to return to Lisbon. Sailing on the 6th both forces were at Lisbon on March 12th.

[1] The 5/60th had been sent back by Moore.

A few days after the British army sailed from Corunna Soult marched for Portugal. His adventures on the way, his fights with the Portuguese and the peasants are not relevant in a regimental history. By March 29, 1809, he had taken Oporto, but the whole country behind him had risen against him.

Just at this juncture the British Government had come to a momentous decision to appoint Sir A. Wellesley to supersede Cradock in the command in Portugal, and to send out Beresford to take command of the Portuguese forces under him.

By this time also Cradock's own position had been much improved, as he had gathered some 17,500 British troops, which enabled him, after garrisoning Lisbon, to dispose of 12,000 men as a field army. By April 21st, in order to put some heart into the sadly dejected Portuguese, he had advanced as far north as Leiria. Next day Wellesley landed at Lisbon. On the 24th he took over the command and Cradock departed to his new appointment as Governor of Gibraltar. Soult had halted at Oporto, sending out Loison, who had required more support before he was able to defeat Silveira, now rallied on the Tamega. That was on May 2nd.

By this time Wellesley had with him, or shortly arriving, about 23,000 troops, British and German, besides 15,000 or 16,000 Portuguese whom Beresford had for three weeks past been doing his best to train. A few of the Portuguese were already good, but there was still much to be done before the rest would be really serviceable. Of guns Wellesley had three British and two German batteries, thirty guns in all. He had two more British batteries, but no teams for them. To his infantry force of about 23,000 British and Germans the 2/9th contributed 572 of all ranks.

Wellesley decided to move northwards first against Soult, and then, after driving him out of Portugal, to deal with Victor, who, joined by Lapisse, was at Merida east of Badajoz, and hopelessly out of touch with Soult. To guard against a rather improbable advance by Victor against Portugal, Wellesley left Mackenzie with a mixed British and Portuguese force—about 5,000 of the former and 7,000 of the latter.

Wellesley's own force was organized by him after his arrival at

IXTH EAST NORFOLK REGIMENT OF INFANTRY.
Ensign and Colours. From a contemporary print. (*Ch. XII*)

Coimbra on May 2nd. The infantry consisted of the brigade of Guards and those numbered 1st, 3rd, 4th, 5th, 6th, and 7th, the 2nd being left with Mackenzie. The 7th brigade, under Brigadier-General Cameron of the 9th, contained the 2/9th, 2/10th Portuguese, 2/83rd, and one company of riflemen of the 5/60th.

The artillery with Wellesley was only two British batteries (one of three-pounders and one of light six-pounders) and two German of light six-pounders. Silveira's defeat prevented Wellesley from carrying out his project of cutting Soult from Amarante on the Tamega, and so forcing him to retreat northwards on to the Minho, instead of northeastwards. His object now was to prevent Soult's advance south of the Douro and to compel his retirement out of Portugal. He entrusted Beresford with a mixed force of British and Portuguese about 6,000 strong, and instructed him to march north-eastwards by Vizeu to Lamego. There he was to be joined by Silveira and Sir R. Wilson's Portuguese, to do his best, without risking a defeat, to prevent Soult from crossing the Douro, and to cut off his retreat eastwards.

On May 7th Wellesley's advance from Coimbra began. At this moment Soult, unsuspecting of the storm about to burst on him, had his army considerably dispersed. Oporto was held by Delaborde's division, Loison was still at Amarante with 7,000 men, Lorge with his dragoons was far to the north, Mermet's division and Franceschi's cavalry were alone on the Vouga, about half-way between Oporto and Coimbra; Franceschi's cavalry and a battalion were acting as advance guard at Albergaria Nova on the Vouga. That river falls, not direct into the Atlantic, but into a land-locked lagoon some fifteen miles long, of which about half is north of the river's mouth.

Wellesley's orders for the 10th were as follows : Cotton, with the cavalry, was to advance by the great road to Oporto and endeavour to surprise Franceschi at dawn and cut him off. He would be followed, on the same road, by Steuart's and Murray's brigades, now forming Paget's division. The rest of the army would follow by the same road, except Hill's division, comprising his own brigade and Cameron's, in which latter the 2/9th was a unit commanded by Lieutenant-Colonel Campbell.

When Wellesley's orders were issued on the 8th Hill had already been directed to reach Aveiro, on the lagoon some distance south of the Vouga, early on the 9th. There he would find boats ready for him, on which he was to embark at high tide, about 4 p.m., on the 9th. He would be carried to the north end of the lagoon at Ovar, but was to lie-to five or six miles south of that place, till slack water, about 4 a.m. on the 10th. The object of this delay was explained to be to prevent the enemy getting news of his whereabouts before the frontal attack by the great road began. At Ovar, which was to be seized by a detachment of three companies landing west of it, Hill would land with his own brigade, and at once send back the boats to fetch up Cameron's from Aveiro. He was not to advance till he had certain information that Cotton was at Oliveira, south-east of Ovar on the main road. The battery allotted to Hill's division would be with Cameron's brigade, which, on the 9th, moved to Murtede, short of Aveiro, to which it was to follow Hill on the 10th and embark in the returned boats. When Hill and Cotton had united they would advance on Oporto, endeavouring, if the chance offered, to cross the bridge there with the French rear-guard, or at least to prevent its destruction. All boats on the south bank of the Douro, in any case, were to be seized and collected.

On the morning of the 10th Cotton, finding that Franceschi had infantry, could not risk an attack till he was joined by Trant's Portuguese, and then Franceschi retired in good order towards Oporto. Hill, meanwhile, found himself watched by three battalions of Mermet's division at Feira, six miles to the north-east. He remained at Ovar, waiting for the arrival of Cameron's brigade and the guns. Mermet's three battalions advanced, and there was some skirmishing between them and Hill's men, till the retreat of Franceschi before Cotton compelled the French to fall back northwards to Grijo, between Feira and the coast. Cameron's brigade was apparently not up in time to take part in this skirmishing.

Next morning (the 11th) Hill's division advanced by the direct road from Ovar to Oporto, whilst Wellesley with a large superiority of numbers attacked Mermet and Franceschi by the main road, and, after turning both their flanks, compelled their retreat, and inflicted considerable loss on their rearmost regiment, the 31st Light Infantry.

The British that night occupied the French camp at Grijo, whilst Mermet and Franceschi reached Oporto and broke the bridge over the Douro behind them.

Soult was now thoroughly alarmed, for, in addition to the unfavourable military position, he had discovered Argenton's plot against himself, and felt by no means certain how far its ramifications might extend. As for the military position, he had about 21,000 effective troops, against Wellesley's 16,400 British and 11,400 Portuguese; but the majority of the Portuguese were as yet of small value. Soult's danger was due to the dispersion of his troops, especially in the case of Loison's 7,000 at Amarante.

Under all these circumstances, Soult had decided to retreat to Spain through Tras os Montes, picking up Loison at the important bridge of Amarante. In Oporto itself Soult had only 11,000 or 12,000 men, whilst Wellesley, beyond the Douro, had 18,400, including 2,400 Portuguese, not to mention Beresford's detachment to his right at Lamego, of which Soult was unaware. Nevertheless it was necessary to hold Oporto till the outlying detachments were gathered in, and the problem was to prevent Wellesley's passage of the river. Soult's fear was that the boats which had brought Hill up the lagoon to Ovar might be used to pass the Douro at its mouth. When, therefore, the British arrived in the southern suburb of Oporto, on the left bank of the river, on the morning of the 12th, his attention was devoted to the lower course of the river, and he had his head-quarters in that direction. But the greater part of the British army was higher up, hidden from the view of the city by the rocky and wooded height of the northward bend of the left bank, on which stood the Serra Convent.

Below the convent hill the river was comparatively narrow and deep; above it was broad and shallow.

Wellesley despatched Murray with a small force to cross the Douro at Avintes, four miles higher up. Thanks to the recovery of four large boats from the farther bank, opposite a point above the convent, Wellesley was able to pass over the Buffs, and to occupy the seminary on the northern bank before the French had any inkling of what was happening. Soult's attention was riveted on the lower river, and he believed himself perfectly safe till the boats from Ovar could be brought round. The history of the fight at the seminary against the French endeavouring, too late, to recover this all-important post, and to destroy the British and Portuguese there, need not be described. Hill's own brigade, the leading one of his division, played a prominent part in it, but the other brigade, Cameron's, in which was the 2/9th, is nowhere mentioned in Wellesley's despatch, either in this connexion or in describing Sherbrooke's crossing opposite Porta Nova. Presumably Cameron crossed later, when the battle at the seminary was practically won, and Soult, with Sherbrooke on his right flank, and Murray now across at Avintes and in position on the flank of his line of retreat, was already falling back in disorder to effect a junction with Loison towards Amarante. With much smaller loss on his own side than he had inflicted on the enemy, Wellesley was now in possession of Oporto and the passages of the lower Douro.

That night Soult's badly beaten army encamped at Baltar, ten miles east of Oporto, where he found himself with about 13,000 men.

We may pass over Soult's terrible retreat to meet Loison, who had been in difficulties with Beresford's detached force. When the two French commanders joined, Soult had about 20,000 men but had lost most of his guns.

Wellesley, meanwhile, had been delayed at Oporto by the difficulty (due to the French destruction of the bridge) of getting over his guns and heavy baggage and stores. His men, too, were weary after their march of eighty miles in four days from Coimbra. Therefore, on the 13th only Murray's detachment followed Soult. It was only at 5 p.m. on that day that Wellesley knew of Soult's desperate march across the mountains. His communications with Beresford were circuitous. and he had not heard of all that officer's successes against Loison. That day he issued orders for the march, next morning, of the Guards brigade and those of Campbell, Cameron, and the cavalry, with two batteries. They were to carry provisions for the 14th, 15th and 16th. The commander-in-chief was still uncertain whether Soult was bound for Braga or Chaves ; therefore he marched himself, in two columns, for the former, and sent orders to Beresford, which the latter had anticipated, to march on Chaves.

On the 15th Wellesley was at Braga. On that day Soult, who had arrived the previous evening about eight miles east of Braga, learnt that he was headed off at that place, so fell back to Salamonde, whence, with great difficulty in repairing one bridge and in carrying another, he retreated to Montalegre. But his rear-guard was caught by Wellesley (who was certain on the 15th that he was bound either for Montalegre or Chaves) and defeated with considerable loss. Wellesley states that in this affair only the Guards were engaged. As for Soult's retreat he remarks: "He had lost everything—cannon, ammunition, baggage, military chest; and his retreat is, in every respect, even in weather, a pendant for the retreat to Corunna."[1] He had now managed to slip through the gap between Wellesley and Silveira, the former of whom had achieved the object with which he set out, namely, the ejectment of Soult from Portugal. The Duke of Dalmatia's invasion of Portugal had resulted in little but the loss of 6,000 men, besides guns and much material of all sorts. British head-quarters were at Montalegre on May 18th, but beyond that Soult was not pursued.

Wellesley had now to deal with his second task—the repulse of Victor from the eastern frontier of Portugal; therefore he returned south and the whole army was back at Coimbra by May 27th. The 2/9th, with the 2/83rd, were stationed at Tancos.

As neither it nor the 1st battalion was engaged in the Talavera campaign we have now to follow it to Gibraltar. Before leaving England Wellesley had arranged that he was to have from Gibraltar the 48th and 61st Regiments, sending in exchange for them two battalions, which he would select, from Portugal. By May 27th he had decided on sending the 1/30th, and said he would decide later as to the other battalion to be sent. He eventually decided, on June 15th, that it should be the 2/9th, which embarked at Lisbon on June 18th, and landed at Gibraltar on July 2nd. Whilst they were on their way Wellesley wrote that he regretted not having sent, instead, another battalion which was in a very bad state.[2]

[1] Despatches, 3, 3, p. 239.   [2] Letter to Colonel Donkin: Despatches, 3, p. 320.

CHAPTER XIII

THE 1st BATTALION IN THE PENINSULA—BUSACO AND TORRES VEDRAS (1809–1810). THE 2ND BATTALION AT GIBRALTAR AND BARROSA (1809–1811)

WE must now trace the fortunes of the 1st battalion after its return from Walcheren, when we left it at Canterbury, in a very bad state of health with " Walcheren " fever, which hung about it for months and caused it very heavy losses. Even when the regiment was about to be sent to Lord Wellington in Portugal a report on it says : " 1/9th a very fine battalion, but had better not undertake a long march yet, as many of the men are only just out of hospital : seventy-two sick : only three too young to march."[1] The battalion nevertheless, embarked about 800 strong (having left about a hundred sick behind) at Ramsgate on March 3rd. It was driven into Torbay by bad weather, but eventually anchored off Lisbon on March 27, 1810.

Viscount Wellington, as Sir Arthur Wellesley had now become, had long foreseen that a great French invasion of Portugal, when the Emperor's hands were free, was inevitable. He believed he could defend the country, and in the beginning of 1810 was busy persuading the Home Government to agree to his doing so, and only embarking from Lisbon in the last resort. He was engaged with Beresford in organizing the Portuguese army, in settling the fortresses to be maintained, and above all in designing and preparing the lines of Torres Vedras, from behind which he hoped to be able to preserve inviolate Lisbon and the peninsula on which it stands, between the Atlantic and the Tagus, for a distance of

[1] Fortescue, vol. VII, p. 439 n.

twenty miles north of the capital itself. He never hoped to prevent the enemy from entering a country which he described as "all frontier"; but he hoped by retiring on his lines, if the invasion came from the north, to exhaust his enemy before turning on him and driving him back whence he came. Many months were still to elapse before the actual invasion; but for the present there was no saying when it might come. Wellington's arrangement of forces was made so as to be able to meet it whichever direction it might take. The danger was if it came from north and east simultaneously.

The 1/9th was, on its arrival in Portugal, stationed in the barracks of Campo do Ourique, in the north-west part of Lisbon, till June 10th, when it moved to Thomar, near the right bank of the Tagus and the Zezere. It formed part of the 5th division commanded by Lieutenant-General Leith, and was brigaded with the 3/1st and 2/38th in the British brigade commanded by Lieutenant-Colonel Barnes. It was itself commanded by Lieutenant-Colonel Cameron, who had been transferred from the 2nd battalion in July, 1809. His name will always be remembered in the regiment as that of the gallant commander who in the next few years led the 1st battalion from Lisbon to Bayonne. The rest of the division consisted of Spry's, Eben's, and Douglas's Portuguese.

Massena's advance from Ciudad Rodrigo and Almeida only commenced on September 15, 1810. He had about 65,000 men, almost all of them French regulars. It was not till the 17th that it was quite clear that he was moving by the north side of the Serra da Estrella, aiming at Coimbra by Viseu.

Wellington's orders for the 5th division required it to march to Espinhal, where it arrived on the 19th. Thence it was moved forward to Foz d'Aronce. It was followed by Hill's (2nd) division from beyond the Zezere, which reached Espinhal on the 20th. On that day Wellington ordered the whole of his army, except Hill's division, into positions whence they were within easy reach of the ridge of Busaco. The fourth division (Cole) was moved to the convent of Busaco, its place being taken by Picton's (3rd), and the latter being replaced by Leith's (5th). Though Hill was a day late, the French attack on Wellington's position was delayed long enough to enable him to come up. Wellington also had some anxiety lest his left should be turned by a road which would cut him from Coimbra. The difficulties of Massena's advance had been greatly enhanced by the systematic denudation of the whole country, in which he was now dependent for supplies on what he could carry with him.

On the evening of the 22nd Leith's, Cole's, and Picton's divisions were on the Busaco ridge. There was an advanced guard at Mortagoa, whilst Spencer was away to the left rear at Mealhada, and Hill was still on the left bank of the Mondego opposite Penacova. The position was still the same on the 23rd. That afternoon the light division retired from Mortagoa before the advance of Reynier's French, who, however, halted at Mortagoa. The light division still did not retire beyond the foot of the ridge. On the 25th Craufurd, always impetuous, nearly got into trouble by moving with the light division into the plain, where he found himself opposed to the whole of Reynier's corps.

That night the French advanced guard lay at the foot of the great ridge below the convent of Busaco. The British were not over-supplied with food, and Hale says his mess bought a small sheep of thirty pounds weight, on which they feasted, for 4s. 6d. Seeing their captain hanging about, and evidently envying them, they sent him a joint which he "accepted with a smile."

The ridge of Busaco runs a little west of north from the Mondego at Penacova for eight or nine miles. Mr. Fortescue likens it to Dunkery Hill on Exmoor in general appearance, though it differs in being solid and devoid of bogs, and in the ravines searing its eastern face being less deep, less steep, and broader, though the boulders encumbering them made the movement of troops in them slow and difficult. Its highest part is the southern end near the Mondego. Of the valley between the Busaco ridge and the next eastwards Napier says it is "a chasm so profound that the naked eye could hardly distinguish the troops in the bottom, yet in parts so narrow that twelve-pounders could range to the salient points on the opposite side." The convent and its park, towards the northern end, were on the main road to Coimbra, whilst two other roads south of it crossed the ridge, one through the position held by the 5th division and one through Picton's area. There were two more rough tracks towards the southern end. Any attack in such a country was likely to follow the roads. The position was too long for Wellington's strength (about 52,000 men), but he had excellent lateral communication by a road, rather below the top of the ridge on his side, which enabled him to meet an attack wherever it came. On the extreme right of the British line was Hill's division, with five companies of the Lusitanian Legion in advance at Nossa Senhora do Monte, a projecting hill below his right. On Hill's left was Leith's division, with its three British and two Portuguese battalions on its right wing, across the southernmost of the three roads to Coimbra. Leith's left—five Portuguese battalions—was separated from his right by an interval of two miles. Picton's division, commanding the central road over the San Antonio Pass was on Leith's left, and beyond Picton came Spencer's division, Pack's Portuguese, the light division, Campbell's Portuguese, and Cole's division on the extreme left. The troops were kept a little behind the ridge, so as to be invisible by the enemy on lower ground.

Ney wanted to attack in the morning, but Massena only reached the front at 2 p.m., and then issued orders for an attack next day, the 27th.

Reynier was to attack, with his 15,000 infantry, the ridge a mile south of the convent, whilst Ney, with another 22,000, would be ready to attack, by the main Coimbra road and Sula, as soon as he saw that Reynier had reached the ridge on his left—the eighth corps (Junot), with 16,000 infantry, to remain in reserve at Moura. No artillery position within range of the British position could be found, and Massena was clearly under the impression that there were no troops beyond the point where Picton's right stood. When Reynier's advance, in echelon from his right, began about 5.30 a.m. on the 27th, the upper part of the ridge was still covered with mist, and Reynier's divisions, taking the ascent at an angle, gradually edged to their right, so that they really moved against Spencer's division standing on the higher point of the ridge. We need give no full account of the defeat of Merle's division of Reynier's corps, which was sent down the hill in disorder before the 1/9th came on the scene.

As Merle's beaten battalions descended the hill, Foy, on their left, was on his way up, just north of the central road crossing the ridge by the pass of San Antonio de Cantara. He hoped with his brigade to support the French 31st. Merle's men were making the best of their way down the hill, hotly pursued by the victorious British, who only stopped when they came under the fire of Reynier's guns. Then Foy stopped his men to steady them against the evil influence of the panic. Goaded by Reynier's taunts, he started again up the hill with his 17th leading, followed on the left by the 70th. Instead of going, as intended, for the San Antonio Pass, his men, like their predecessors, inclined to the right, and, in so doing, came under the fire of Wellington's guns at the top of that pass.

Meanwhile Leith had received orders to move leftwards to the support of Picton, always provided his own front were not threatened, as it appeared not to be. What happened is best told in the words of Leith's own report submitted to Wellington [1]:

" At daybreak Major General Leith's corps formed itself posted as follows : the British brigade under Lieutenant-Colonel Barnes, consisting of the 3rd battalion Royals, 1st battalion 9th, and 2nd battalion 38th Regiments, were behind the ridge where the high roads from Gondolem and Carvalhos meet and cross the Serra do Busaco as one. At this point, and commanding the passage of the Serra, were placed four guns of the six-pounder brigade of Portuguese artillery. In pursuance of directions received from Lord Wellington on the 26th, Brigadier-General Spry had moved from this point with his Portuguese brigade, consisting of the 3rd Regiment (two battalions), the 15th (two battalions), and the Thomar Militia ; the 8th Portuguese regiment were also attached to him. They moved by their left till the leading regiment (the 8th) had nearly formed a junction with the right of Major-General Picton's division, posted to command near the high road leading across the Serra from St. Antonio de Cantara. The two battalions of the Lusitanian Legion, under Colonel Baron Eben, were posted about half-distance between the British brigade and Brigadier-General Spry. Two six-pounders and 300 of the Lusitanian Legion, under Major Fearon, were posted

[1] Supplementary Despatches, vol. 6, p. 636.

in the redoubt of the chapel of N.S. de Monte Alto, on the right of the whole line.

"The firing, which commenced towards the centre and left soon after daybreak, seemed to indicate a serious attack before 6 a.m.; that nearest on the left appeared principally directed against the position of St. Antonio de Cantara, occupied by the 3rd division. Lord Wellington had generally directed, on taking up the position that the divisions should, in case of necessity, mutually support each other; finding that there was no attack on his right or front Major-General Leith immediately put the brigades of his corps in motion by their left, the six-pounder Portuguese artillery moving with the British brigade. During this movement, Major-General Leith received a pencil note from Lord Wellington, which he communicated to Lieutenant-General Hill, directing that he should move to his left to support Major-General Picton, unless Lieutenant-General Hill's position on his right, or his own front, were attacked; to which the Major-General replied that no attack was made or threatened, and that his corps had already been put in motion by its left for that purpose. Major-General Leith rode on to ascertain the nature of the attack, and arrived at the commanding part of the Serra, where some Portuguese guns were posted on Major-General Picton's right, and were firing on the road which passes over the Serra from St. Antonio de Cantara, near which the enemy were endeavouring to ascend. The ammunition of these guns being expended, and it being of much importance to have artillery at that point, Major-General Leith immediately ordered the six-pounder brigade of his corps to be placed there as soon as possible, which was accordingly done. Brigadier-General Spry's brigade and one battalion of the 8th Portuguese Regiment under Lieutenant-Colonel Douglas were in line in front of the rocky ridge near those guns, on both of which the enemy kept up a heavy cannonade, and succeeded in dismounting two of the guns and wounding some officers and men. The 9th Portuguese Regiment under the command of Lieutenant-Colonel Sutton (belonging to Major-General Picton's division) was also in line there. The enemy, who was sometimes driven back and sometimes driving our troops, had, in conformity to his usual custom, a succession of columns to support the attack on Major-General Picton's position, and now appeared evidently to gain ground on the face of the Serra to the left of the road of St. Antonio de Cantara; Major-General Leith accordingly directed a movement of succession, ordering Lieutenant-Colonel Douglas, with the right battalion 8th Portuguese Regiment, to move by his left to support the point attacked; he also ordered the 9th Portuguese Regiment under Lieutenant-Colonel Sutton (belonging to Major-General Picton's division) to move to the support of Major-General Picton's position; and Brigadier-General Spry's brigade was also ordered to move to its left, partly as a reserve and to support the Portuguese artillery, under Major Arentschild, near the road of St. Antonio de Cantara. The enemy, during this movement, disengaged part of his leading column, and branched into two, the first continuing to its right, the head of the second pointing towards its left, and threatening the position on the right of the road from St. Antonio de Cantara, which caused Brigadier-General Spry's brigade to be formed; this column, however, when the first column had succeeded, turned towards its right also, and followed the other, which was gaining the ascent of the Serra; the enemy was still advancing, and had every appearance of succeeding in forcing that part of Major-General Picton's position which is on the left of the road of St. Antonio de Cantara, where several rocky eminences crown the ridge of the Serra. Major-General Leith, who had directed the British brigade and Lusitanian Legion to move by the road of communication in rear of and nearly parallel to the ridge of the Serra, till it should appear where their support might be most necessary, now ordered the Lusitanian Legion to remain in column behind that part of the ridge which concealed its movements and those of the British brigade from the view of the enemy, with its head resting so as to be ready to support, near the road, the Portuguese artillery under Major Arentschild, and the 8th and 9th Portuguese Regiments, which he had ordered (as before stated) to support the point attacked and where the enemy were fast gaining ground, while Major-General Leith led the British brigade by the shortest line to where it was evident their support was become essentially necessary. The ground where the British brigade was now moving behind a chain of rocky eminences, where it had appeared clearly the enemy was pushing to establish himself, precluded Major-General Leith from seeing at that moment the progress the enemy was making; but by the information of staff officers, stationed on purpose, who communicated his direction and progress, Major-General Leith moved the British brigade so as to endeavour to meet and check the enemy when he had gained the ascendancy. At this time a heavy fire of musketry was kept up on the height, the smoke of which prevented a clear view of the state of things; when, however, the rock forming the high part of the Serra, where Major-General Picton's division was originally, became visible, the enemy appeared in full possession of it, and a French officer was in the act of cheering, with his hat off, while a continued firing was kept up from thence and along the whole face of the slope of the Serra in a diagonal direction towards the bottom by the enemy (ascending rapidly from the successive columns formed for the attack) on a mass of soldiers of the left battalion of the 8th and 9th Portuguese Regiments, who, having been severely pressed, had given way, and were rapidly retiring in complete confusion and disorder. Major-General Leith, on that occasion, spoke to Major Birmingham (who was on foot, having had his horse killed), who stated that the fugitives were of the 9th[1] as well as of the 8th[1] Regiment, and that he had ineffectually tried to check their retreat. Major-General Leith addressed and succeeded in stopping them, and they cheered, when he ordered them to be collected and formed in the rear; they were passing, as they retired, diagonally to the right of the 9th British Regiment. The face of affairs in this quarter now wore a different aspect, for the enemy, who had been the assailant, having dispersed or driven everything there opposed to him, was in possession of the rocky eminence of the Serra at this part of Major-General Picton's position without a shot being then fired at him. Not a moment was to be lost; Major General Leith

[1] Portuguese.

accordingly resolved instantly to attack the enemy with the bayonet; he therefore ordered the 9th British Regiment, which had hitherto been moving rapidly by its left in column (in order to gain the most advantageous ground for checking the enemy), to form the line, which they did with the greatest promptitude, accuracy, and coolness, under the fire of the enemy, who had just appeared formed on that part of the rocky eminence which overlooks the back of the ridge, and who had then, for the first time, also perceived the British brigade under him. Major-General Leith had intended that the

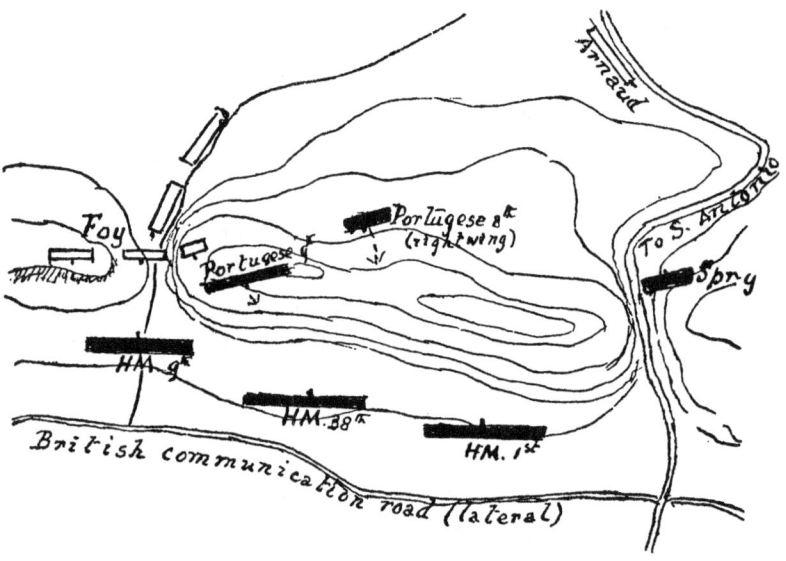

BUSACO—MOVEMENT OF 9TH FOOT

38th Regiment should have moved on in rear and to the left of the 9th Regiment, to have turned the enemy beyond the rocky eminence, which was quite inaccessible towards the rear of the Serra, while the 9th should have gained the ridge on the right of the rocky height—the Royals to have been posted, as they were, in reserve; but the enemy, having driven everything before him in that quarter, afforded him the advantage of gaining the top of the rocky ridge, which is accessible in front, before it was possible for the British brigade to reach that position, although not a moment had been lost in marching to support the point attacked, and for that purpose it had made a rapid movement of more than two miles without halting, (and frequently in double time); the 38th Regiment were therefore directed to form also and support, when Major-General Leith had the honour, to lead the 9th Regiment to attack the enemy on the rocky ridge which they did without firing a shot. That part which looks behind the Serra (as already stated) was inaccessible, and afforded the enemy the advantage of outflanking the 9th on the left as they advanced; but the order, celerity, and coolness with which they attacked, panic-struck the enemy, who immediately gave way on being charged with the bayonet, and the whole were driven down the face of the Serra in confusion and with immense loss, from a destructive fire which the 9th Regiment opened on him as he fled with precipitation after the charge. The 38th Regiment advanced with great coolness and spirit under a heavy fire to support the 9th while they were ascending to attack the enemy on the top of the rocky ridge, and after the charge they moved up on the right of the 9th and joined in the destructive pursuit of the enemy till the whole were ordered back, the action having entirely ceased after this, excepting a cannonade. The steadiness and accuracy with which the 9th Regiment altered the direction of march, which, before they were engaged, was continually changing in order to form in the most advantageous manner for the attack of the enemy, the quickness and precision with which they formed line under a heavy fire, their instantaneous and orderly charge, by which they drove the enemy, so much superior in numbers, from a formidable position, and the promptitude with which they obeyed Major-General Leith's order to cease firing, in his humble opinion was altogether conduct as distinguished as any regiment could have shown, and perhaps not the less worthy of notice that it is well known the attack was made by the flower of Reynier's corps, who had volunteered the service in which the enemy was there ultimately defeated. Lieutenant-Colonel Barnes, commanding the British brigade, with great zeal and gallantry accompanied the 9th Regiment, which was commanded by Lieutenant-Colonel Cameron, who, notwithstanding his being extremely ill, exerted himself with the greatest gallantry in front during the charge, when his horse was killed under him; Lieutenant-Colonel Crauford, who had been on duty during the night with the pickets, by a zealous exertion arrived in time also to distinguish himself in front of his regiment."

At the end of this report Captain Gomm of the 9th is included in the "mentions" of the staff. His account of the action of the 9th, though brief, agrees with that of Leith, except that in describing the attack on the height he says[1]: "Both sides fired" before the 9th charged. Elsewhere he says:

"The 9th are out of humour with the despatches. They will have it that they did not *assist* in driving the enemy from the heights, nor had the 38th and Royals an opportunity of doing as they did; but, according to their own story, they found the French crowning the top of the hill, after having driven whatever had been opposed to them, waving their caps with exultation and increasing in number every instant; they climbed up at them and hurried them down the hill one over the other, while the alarm was spreading to the right and left that the French had succeeded in breaking through our line. This, you see, was a good moment to arrive, but I can promise you that, if we had arrived a little later, our praises would have sounded louder, and what was really the work of ten minutes might in that case have been the labour of half as many hours, or it might not have been done at all. This is the way the 9th tell the story, and I promise you it is a true one."

Hale's account of Busaco says that the 9th were ordered to proceed to the top of the heights about a mile to their left, and when they came up they found the enemy on the top.

---

[1] Mr. Fortescue (vol. VII, p. 520), preferring the accounts of Picton and Douglas, thinks that, though it is not mentioned by Leith, the attack of the 9th was aided by Douglas's battalion of the 8th Portuguese and Meade's five companies of the 45th firing on the left flank of the French lower down. In any case this does not detract from the merit of the 9th in storming the rocky height. Cameron always vigorously maintained, in correspondence quoted in Colonel Chambers's "Bussaco" that the 9th had no assistance from the Portuguese or anyone else in their attack.

THE IXth AT BATALHA ON THE WAY TO ROLIÇA, August, 1808.
Batalha is the Battle Abbey of Portugal.

"We were then ordered to load, but not to fire a shot till ordered. So we continued moving on in open column of companies, until we got within one hundred yards of them, when we were ordered to wheel into line and give them a volley, which we immediately did, and saluted them with three cheers and a charge, taking the signal from General Leith who commanded our brigade [*sic*]; he made the signal by taking off his hat and twirling it over his head. The enemy stood their ground till we got within twenty yards of them, but seeing that it was our intention to use the bayonet, they took to their heels and made off as well as they could. We continued to fire, advancing down the hill as far as it was thought necessary, and being so close to their heels there was great slaughter among them. So, the enemy being got near the bottom of the hill and having a brigade of guns placed on a little hill just on the other side of the valley, cannon shot and shells began to fly among us very sharply; in consequence of that the brigade was obliged to retreat to the top of the hill, leaving the light companies extended along about the middle of the hill, with an order to lie down behind anything that would cover them, but not two to be together."

The story of the defeat of Ney's attack near the convent is perhaps better known than any other part of the battle and need not be repeated.

The battle of Busaco cost Massena a loss in killed, wounded, and prisoners of nearly 4,500. On the British side the losses of British and Portuguese were exactly equal, in all only 1,252. The losses of the 9th were five men killed, one officer (Lieutenant Lindsay) and eighteen men wounded—a very light loss considering the very large share they took in the repulse of Foy's brigade (seven battalions), which alone lost 670. Colonel Cameron, who had risen from a sick bed in order to command in the battle, had a horse killed under him and was hurt by the fall. Foy himself was wounded in the arm by a bullet fired by the 9th.

Sir C. Oman's note on the crises at Busaco[1] considers Leith's account correct. That account goes to show that Picton's division was in a very critical position when it was pulled out of the fire by the intervention of

---

[1] "Peninsular War," vol. III, p. 388.

Leith, and especially of the 9th Regiment headed by him. Picton attempted to contest this view, and would allow but small credit to Leith. "Picton," says Sir C. Oman, "cannot be acquitted of deliberate belittling of the part taken by his colleague in the action." The night after the battle the 9th camped on the scene of their fight and Hale says: "There the dead lay so thick that we could not make it convenient to lie down in any comfort; therefore we set to work and drew them a little distance away; thirty-two were on that bit of ground that our company was to lie down on."

Wellington's hopes of stopping Massena for good at Busaco vanished on the 28th, when he was certain that the French cavalry had discovered and seized the road to Sandao, which he blamed the Portuguese for failing to defend in time. As by this road Massena could turn his left, he ordered the retreat to commence that night on Coimbra, camp-fires being kept up on the ridge by the light division and cavalry, in order to deceive the French. The latter had not completely quitted their position till the 29th, on which day Wellington's army was all gone, except the cavalry watching the French move off. Hill had been sent by Thomar, whilst Wellington with the bulk of the army, including the 5th division, passed the Mondego at Coimbra and west of it. Hale says the enemy were so close up at Coimbra that they entered on one side as the 9th were leaving on the other. Intent on preserving the capital, and confident in the impregnability of the lines he had prepared with such care, Wellington was now retreating on Torres Vedras. His whole army had left Coimbra by September 30th. Next day the French arrived and lost two days in sacking the town. Wellington was back unmolested at Leiria on October 4th. There was a cavalry skirmish on the 5th with his rear-guard, and there were other small affairs which we need not describe as the 9th were not engaged in them. The great lines were safely reached and Leith's division found itself posted on the heights of Monte Agraça behind Sobral, between the Lisbon-Coimbra road and the eastern end of the lines on the Tagus. In front of Leith was Pack, and on his right Craufurd.

For the defence of the lines of Torres Vedras, Wellington had by November 1, 1810, 34,000 British troops, 24,600 Portuguese, and

8,000 Spanish—in all about 66,000 effective regular troops, besides Portuguese militia, etc. His numbers were now superior to Massena's.

Wellington had the 3rd division at Torres Vedras, and the rest of his 66,000 regular troops were in two masses, behind Sobral on the left and Alhandra on the right, within half a day's march of one another, available for employment in mass at any point. The forts of the double line of defensive works were held by the best of the secondary troops.

On October 12th there was a skirmish at Sobral with Junot's advanced guard, which resulted in the British retirement from that village, which was outside the lines. The 9th were not engaged in this affair. There was further skirmishing on the 13th and 14th near Sobral, but, as Wellington had now in line there some 30,000 men against Junot's 12,000, no serious attack was made. The 5th division, being in reserve, was not called upon to take part in these affairs.

Massena, by no means relishing the idea of a second Busaco by attacking vastly superior numbers in an even stronger position, began to settle down in front of the lines and to fortify his own front. For a whole month he held on obstinately, though he was in great difficulties, for the country had been almost entirely cleared of supplies by Wellington, and even that prince of marauders, the French soldier of Napoleon's day, could extract very little from the empty villages. Coimbra had been retaken, behind Massena, by Trant.

By November 14th Massena was at last obliged to retreat, in the hope of finding better subsistence in the plains about Santarem. That night, as the retreat commenced, it was concealed from the British by a fog, and it was not till well on in the morning of the 15th that the disappearance of the French was made clear by the lifting of the fog.

Wellington followed cautiously, being very uncertain as to whether Massena was retreating to Spain by the northern route or by Abrantes, or meant to stop at Santarem. Finding the French in force at Santarem he eventually decided to go into winter quarters, leaving a corps of observation in front of Massena.

During the advance the 5th division had no fighting. The following extracts from Captain Gomm's correspondence give the history of its movements, and those of the 9th :

"*Before Santarem*, November 21, 1810.—The French left their position in front of our lines, I think, the day after I wrote my last letter to you, in full retreat upon Santarem. Lord Wellington put the army in motion immediately, and the 5th division arrived at Cartaxo yesterday, two leagues from Santarem. An attack has been meditated upon the French position by the light troops, 1st and 5th divisions of the army. It was intended to have taken place yesterday, but the heavy rains which began to fall at daybreak, and continued almost without interval during the whole course of it, rendered the rivers necessary to be crossed, fordable in general, impassable for the time; and the attack has been, at least, suspended."

"*Torres Vedras, December* 28, 1810.—We played Bo-peep with the French at Santarem for a day or two after I wrote to you from Cartaxo, and the 5th division were then moved to Alcoentre and the neighbourhood. Here, I am sorry to say, we have had leisure to become very sickly, so much so that it has been found necessary to remove us to this place, and to occupy our post in the line with the 4th division. We have been here very few days; but the change is so much for the better in point of quarters that I have great hopes we shall soon experience all the good effects our move was intended to produce."

He mentions that Leith had gone to England ill.

Hale says—"The enemy never made an attack on our brigade during the time we remained at that place [Torres Vedras]." He mentions an earthquake there, which alarmed the soldiers, but which the inhabitants took very quietly, this being by no means the first.

Nothing of importance happened during the winter till Massena, having held out at Santarem as long as he could subsist his army there, began his retreat from Portugal on March 1, 1811.

The Second Battalion

Leaving the 1/9th in their winter quarters for the moment, we must bring up to date the story of the 2nd battalion, which we left in garrison at Gibraltar on July 3, 1809.

In April, 1810, the light company of the 2/9th was sent, with those of the 30th and 47th, a battalion company of the 28th, and a detachment of thirty artillerymen, from Gibraltar to Tarifa, the fort at which place was threatened by the French. The Spanish Governor had appealed for help. They crossed Gibraltar Bay to Algeçiras by ship, and marched thence to Tarifa on April 14th. On the 21st the place was attacked by about 500 French troops, who surrounded it and fired heavily on it all that day from a large convent which they had occupied within thirty yards of the gate. About 4 p.m. a party of volunteers under Stovin, the adjutant of the 28th, drove the enemy with the bayonet from this convent, whereupon the French gave up the enterprise and retreated. The light companies remained at Tarifa till September 15th, when, on relief by the 28th, they returned to Gibraltar.

From February 23, 1809, there was established in England a recruiting company of one captain, two lieutenants, one ensign, eight sergeants, eight corporals, and four drummers.

On June 22nd the battalion, less its light company, still at Tarifa, embarked with a detachment of the Royal Naval Battalion, under the command of Major-General Bowes, for Malaga. Finding the enemy there in too great strength, the expedition returned, without landing, to Gibraltar on July 2nd. On September 24th the battalion was rejoined by the light company from Tarifa. At the beginning of February, 1811, orders were received to complete the flank companies to eighty men each. They were destined to go on an expedition now to be described.

At the close of 1810 the French were still blockading Cadiz; but on December 22nd news was received of the weakening of the blockading force, and it was determined to carry out a diversion on the enemy's rear with a force from Cadiz, which could easily be sent, owing to the British command of the sea and the strength of Cadiz as a fortress in those days. This force was under the command of Lieutenant-General Thomas Graham. That patriotic officer was willing to use the greater part of his British troops in Cadiz, and moreover to serve as 2nd in command, under the Spanish General La Peña.

The British troops sailed on February 21st, intending to land at Tarifa, but a westerly gale drove them past it into Gibraltar Bay, on the west side of which they landed at Algeciras on February 23rd, but without the artillery, which could not be disembarked owing to the continuance of the gale. Nevertheless, Graham marched to Tarifa on the 24th, where he found reinforcements, sent by the Governor of Gibraltar, consisting of the 1/28th (less its flank companies) and what was known as "Browne's Battalion," consisting of two flank companies each from the 2/9th, 1/28th, and 2/82nd, numbering 475 rank and file.

With these reinforcements and his artillery, which was landed on the 25th, Graham commanded a British force of about 5,100 of all ranks with twelve guns, but only two squadrons of the 2nd Hussars of the King's German Legion.

He organized his infantry in the brigades of Dilkes and Wheatley and the two flank company battalions of Barnard and Browne, the latter containing the flank companies of the 2/9th. Lieutenant-Colonel Browne belonged to the 28th.

La Peña with 7,000 Spanish troops joined Graham on the 27th. The Spanish general mismanaged his marches on Cadiz, thereby inflicting much hardship and fatigue on his men, both British and Spanish.

Early on the morning of March 5th the allied troops were approaching the south of Cadiz by the strip of land between the sea and the Almansa creek. This strip gradually diminishes in breadth as it approaches Cadiz. Across it was drawn up Vilatte's division, whilst Ruffin and Leval were posted at Chiclana so as to be able to fall on the right flank of a force moving on Cadiz. La Peña, who was ignorant of the position of these two divisions, decided to attack with his troops already exhausted by a night march.

Vilatte, attacked in front, and also threatened by an attack in rear from Cadiz, succeeded in slipping away across the Almansa creek.

Graham, meanwhile, had taken up his position, under La Peña's orders, on the hill of Barrosa, on the coast at the broadest part of the strip of land.

Having driven the French from Bermeja, La Peña wanted to do no more, and was with difficulty persuaded by Graham to maintain the hill of Barrosa with a garrison consisting of Browne's Battalion (including the flank companies of the 2/9th) and five Spanish battalions. Graham had already sent out patrols towards Chiclana, but they had, so far, reported no enemy. He therefore, as required by La Peña, began to move through the thick woods north-westwards. Half an hour later Graham's patrols reported French troops marching from the Chiclana direction.

Victor, seeing no British troops on Barrosa Hill (for Browne's men were on the seaward slope), resolved to seize it, thus penning in towards the Santi Petri River all who had passed north to Bermeja.

When the approach of the French was announced most of the troops on the hill were resting after their fatigues of the night before. La Peña himself was there, and, as usual, lost his head and ordered an immediate retreat on Cadiz, which he had so recently left by sea. The hill was presently abandoned by all, including Browne's Battalion, which followed Graham north-westwards. As they retired they were seen by Ruffin, now on the top of Barrosa Hill, who sent a squadron after them. Browne promptly formed square, but before the French squadron reached the battalion they were charged by a German squadron and dispersed.

Graham, aware that the French were marching on Barrosa Hill, promptly decided to return to the assistance of La Peña, whom he believed to be still there. Riding back, he met Browne's Battalion just entering the woods and learnt that the hill was lost. Realizing the danger of being crowded up with the Spaniards at the narrow end of the peninsula between the sea and the Almansa creek, and that, even if they all got safely into Cadiz, the whole operation would have ended in nothing, he decided to attack at once, despite the fatigue of his men.

Browne's Battalion was, of course, now the nearest to Barrosa Hill, and was sent alone against it in line.

Ruffin was forming his division on the hill, on the top of which he had eight guns. As Browne's men re-formed after passing the ravine at the foot of the hill they were met by such a storm of musketry and grape that they lost half their officers and 200 out of their 470 men. With admirable coolness they closed on their centre, and as they did so another storm of fire put *hors de combat* more officers and another fifty men. Having suffered a loss of more than half their numbers, it is hardly to be wondered at that Browne was unable to get them to form again, or that they would do no more than continue firing vigorously from the shelter of the ravine. All the same they were by no means knocked out ; for, as the Guards passed to the attack of the hill Browne's men formed on their left and were able to have some revenge by firing into the left flank of the French 96th as it moved, by Victor's orders, towards his right. Beyond this point it is hardly necessary to follow the course of the battle in detail—to describe how Ruffin was driven from Barrosa Hill, Leval on his right was defeated, and both divisions compelled to retreat again towards Chiclana. Browne's Battalion is said, at a later stage of the battle, to have sent out skirmishers, who were, however, withdrawn. The battalion had already suffered heavily enough in all conscience, and it is only wonderful how pluckily they held together to the last. With regard to Graham's use of Browne's Battalion against Barrosa, according to Blakeney's account, Graham had actually ordered Browne to advance in skirmishing order, but changed his mind, saying he " must show something more serious than mere skirmishing." This bloody battle might have been a decisive victory, but for the incapacity and slackness of La Peña in affording no support to the British with his Spanish troops.

The total loss on the British side was 1,238 (out of 5,000) killed and wounded, of whom no less than 236 were the share of Browne's 536 present of all ranks. The flank companies of the 2/9th numbered 160, besides officers, and their losses on this day were, one drummer and ten men killed ; Captain Godwin, Lieutenants Seward, A. Taylor, Robinson, five sergeants, one drummer and seventy men wounded. Lieutenant Colin Campbell found himself, as the only unwounded officer, left in command of the two flank companies of the 2/9th.[1]

The French loss, out of 7,000 present, was 2,062 killed, wounded, and prisoners.

On March 6th both British and Spanish were back again in Cadiz. Victor, after practically raising the siege, was able again to renew it.

---

[1] In " Military Extracts " (vol. VI, col. 390) it is mentioned that the Jews of Gibraltar subscribed 738 Spanish dollars for the widows and orphans of those killed at Barossa.

On March 8th the flank companies embarked for Tarifa, landed there on the 11th, and on April 2nd rejoined the battalion at Gibraltar.

On June 20, 1811, the battalion sailed from Gibraltar, with the 47th and a detachment of artillery, under the command of Colonel Skerrett of the 47th. Their mission was to try and relieve Tarragona, then besieged by the French. Arriving there on the 26th, they found the fortress had surrendered two days before. They therefore sailed again for Port Mahon in Minorca, and thence back to Gibraltar, which was reached on July 26th.

Here it will be convenient to wind up the history of the 2nd battalion during its second period of embodiment. It remained at Gibraltar doing garrison duty, and not otherwise employed, but generally having a detachment at Tarifa of about 200 officers and men till April, 1812, when it was withdrawn on relief by the 87th. In April, 1812, one company from each regiment at Gibraltar, including the 2/9th, went over to Ceuta to protect the Spanish sick and wounded there against the Moors. After remaining in garrison there till the end of June they returned to Gibraltar on relief by a detachment of the 37th. In the beginning of 1813 the 2nd battalion was sent home after it had contributed a large draft of over 400 men to fill up the ranks of the 1st battalion. It was at Canterbury in April, 1813, whence it contributed another 141 men and six officers to the 1st battalion.

In 1814 it was at Chatham, Sheerness, and the Isle of Sheppey till it was disbanded, after the final fall of Napoleon, on December 24, 1815. It remained in abeyance till its final revival in 1857.

CHAPTER XIV

THE 1st BATTALION IN THE PENINSULA—FUENTES DE OÑORO—BADAJOZ—SALAMANCA. 1810-1812

WE parted with the 1st battalion spending the winter of 1810–11 at Alcoentre and Torres Vedras. Hale states that in the beginning of January, 1811, the brigade was sent to Sobral fort. The enemy were in possession of the town two miles off, and there was occasional firing between the piquets. There they were joined by 150 men, some of them from the 2nd battalion, and some men who had been left behind in England. Wellington was determined not to risk an attack on Massena's strong position. He preferred to wait till starvation had compelled his opponent to fall back. But the Portuguese, perhaps it was not to be wondered at, had not cleared the country of provisions so completely as he would have desired, and there were many hidden and buried stores which the peasants had believed to be undiscoverable. But the French soldier of those days was a forager of unlimited ingenuity, and quite devoid of scruples. Thus, though Massena at the beginning of December had only 45,000 effective men, with 8,000 or 9,000 more in hospital, he managed to hold on where he was all through the winter.

At last, in the beginning of March, he made up his mind that he could hold on no longer. He had received some reinforcements during the winter, but nothing to justify a resumption of the offensive.

On the 4th March the retreat began in the direction of Coimbra, but it was only on the morning of the 6th that Wellington occupied Santarem after its evacuation, and was finally convinced that Massena was retreating on Coimbra and did not mean fighting.

We may pass rapidly over the early days of the pursuit, for the 5th division, now commanded by Hay, in Leith's absence sick, was far behind, and was not called upon to do any fighting.

It was only late on March 11th that it was reported to be close up to the front. Writing from " One league in front of Miranda do Corvo " on March 16th, Gomm says : " The 5th division has not been engaged, neither have several others " ; and it was the same again on the 24th at Venda do Valle, just beyond the Alva River, and at Misarelhu, one league short of Guarda, from which the French had been driven by March 31st. Nave de Haver was reached on April 8th. At Sabugal, on the 3rd, the 5th division had been held ready to assist, but had not been called up to the fighting line.[1] In his letter from Nave de Haver, Gomm mentions the arrival of Leith from England in Portugal, at which he expresses his special pleasure, " as I dislike the person I am with [Erskine apparently] exceedingly."

At Aldea do Bispo,[2] just over the Spanish frontier, on the 11th April, he mentions that all the French are reported to have gone to Salamanca. All through his letters he dwells on the atrocities committed everywhere by the retreating French. As for Massena, whilst expressing his reprobation of the Marshal's character as a man, he renders full justice to the military abilities of this " able, wily, profligate soldier." Hale also speaks of the French atrocities and plunder, and the British shortness of provisions. At one place he describes how they found some Indian corn and oil which had escaped the French. " Being very hungry," he writes, " and having some of the Indian corn, we set to work with our camp kettle lids (which we in general used for frying pans) and fried some of it with the oil. It was something like eating parched peas ; but, however, most of us made a hearty meal, for hunger is very bad." At the same time he writes : " Every day, as soon as our butchers arrived with the bullocks, the men would flock round them with their mess kettles, like a swarm of bees in comparison, and the moment a bullock was stuck there was such pushing and thronging to

[1] The " Regimental Record," however, speaks of the enemy " whom the Battalion charged over the bridge and through the town of Sabugal."
[2] Aldea del Obispo.

catch the blood, almost as if it was good wine, and frequently some dispute would take place in the scuffle."

Wellington had started the pursuit with about 45,000 men—a strength almost exactly equal to Massena's; but when he had detached Beresford against Soult, with two British divisions and one Portuguese, besides cavalry and artillery, Wellington's own force was reduced to about 30,000, whilst Massena's, thanks to reinforcements compensating for his losses, was still about 44,000. Wellington had himself gone to look after affairs in the Alemtejo when Gomm wrote, on April 19th, still from Aldea do Bispo. The French in Almeida were still invested, for Wellington had no heavy artillery with him.

The commander-in-chief was back again with his own army at Alameda on April 28th.

Massena, meanwhile, beyond the Agueda, had been reinforced, though by no means to the extent he had demanded. He now had at his command rather over 47,000 men, of whom 4,500 were cavalry, useless in the mountains of Portugal, but very much the reverse in the plains. Feeling himself strong enough, he again began to advance, crossing the Agueda on May 2nd, at Ciudad Rodrigo, whence his right column moved on Marialva and his left on Espeja, the British advanced guard falling back before him from Gallegos.

Wellington now had, to oppose Massena's 47,000 or more,

	British.	Portuguese, etc.	Total.
Infantry	23,000	11,000	34,000
Cavalry	1,800	50	1,850
Guns	24	24	48

In guns only was he slightly superior to Massena, who had only thirty-eight.

The position which Wellington had chosen for a defensive battle was just on the Spanish frontier, north of Nave de Haver, in the space between two streams running northward—the Turones on the Portuguese side, and the Dos Casas on the Spanish side of the frontier. He faced due east on the slope of the watershed between the two streams, facing the Dos Casas. This stream passes along the east side of the village of Fuentes de Oñoro. As it flows northwards, the stream furrows deeper and deeper into the face of the country for the next eight miles, having been, above Fuentes de Oñoro, hitherto an inconsiderable obstacle, except where it passed through swamps. The village, with its walls and hedges, and its church on higher ground than the rest, was a strong defensive post.

On May 3rd Wellington had his right beyond Fuentes de Oñoro on the slope, with Spencer's and Picton's divisions in first line, and Houston's and Craufurd's in second. His left was separated by a considerable interval from his right, for the position was much stronger naturally at the northern end, and if it was to be turned it would be so by its right, through the flat country about Nave de Haver. Accordingly, Campbell with the 6th division was posted across the road crossing the frontier west of Alameda, whilst the 5th division (under Erskine) was about two miles north of it. Wellington's intended line of retreat, if he were worsted, was towards his right; but if that were turned he might be compelled to cross the Coa by Castello Bom only.

Outside his main line he had a small Spanish detachment in Nave de Haver, and the village of Fuentes de Oñoro, in front of his right wing, was strongly occupied by twenty-eight light companies from Spencer's and Picton's divisions, with the 83rd in support—about 2,000 men in all.

On the French side Reynier's corps was moving westwards against the 5th division, and the space between it and the 6th, Solignac, south of Alameda, was facing the space on the right of the 6th division, whilst Loison (now in command of the 6th corps, *vice* Ney sent home) was to attack Fuentes de Oñoro, with d'Erlon's 9th corps supporting him. The cavalry under Montbrun was on Loison's left.

On the front of the 5th and 6th divisions Reynier began to advance against the very strong position as if to attack. Wellington at once moved Craufurd's division northwards, but withdrew it when it was recognized that the French were only making a feint. Neither the 5th nor the 6th division was engaged or had a single casualty on this day.

The desperate fighting for the possession of Fuentes de Oñoro on the afternoon of May 3rd does not concern us, for it took place nearly five miles from the 5th division and the 1/9th Regiment.

Next day was spent, on Massena's part, in reconnaissances, and in revising his method of attack, after his failure to take Fuentes de Oñoro. He discovered that there was nothing to prevent the turning of Wellington's right by Nave de Haver, except the small Spanish force in that village.

His new plan contemplated a fresh demonstration against Wellington's left by Reynier, who, if he found that wing moving south to support the right, was to follow the 5th and 6th divisions as they did so.

Solignac would move to his right to support Loison, also moving south in the night with Marchand's and Mermet's divisions ready to attack Poco Velho at daybreak, whilst the cavalry on his left would turn Nave de Haver. Ferey's division of Loison's corps, which had borne the brunt of the fighting on the 3rd, would remain facing Fuentes de Oñoro, supported by d'Erlon, with his troops at large intervals, to give the impression that the whole 6th corps was still there.

Wellington also moved his 7th division so as to guard the crossing of the Dos Casas at Poco Velho. Otherwise he made little change. That night Craufurd returned to the command of the light division from England. The battle of the 3rd was resumed early in the morning of May 5th. Again we must resist the temptation to describe the struggle on Wellington's right, the defence and loss of Poco Velho, the great cavalry combats in which the British, vastly outnumbered, covered themselves with glory, or the " artillery charge " of Norman Ramsay's battery. Fuentes de Oñoro was taken by the French after a desperate struggle, which was repeated when they were once more driven from it and it remained for the rest of the day in the hands of the British. When the battle died down into a long range cannonade, Wellington's army stood with its main front facing south on a line extending from just north of Fuentes de Oñoro to the eastern edge of the Coa valley. The bloodstained village was on its left, and the left wing of the army, the 6th and 5th divisions, still stood where they had been on May 3rd, along the ridge farther north and facing east, at right angles to the greater part of the army. Reynier, who alone was opposed to these two divisions on May 5th, had orders to make no serious attack, but merely to detain the two divisions where they were. He therefore confined himself to small skirmishes with the light troops in front, which served his purpose by keeping the 5th and 6th divisions on the alert but stationary. The 6th division had no losses whatever on this day, and those of the 5th were only twenty-one rank and file wounded, of whom four belonged to the 1/9th. The Regimental Record says " the light company was employed for some hours in bush fighting ".

Wellington was determined, if possible, to gather in Almeida, the French garrison of which still held out, and it was for this reason that he eld on between Fuentes de Oñoro and the Coa, which enabled him to cover the siege. He was still busy fortifying his new front on May 6th and 7th, but a few hours after the work was completed Massena, who knew that he had succeeded in conveying orders to Brennier at Almeida to blow up the fortifications and escape, gave orders for retreat at daybreak on the 8th. On the morning of the 10th he had once more passed behind the Agueda at Ciudad Rodrigo and Barba del Puerco.

In the night of the 10th Brennier blew up his works at Almeida and evacuated the fortress, making for Barba del Puerco. To endeavour to intercept him Erskine sent the 1/4th and the light companies of the brigade, including that of the 9th, in which was Hale. Hale's account says that they were despatched in very light order, without their knapsacks. They came up with the enemy at what he calls " Barbadepork " and skirmished for five hours, finally charging with the bayonet " which we did with great vigour ; for having no knapsacks we could outrun the enemy, as they were loaded with the plunder of Almeida." The charge was downhill towards the river, and a number of the French, not knowing the locality, fell over a small cliff. Their sudden disappearance warned the pursuers in time to prevent their also falling over. Stopping at the top of the cliff, they began firing at the French as they passed the river, in which several were drowned. At 7 p.m. there was a truce for collecting the wounded, and after that the three light companies were ordered back to their regiments, now twelve miles off. They reached them, quite worn out by their exertions, at 2 a.m. After this Hale, being ill with fever, was sent to Lisbon and only rejoined the regiment six or seven weeks later.

The 5th division was now destined to some time of repose, whilst the principal scene of the war was transferred to the Alemtejo. Marmont, who had succeeded Massena in command, was gone for Salamanca, but still had to be watched. Wellington sent his 3rd and 7th divisions to support Beresford, whilst the rest of the army remained in the north doing little or nothing. The 1/9th, with the 5th division, was at Sabugal on June 11th, having withdrawn before a threatened advance of the French, after having remained at Nave de Haver till the early part of the month. Gomm writes on that date that the army had " in conformity with the movements of the enemy, extended itself from hence towards Peñamacor, Castel Branco, and the Tagus," and he believed was tending towards Badajoz. He adds that " for some days past I have . . . played cricket till our legs were tired, and chess till our heads were; and, in fact, we have almost forgot the sound of drums." Almost immediately after this they marched for Castel Branco and Villa Velha, and when Gomm next wrote, on June 24th, they had arrived at Arronches, having left Portalegre that morning. There they remained till orders of July 1st sent them back next day to quiet quarters at Portalegre. By July 25th they had been moved from that place, and, after a week's living " under the canopy of birds and beasts," were at the Quinta of Alameira, a league south of it.

A few days later they again turned their faces northwards, and by August 16th were at Payo, the summit of the Pass of Perales over the Sierra de Gata. Their mission was to cover the passes of the Sierra against any attempt of the French from Plasencia and Coria to relieve Ciudad Rodrigo, then besieged by the British. They were still there on September 19th. At this time, the whole strength of the 5th division (temporarily under command of Brigadier-General Dunlop) was scarcely 3,000 of all ranks, the 1/9th accounting for 626 rank and file.

The French, under Marmont and Dorsenne, were now in great force, estimated at 50,000 men, and were preparing to revictual Ciudad Rodrigo by a combined movement. Wellington was not strong enough to prevent this, and temporarily raised the siege. The 5th division was still at Payo on September 26th. Marmont had crossed the Sierra farther east on the previous day, leaving Foy only to watch the Pass of Perales from the south. The 9th was therefore not present at the combat of

El Bodon on the 25th. It was not till the 26th that the division was moved to Wellington's new position at Alfayates, where it took post on the 27th at Aldea Velha on the right, along with the light division. Marmont, who had started his retirement on the 26th after demonstrating, but not fighting, before the British position, countermarched on the 27th, when he found Wellington had retreated on the Alfayates position. His right column, finding the 5th and light division in position at Aldea Velha, stopped without attacking. What fighting there was, was for the village of Aldea da Ponte. The 9th were not involved in this affair, which was far to their left front.

On the 28th Wellington was in a position which he had selected, extending from Rendo to Quadrazaes, at which latter place the 5th division stood on his right with Hay's brigade (including the 1/9th) at Valle d'Espinho. On this strong position Marmont decided against attempting an attack. He had revictualled Ciudad Rodrigo and compelled Wellington to retire, and with this he was content. On October 1st he and Dorsenne separated, the latter for the direction of Salamanca, Marmont himself for Talavera and winter quarters in the valley of the upper Tagus. Wellington also went into winter quarters for the moment, nd it fell to the lot of the 5th division to go to Guarda, well on the Portuguese side of the frontier. Here, on October 10th, Gomm got his promotion to major, and afterwards from D.A.Q.M.G. to A.Q.M.G. of the 5th division. At Guarda the 9th remained all through October and November. On December 7th Gomm, writing from Travinhas, a village somewhat farther west, mentions that the 9th were there with the divisional head-quarters, the rest being in neighbouring villages. His next letter, January 18, 1812, is from Albergueria, where the division had just arrived after five marches from Travinhas. Wellington was now again besieging Ciudad Rodrigo with the 1st, 3rd, 4th, and light divisions.

On December 8th the 5th division moved on to Casillas de Flores and Fuente Guinaldo. Writing of the sound of the guns from Ciudad Rodrigo, twenty miles off, and of the progress of the siege, Gomm says : " The 5th, 6th, and 7th divisions have nothing to say to all this ; they are taking too good care of us." Their turn would have come had there been another attempt by Marmont to raise this second siege of Ciudad Rodrigo; but that marshal heard nothing of it till January 15th, by which time it was too late to intervene, for the fortress was taken by assault on the night of the 19th. The storm was followed by an orgy of plunder and indiscipline, destined only to be surpassed by what occurred at Badajoz and San Sebastian later. The British army was unaccustomed to the capture of large fortresses by storm, and the troops got completely out of hand. In the morning of the 20th, the 5th division marched in, as Gomm says," to mend holes and repair damages." They probably also had to restore order amongst the victorious troops. The army had suffered a heavy loss in the death during the assault of Craufurd, the famous commander of the light division. On the other hand, Leith, recuperated in health, had just rejoined the 5th division. Here, at Ciudad Rodrigo, the 5th division remained, at the unpalatable work of repairing breaches and improving fortifications, till March 9, 1812, when most of the army was on the way to Badajoz, the last of the frontier fortresses requiring to be taken.

The 9th marched by Aurela, Calagas, San Vicente, Castello Branco, Villa Velha (where they crossed the Tagus), Niza, Portalegre, Arronches, Campo Mayor, and Elvas to Olivenza. Thence they marched to within a league of Badajoz, Wellington's[1] siege of which was then (March 26th) well in progress.

That famous fortress, so often besieged, had been invested on March 16th. That night the 3rd and 4th divisions bivouacked on the heights to the south. The 1st, 6th, and 7th divisions had marched that morning for Zafra to cover the siege against the French of Soult and d'Erlon. On the 17th the light division arrived before Badajoz; the 5th was, on arrival, kept in the neighbourhood of Badajoz in reserve, and was only brought up to the front on the evening of April 6th, just before the final assault.[2] It was then posted on the Cerro del Viento, the hill facing the great outwork of Fort Pardaleras.

---

[1] Viscount Wellington had been raised to an earldom for the capture of Ciudad Rodrigo.

[2] Wellington to Earl of Liverpool, April 7, 1812: "Despatches," vol. IX, p. 37, Edition of 1838.

In the "Memorandum for the Attack of Badajoz," paragraph 26, it is noted that an arrangement had been made with Leith to attempt to escalade the San Vicente bastion, the last at the western end of the enceinte on the left bank of the Guadiana, or the curtain between that bastion and the bridge. The piquets of the brigades on the Cerro del Viento were to alarm the enemy by firing at the Pardaleras and the covered way of the neighbouring works. Unfortunately the rôle of the 1/9th was confined to this latter operation, for Leith sent to the escalade of San Vicente only Major-General Walker's brigade, supported by the 2/38th from Hay's brigade.

Under these circumstances it would be useless to repeat the oft-told story of the memorable assault, in which the 9th played only the smallest part. The storm of Badajoz was followed by horrors which have often been described and reprobated far more strongly than they were in Wellington's order of April 7, 1812 :[1] "It is now full time that the plunder of Badajoz should cease ; and the Commander of the Forces requests that an officer and six steady non-commissioned officers may be sent from each regiment, British and Portuguese, of the 3rd, 4th, 5th, and light divisions into the town to-morrow morning at 5 o'clock, in order to bring away any men that may be straggling there." The provost marshal was to execute any plunderers caught red-handed after his arrival. The 9th sent their party on this unpleasant and by no means safe duty. During it, says Hale, "we likewise found a large vault underground nearly full of French brandy, which contained several thousand gallons." The total British and Portuguese loss in the assault was 3,713 killed, wounded, and missing, a number nearly equal to the whole effective strength of the garrison at the time. Of Hay's brigade the 2/38th had forty-two casualties, the 3/1st and 1/9th none at all.

In the meanwhile Marmont had advanced on Ciudad Rodrigo, where he left a division to blockade the fortress, and himself moved south through Sabugal and Peñamacor. Castello Branco was evacuated by the Portuguese on April 12th, but here Marmont had come to the end

[1] "Supplementary Despatches," vol. VII, p. 311. Hour not stated, but Oman puts it late in the day, when the sack had already been going on for fifteen or eighteen hours.

of his tether in the matter of supplies, and found himself compelled to retreat. Wellington, having satisfied himself that he was no longer in danger from Soult in the south, proceeded to march northwards against Marmont.

By April 20th the 5th division was back again at Castello Branco, after a very trying march in heavy rains. The light and 3rd divisions were in front of them. By April 24th, when the division had reached Moimenta da Beira, Wellington, satisfied that Marmont was gone behind the Tormes, halted his army. At Moimenta da Beira the 5th division remained till the advance on Salamanca began. On June 10th the 1/9th were back again at Fuentes de Oñoro in the centre column of the army, commanded now by General Leith. On June 13th the army crossed the Agueda with a strength of nearly 43,000 all ranks, of whom the British and Germans were over 27,000, the rest Portuguese. The strength of the 1/9th was 666 of all ranks. There were, besides, 3,000 or 4,000 Spaniards under Carlos de España. On June 17th the Tormes was reached at Salamanca and passed by fording above and below the city, since Marmont had broken down the bridges except that of Salamanca itself, which, being under the guns of three forts, could not be used. Marmont himself had gone off north-eastwards, but had left garrisons in the forts which he had built, by Napoleon's orders, by converting three convents near the river. On June 19th, Gomm writes from "Camp on the Tormes, one league below Salamanca," saying they had arrived there on the 17th, and that the sound of guns showed that the siege of the forts was in progress by the 6th division told off for that duty. The siege was not such an easy matter, as Wellington was short of heavy artillery, and it had to be suspended on the 20th. Marmont had returned with 25,000 men, and Wellington was compelled to draw out his army, less one brigade of the 6th division left before the forts, on the heights of San Christobal, north of the city. Though Marmont advanced to the foot of the heights on the 20th, he did not venture to attack, and nothing happened beyond a cavalry skirmish. On the 21st the arrival of Bonnet's division brought Marmont's strength up to about 35,000. On that evening the 68th took a village from the French, but Marmont decided that Wellington's position was too strong for attack and, except at one height on the British right, from which the French were dislodged by the 7th division, after they had occupied it, there was no fighting on the 22nd. Marmont then retired to Aldea Rubia, nine miles north-east of Salamanca. To face this new position Wellington moved his right to the ford of Santa Marta and his left to Moriscos, with his centre at Aldea Lengua. On the 24th Marmont attempted to turn Wellington's right by passing the Tormes above it near Huerta, but was forced to retire. The 5th division was not actively engaged in any of these manœuvres. On the 27th the Salamanca forts were taken, and that night Marmont retreated on Toro and Tordesillas towards Valladolid.

At dawn on the 29th Wellington followed in three columns, and on June 30th the 5th division was at Fuente la Peña, fifteen miles south of Toro. Marmont was about to cross the Douro, and, having broken down all the bridges except that of Tordesillas, he fixed his centre there. On July 7th Gomm's letter is dated from Torrecilla de Medina, near Medina del Campo. That is his last before the battle of Salamanca. Wellington kept the bulk of his army in this neighbourhood, where the men passed quite a comfortable time. The troops on the Douro were on the best of terms with the French opposite them, and the bathing from either bank was never interrupted by firing. The country, as Gomm describes it, was devoid of trees and the weather very hot. So hot was it that Hale says that, after midday, only the piquets were left out, the rest being withdrawn into the shelter of Nava del Rey. So matters continued till the night of July 16th, when Marmont, after inducing Wellington to move to his left by a threat of crossing at Toro, suddenly crossed at Tordesillas, reaching Nava del Rey on the 17th.

In the night of the 16th the 4th and light divisions and Anson's cavalry had marched to Castrejon, where they stood on the 17th under the orders of Sir Stapleton Cotton. Wellington took measures to provide for their retreat and junction by moving the 5th division to Torrecilla de la Orden, five miles south-west of Castrejon. At Castrejon, Cotton was attacked at dawn on the 18th, and when his left was turned by Alaejos he retired through Torrecilla de la Orden to the Guarena stream. During this march, in which the 5th division was in the left.

the light in the right column, the enemy was marching parallel to and not more than 500 yards from the British column. Officers on either side could exchange complimentary salutes, which were often interrupted by the French guns unlimbering and firing on the British. The heat and dust were terrific, and when the British at last reached the Guarena nothing could stop them from rushing to quench their raging thirst with its muddy water. The French artillery promptly opened on the 5th division, which reached the stream at the same time as the light division, but higher up. Under the fire of forty French guns they crossed to the slopes of the left bank.

Having crossed the Guarena, the three British divisions took post, facing east, on the heights of the left bank, the 5th division being on the right at Canizal. The remainder of the army was ordered to cross the Guarena above at Valesa. The French now attempted to turn the left where the light division stood, but were repulsed with considerable loss on both sides. On the afternoon of the 19th the enemy started to march by his left to turn the British right by Vallesa, to meet which Wellington again crossed the Guarena at Vallesa and prepared to meet an attack on the 20th, facing north. Again, on the morning of the 20th, Marmont moved by his left, across the eastern branch of the Guarena at Cantalpiedra, and encamped that night at Villaruela and Babila Fuente. Wellington replied by moving to his right to Cabeza Vellosa, with cavalry at Aldea Lengua. Occasional artillery fire during these manœuvres caused no loss to the British. Marmont's object was to cut Wellington's communications with Salamanca and Ciudad Rodrigo. He was probably going to cross the Tormes in continuation of the same plan.

On the 21st Wellington was in the position of San Christobal, where he had been on June 22nd. Marmont seized Alba de Tormes, which had been evacuated by Carlos de España without Wellington's knowledge. He then passed the Tormes by fords between Alba and Huerta, and camped behind Calvariza de Ariba on the western edge of the forest.

The same evening Wellington also passed the Tormes by the bridges and the fords at Santa Marta and Aldea Lengua, except the 3rd division and d'Urban's cavalry left on the right bank at Cabrerizos. The light division passed, in a terrible thunderstorm, at Aldea Lengua late in the evening. They lost a number of men by lightning. Hale, describing the storm, says they had a very unpleasant time, though the storm lasted only about half an hour. The claps of thunder stampeded some of the dragoons' horses, which were supposed to have bolted into the enemy's lines. Marmont was about to play into Wellington's hands by fighting a great battle before he had received the reinforcements he expected from Madrid.

He had for this battle nearly 50,000 officers and men, with seventy-eight guns. Of infantry he had 43,000, with 4,500 cavalry. Wellington had about 52,000 men with fifty-four guns; but of these 30,500 only were British, 18,000 Portuguese, and the rest Spaniards. His cavalry numbered 3,500 British and 500 Portuguese and Spanish. In numbers the armies were approximately equal, but in quality Wellington's Portuguese and Spanish, more than two-fifths of the whole, could certainly not be reckoned as the equivalent of an equal number of French.

Marmont was still playing the game of the last few days, trying by turning Wellington's right to separate him from Salamanca and Ciudad Rodrigo before fighting him on more advantageous terms. The scene of the coming battle was in an undulating country, which Mr. Fortescue compares to Salisbury Plain, adding that, though favourable to cavalry action, it was " far blinder than the inexperienced would suppose." To the east, stretching back to Alba de Tormes from behind Calvariza de Ariba was forest, which extended some distance westwards from the Alba road. The only marked features were two flat-topped hills—the Lesser Arapile to the north, and the Greater some one-third of a mile south-east of it. Both, though of no great height, were difficult of ascent, and easily held by the force in possession. The Greater Arapile had a larger flat summit than the Lesser, which it commanded by a few feet. It rose about 100 feet above the surrounding ridges. Neither Marmont nor Wellington had any definite intention of fighting a battle; the former aimed, by continuing movements similar to those of the last few days, at separating Wellington from his line of retreat on Ciudad Rodrigo, whilst the latter had already started his baggage towards that fortress. He would only fight if he saw a very advantageous opportunity.

When the French began reconnoitring westwards in the morning at Calvariza de Ariba they could only see the 7th division, with which there was some skirmishing; the rest of Wellington's army was hidden in the folds of the ground farther west.

Marmont, meaning to move by his left round the allied right as on previous days, required the Arapiles, or at least the Greater, as a strong post where he could cover the movement to his left, and, when that movement was complete, as a support for his right.

Wellington held the northern hill, but was too late to anticipate the French at the southern. The two hills were within easy artillery range of one another, and each side managed to get guns on to the top of its own hill.

As Wellington saw, from the top of his Arapile, the movement of Marmont's left wing round the right of his existing line, which faced eastwards, with the Lesser Arapile on its right, he made corresponding dispositions. From his eastern front he withdrew the 7th division, leaving there the light division, with the 1st behind it, to oppose Foy's division. The 4th division held the Lesser Arapile and the space on its right, with light troops in the village of Arapiles. The 5th and 6th divisions, España's Spaniards, and Bradford's Portuguese, hitherto hidden in the depression east of Carbajosa, were brought forward, so as to be able to support either the left eastwards or the right southwards. At the same time Wellington ordered the 3rd division (now under Pakenham, *vice* Picton, sick) and d'Urban's Portuguese cavalry to cross the Tormes and pass to Aldea Tejada, far away to his right. It was the dust raised by this movement which confirmed Marmont's belief that Wellington was off to Ciudad Rodrigo. About noon Wellington seems to have had an idea of trying to storm the Greater Arapile with the 1st division, but abandoned it. Then he thought he might have to abandon Salamanca and retreat by Aldea Tejada, always supposing Marmont did not make the mistake he actually did. The Marshal, judging as he did Wellington's intentions, proceeded to push on his left wing from the woods south of the Greater Arapile, behind which he had five divisions, protected by Bonnet at and north of the Arapile. He says he intended the divisions of Maucune, Thomières, and Clausel to take post in three lines in the order named on the near end of this plateau facing the village of Arapiles. It was about 2 p.m. when this order was issued, but it appears to have been misunderstood, and Thomières, instead of halting behind Maucune, was pushing on

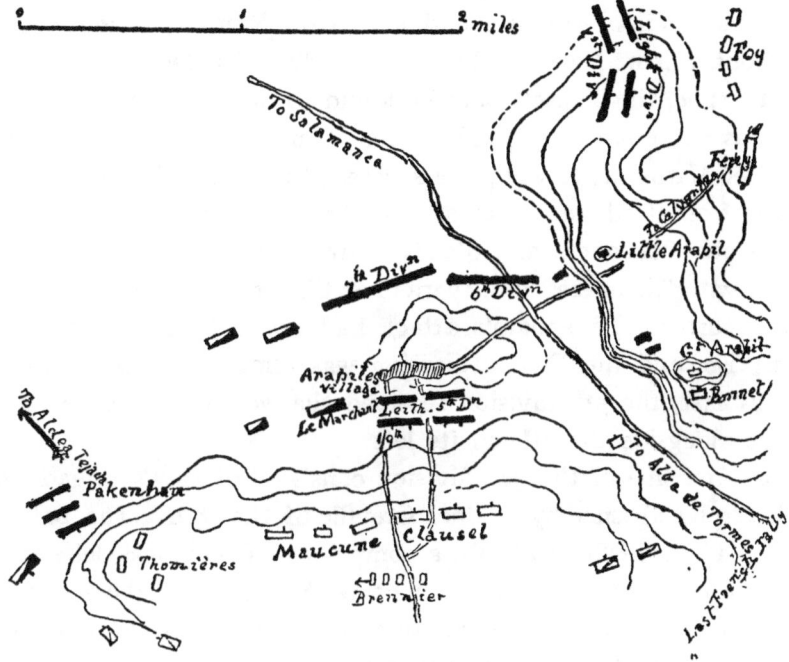

BATTLE OF SALAMANCA—5TH DIVISION ABOUT TO ATTACK

beyond him, and thus unduly extending the left. It seems probable that Marmont really intended what was actually done, for he believed Wellington to be retreating by Aldea Tejada.

Wellington at once saw that Marmont had delivered himself into his hands, and acted accordingly. Whilst a fierce artillery action was going on in front of Maucune, in which the English guns were outmatched, Wellington sent off Pakenham with orders to advance, from his position of concealment at Aldea Tejada, against the head and right flank of Thomières's column. The 5th division was pushed forward on to the crest on the right of the 4th; the 6th was placed behind the 4th; the 7th, still on the left wing, was brought up to support the 5th, in line with the 6th. Bradford's Portuguese, the Spaniards, and most of the allied cavalry were in reserve at Las Torres, a mile behind Arapiles.

Under the storm of artillery fire the men of the 5th division lay down to wait, with Leith slowly riding amongst them and encouraging them, the light companies only being engaged in skirmishing towards Maucune's position. Clausel had halted on Maucune's right.

About 4 p.m. Marmont had been badly wounded by a shell, and for some time, till Clausel could be found to take his place, the French army was without a commander; for Bonnet also had been wounded soon after Marmont, to whom he succeeded by right of seniority.

The frontal advance against Maucune's position was only to commence when Pakenham and d'Urban, from Aldea Tejada, were clearly engaged with Thomières, and it was not till after 4.30 that that contingency occurred. Pakenham's attack had taken Thomières completely by surprise, and the French division was almost completely defeated when, at last, the 5th division received the welcome order to rise and advance alongside the 4th on its left.

The first line of the 5th division consisted of Hay's brigade, commanded in his absence by Colonel Greville of the 38th. The battalions were the 1/9th, 1/38th,[1] 2/38th, a company of Brunswick Oels, and the 1/4th, the last named drawn from Pringle's brigade of the second line.

For a description of the advance we cannot improve upon this of Leith Hay, who himself took part in it.

"The ground between the advancing force and that which it was to assail was crowded by the light troops of both sides in extended order, carrying on a very incessant 'tiraillade.' The general desired me to ride forward, to make our light infantry press up the heights to cover his line of march, and bid them, if practicable, make a rush at the enemy's guns. Our light troops soon drove in those opposed to them; the cannon were removed to the rear; every obstruction to the general advance of our line vanished. In front of the centre of that beautiful line rode General Leith, directing

[1] The 1/38th had only reached the army that morning.

its movements. Occasionally every soldier was visible, the sun shining bright upon their arms, though at intervals all were enveloped in a dense cloud of dust, from whence at times issued the animating cheer of the British infantry. The French columns, retired from the crest of the heights, were formed in squares about fifty yards behind the line at which, when arrived, the British regiments would become visible. Their artillery, though placed more to the rear, still poured its fire upon our advancing troops. We were now near the summit of the ridge. The men marched with the same orderly steadiness as at the first; no advance in line at a review was ever more correctly executed; the dressing was admirable, and the gaps caused by casualties were filled up with the most perfect regularity. General Leith and the officers of his staff, being on horseback, first perceived the enemy, and had time to observe his formation, before our infantry became so visible as to induce him to commence firing. He was drawn up in contiguous squares,[1] the front rank kneeling, and prepared to fire when the drum should beat. All was still and quiet in these squares; not a musket was discharged till the whole opened. Nearly at the same instant, General Leith ordered our line to fire and charge. At this moment, the last thing I saw through the smoke was the plunge of the horse of Colonel Greville, commanding the leading brigade, who, shot through the head, reared and fell back on his rider. In an instant every individual present was enveloped in smoke and obscurity. No serious struggle for ascendancy followed, for the French squares were penetrated, broken, and discomfited, and the victorious 5th division pressed forward, no longer against troops formed up, but against a mass of disorganized men flying in all directions."

General Leith had been wounded in the arm by a bullet close up to the enemy and forced to leave the field; Pringle, as senior brigadier, assumed command of the division. Leith Hay himself, also being wounded, knows no more of the battle from personal observation.

Meanwhile Pakenham and D'Urban had been completing the defeat of Thomières, and were now so close upon Maucune's left, and the right

[1] Other accounts say contiguous columns, which seems more probable.

of the 5th division, that men of the 3rd and 5th divisions, lost in the smoke found themselves in one another's divisions. The defeat of Maucune's division was completed by a splendid charge of Le Marchant's heavy dragoons, who destroyed the 66th of the line, and fell also on the leading regiment of Brennier's division, which was attempting to cover the retreat of Maucune.

In less than an hour the whole of Marmont's left wing had been almost destroyed. On the left of the 5th division the success had been less decisive, and Clausel was able to make a heavy counter-attack, which placed the allied troops in that direction for some time in a critical position. An attack on the Greater Arapile had failed, and the 4th division had been defeated when the counter-attack was stopped by Beresford with the 6th division, aided by an attack on Clausel's left flank by Spry's Portuguese brigade of the second line of the 5th division. The Greater Arapile was evacuated, as the French regiment holding it found itself in danger of isolation.

The counter-attack having been repulsed, the 3rd and 5th divisions now formed in one line, supported by the 7th and Bradford's Portuguese. They advanced eastwards against Sarrut's division standing on the plateau south-east of the Greater Arapile, endeavouring to save the broken remains of the French left. Whilst the 3rd and 5th divisions pressed Sarrut in front, his left was threatened by cavalry, and he was forced to give way. The last stand was made by Ferey, who, after inflicting heavy loss on the 6th division, was again able to form just in front of the forest. Here Ferey was killed, but his men stood firm, and it was again the 5th division which, after its defeat of Sarrut, came up on the French left flank, completed their defeat, and drove them in the gathering darkness into the forest. There the wildest confusion prevailed, and again the French had lost their commander, for Clausel was wounded and at Alba de Tormes. It was only the unfortunate evacuation of Alba de Tormes by Carlos de España that saved the French left and centre from surrender in the forest and enabled them to cross the Tormes. The last of the French on the west of the forest was Foy's division, covering the right of the retreat, which, though pressed by the light and 1st divisions, was able, thanks to the skill of its commander, to get safely away to Alba de Tormes. Wellington, still thinking Carlos de España was at Alba, sent the light division to Huerta, where it arrived at 11 p.m. Beyond that there was practically no pursuit that night.

The allied loss in this battle, generally reckoned as Wellington's tactical *chef d'œuvre*, amounted in all to 5,220. The British losses were twenty-eight officers and 360 men killed, 178 officers and 2,536 men wounded, and seventy-four men missing. Looking to its position, in the first line of the 5th division in the great attack, the 9th got off lightly in the matter of casualties. It lost three men killed—one officer (Lieutenant Ackland), two sergeants—and forty men wounded. General Leith, with all his coolness and bravery under fire, was lucky to escape with a bullet wound in the arm, which turned out to be not so serious as was at first anticipated. Colonel Cameron, who led the 1/9th on this great day with his usual skill and courage, was unscathed. He had actually started for England on sick leave on July 17th, when the sound of the guns on that day reaching his ears brought him back to share in the glories of Salamanca.

The French loss was about 14,000 men and twenty guns.

CHAPTER XV

THE 1st BATTALION IN THE PENINSULA—MADRID—THE RETREAT FROM BURGOS—VITTORIA—SAN SEBASTIAN
1812-13

ON July 23, 1812, the 5th division, and other infantry which had been heavily engaged the day before, were allowed a day's rest whilst Wellington, with the 1st and light divisions and cavalry, pursued by Garcia Hernandez, where there was an action with the French rear-guard.

Clausel was marching with the remnants of Marmont's army north-eastwards, in the direction of Valladolid. Wellington's pursuit was not vigorous, as he could not afford to wear out his scanty force of British, and on the 25th he was out of touch with Clausel, who had scarcely over 20,000 men, some 12,000 or 14,000 being stragglers or unarmed fugitives who had not yet rejoined the army.

On that same 25th of July the 5th division had reached Nova de Setraval, and on the 31st they were camped on the River Cega, only six miles from Valladolid. Joseph Bonaparte had left Madrid with about 14,000 men to join Marmont, but hearing of his defeat at Salamanca, and being assured by Clausel that, even if the two forces could join, they were powerless to resist Wellington, he turned back towards Madrid. Wellington decided to leave him alone for the moment, till he had driven Clausel well beyond Valladolid. That general, by July 29th, was two-thirds of the way from Valladolid to Burgos, and finding Wellington's pursuit had ceased and that none of his infantry was north of the Douro, was busy reorganizing his army.

Wellington now determined to turn on Joseph and Madrid. He

marched by Segovia, because Joseph, cheered by more hopeful news from the north, had gone there with the idea of joining Clausel, though he presently reverted to the idea of an immediate return to Madrid. He left Segovia on August 1st.

Wellington, leaving only Santocildes's two Spanish divisions, called in from Astorga, on the Douro to support Anson's cavalry in containing Clausel, marched with the rest of his army, including the 5th division and the 1/9th, by Segovia and the Guadarama and Nava Cerrada passes. His advanced guard was in Segovia on August 3rd, and for the three following days the army halted about Cuellar. He now left the 6th division as part of the containing force, and added to it five battalions which were still suffering from the effects of Walcheren. The 1/9th was not among them. In all, the force numbered about 7,000 men, besides the 11,000 Spaniards from Astorga. With himself Wellington took about 36,000 men. Leaving Segovia on August 8th the 5th division, with the rest of the main body, were across the Guadarama pass by the 10th and near the Escorial by the 11th.

That day Joseph had evacuated Madrid, leaving a ramshackle garrison of over 2,000, mostly recruits, in the fortified arsenal of the Retiro, outside the eastern gate of Madrid.

D'Urban, with Wellington's advanced guard, had what Wellington described as "a devil of an affair" on the 11th with 2,000 cavalry, under Treilhard, sent back by Joseph to see if Wellington was really at hand. In that the 9th were of course not engaged.

On the 12th Wellington entered Madrid amidst scenes of wild enthusiasm, which he hoped, but, perhaps, as Sir C. Oman suggests, did not believe, indicated exertions on the part of the inhabitants in the cause of their country's liberation from the French.

On the 13th the first line of the Retiro defences was stormed, and next morning the garrison surrendered on easy terms. The 5th division took no hand in this, though they were near the Retiro. Hale says the 9th marched through Madrid, with drums beating and colours flying, to the side on which was the Retiro.

Wellington probably had before his eyes the disastrous effects on Galway's army of 1706 of a prolonged stay in a capital where attractive but destructive pleasures could still be fostered by French agents. Anyhow, Gomm, who had now been promoted lieutenant-colonel at the age of twenty-seven, writes on the 21st August from the Escorial: "They have taken care for the present that Madrid shall not be our Capua, and have quartered four divisions of us in and about this very large house; two divisions still continue in the neighbourhood of Madrid."

At the Escorial the 1/9th remained till the last days of August, when Wellington was about to march again in pursuit of Clausel, who, after the occupation of Madrid, had been showing considerable activity. Marching by Arevalo, the 5th division was on September 4th once more on the march for Valladolid. On the 6th they passed the Douro with the rest of the army by fording at Herrera de Duero. The French posted beyond the river withdrew without fighting and marched up the right bank of the Pisuerga. After a day's halt on the 9th Wellington passed the Pisuerga at Cabezon and Valladolid, the latter being the crossing-place for the 5th division. Clausel continued his retreat slowly on Burgos, followed by the Allies. He took up a position on the 16th to cover that fortress, but finding Wellington had now received a reinforcement of 11,000 Spaniards under Castaños, he again retreated almost unharmed. On the night of the 17th he passed through Burgos, leaving behind him a garrison of 2,000 men under du Breton in the castle. Wellington proceeded to lay siege to this fortress, using for the purpose the 1st division only. The 5th and 7th, with Pack's Portuguese and other troops, moved on to cover the siege against any return of Clausel by the great road from France.

On October 9th Gomm writes from head-quarters of the 5th division at Hurones rather despondent about the siege of the Castle of Burgos, a siege to the actual conduct of which the 1/9th only contributed to the extent of lending the services of Captain Kennedy and Lieutenant Dumaresque, as assistant engineers. The former was killed and the latter wounded during the siege. Gomm's letter of the 9th October mentions that the 5th and 7th divisions had remained in position on the Vittoria road.

All this time the French had been gathering strength, and there had been constant bickerings on the British front, which culminated,

FIELD-MARSHAL LORD CLYDE (Colin Campbell), G.C.B., 1792–1863. (*Ch. XV*)

on the 18th, in a somewhat sharper affair when the French forced back the outposts and captured a piquet of Brunswickers north of Monasterio de Rodilla. On the 20th Wellington took post with the 1st division in front, and the 5th behind it, at Rabena, five or six miles out of Burgos, ready to offer battle next day. On the 20th Maucune advanced with two divisions and some cavalry against Wellington's force; but the 1st division, followed by the 5th, descending on his flank, he gave way and escaped, thanks to darkness, with small loss. Souham, now commanding the French on this front, only came up with his main body late on the 21st.

Meanwhile Wellington, learning that Madrid was about to be evacuated by Hill and the troops left there, before the advance of Soult's and Joseph's superior forces from the south, resolved to abandon the siege of Burgos and retreat towards Portugal. In the night of the 21st–22nd the retreat commenced; the 5th division, with two Spanish divisions, passed back to the west of Burgos, crossing the River Urbel at Tardajos. Thence they followed the left bank of the Pisuerga and rejoined the rest of the army near the junction of the Arlanza and the Pisuerga. The Pisuerga was crossed on the 23rd, under protection of a rear-guard in whose action that day the 1/9th of course had no share. At Torquemada indiscipline began to set in, and it was said that 12,000 men were drunk at one time on the new wine found in the villages. The retreat threatened to be a repetition of Corunna in this respect.

On the 24th the army halted after passing the Carrion a short distance above its junction with the Pisuerga, and took post, with its right resting on the Pisuerga and its left posted on the ridge of the right bank of the Carrion. Orders were issued for the destruction of the bridges over the Carrion at Palencia, Villa Muriel, and Dueñas.

On the 25th Foy's division moved on Palencia in front of the British left, Maucune's against Villa Muriel in the centre, and some cavalry against the bridge at Tariego over the Pisuerga on the right rear of Wellington's position. The passages on the flanks were carried; but at Villa Muriel the bridge had been blown up properly, and the 1/9th, mustering now only 300 men, with scarcely an officer to each company, were defending it and an adjacent ford. They held on gallantly, and so hot was the fight that they had to have their ammunition replenished twice. When at last they were forced to retreat, they had lost one sergeant and sixteen men killed, six officers,[1] four sergeants, and fifty men wounded. One company at the ford, commanded by Lieutenant Whitley, was surrounded and captured by French cavalry. The 5th division remained behind as rear-guard when the army retreated in the night of the 25th-26th.

Hale gives the following account of this affair: "About 200 of our regiment were placed very convenient to the bridge, and the remaining part of the regiment was extended along the river. The enemy seeing so small a party left to defend the bridge, they made a grand push for that place; but, fortunately, before they could make their object, the bridge blew up, which put a stop to their pursuit, so then they extended themselves along the river in about the same direction that we were, by which a sharp skirmish immediately took place and continued about four hours. One company of our regiment was very convenient to a grist mill that was on this river, and while they were busily skirmishing with the infantry that was on the opposite side of the river, a troop of the French cavalry rushed out from behind the mill, quite unawares to us, and swept away the whole company as prisoners of war, before we could give them any assistance." He adds that after four hours a Spanish brigade took the place on the river of the British, who retired half a mile to rest. Half an hour later the enemy were seen fording the river, and the Spaniards, "retreating in an unsoldierlike manner, in consequence of which our brigade was again ordered to stand to our arms and give them a charge, which we immediately did with great vigour, and in a few minutes we captured about four hundred prisoners; there were also a great number of killed and wounded in endeavouring to make their escape back across the river; therefore they did not make any further attack that day."

The whole 5th division had recrossed to the left bank of the Pisuerga at Cabezon by 3 a.m., when they halted to cover the bridge, whilst the

[1] Lieutenants Ackland, Taylor, Curzon, and Dumaresque; Ensign Ross Sewen and Surgeon Buckley.

7th division hastened on to secure the bridges of the Pisuerga at Valladolid and Simancas, and of the Douro at Tordesillas, thus assuring the safe passage of the latter river. On the 28th Souham failed in an attempt to wrest from the 7th division the Pisuerga passages at Valladolid and Simancas. That night Wellington marched for the Douro, which he crossed at Tudela and Puente de Duero, above the inflow of the Pisuerga. Souham, during the 29th, got possession of the Tordesillas bridge, but Wellington, hurrying down the left bank, was just in time to prevent his repairing it, and to destroy the bridges at Toro and Zamora. When Gomm wrote on November 1st from opposite Tordesillas, the 9th were watching the French manœuvring on the north bank of the swollen river, unable to cross it.

On November 6th, Wellington's army fell back unmolested by Tordesillas, de la Orden, and on the 8th stood for the third time on the position of San Christobal, north of Salamanca. On the same day Hill crossed the Tormes at Alba de Tormes in his retreat from Madrid before Joseph and Soult, who, on the 9th, joined hands with Souham now on the south bank of the Douro.

Wellington, when joined by Hill, was at the head of 52,000 British and Portuguese, and 16,000 Spaniards, standing with his right at Alba de Tormes, his centre at Aldea Lengua, and his left at San Christobal; but both fractions of the army were disorganized by a long campaign and by heavy drinking in the retreat. Moreover, the transport and supply organization was in a very bad state.

On the 14th the right was turned by Soult's passage of the Tormes above Alba.

Wellington now assembled his whole army in the old position of Salamanca. The weather was of the worst in the night of the 14th–15th, and Soult made no attack on the 15th. Wellington retreated unmolested towards Ciudad Rodrigo.

For some time after this the retreat, generally in heavy rain, great discomfort, and shortage of food, was described by Gomm as reviving " many recollections of the dreadful race to Corunna." Fortunately the French pursuit was far from energetic. On the 18th matters were so bad that Generals Clinton, Stewart, and Dalhousie deliberately disobeyed Wellington, thereby endangering the safety of the whole army. On the 19th Ciudad Rodrigo was at last reached in safety.

Wellington was furious, and hardly just, in his condemnation of the conduct of his army in this retreat. The 9th claim that their conduct in it was distinguished for order and discipline, that they only lost two men by desertion between Salamanca and Lamego, and that they therefore were not covered by Wellington's general censure.

The 9th now went into quarters about Lamego, where we find Gomm writing, on December 28th, and at intervals up to May 13, 1813, when he announces, " We cross the Douro to-morrow, and proceed through Villa Real, Murcia, and Mirandela to the neighbourhood of Braganza, where we expect further instructions." At Lamego, says Hale, the men got the balance of six months' arrears of pay, " for during this campaign we never received any money whatever." That, however, he says was not so bad as shortage of provisions, for " if we lost three days' provisions out of four (which we several times did) we never got a bit more than our allowance at any other time when it could be got, and we always paid the same if it was ever so short."

The sadly depleted 1/9th had now been raised to a strength of over 900, partly by recruits from home, but still more by a draft of ten sergeants and 400 men from the 2/9th, sent just as it started for England, whence it sent a further draft of six officers and 141 men. The draft from Gibraltar was commanded by Colin Campbell, who now found himself once more under the command of Colonel Cameron, to remain under it till nearly the end of the war. The 1/9th was still commanded in the field by Lieutenant-Colonel Cameron.

The winter had been very unhealthy in the British army, and in the epidemic of typhus the 5th and 7th divisions had been the greatest sufferers, with the exception of the Guards. But when the army was about to start on its last campaign in Spain health had been completely restored.

On this occasion Wellington had decided to enter Spain by the north side of the Douro, threatening the communications of the French with their own country by Valladolid, Burgos, Vittoria, and the western Pyrenees. His concentration was to be on the line from Braganza to

Miranda de Duero, and the 5th division was directed on Onteiro, where they arrived on May 23, 1813, after a march over very rough roads, practicable enough for infantry, but extremely difficult and unpleasant for artillery or wheeled transport. By June 5th, they had reached Medina de Rio Seco without opposition. They formed part of the left column under the command of Sir Thomas Graham, some 52,000 strong, whilst the right column of about half that strength, under Hill, was now marching by Tordesillas and the left bank of the Douro and the Pisuerga. What fighting there had been on the left was only with the advanced guard.

By June 12th the 5th division was at Sotresgudo, only one day's march from the Ebro, the farthest point on the road to France yet reached. The march had been uneventful from the point of view of fighting. The French had fallen back steadily through Burgos to the right of the allied advance, in the direction of Vittoria. Wellington, always threatening the right of Joseph and Jourdan, his present opponents, kept his left column well to the northward. At Sotresgudo there was a halt for the supplies to catch up the columns. There had been some trouble with the plunderings of wine vaults, but nothing to be compared to what had happened in the previous retreat. On the whole, Wellington was able to write: "The army is in better order than I have ever known them."

When the March was resumed on June 13th it continued by La Piedra (13th), San Martin (14th), Villarcayo (15th). On the 16th the army began to wheel eastwards and was all united on a narrow front. On the 17th the march continued over extremely bad roads.

On June 18th Maucune's division of the French army was found, at San Millan, whither it had retreated from Frias, whilst Reille with two more divisions moved along the Bilbao road northwards from Espejo on Osma, where Jourdan had ordered him to assemble the remains of the old "Army of Portugal." He was to be joined by Maucune from Frias. At Osma he met the 5th and 6th divisions as they marched. According to Wellington's despatch of June 19th, "the corps from Espejo was considerably stronger than the allied corps, which had arrived nearly at the same time at Osma. The enemy moved on to the attack, but were soon obliged to retire; and they were followed to Espejo, from whence they retired through the hills to this place (Subijana, de Morillos)." Gomm writes of this fight: "One of our brigades, General Hay's, had an affair the other day with part of Macune's division." Colin Campbell's diary says: "The light companies of the 1st brigade, with a portion of the 8th Caçadores, were employed against the enemy, and were supported, in the first instance, by the fire of a brigade of Royal Artillery. Colonel Cameron sent a battalion company to support his own light company [which the writer himself commanded]. This being our first encounter this campaign, the men were ardent and eager. . . . We continued the pursuit until dark, when we were relieved by the light troops of the 4th division." Hale (of the light company) gives the following account: He states that they fell in with the French about midday. The latter were being pursued by the 4th division, which they had succeeded in evading during the previous night. Now they had fallen to the lot of the 5th division. After a fight of two hours' duration the French retreated so rapidly that the division was halted, and only the light companies were sent in pursuit. They followed for six miles, during which the light company of the 9th lost five men wounded. They rejoined the 5th division the same evening.

It seems that the French on this occasion were Maucune's division, which Reille had been expecting to join him.

On the night of June 20th, when Wellington's orders issued for the approaching battle, he still had his head-quarters at Subijana de Morillos. His divisions all bivouacked in the valley of the Bayas, except Hill's, which was somewhat in rear. The 5th division was on the left about Murguia.

The so-called plain of Vittoria is by no means level, for it has at the great bend of the Zadorra, above Tres Puentes, a hill rising 300 feet above the river, and the hill of Arinez is about the same height. The true plain lies east of these points, and it is with that that we are principally concerned.

The plain is enclosed on the north and west by the Zadorra, a considerable mountain stream, with many fords and bridges. The mountains through which the British advance had to be made came close down to the right bank of the Zadorra on the western and southern sides, but stood farther back on the north, where the plain extended beyond the right bank for some distance, save where a spur between the Bilbao and Bayonne roads reached to the river.

Wellington's army now numbered about 72,000 men, of whom about 61,000 were British or Portuguese, the latter now, thanks to British training and officers, of a very different value from the levies of 1808. The remainder were Spanish, including Longa's guerillas. There were about 7,000 cavalry and ninety guns.

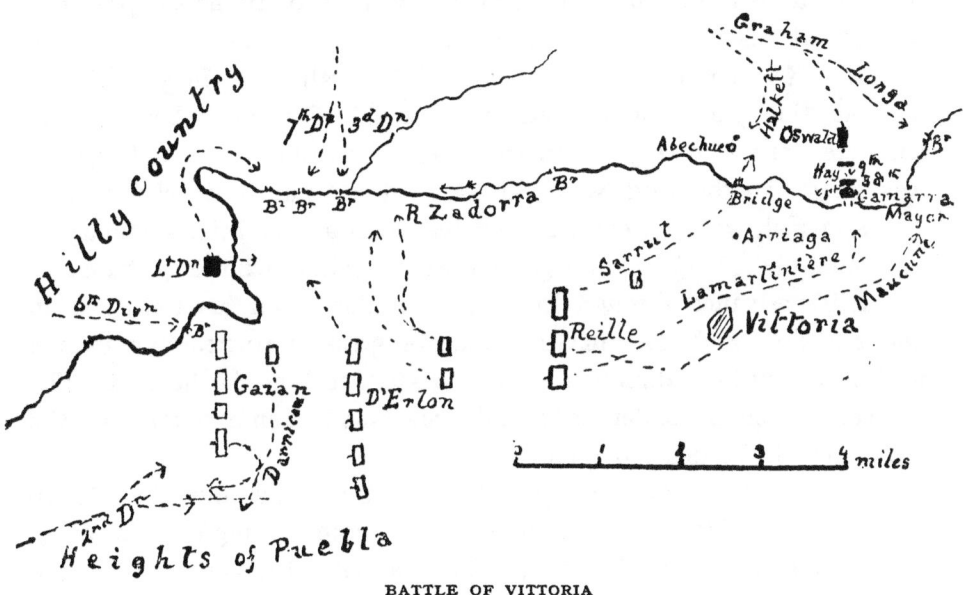

BATTLE OF VITTORIA

To these Joseph and Jourdon could oppose about 43,000 infantry, 6,000 or 7,000 cavalry, and 150 guns. Their approximate equality in cavalry, and their great superiority in artillery, by no means compensated for their great inferiority in infantry. They had posted their army in three lines—Gazan with the " Army of the South " in front, d'Erlon with the " Army of the Centre " behind Gazan, and Reille with the " Army of Portugal " behind d'Erlon.

Wellington's plan of attack provided for the advance of four columns :

The right.—Hill's division and Morillo's Spaniards, across the Zadorra over the heights of Puebla.

The right centre.—The light and 4th divisions by Nanclares.

The left centre.—The 3rd and 7th divisions, from the north above the bend of the Zadorra, against the French right flank.

The left.—The 1st and 5th divisions to descend by Arriaga on Vittoria in the French rear. Beyond the 5th, Longa's guerillas would operate higher up the Zadorra. Pack's and Bradford's Portuguese and Bock's and Anson's cavalry were with this column. Its march through the mountains was so difficult that it is said that, on its first appearance on the battlefield, the French felt certain that it could have no guns with it. It was under the command of Sir T. Graham. The 5th division was at this time commanded by General Oswald, whom Gomm characterizes as " a very able man and excellent officer," ; the brigadier was Hay, and the 1/9th was still led by Lieutenant-Colonel Cameron.

As usual, we must content ourselves with a very brief summary of the course of the battle to the right of the column in which the 1/9th fought.

Hill's advance through Puebla, with Morillo on his right, began about 8 a.m., and after making some progress and attracting French movements in their direction came to a standstill on the heights. The left centre column, under Lord Dalhousie, was late in arriving, and the battle had to be delayed for it.

It was not till towards 2 p.m. that Wellington, seeing Hill held up at Subijana de Alava, and also seeing smoke and hearing guns far away on the hills about Mendigueren, ordered a general advance of the two centre columns. What he had seen and heard on his left front showed him that Graham, on his own initiative, had commenced his advance against the French right rear.

Whilst the three right columns were steadily pushing back the armies of the centre and the south, Reille, finding himself threatened by Graham, of whose presence he had some inkling since noon, already had Sarrut's division beyond the bridge of Arriaga to meet the new danger towards the western front of the spur which descends to the Zadorra east of that bridge. He now sent Lamartinière's division to hold Gamarra and its bridge, whilst that of Arriaga would be held by Sarrut, now retreating before the British 1st division, with his right flank threatened by the 5th. Graham had sent Longa's guerillas farther to his left, towards Durana, where the French Spaniards had given way to their countrymen without resistance. To support them Reille sent some cavalry.

Graham's 1st division pushed Sarrut back on the bridge of Arriaga, but seems to have made no serious effort to pass it.

Meanwhile the 5th division, moving to the left of the 1st, advanced on Gamarra Mayor and its bridge. The French were driven from the hills on the left of the road near Abechuco by Caçadores followed by the 5th. During this movement Colin Campbell was detached with the light company of the 1/9th to cover the right flank of Hay's brigade. The river, from the mill dam below Arriaga up to and above Gamarra Mayor, seems not to have been fordable. Oswald now brought up two guns against Gamarra Mayor, to storm which he sent forward Robinson's brigade with the bayonet. Its right was covered by the light companies of the 9th and the rest of Hay's brigade. As it moved forward it encountered so severe a fire of grape from a French battery, and of musketry from Lamartinère's infantry, that it got into some confusion and began firing. Robinson, putting himself at the head of his brigade, gallantly led it forward and drove the French from the village and across the bridge, where he captured a gun. There, however, under the fire of a second French battery, covering a furious counter-attack by Lamartinère's rallied men, it was driven back across the bridge, and probably out of part, if not the whole, of the village. The fighting was very furious, each attack being followed by a counter-attack. This brigade was clearly unable to make any progress, and Oswald put in Hay's brigade to relieve it. The new attack was headed by the Royal Scots, followed by the 1/38th and 1/9th. Driving the French from the village, they carried the bridge for the second time, only to be driven back across it by a counter-attack.

Hale states that the light companies were extended along the river bank, with orders not to expose themselves or to advance without orders. They found cover from behind which to fire on the enemy across the river in an embankment about knee high on their own side. Whilst they were so employed the rest of the brigade held the village. This is confirmed by Colin Campbell, who says the light companies were first moved leftwards into the village to support the 1st brigade and later still more to the left to line the river bank. In this position the attack on the Gamarra bridge was brought to a standstill, and it was only when the French began to retreat before Wellington's frontal attack that Hay's brigade could cross and join in the pursuit. According to Hale there was a sharp fight to get across the bridge even then.

Though the bridges of Arriaga and Gamarra were not finally carried by force, there can be no doubt that the attack on them of the 1st, and still more that of the 5th, division was decisive in determining the retreat of the French, in preventing its being carried out in an orderly manner, and above all in forcing it from the main road to the Bidassoa and Bayonne on to the Pamplona road due east.

The rout of Joseph's army was complete; he lost the whole of his 151 guns, his ammunition, his transport, his treasure, his ciphers, everything, except the clothes he stood up in. Even Jourdan's marshal's bâton fell into the hands of the victors. In killed, wounded, and prisoners (Gomm says there were only about 1,000) the French loss was probably between 7,000 and 8,000.

The allied losses were 5,180 killed, wounded, and missing. Of the missing it was believed but few had fallen into the hands of the enemy. Of the total losses, 3,308 fell upon the British troops.

The 1/9th lost Ensign Saunders and 9 men killed and 15 men wounded.

That their losses were so small, as compared with the 111 lost by the Royal Scots, appears to be due to the ravaging effects of the first French fire of grape and musketry from Gamarra Mayor, which caught the Royal Scots before the 1/9th got up.

The pursuit along the Pampeluna road ended for the night of the 21st, at Metanco. Darkness had fallen and the victorious army was exhausted. The French retreat continued unmolested during the night till 2 a.m., when its rear-guard was at Allegria on its way to Pampeluna.

After the battle Wellington left at Vittoria the 5th division, the heavy cavalry, d'Urban's Portuguese and Pakenham's division now coming up from Medina de Pomar. Their business was to restore order in the town, where a wild orgy of plunder and drunkenness had broken out, which excited Wellington's wrath and drew from him, in his despatch of June 29th, many hard words as to the discipline of the British army, whose common soldiers he described as "the scum of the earth." This force was also required to guard against any enterprise by Clausel's corps, which was known to be approaching Vittoria at the time of the battle by the line of the Ebro.

When Wellington abandoned the pursuit of Joseph at Pampeluna he decided to go in search of Clausel. He had already ordered the 5th and 6th divisions, with two cavalry brigades, down the Ebro.

The 5th division appears, from the regimental records of the 9th Regiment, to have reached Salvatierra on the Pampeluna road on the 23rd, and to have started over the mountains to the Ebro valley on the 25th. Reaching that valley at Laguardia it marched in the direction of Logroño. Clausel, however, had already passed on his way to join Suchet at Tudela, and it was useless to pursue him farther down the Ebro. The 5th division was therefore recalled, and, passing within a mile of Vittoria, went by the Bayonne road to rejoin Graham's column, the main portion of which was before San Sebastian.[1] An advanced guard had followed Reille and Foy in their retreat over the Bidassoa at Irun. There they had passed into France, where, for the present, they were not to be followed.

On July 6th the division arrived in the neighbourhood of San Sebastian, in the siege of which the 1/9th was destined to play an important part.

Some description of this small but famous stronghold is required. It was now held by General Rey with a garrison of only 2,300 at first, inclusive of four battalions left by Foy. The number was raised to 3,000 by the addition of the garrison of Guetaria, which succeeded in getting in after the failure, on July 1st, of a feeble attack by the Spaniards blockading San Sebastian under Mendizabal.

The main fortress of San Sebastian consisted of two parts, situated

[1] This account of the movements of the 5th division agrees with that in General Shadwell's "Life of Colin Campbell."

at the outer end of a low-lying isthmus projecting northwards towards the Bay of Biscay. At the end of this isthmus there rose, to a height of over 400 feet, a considerable and precipitous hill, Monte Orgullo, which but for the connecting isthmus would have been an island. This was the citadel, at the foot of which, on the isthmus. lay the town, protected towards the mainland by a strong horn work covering a bastioned

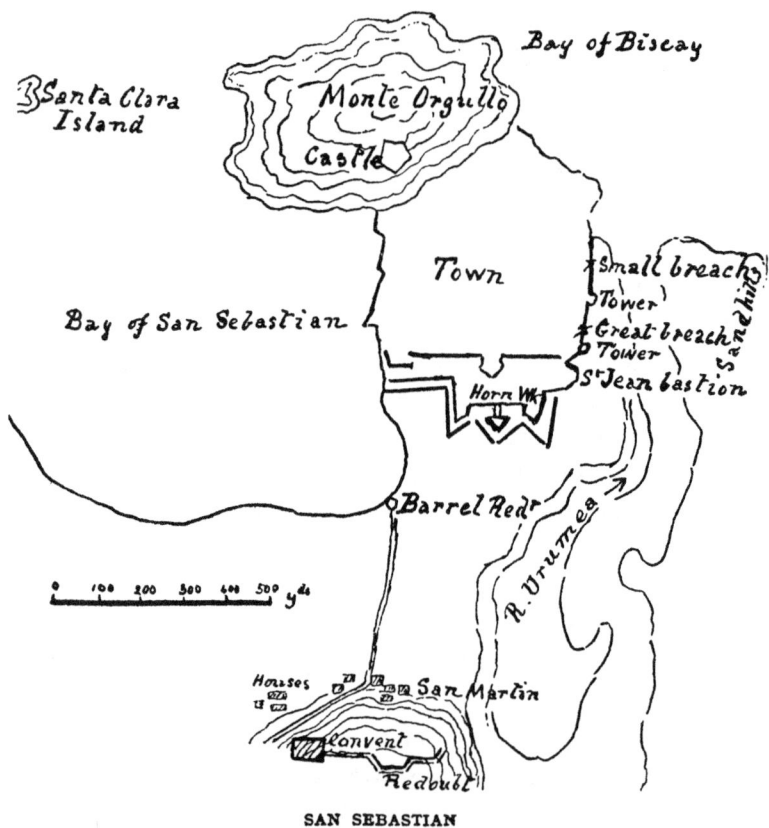

SAN SEBASTIAN

enceinte. The eastern side of the peninsula is formed by the river Urumea, unfordable except for two hours before and after low water. On the western side is a little bay only about three-quarters of a mile across at its mouth, where Monte Orgullo stands sentinel on the eastern side, the still more commanding Mont Iguedo on the western. Midway between the two is the small island of Santa Clara commanded by both these heights.

The front of the town was strong, but its flanks consisted only of an eight-feet thick wall facing the Urumea and the bay respectively. The Urumea flank was to some extent strengthened by a small bastion at its northern end and two towers. As a defence it was very weak. Except about the period of low water these flanks were unassailable; but during the hours the Urumea was fordable there was also a stretch of sand in the bay, so that both flanks could be approached dryshod. The guns of the citadel could sweep from their elevation the whole peninsula in front of the town, right up to and beyond the foot of the landward heights, on which stood the convent of San Bartolomeo, which Rey had fortified as an outwork and occupied with a battalion. He had also cleared the nearer part of the isthmus of its suburbs and trees. It could be swept by fire from San Bartolomeo, as well as from Monte Orgullo and the town front; indeed, the town, as well as the isthmus, was commanded by all the neighbouring heights. The town itself was so close under the cliffs of Monte Orgullo that the citadel guns could not be depressed sufficiently to command it. On the east bank of the Urumea, at its mouth, were sandhills suitable enough in those days for trenches and batteries. The plan of attack was settled by Wellington on July 11th, and two days later Graham was ordered to relieve Mendizabal's Spaniards then blockading the fortress. It was decided to attack on two fronts—the eastern on the right bank of the Urumea which could be crossed at low tide by stormers, and the southern against the front on the isthmus. For the eastern attack Bradford's Portuguese, for the southern the 5th division, were told off.

Evidently the first thing to be done was to gain possession of the out work of San Bartolomeo. During three days (14th to 17th July) the convent was battered almost into ruins by two batteries within 250 yards of it.

On the morning of the 17th the convent was ripe for assault, and the 1/9th was told off to play the principal part. The attack was made on the right by the piquets of the 4th Caçadores, followed by the 150 men of the 1st Portuguese infantry, backed by three companies of the 1/9th.

Three companies of the Royals were in reserve. This column was directed on a lunette to the east of the convent, with which it was connected by a trench. The left attack was headed by 200 men of the 5th Caçadores and 200 of the 13th Portuguese. Behind these came the rest of the 1/9th, the whole commanded by Lieutenant-Colonel Cameron.[1] He appears to have directed part of his attack directly against the front of the convent, whilst he himself led the rest against the western flank of that building and the outlying loopholed houses of the Faubourg St. Martin lower down the hill.

At 10 a.m. two six-pounders began firing against the lunette on the east of the convent, which appears to have required some further demolition. It was soon after noon that the signal for the infantry attack was given, but the Portuguese leading both attacks displayed some hesitation in facing the heavy French fire. They got as far as a road with trees on either side which they had to cross to reach their objective. Instead of crossing it, they began firing from behind the trees on the near side at the French behind those on the farther side. Then Colonel Cameron, losing patience at their slowness, passed through them with the 9th. The three companies on the right, led by Lieutenant-Colonel Craufurd, got forward to the counterscarp of the lunette, where they were temporarily checked under a heavy fire. Colin Campbell was with this attack.

Meanwhile Colonel Cameron, with three more companies of the 9th, leading the left of his attack down the hill to the main road from Hernani, encountered a heavy artillery fire from the horn work on the town front. From this he found shelter in a wall about fifty yards from the west side of the convent.

The right portion of his attack had been stopped on the breach in front of the convent, partly by a fire raging in the debris, and partly by a fusillade from the convent itself and from the houses to its left.

---

[1] Belmas mentions three attacks. He probably considered the left as two—one on the front and one on the west flank of the convent. He also describes the repulse of a previous assault on the 15th, which is evidently that of which Colin Campbell says " An attack was made on the convent by the 4th and 5th Caçadores to ascertain what numbers the enemy kept in his works." His biographer adds that this attack was repulsed with great loss.

When Colonel Cameron's section had taken these houses, and was, moreover, threatening the retreat of the garrison, the convent was cleared of the enemy. Cameron, not content with this, pushed on into the San Martin suburb by the main road. Here he and the three companies with him encountered a strong French reserve placed there by Rey and had to call up the rest of the 9th to aid him.

When the lunette on the right was abandoned by the defenders, simultaneously with the evacuation of the convent, the right column also passed on beyond it, down the hill, and along the isthmus to the " Barrel "[1] redoubt, more than two-thirds of the way to the horn work. From that redoubt they were, as was natural, beaten back by the fire of the horn work and forced to retreat up the hill.

Meanwhile Cameron's small party, largely outnumbered, was driven back from San Martin, and, according to Belmas, the convent, as well as the lunette, was temporarily recaptured, but lost again on the arrival of British reinforcements.

The convent position remained in British hands, but the loss had been heavy. Of officers of the 9th there were killed, Captain Woodham and Adjutant Thornhill; wounded, Lieutenant-Colonel Cameron, Captains Hector Cameron, Isaac Jervoise, and Lieutenant Richard Ruse. Captain Woodham was killed in the upper room of a house in the suburb, into which he had fought his way. About seventy men were killed or wounded—Colin Campbell was specially mentioned in Graham's report as the first to enter the redoubt. Cameron's name was not mentioned, but years later, when he first saw Graham's report, he referred to Colin Campbell, who frankly admitted that the resistance at the redoubt was not great, and was overcome largely owing to Cameron's success on the left.

The French troops now retired into the place, evacuating San Martin and only leaving a small detachment in the " Barrel " redoubt and some sharpshooters in the ruins in front of it.

The besiegers, being in possession of the convent hill, were now able to erect batteries and approach the horn work by trenches in regular form along the isthmus, as well as on the eastern bank of the Urumea,

---

[1] So called, as the parapets were made of casks of earth.

where progress in the sandhills had already been made. The details of these works are a matter for the artillery and engineers and need not be entered into in the history of an infantry regiment. Lieutenant Robertson of the 9th was killed whilst acting as engineer.

By the morning of July 23rd, the artillery had made a practicable breach between the two towers at the south-eastern end of the town defences facing the Urumea. During the day a second breach was made between the northern tower and the St. Elmo battery, and the town was set on fire. During the ensuing night Rey was busy making retrenchments to the breaches and combating the fire, which, for want of water, was very difficult to deal with. To an assailant it was also likely to form an obstacle, and the assault, for which preparations had been made on the morning of the 24th, was therefore postponed. All that day the British artillery fired upon Rey's retrenchments. The assault was then fixed by Sir Thomas Graham for the morning of the 25th, at the time near low tide when the exposed margin of the Urumea would be broadest. It had been ascertained that the tide would be suitable at daybreak on the 24th. When the date was fixed for the 25th, as a matter of fact low tide would have been some forty or fifty minutes after daybreak, if the calculations for the 24th were correct.

Wellington had recommended that an assault should be carried out in full daylight, soon after daybreak. That of July 25th started at 4.30 a.m., when it was still dark. The troops of the 5th division detailed were the 3/1st under Major Fraser; the 1/9th under Colonel Cameron, and the 1/38th under Colonel Greville. The Royals were to attack the nearer and larger breach, supported by the 9th, whilst the 38th were to storm the farther one; yet the 38th were placed in rear, instead of at the head of the column. A special storming party was placed under the orders of Lieutenant Colin Campbell of the 9th. It was made up of men selected from the light companies of all three regiments, and was in fact a forlorn hope.

From the most advanced trench, in front of the eastern demi-bastion of the horn work, it was 300 yards to the nearer breach, and that distance was difficult to traverse, especially in the dark, for there were in it pools left by the tide, and slippery rocks.

To cover the advance a Portuguese detachment was placed in a trench outside the starting-point, only sixty yards from the horn work. Their fire was to distract the attention of the garrison from the real attack farther north, and to keep down, as far as possible, that directed on the stormers. Moreover, as the troops left the trenches a mine, which had been placed in a drain under the counterscarp of the horn work, was fired, destroying the *place d'armes* in the covered way. Stormers planted scaling ladders in the ditch—but the assault here was repulsed with heavy loss by the flanking fire of the defenders. As the stormers rushed forward for the breaches, Napier alleges that they suffered heavily from the fire of their own guns beyond the Urumea— more heavily than they did from the projectiles hurled on them from the *fausse braie* of the eastern flank of the horn work, close under which they passed. As the Royals, floundering in the darkness through the pools, and slipping on the rocks, reached the first breach, they were led to it by the gallant Frazer and Lieutenant Harry Jones, R.E. The column behind these brave officers was already in confusion in the darkness and difficulties of the way, and their following was small. Many had stayed behind at the demi-bastion of the horn work, to join in the abortive assault there and to exchange fire with the defenders.

When Frazer and Jones reached the top of the breach they found a sheer drop of twelve feet or more in front of them before they could get into the town, where the defenders were now rallying and firing heavily on the head of the column, on which also there rained a storm of shells and musketry from the towers on the flanks. Frazer was killed, Jones wounded, and little or no assistance came to the few who still remained on the breach. The ladders were not forthcoming and everything was in confusion in the rear of the column. This confusion was added to as the 38th, so foolishly placed at the rear of the column, endeavoured to pass through to their point of attack farther north. With these were some companies of the 9th, also pushing northwards and meeting the now retiring Royals. Colonels Greville and Cameron (9th) and many other regimental officers exerted themselves to the utmost to bring up fresh troops into the breach—in vain, the disorder was too widespread. Lieutenant Campbell and his forlorn hope covered themselves with glory; for twice they mounted, twice they were forced by terrible losses to retire, twice was Campbell wounded before he at last desisted. He had been placed with twenty of his own light company in the centre of the Royals, whose light company was to support him under his orders. His letter of April 10, 1836,[1] to Sir J. Cameron gives a graphic account of the confusion in the attack, of the difficulties of advancing in column of fours in a trench which was barely wide enough to hold them standing still, and from which the exit was still narrower. He also describes the difficulties due to many men halting and firing long before they had reached the breach. He was twice wounded—in the right hip and left thigh—and the second wound knocked him from the breach into the ditch.

The whole column, or what was left of it, was now confined in the narrow space between the *fausse braie* and the rising river, as far forward as the nearer breach, for the 38th had never succeeded in getting forward to the farther breach. Under the storm of musketry and shell fire, added to the grenades and other projectiles hurled on their left flank, no troops could hold long, and presently they turned and ran for the trenches from which they had issued. A truce for an hour was agreed to, to enable the French to remove the British wounded from the shore, on which they were in imminent danger of drowning in the rising tide.

The British loss in this mismanaged and disastrous assault amounted to eight officers and 121 men killed, thirty officers and 142 men wounded, six officers and 118 men taken prisoners—total 425 out of about 2,000 who left the trenches that morning. Of the 1/9th the losses in this attack are not separately distinguishable from those in the attack of the convent and the subsequent successful assault.

In the 5th division this repulse was felt not only on account of the slur of the failure and of the heavy losses, but perhaps almost more from a sense that the troops had been sacrificed by mismanagement, especially on the part of the scientific corps. General Oswald had protested beforehand against the assault as planned, and now, when it had so signally failed, there was throughout the corps of officers, and apparently amongst the men, a feeling of bitter resentment at having

[1] Printed in full in Shadwell's " Life of Colin Campbell," p. 25.

been, as they held, sacrificed unnecessarily. The talk reached Wellington's ears and drew from him reprobation which, at any rate as far as the bravery and devotion of officers and men were concerned, was undeserved. It is easy to see what was the conversation amongst the officers when we read Gomm's letter to his sister, written the day after the assault.[1] Remembering that he was Assistant Q.M.G. on the staff of the 5th division, and that he was the most loyal of men, it is easy to infer what the general talk among the officers must have been. The following are extracts from the letter :—

"We attacked the town yesterday and failed. I do not think we have been engaged in so hazardous an attempt since this country became the scene of our adventures, not even at Badajoz. . . . I have always had a dread of being engaged in any of these sieges. We are used to set so much to the hazard, and to dispense with the common precautions which theory would make us believe are necessary to be taken where success is in any degree to be ensured, and which our own repeated experience confirms. . . . I am afraid the success on these occasions, owing to the almost miraculous efforts of our troops, has checked the progress of science among our engineers, and perhaps some more ; for it seems to have inspired them with a contempt for as much of it as they had attained. Our soldiers have on all occasions stood fire so well that our artillery have become as summary in their proceedings as our engineers ; and provided they can make a hole in the wall by which we can claw up,[2] they care not about destroying its defences, or facilitating in any degree what is, under the most favourable auspices, the most desperate of all military enterprises. In fact, we have been so called upon hitherto to ensure the success of our sieges by the sacrifice of lives, that our chief engineers and commandants of artillery remind us of what Burke says of the Revolutionary philosophers : ' The mathematicians, from the dry bones of their diagrams,

[1] It is dated July 25th, apparently a mistake for 26th.
[2] This expression can hardly fail to recall the remark of that hard-bitten old soldier Lefèbvre to his artillery officers at the siege of Danzig in 1807 : "Je n'entends rien de votre affaire ; mais fichez moi un trou et j'y passerai."

and the chymists from the soot of their furnaces, bring with them dispositions which make them more than indifferent to the cause of humanity.' They seem to consider men as no more than mice in an air pump, and calculate upon the expense we shall incur in carrying such and such a post with as much sang-froid as they do upon the supply of ammunition necessary to bring down the wall."

If the expressions are sometimes perhaps a little too harsh, they at least indicate the prevalent feeling. One more remark of Gomm's is: " The 9th, fortunately, had not time to suffer much; but they lost nearly as many heads as they showed." Sir T. Graham's report to Wellington highly commends Colonel Cameron and Lieutenant Colin Campbell, the leader of the forlorn hope, who was severely wounded.

In addition to Napier's and Fortescue's statement of the causes of failure, it may be suggested that the explosion of the mine at the horn work, without properly warning the officers and men that no assault was intended at that point, and that the explosion was merely a diversion, may have added considerably to the confusion by drawing off men, and especially ladder bearers, to that point instead of to the real breaches. Colin Campbell's account seems to point to this conclusion.

After the failure of this assault supplies and ammunition for the siege began to fail, owing to the difficulty of getting them into and out of the tiny harbour at Passage. On the other hand, the naval blockade of San Sebastian was so feeble that the French were always able to run small boats into and out of it by night, bringing ammunition and taking away the wounded. It was now, therefore, decided for the present to turn the siege into a blockade, which was easy on the land side, looking to the small garrison in the place. On the 27th, however, the French attempted a sortie, in which they surprised the Portuguese and took more than 200 prisoners, including a few British.

The 9th remained in the neighbourhood till siege operations were recommenced in earnest on August 22nd. Fresh batteries were then constructed, and a fire, tremendous for those days, was opened from seventy-three pieces of artillery, one battery being within 300 yards of the eastern demi-bastion of the horn work.

At 3 a.m. on August 27th 100 men of the 9th, under the command of Captain Hector Cameron, Lieutenant John Chadwick, and Ensign Robert Brooke, set out in boats across the harbour against the island of Santa Clara, on which there was a French garrison. Its capture would enable a battery erected on it to enfilade or take in reverse the defences of the town, the horn work, and the castle. As the boats approached the island a heavy fire was opened upon them, which cost the 9th the lives of Lieutenant Chadwick and ten men, besides twelve seamen killed or wounded. Nevertheless, the landing was carried out and the whole French garrison captured. In Wellington's despatch of the 2nd September he says: "Captain Cameron of the 9th had the command of the detachment which effected this operation, and Lieutenant-General Sir T. Graham particularly applauds his conduct." During the ensuing night Rey made a sortie which was repulsed without difficulty. The garrison were now with difficulty maintaining their fire against the heavy bombardment of the allied batteries, but they had not lost heart.

The grumbling in the 5th division which was described by Gomm still continued and had reached Wellington's ears. Such a feeling and the publication of it were clearly subversive of discipline, and Wellington determined to stop them.

He wrote to Graham that he understood the general and superior officers were so indiscreet as to talk before their men of the impossibility of success, and were still continuing the conversation. He said that he would "make them continue the operations of the siege, and bring other troops to storm the place, when it is ready to be stormed, who will not find success impossible." He called for volunteers from other divisions "to show the Fifth Division how to mount a breach," and actually sent 750 such men to Leith, who had now returned to his command. He was probably not surprised that Leith did not put them at the head of the assault, but kept them in reserve, or to cover the assault by their fire from the trenches.

Except for the reflection on the conduct of the troops in the late attack Wellington's censure was no doubt justified, even in threatening to disgrace the division if the dangerous talk continued. The circumstances of the case demanded the severest comment, followed by sterner measures if the talk, and especially the use of the word "impossible," should continue.

The assault was fixed for August 31st, this time in broad daylight, and the lead in the attack was given to Robinson's brigade, Hay's, in which was the 1/9th, being kept back in the trenches to feed the attack as required.

By this time, in addition to the two former breaches which had been greatly extended, a new one had been made, by the practical destruction of the St. Jean bastion, at the south-east angle of the town defences, whilst the *fausse braie* on the east of the horn work had been blown up by mines, and yet another breach had been made in the south face of the eastern demi-bastion of the horn work.

Rey had done everything possible in the way of retrenching the breaches, even to the extent of building a very thick wall in the nearest street parallel to the eastern wall. He was fully prepared for the assault, and had all his troops and guns ready in place when the forlorn hope, led by Lieutenant MacGuire of the 4th,[1] rushed forward from the trenches about 11 a.m. The French fired a mine prematurely as they passed the horn work, but it did not touch the main column, which was not yet up. That column consisted of 1,000 men of the 4th, 47th, and 59th, only about half the numbers sent forward on the former occasion. Half of it was directed against the breach between the two towers, the rest against the ruined bastion of St. Jean. The former mounted the great breach, only to find themselves stopped by a drop of sixteen feet, the ground at the foot of which was thickly planted with obstacles of every sort. After suffering very heavy losses from the fire of the besieged on their front and both flanks, the men at last fell back to such cover as they could find at the foot of the breach. The attack on the St. Jean bastion was equally unsuccessful. The reserve of Robinson's brigade was used up in supporting these attacks, and Hay's brigade also was sent in, with the exception of one wing of the 9th left to hold the trenches in case of a counter-attack. In this desperate fighting one wing of the 9th was engaged, but it is impossible to disentangle their precise work from the rest of the troops, with whom they were mixed up to such an extent that

[1] Colin Campbell was still in hospital suffering from his wounds in the first assault.

in the end the assaulting force was a mob of soldiers rather than a distinctly organized body of units. An hour had passed and this assault seemed to be almost as hopeless of success as that of the month before.

Graham now directed a terrific fire from the batteries beyond the Urumea, over the heads of his troops, against the interior of the horn work. This continued for half an hour, when two Portuguese regiments forded the river opposite the breaches north of the towers, which they attacked, whilst the British, on their left, again mounted the other breaches. Some of the 85th, in boats, attempted to divert the enemy's attention by threatening a landing on the north side of the citadel. Still the assault made no progress, and the rising tide threatened to bring it to an end when, fortunately, the French reserves of ammunition behind the breaches caught fire and caused heavy losses to the defenders.

Now, at last, Rey recognized that the town was lost and withdrew the 1,200 or 1,300 men he had left into the citadel, leaving the allies to rush into the town. It is perhaps well to draw a veil over what happened in San Sebastian during the rest of this and the two succeeding days. The conduct of the French troops after the storming of Lübeck in 1806 had been bad, but the British at Badajoz were worse, and at San Sebastian the scenes were worse even that at Badajoz. The Portuguese, too, hating the Spaniards with a bitter hatred, were only too ready to join the work of plunder, murder, and rape. The conquerors were a mob over whom their officers, owing partly to the intermixture of units, had no control, and the men were exasperated by the resistance they had experienced. It must be remembered, too, that the ranks of British regiments contained a proportion of very rough characters, criminal, brutal, and ignorant, only kept in order by very stern discipline.

Rey's little force, encumbered though it was by numerous prisoners and wounded, would still have been a difficult nut to crack, for Monte Orgullo, on the landward side at any rate, is so precipitous that an assault must have been a desperate affair. But Rey had at last lost hope and felt that relief from outside was not to be expected. As Gomm says of the French, "There is little *acharnement* left among them."

For the next week there was continuous bombardment, culminating on September 8th with the opening of fire from sixty pieces. Two hours of this induced Rey to surrender, with about 1,400 sound men and 500 wounded. There were recovered 670 allied prisoners, taken on July 25th and August 31st. The town had practically been obliterated by fire. Rey may have been, as Gomm calls him, " a coarse fellow," and Sougeon, his chief of the staff, " a great rogue," but they had put up a fine soldierly and honourable defence, which cost the assailants, in killed and wounded, considerably more than the whole strength of the garrison. The losses of the 1/9th in the successful assault—and it will be remembered only half the battalion went to the front—were four officers (Brevet Lieutenant-Colonel Crawfurd,[1] Lieutenants E. Frazer, E. R. Lewyn, and Ensign R. Morant), five sergeants, and forty-two men killed; six officers (Lieutenant-Colonel Cameron, Captains T. Ferrars, J. Shelton, Lieutenants R. Dale, W. McAdam, J. Ogle), two sergeants, two drummers, and ninety-eight men wounded, and six men missing—in all 178 of all ranks, a loss which shows how heavily they were engaged. Amongst the wounded was Hale, who had been made a sergeant on the evening after Vittoria. He was sent to Bilbao, where he had a very poor time in hospital. He did no more fighting, and when we quote his diary again it must be understood that he is giving second-hand news received from his brother. He does not say if the brother kept a regular diary. Adding the losses at the storming of the convent and at the unsuccessful assault, San Sebastian cost the regiment in casualties, six officers killed and twelve wounded, and of other ranks sixty-two killed and 177 wounded.

[1] One of the " Military Extracts " (vol. II, col. 429) at the R.U.S.I. describes a monument to Crawfurd, apparently at Greenock. Amongst the trophies depicted on it is a representation of a sword presented to him by the 9th and the names Roleia, Vimiera, Busaco, Badajoz, Salamanca, Vittoria. The inscription is as follows:—

" To the memory of
LT.-COL. HENRY CRAWFURD
Of His Majesty's 45th Regiment of Foot
Who fell gloriously on the 31st August, 1813,
In the breach at the storming of San Sebastian
While leading on a division
Of His Majesty's 9th Regiment
This Monument is erected
by his school fellows and early friends."

CHAPTER XVI

THE 1st BATTALION, 1813–1827—CROIX DES BOUQUETS—THE NIVE—BAYONNE—CANADA—THE ARMY OF OCCUPATION

THE risk, such as it was, of leaving San Sebastian untaken on Wellington's rear being removed at so great a cost, the 5th division was now called forward to the front on the Bidassoa. On September 25th San Sebastian was taken over by a Spanish garrison, and two days later the division was established at Ozarzun, half-way to the Bidassoa, in the second line of the army, where they remained till October 6th. Leith and Oswald had both been wounded at the taking of San Sebastian, and Hay, as senior brigadier, now commanded the division, Greville taking his place as brigadier.

On October 6th the 5th division moved up to the neighbourhood of Irun, though that was not the point at which it was to cross the Bidassoa next day. It was to march to Fuentarabia, turn to the right and pass by two fords, between that town and Hendaye on the French side of the river, which had been reconnoitred and found to be passable by infantry at low tide when a sandbank broke the crossing midway.[1] On the right of the 5th division the 1st was to cross and attack the French front about Béhobie whilst the 5th turned their right. The rest of the army were to cross higher up on a broad front. Greville's brigade, in which was the 1/9th, was the right column of Hay's division, with a Portuguese brigade on its left separating it from Robinson's brigade

[1] There were two fords to the sandbank, and three from it to the right bank of the Bidassoa—one for each column.

still farther to the left. The crossing would be covered by batteries on the heights of the left bank above Irun.

The troops were under arms at 3 a.m., and in the midst of a heavy thunderstorm took post, concealed by the embankment of the river, till 7 a.m., when they passed the first of the fords, to the sandbank, up to their waists in water. A quarter of an hour later a rocket from Fuentarabia gave the signal for the farther advance. The storm of the night had passed to the French side and helped to conceal the movement.

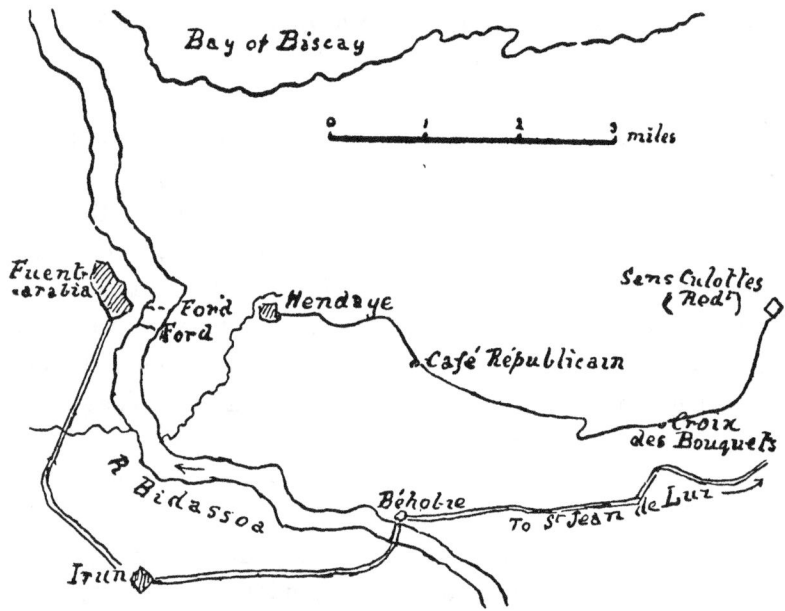

WELLINGTON'S PASSAGE OF THE BIDASSOA

Beyond the sandbank the men only got forward slowly in the deep water and mud, and as they reached the French bank they were met by the fire of the 3rd of the line. That regiment and the 17th light were soon swept back, and Greville's brigade, with which was Hay himself, their old commander, moved steadily up the hills, the centre and left columns by Café Républicain towards the hill of the Sansculottes.

The 9th, leading Greville's brigade, kept more to the right, advancing on Croix des Bouquets in such close touch with the Germans, on the left of the 1st division, that, when they charged the first position taken up by the French, they had to pass through German skirmishers. Cameron, as always, led them with the greatest gallantry to the attack, before which the French retired hurriedly to a second position on the next ridge, where they took post in a curve, concave towards the advancing 9th, who naturally suffered heavily from a fire which struck them in both flanks as well as in front. Moving steadily forward, notwithstanding their losses, they were within a dozen yards of the French when, with a cheer, they charged with the bayonet. Maucune's men would not stand up to this, and were driven in confusion from the Croix des Bouquets, only a short way west of the great road from Bayonne to Spain, as it begins the descent into the valley of the Bidassoa.[1]

Hale's, or rather his brother's, account of this affair is as follows : " About one mile and half distance from the river, on the other side, the enemy had formed a four-gun battery, which place our regiment was ordered to attack." He says there was no opposition encountered in the passage of the river, but they had not advanced a mile beyond it when the battery opened fire on them ; " Nevertheless we continued advancing very regularly in column of companies till we got within musket shot distance, and then we fired one volley and gave them one charge (according to the English fashion) with as much vigour as the strength of our bodies would permit, by which we drove them from their battery and occupied their ground in less than fifteen minutes, and from thence we continued advancing and driving them before us for nearly two miles, when we were ordered to halt and cease firing, for we were getting very near to their main body." Another account is given in " A Boy in the Peninsular War," by Robert Blakeney of the 28th, as follows :

"On fording the Bidassoa Halket's light Germans drove up all the enemy's advanced parties close to the summit of the Croix des Bouquets ; but this being the key of the position, the enemy were strengthening it continually from the first onset both with guns and troops ; so that when the Germans approached, the position had become so strong that Halket, having lost many men during his

[1] The scene of the fight is easily seen from the road by those who drive from St. Jean de Luz to Irun.

ascent, was brought to a stand. At this critical moment Colonel Cameron with the 9th Regiment, having arrived just as the Germans were checked, put them aside, and making a desperate charge gained the summit. The enemy's guns had just time to retire through their infantry, who also quickly retreated to a second ridge, The approach to this was narrow; but Cameron, reducing his front quickly, followed. However, the enemy having the start were soon formed, and the approach being winding with sharp turns, they poured a destructive fire both in front and flank into the regiment. Yet this did not retard their quick advance for a moment; while the enemy seemed in no way moved by the vehement advance of Cameron until the regiment approached within a few yards, when a loud cheer and rapid charge so astonished them that they scarcely knew what they were about until they found themselves borne off the hill. Thus the 9th regiment gallantly carried the key of the position, but with a heavy loss both in officers and men."

Colin Campbell, though by no means cured of his wounds, had got out of hospital without a proper discharge. He was determined to lead his light company, and in doing so was again badly wounded. Cameron, bound by his strict notions of discipline, censured Campbell for his conduct in irregularly leaving hospital, for which he said the only palliative was his conduct at San Sebastian. Campbell's connexion with the 9th ceased soon after.

The 1st division had driven in Reille's front on the Bidassoa, Robinson's brigade was threatening his extreme right on the Sansculottes' Hill, and his left was also turned farther east. He took up a new position with his right resting on the old redoubt on Sansculottes' hill, his centre on the hill of Socorro and his left on the Camp des Gendarmes. Against this no further attack was made.

Gomm writes of October 7th as "a fatiguing day, though not a very hard fighting one." That hardly applies to the 9th, who lost eight men killed, ten officers,[1] two sergeants, and sixty-two men wounded.

[1] Captain I. Jervoise; Lieutenants R. Dale, T. Sheppard, W. McAdam, G. Stirling, Colin Campbell, Peter Le Mesurier, R. Brooks; Ensigns J. Nash and E. Kenney.

The conduct of the regiment was generally commended by those superior officers who witnessed it, and Wellington himself, in his despatch of October 9, 1813, says, " I had particular satisfaction in observing the steadiness and gallantry of all the troops. The 9th British regiment were very strongly opposed, charged with bayonets more than once and have suffered." He had himself come up after the last charge, had been received with cheers, and had personally thanked the regiment.

The allies took post in this part of the field along the well-marked ridge which forms the northern edge of the Bidassoa valley, the 5th division on the extreme left, extending to the sea coast. We find Gomm accordingly dating his letter of November 7th from " Camp des Sansculottes."

During this period Reille, acting under Soult, had been busy entrenching his army in this quarter on both sides of the Nivelle. His entrenchments, far too extensive for all to be held by the force available, were in themselves a danger, as a temptation to undue dispersion of forces. Wellington, too, did a great deal of fortification, for he was still by no means sure how far it would be advisable to advance on French soil. By the beginning of November he had made up his mind to force the French back on Bayonne. Pampeluna had fallen on October 30th, and the allied right was therefore relieved of the duty of covering the blockade of that fortress.

Very bad weather in the early days of November deferred the passage of the Nivelle till the 10th. The main attack was to be delivered against the area about Sare, some six miles south-east of St. Jean de Luz. The function of the left of the army, commanded by Sir John Hope,[1] was to make a feint against the French right in front of St. Jean de Luz, where Soult expected to be attacked, in order to keep as many French as possible away from the real attack about Sare. The 5th division, still on the extreme left of Wellington's army, would move with its left on the coast by the road leading to the fort of Socoa, on the south-

[1] It consisted of the 1st and 5th divisions, Aylmer's brigade, Bradford's and Wilson's Portuguese, Vandeleur's light brigade, and the German brigade of heavy cavalry.

western horn of St. Jean de Luz harbour, which was to be bombarded from the sea.

In this operation Hope's force moved forward from the Camp des Sansculottes at daybreak and stormed the redoubt which the French still held. The 1/9th was too far to the left to be engaged in this affair. They advanced next day to the inundations of the stream covering the southern foot of the heights of Bordegain in front of Ciboure, the suburb of St. Jean de Luz, after the French had been driven over the Nivelle as a result of the main attack at Sare. Thence they moved on to cantonments at Guéthary. Here they remained undisturbed till December 9th, the date of the commencement of the battle of the Nive.

Soult was now occupying a very strong entrenched camp round Bayonne which fortress formed its citadel. Within that city the Adour, flowing into the Bay of Biscay a few miles north-west of the city, is joined by the Nive from the south. Protected on the west and south-west by artificial inundations backed by numerous works, and by a bend of the Nive on the south, Bayonne was not open to a turning movement, either on the east or the west, by the course of the Adour.

Wellington's army was cooped up in the somewhat narrow space between the Nive, the Nivelle, and the sea. He had already resolved on an advance when, in consequence of Napoleon's disasters in Germany, the Home Government sent him positive orders to push on in France. The first requisite for this was the passage of the Nive, which Wellington decided to carry out by moving his right across at Cambo and Ustariz, where Soult could not seriously interfere with him, except by letting go his hold on Bayonne. To fix him there the left and centre of the allied army was to move forward, Hope's wing pushing well on towards Bayonne and the Adour below it. Once Wellington was across the Nive with his right his army would be cut in two by the Nive, which was devoid of bridges in its lower reaches and difficult to pass when swollen by the prevailing heavy rains. Soult, on the other hand, could pass it at pleasure within his camp of Bayonne.

The passage of the Nive was fixed for December 9th, and in the preceding night the 1/9th was marched from Guéthary, by the St. Jean de Luz-Bayonne road, through Bidart, the head-quarters of the 5th division. As the division moved by the main road the 1st division, after a few hours' march, was halted on the heights of Barouillet. The two divisions then wheeled half-right and skirmishing began on their front with the French about 8 a.m. Steadily pushing the enemy back, the 1st division had by 1 o clock got to Anglet on the main road, whilst the 5th had gone still farther and occupied the Forest of Bayonne, facing the inundations and other defences of the western front of the fortress. In this position they remained till nightfall, gathering for Wellington information as to the French defences and as to the possibility of a passage of the Adour below Bayonne. Then the whole retired, the

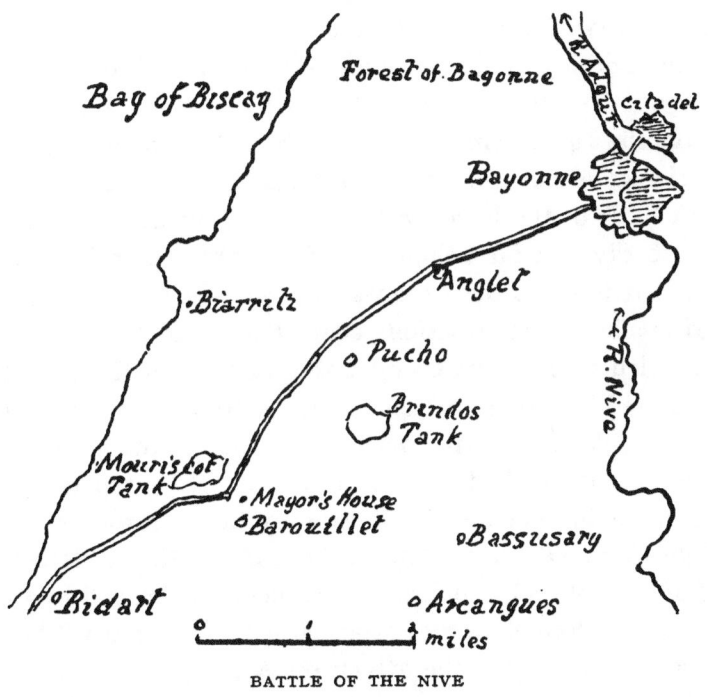

BATTLE OF THE NIVE

retreat being covered by the 5th division. Hale's journal states that the 9th were the rear-guard in the retirement. Hope's advance had been opposed only by two French brigades of the divisions of Leval and Boyer. The fighting had not been very severe, but the 1st and 5th divisions had suffered about 250 casualties, to which the 1/9th contributed one sergeant and one man killed. On this day Gomm, who was on the staff of the division, was slightly wounded, but had not to go off duty.

That night the 1/9th were back at Bidart with the rest of the 5th division, but the 1st division and Aylmer's brigade were sent right back to St. Jean de Luz—a move which might have had serious consequences on the next day.

Soult had now decided to contain the allies who were on the right bank of the Nive, and had no safe communication with the rest of the army below Ustariz, whilst he attacked those on the left bank with nine divisions of infantry (four of them brought over the Nive in Bayonne), a division of cavalry, and forty guns.

On the morning of the 10th the position from Barouillet to Bidart was held by the 5th division and Bradford's Portuguese, Robinson's brigade on the right being at Barouillet. Beyond his right were the light division at Arcangues, and one brigade of the 7th division extending to the left bank of the Nive, with the other brigade three miles in rear and the 4th division far behind it. The French attack on Arcangues and beyond it towards the Nive was, on the whole, very feeble, though they had available four divisions against one and half British. Foy's division, which would have brought the number on the left up to five, was transferred by Soult to Reille's attack from Beyris on the west of Bayonne. Reille only started his advance against the 5th division after 9 a.m., when Clausel had driven in the British outposts of the light division. Then he sent Leval's division by the high road on Barouillet, whilst Boyer's moved on its left by Pucho. In the defile between the tanks of Mouriscot and Brindos the advance was delayed by Campbell's Portuguese, and Reille's actual attack was not ordered till he saw that Clausel had deployed for the attack on Arcangues, and that Foy was moving on Croix d'Olhar against the eastern flank of the position at Barouillet, where Robinson's brigade was now firmly established in the coppice in front of the village and the mayor's house and orchard near the main road.

It was noon when Boyer's division in columns of battalions advanced against Barouillet from the north, and Foy's from the east. Split up

SIR JOHN CAMERON, K.C.B.
Born 1773. Commanded 1st Battalion, 1808–22. Colonel, 1833–1844. (*Ch. XVI*)

by the nature of the country into combats between small bodies of men, the first attack of Boyer was repulsed.

The attack was renewed by one of Leval's brigades on the road against Robinson's left, one of Boyer's brigades in the centre, and one of Foy's against the right.

Now, however, Aylmer's brigade and Bradford's Portuguese were arriving from St. Jean de Luz, and Hay was able to release Greville's brigade, which he had so far held in reserve. The three French brigades attacking Robinson soon got entangled in their converging advance, so that when they at last reached the garden and orchard of the mayor's house, where Robinson had his stronghold, they were a confused and disorderly crowd which suffered heavily from the fire from the house. It was at this juncture that the 1/9th, preceded by a Portuguese battalion, arrived at the head of Greville's brigade by the main road. These two regiments—the 9th on the right and the Portuguese on the left—wheeled inwards and fell upon the flank and rear of the attacking French, whom they soon drove back with heavy losses in killed and wounded, and especially in prisoners.

It was after 2 p.m. when this attack was finally disposed of, and now fresh help was in sight as the 1st division came up from St. Jean de Luz, where it had been so unwisely sent the night before. Nevertheless, Soult was already arranging a fresh attack by a German brigade of Vilatte's division against Barouillet in front, whilst Foy's second brigade was to turn it from the east.

Meanwhile the course of the battle farther east disturbed Soult and induced him to give up this attack on the 5th division.

Foy and Vilatte fell back to Pucho, Boyer to Plaisance, and only Leval remained behind to hold the line of outposts. The German brigade of Vilatte's division took the opportunity of this retreat to lag behind and pass over *en masse* to the British. The following incident of the action of the 1/9th on this day is recounted by Napier:

> " Colonel Cameron was on the extreme left of Greville's brigade, Robinson being then shifted into the second line and towards the right, Bradford's brigade was at the mayor's house, some distance to the left of the 9th Regiment, and the space between was occupied

by a Portuguese battalion. There was in front of Greville's brigade a thick hedge, but immediately opposite the 9th was a coppice wood possessed by the enemy, whose skirmishers were continually gathering in masses and rushing out as if to assail the 9th; they were as often driven back, yet the ground was so broken that nothing could be seen beyond the flanks; and when some time had passed in this manner, Colonel Cameron, who had received no orders, heard a sudden firing along the main road to his left. His adjutant was sent to investigate the cause of the firing, and returned immediately with intelligence that there was little fighting on the road, but a French regiment, which must have passed unseen in small bodies through the Portuguese, between the 9th and the mayor's house, was rapidly filing into line in the rear. The 4th British regiment was in close column at a short distance, and its commander, Colonel Piper, was directed by Colonel Cameron to face about, march to the rear, and then bring up his left shoulder, when he would fall in with the French regiment. Piper marched, but whether he misunderstood the order, took a wrong direction, or mistook the enemy for Portuguese, he passed them. No firing was heard by the 9th, so the adjutant again hurried to the rear and returned with the news that the 4th Regiment was not to be seen, but that the enemy's line was nearly formed. Colonel Cameron, leaving fifty men of the 9th to answer the skirmishing fire, which had now increased from the coppice, immediately faced about and marched in line against the new enemy as fast as the rough nature of the ground would permit. The French fire, slow at first, increased as the distance lessened, but when the 9th, coming close up, sprang forward to the charge, the French line broke and fled to the flanks in the utmost disorder. Those who made for their own right brushed the left of Greville's brigade and even carried off an officer of the Royals in their rush, yet the greatest number were made prisoners, and the 9th, having lost several men, resumed their old ground."

The account in Hale's diary makes the matter clearer. He says that Robinson's and the Portuguese brigades were called up first,

Greville's being a little in rear in reserve. Towards midday Greville's brigade was sent up to relieve Robinson's, which had suffered heavily. The Portuguese had not lost much. Robinson then fell back to Greville's old position of reserve. A little distance on the left of Greville's brigade were the Portuguese, separated from him by a coppice. Soon after Greville relieved Robinson the French began to devote more attention to the Portuguese, who were not very reliable against a bayonet charge, and gave way before one about half an hour after the relief. The result was that the 9th were almost surrounded. The 9th could see very little of what was going on, and did not know the Portuguese had given way. As soon as Cameron found he had French in his rear, he at once turned the regiment right about and charged to his rear, broke the French, and took about 400 prisoners, whom they made over to the care of Robinson's brigade, which was just coming up again. Then the 9th returned to deal with the enemy in their front, who had almost got into the British position. Another charge with the bayonet drove them completely out and replaced the 9th in its old position. After that there were several attempts by the French, which all broke down. Colonel Cameron's prompt action against the French in his rear probably saved a very awkward situation.

Cameron's direction to Piper to face about, march to the rear, and bring up his left shoulder, indicates the 4th as being on Cameron's right or right rear. If that were so, the direction would bring the 4th on the right flank of the French in Cameron's rear.

The following is another anecdote of this day. Major-General Bainbrigge in 1848 wrote to Lieutenant-Colonel Davis of the 9th :—
" I forgot in my address [on presentation of colours at Newry] to mention an anecdote of Lieutenant Dale of the 9th, which was this : At the battle called the Nive in December, 1813, the 9th was in small parties skirmishing, defending a coppice wood near the mayor's house at Bassusary. A party of the enemy under an officer came round by the rear upon a party of the 9th whom Lieutenant Dale commanded, and the French officer in exultation, thinking he had surrounded them, called out ' Rendez vous, vous etes prisonniers ! ' ' No,' said Dale, ' I'll be d——d if we are,' on which his party faced about and, after a sharp

scuffle hand to hand with the bayonet, it ended in the whole French party being taken prisoners or killed. Here was again shown an example of British determination and no surrender under any circumstances. Sir J. Cameron told me the above anecdote was true, at Plymouth."

On this day the 9th lost Lieutenant P. Le Mesurier, Ensign G. Bolton, and ten men killed ; Captain B. Siborn, Lieutenants E. Watkins, Dallas, R. Brookes, one sergeant, and sixty-four men wounded. On the other hand, they took 160 prisoners.

A thick fog covered the neighbourhood of Barouillet in the early morning of the 11th. At dawn, by Wellington's personal orders, an advance was made to clear Leval's pickets from the hill towards Bassusary but they were withdrawn without fighting. At 10 a.m. Wellington ordered the 9th forward towards Pucho to ascertain what the French were doing. Colonel Cameron with the regiment was soon engaged in a sharp skirmish in front of Pucho, but apparently did not intend to advance into the village, which would be a dangerous operation in the uncertainty as to the French strength. At that moment, however, Colonel Delancy of the staff rode up and directed Cameron to occupy the village. Soon after he had done so the fog lifted and revealed the French in great strength, about to counter-attack in front and on both flanks. So heavy and sudden was the attack that the 9th was practically surrounded, and in imminent risk of capture, when Hope, bringing up some of the Portuguese to their rescue, enabled Cameron's men to retreat. The fighting ended here and Wellington rode off to look after his right, leaving Hope with orders to push back the enemy's piquets and reoccupy his former outposts on the ridge towards Bassusary.

After this morning affair there seems to have been an idea in Hope's force that the fighting was over for the day. The men, weary with hard work and suffering from the cold rain and wind of the previous days, were enjoying the improvement which had now set in, and were eating their rations or searching for fuel, when, about 2 p.m., the French suddenly came forward again along the road. Hope had been careless in allowing this incautious conduct of his troops, and before his great personal exertions could get them ready again the French with loud cries of " En avant " were upon them all over the scene of the fighting of the

10th. The coppice in front of the mayor's house and even its outbuildings were lost, and a confused fight raged about the house itself. The British were in complete disorder, units intermixed, and fatigue parties hurrying back to the struggle.

Fortunately a British battalion on the road was able, by its fire on the right flank of Boyer's attack, to check it long enough for order to be restored amongst the British at Barouillet. The 5th division, with part of Aylmer's brigade and the Portuguese, now took up a line with its left resting on the Mouriscot tank west of the road, and extending through the coppice and orchard in front of the mayor's house to the right bank of the valley of the Ouhabia, the little stream which flows down to the sea between Bidart and Guéthary. In second line, on a ridge behind Barouillet, were the Guards and the rest of Aylmer's brigade. In this formation the French attack was beaten off, and Boyer's men retired to their position of the morning, whence they kept up a cannonade till nightfall.

The 5th division was then withdrawn to the second line, for it had suffered heavily in both its brigades. The 9th had lost fourteen men killed; Ensigns David Holmes, Robert Story, three sergeants, and seventy-two men wounded; two sergeants and ten men missing, the latter probably in the unfortunate affair at Pucho when the regiment was sacrificed by the indiscretion of a staff officer. In three days' fighting it had had casualties numbering over 200.

December 12th passed in comparative peace on the British front between the Nive and the sea, though the tension due to the recent fighting was so great that there was a sudden outburst of firing between the piquets when a visit of the Adjutant-General to those on the British side created an alarm, among the French, of an impending attack.

The 13th again was peaceful on the front of the 5th division, for on that day Soult had transferred a large force to the right bank of the Nive and made a heavy attack on Hill. In this battle of St. Pierre the 9th of course had no hand. It resulted in Soult's repulse on that side of the Nive also.

The 1/9th now again went into cantonments at Guéthary and Bidart, where they remained peaceably till February 4, 1814, when they moved to Garat's house behind the bridge of Urdain on the Cambo-Bayonne road, and on the 8th to Arcangues. On the 21st it passed, with the rest of the 5th division, now commanded by General Colville, to Villefranque, on the right bank of the Nive, just below the pontoon bridge constructed by Wellington in December to connect the two wings of his army.

Soult had now abandoned Bayonne as the support of his right and St. Jean Pied de Port as that of his left, and was concentrating for his retreat, which ended at Toulouse.

Hope was left behind to invest the fortress of Bayonne. By the end of February, when Hope had passed the Adour near its mouth, the fortress was completely surrounded with its garrison of 11,000 men under Thouvenot. On March 24th the 9th was moved from Villefranque to Anglet, opposite the south-western outworks of the fortress, and here it remained till the surrender of Bayonne. It was employed merely on blockade work and had no fighting. It had had some of its recent losses replaced by a draft of 150 men from the 2nd battalion, in which they were replaced by recruits from the Militia.

The great sortie on the night of April 14th, eight days after Napoleon's abdication, issued from the north side of the fortress, beyond the Adour, though there was a small demonstration towards Anglet to divert attention from the north and to retain British troops on that side. It is true that Hay's brigade is stated to have furnished the piquets on the night of the sortie on the northern front. Hay himself was killed there; nevertheless it seems certain that the 9th was left at Anglet and that it was only its piquets which were engaged. Its losses were two rank and file killed and eight wounded. This disastrous sortie cost both sides dearly and should never have been made had it been made clear to Thouvenot that Napoleon had abdicated. In it Sir John Hope, in the dark, got amongst French troops and was wounded and taken prisoner.[1]

The war in France being now over, there remained only the war

[1] From this time we lose the advantage of Gomm's admirable letters and diaries. He served no more with the 9th, and on July 25, 1814, became captain of a company, and lieutenant-colonel, in the Coldstream Guards.

with America. In May, 1814, the 1/9th was marched from Bayonne to Bordeaux, where it arrived on the 22nd and encamped seven miles lower down the Garonne until June 3rd, when it embarked on transports. Next day it was transferred to H.M.S. " York " and H.M.S. " Vengeur," of 74 guns each, for transport to Canada. From the mouth of the St. Lawrence the regiment was sent in transports to Quebec, whence, after a week's halt, it proceeded to Montreal, arriving there on August 22nd. They were now encamped north of the St. Lawrence, below Prescott. Here they remained, without taking any part in Sir G. Prevost's advance on Plattsburg. In October they moved up the left bank of the St. Lawrence to Kingston. At this time the battalion had been reinforced by two strong drafts from the 2nd battalion in England.

Though the 1st battalion was not actively engaged in the American War on the Canadian frontier, they were exposed to many temptations by American agents, who, when both sides spoke the same language, could easily approach the British troops. As had been the case with Burgoyne's captured soldiers after Saratoga, many inducements to desertion were held out, and the risk was small. The temptation was by no means always resisted, and it speaks highly for the patriotism and discipline of the 9th when we find it stated publicly by Sir George Murray, the Governor and Commander-in-Chief, when the regiment was leaving Canada, that not a single man of the 9th had deserted to the enemy. After the review of the regiment previous to its embarkation at Kingston, Sir George Murray addressed the regiment as follows :—

"I have detained the 9th Regiment on the field a little after the other troops, that I might have an opportunity of thanking the officers and soldiers for their good conduct since they have been in this province. Sir Frederick Robinson, who had before an opportunity of witnessing the gallantry of the regiment when opposed to the enemy, and having been in a situation to bear testimony to its exemplary conduct in quarters, has made to me the most favourable report of the regiment. You have not been, I am sorry to say, without bad examples in your neighbourhood, and I regret it the more because they have taken place in regiments which have, prior to that, borne high characters. It has given me very great pleasure that the ninth has borne itself entirely free from any stain, such as that to which I allude, that the men have shown they are justly impressed with the sacredness of the obligation which binds them to the service of their King, and that they have a due regard to their own characters, and the unsullied reputation of the regiment. The praise for such conduct is equally due to all the individuals composing the corps: to the absent Colonel Cameron, whose zeal and ability in the service have long been conspicuous; to the commanding officer, and the other officers of the first battalion now present; to that useful and respectable body of men, the non-commissioned officers; and to the private soldiers themselves, whose good conduct is the best and most honourable return that the officers can receive for the pains they have bestowed upon the discipline of the corps. I have only now to take my leave of you with my best wishes for your honour and success, wherever you may go, and to assure you that, in whatever part of the world it may be my lot to serve, it will at all times be a matter of satisfaction to me, if I should find myself in company with the 9th Regiment."

The only other regiment which could show as clean a sheet was the 88th. Meanwhile, in March, 1815, Napoleon had landed and the Hundred Days had commenced, but the battle of Waterloo had not yet been fought when, early in June, 1815, the 1/9th was called back to England, expecting to take part in the coming campaign against the returned Emperor. Going down the St. Lawrence in boats from Kingston, the regiment was transferred to transports at Quebec, and reached Spithead on July 15th, having missed the chance of taking part in Wellington's and Napoleon's last campaign.

Naturally enough the regiment was detailed to form part of the Army of Occupation in France. Again reinforced from the 2nd battalion, they landed at Ostend on August 17, 1815, went by boats on the canal to Ghent, and marched thence to Paris. Arriving there on September 5th they were sent into camp at St. Denis, where they constituted the 16th brigade under Major-General Sir Thomas Bradford, with the 57th, 81st, and 90th Regiments, and were reviewed by Wellington between the Porte Maillot and St. Denis on September 18th. In November they were brigaded with the 5th and 21st under Sir Thomas Brisbane and sent back to Boulogne, whence, in December, they again marched to Compiègne. In January, 1816, they marched to new quarters at St. Amand, north of Valenciennes, a neighbourhood the future celebrity of which no one could then foresee. In August they moved a short way to Aire, and later to the glacis of Valenciennes itself. Here they were reviewed, with other British troops and Danish and Saxon contingents on the plain of Denain, whence they returned to St. Amand.

In the spring of 1817 the strength of the battalion was reduced to ten companies with a staff of one colonel, one lieutenant-colonel, two majors, ten captains, twelve lieutenants, eight ensigns, one paymaster, one adjutant, one quartermaster, one surgeon, two assistant-surgeons, one sergeant-major, one quartermaster-sergeant, one paymaster-sergeant, one armourer as sergeant, ten colour-sergeants, one schoolmaster-sergeant, thirty sergeants, forty corporals, one drum-major, twenty-one drummers and fifers, 760 privates. Total, all ranks, 907.

The 9th was now brigaded, on the reduction of the strength of the Army of Occupation, with the 5th and a battalion of the Rifle Brigade, under Major-General Sir J. Lambert.

In April, 1816, the 9th moved to cantonments in villages about Cambrai, and in July to camp on the glacis of the fortress. Here it lost Major Ferrars, killed accidentally by falling into the ditch. In September the regiment again camped on the glacis of Valenciennes, where, on the 6th, it was reviewed, with the other British forces, by the King of Prussia. It was present at another review, near Bouchain, by the Duke of Kent, previous to returning for the winter to cantonments in the villages about Cambrai.

In June, 1818, it again went into camp on the glacis of Cambrai, and in October marched to Neuilly-sur-Seine for the general review of the Army of Occupation before its withdrawal from France. The review took place on October 23rd before the Emperor of Russia, the King of Prussia, the Prince of Orange, and the Grand Dukes Constantine and Michael.

The 9th then marched to Calais, where it embarked for England, landing at Dover and Ramsgate. Thence it marched to Winchester, where its establishment was reduced by one assistant-surgeon, ten sergeants, ten corporals and 140 privates, to a total of 746 of all ranks. Here it received orders to proceed to the West Indies, of which it had such unpleasant experiences in the latter part of the eighteenth century. Leaving Winchester on January 30, 1819, it embarked at Gosport on February 3rd, and arrived at Carlisle Bay in the island of Barbados on April 3rd. It landed on the 7th to be inspected by Lieutentant-General Lord Combermere, and then re-embarked for various destinations in the islands.

The headquarters and five companies, under Lieutenant-Colonel Campbell, sailed to St. Vincent; Brevet Lieutenant-Colonel Peebles took three companies to Dominica, and the remaining two went with Brevet Lieutenant-Colonel Lambert to St. Lucia.

Health conditions in the West Indies were not much better than they had been, though of course now, in peace time, the effects of climate were not aggravated by the harships and exposure of war, as they were when the regiment was last in this region. On July 14th occurred the first loss of an officer by disease in the death of Captain Siborn, a veteran of the Peninsula, who, it will be remembered, was wounded at the battle of the Nive.

At these stations the regiment remained till February, 1821, when, in a general shuffle of West Indian stations, it was allotted to Grenada and Trinidad. In April two companies were detached to Tobago, an island in the taking of which part of the regiment had assisted in 1795.

From 1821 the establishment was reduced from ten companies to eight. Four of them were at Grenada and two each at Trinidad and Tobago.

At this time Colonel Cameron was promoted to Major-General, and his place, after fourteen eventful years of command of the battalion, was taken by Colonel N. Blackwell, who reached Grenada at the end of 1821.

The year 1822 was a disastrous one. Thirty-two recruits had been sent out from England under Major Loftus. Before they landed yellow fever broke out amongst them, and no less than twenty-seven, including Major Loftus, died of it. Presumably the transport was already infected from a previous voyage, and, of course, in those days no one would have thought of disinfecting her.

The head-quarters of the regiment were at first in Grenada, with detachments in Trinidad and Tobago, but in 1825 they were removed to Trinidad. Otherwise, beyond slight alterations of the strength of the detachments in one or other of the three islands, there is nothing to record of their sojourn there, save that they were always suffering off and on from yellow fever and other diseases of the region.

The year 1825 is remarkable as that in which a regular regimental depot was first established. In order to do this the establishment of the regiment was increased from eight to ten companies, of which six were service and four depot companies. Some officers and men were withdrawn from the West Indies and sent home as the nucleus of the four depot companies, which were first established at Albany Barracks in the Isle of Wight.[1]

In December, 1826, the companies at Grenada and Tobago embarked for England and were followed by the others. The last company reached Portsmouth in the beginning of February, 1827. The regiment had been eight years in the West Indies, and had suffered severely, losing eight officers and 271 men dead of disease, not to speak of constant shortages owing to men being in hospital.

Soon after its arrival in England Colonel Campbell, who had been appointed to the lieutenant-colonelcy in 1826, was succeeded by Major Taylor. The regiment also received new arms.

During the summer the adjutant (Brownrigg) was very busy training 400 recruits, and his energy was acknowledged when the regiment was inspected in June by Major-General Sir John Cameron, the officer whose name, as lieutenant-colonel, is inseparably connected with the achievements in the Peninsula of the 2nd, and afterwards still more so with those of the 1st, battalion. He expressed the great pleasure he should have in reporting the very gratifying results of the exertions of the officers, in the high conditions into which the corps had been so speedily brought after its return from the West Indies.

[1] It will be recalled that there had been formed something resembling a depot when, in 1776, two out of twelve companies were left in Ireland for recruiting purposes, one of them being afterwards sent to India with Medows in 1781.

CHAPTER XVII

THE 1st BATTALION IN INDIA—FIRST KABUL CAMPAIGN.
1827-1842

A NEW set of colours, bearing the battle honours of the regiment so far sanctioned, had been prepared by the colonel, General Sir Robert Brownrigg. On September 25, 1827, a parade of the whole garrison of Plymouth was held at which the new colours were presented to the regiment by Lady Cameron, wife of their old leader of the Peninsula, in the Grand Square, Devonport. Major-General Sir John Cameron was himself commanding the Plymouth garrison.

A few days later the regiment left Plymouth by sea for Liverpool, and the following garrison order was issued on the 4th October :—

> " The first division of the ninth regiment will embark from the dockyard on Saturday morning at 7 o'clock, and the baggage at 4 p.m. on Friday. The remaining companies will be concentrated in the citadel.
>
> " This regiment is naturally endeared to Major-General Sir John Cameron by long and intimate association ; expressions of marked approval, which the appearance, interior system, and conduct of the corps undeniably claim from the General Commanding, are therefore particularly in accordance with his private feelings.
>
> " The Major-General has watched with lively interest the unremitting exertions of Lieutenant-Colonel Taylor and the officers under him, to form the numerous recruits and improve the battalion, and warmly congratulates the Lieutenant-Colonel on the proof of success exhibited by the steadiness and correct movement of the men at the inspection of the 1st instant. The Major-General takes leave of

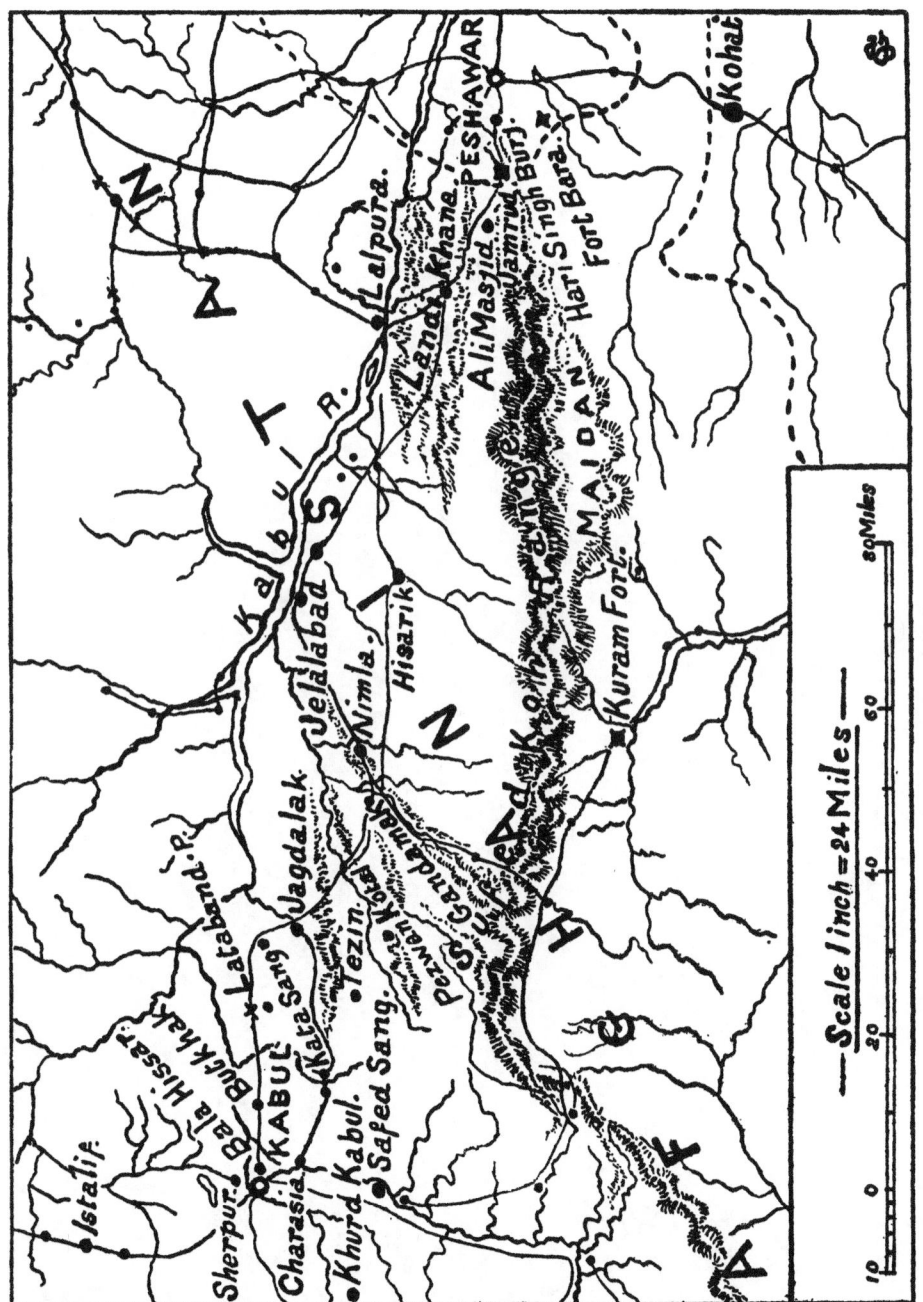

AFGHANISTAN—KHYBER PASS TO KABUL

the ninth regiment with sensible regret ; his best wishes will ever attend the officers, non-commissioned officers, and private soldiers." Landing at Liverpool, the regiment was marched to Manchester, Stockport, and Oldham. At the inspection on May 12, 1828, at Manchester Barracks, Major-General Harris described the battalion as " in very excellent order."

In the summer of 1828 the regiment moved to Bolton and Blackburn, and in October embarked at Liverpool for Belfast, where it was stationed, with a company each at Downpatrick and Carrickfergus. Between that and June, 1830, it was three times inspected by Major-General Thornton. At the inspection of May 22, 1829, he recorded the following remarks : " The regiment is fairly composed, both as to its officers and men, and is fairly commanded. Its field movements are excellent, and generally it has advanced considerably in good order and other respects, although some of its companies have not yet improved to the perfect state I had expected." On May 17, 1830, he said : " The regiment is a fair body of men on the whole, but some are short and of puny appearance. It is well officered and drilled, and has improved." The officer commanding at this last inspection was Major Watkins.

It then marched to Newry, Armagh, and Cavan, where it was employed on more than one occasion in stopping threatened riots.

September, 1830, saw it transferred to Richmond Barracks, Dublin. Thence, in May, 1831, it marched to Limerick. On May 31st Lieutenant-Colonel Custance took over command from Lieutenant-Colonel Taylor, placed on half-pay. From October to December the head-quarters were in Galway, but returned in the latter month to Limerick. In January, 1832, the regiment marched to Fermoy and on to Cork.

The whole of this tour of service in Ireland was most disturbed and irksome. The regiment was constantly being marched about all over the country to keep order. It is hardly worth while to record the numerous places, small and large, thus visited. The duties were generally unpleasant, consisting largely in dispersing illegal meetings and protecting the well-disposed. On January 11, 1832, the battalion was under orders to embark for Gibraltar when, owing to the disturbed state of the country, it had to be stopped and again sent marching in detachments about the south of Ireland on the usual duties.

On November 4, 1832, the six service companies were embarked for Plymouth, the four depot companies being left at Fermoy.

Sailing on January 8, 1833, from Plymouth, after being twice driven back by bad weather, the service companies landed in Mauritius in April, and were stationed at Mahebourg, on the south-east coast, till April, 1834, when they returned to Port Louis on the west coast. In May, 1833, General Sir R. Brownrigg, colonel of the regiment, having died, the colonelcy was bestowed on Sir John Cameron, K.C.B., whose long connexion with the regiment only ended with his death in November, 1844. The service companies left Port Louis in September, 1835, for India, and landed at Calcutta in November.

In February of the same year the depot companies had been removed from Ireland to Chatham. There they embarked in June for India and had already arrived (in October) in Calcutta when the service companies reached it from Mauritius. It was in this year also that, on June 9th, an order was issued by the War Office that

> "His Majesty has been graciously pleased to permit the Ninth of Foot to bear on its colours and appointments, in addition to any other badges and devices which may have heretofore been granted, the word 'Corunna,' in commemoration of the distinguished conduct of the regiment before Corunna in January, 1809."

After two months in Fort William at Calcutta[1] the whole regiment marched to Chinsura, in January, 1836, and in December, 1838, to Hazaribagh. At Chinsura Lieutenant-Colonel (afterwards Sir John) McCaskill succeeded Lieutenant-Colonel Custance in command of the battalion. With the regiment in India was Lieutenant James Slater Cumming, whose diary and letters during six years in it were published

---

[1] In March, 1836, it is stated that Private Febble was transported for life for desertion. In April it is noted that there were several fatal cases of cholera in the regiment at Calcutta ("United Service Gazette," March 12 and April 23, 1836). Looking to the time it took then to communicate with India these events probably occurred in the autumn of 1835.

by his relatives after he was killed at the forcing of the Khyber Pass in 1842. There is a monument to his memory in St. Patrick's Cathedral, Dublin. His father was a clergyman of the Irish Church whose circumstances did not admit of the idea of purchase of commissions, and the young officer's diary throws a few interesting sidelights on regimental life under those circumstances.

He joined the regiment at Chinsura on July 13, 1837, after a weary voyage of six months. He says, in his letters from Chinsura, that he found he could live comfortably on his pay as ensign of Rs. 130 per mensem (less deductions), and we even find him, rather later, remitting money to help his father, and investing in a bungalow at Hazar bagh, for which he paid Rs. 700. In November, 1837, Colonel McCaskill being appointed to command the Meerut division was succeeded by Major A. B. Taylor. The regiment moved from Chinsura to Hazaribagh in January, 1838. Four months later there is a letter from Cumming in which he mentions that he had written to " Mrs. General Churchill " to ask her interest in getting him his promotion to lieutenant without purchase, in the vacancy created by the recent death from cholera of Lieutenant French. He was luckier than many of the poorer officers, for when he was killed in April, 1842, he was the senior subaltern. What the lot of some others under the purchase system was is described in his letter of December, 1840 : " I have been fortunate," he writes, " but in the 9th I have seen three old lieutenants—one of sixty and two of forty years—men who were not born when these entered the army have passed over their heads ; but yet the finest profession is the army."

From Hazaribagh the 9th marched, in the cold weather season of 1839–40, to Agra, where it arrived in the beginning of March without losing a single man on the march. The sick and the women and children were brought up the Ganges and Jumna in boats. Cumming was sent down to meet them on March 15th, expecting to find them as far back as Calpi ; but they had travelled quicker than was anticipated, and he found them at Secundra. Colonel McCaskill was again in command from October, 1840, till December, 1841, when he became brigadier-general. In the ensuing cold weather the 9th marched to Meerut, and stayed there till the 1st December, 1841, when they marched for Firozpur, the British frontier station near the River Sutlej, which then formed the boundary between British territory and the Sikh Kingdom ruled by the famous Maharaja Ranjit Sing.

The regiment was under orders for active service beyond the Indus in Afghanistan. The origin of the expedition on which the 9th were now starting, put very briefly, was this : In 1839 the Government, both at home and in India, suffering from a very acute attack of Russophobia, looked upon Afghanistan as a probable instrument in the hands of the Tsar for the invasion of India. To cut the ground from under the Russian's feet it was decided to set up in Afghanistan a prince friendly to and protected by the British. The man selected was Shah Sujah, a former ruler of Afghanistan, who had been defeated and driven out of the country by his brother Mahmud Shah. He in turn had fallen before Dost Muhammad Barukzai, who in 1837 was firmly established in power at Kabul, whilst Shah Sujah was an exile in the Punjab. Negotiations with Dost Muhammad having failed to enlist him as an ally of the British, it was decided to replace Shah Sujah by force on the throne. The advance on Kabul through the Bolan Pass was successful. Kandahar and Ghazni were taken, Shah Sujah entered Kabul in triumph in August, 1839, and Dost Muhammad fled. For the next two years Afghanistan was occupied by British troops, to whose presence alone was due the power of the unpopular Shah Sujah to maintain himself as ruler.

In November, 1841, Sir Alexander Burnes, the British envoy, was assassinated in Kabul, and shortly afterwards followed the treacherous murder of Sir W. Macnaghten. The British force of 4,000 troops, with thrice that number of followers, surrounded by a hostile population, started in midwinter to return to the Khyber Pass and India. Before it reached Jellalabad, where General Sir R. Sale held the fort, the whole had been destroyed, save a few officers, women, and children taken prisoners by Akbar Khan, the son of Dost Muhammad. Only one survivor, Dr. Brydon, exhausted by hardships, succeeded in reaching Jellalabad.

General Pollock was already marching through the Punjab to bring back the garrisons of Kabul and Jellalabad when the news of this disaster arrived in India. He was at once ordered to avenge the massacre

SIR JOHN McCASKILL, K.C.B., K.H.
Commanded 1st Battalion, 1838–46. Killed whilst commanding a Division at Moodkee, 1845. (*Ch. XVII*)

and to retake Kabul, where he was to be joined by General Nott from Kandahar.

The 9th, ordered to form part of General Pollock's force, marched from Firozpur on January 4, 1842. The advanced guard of the relieving army was a brigade of four native regiments under General Wild, which reached Peshawar at the end of December, 1841. It was unsupported till early in February, when the brigade under Colonel John McCaskill of the 9th, and including that regiment, arrived.

Meanwhile, in January, Wild had failed in an attempt to occupy and hold the fort of Ali Masjid, five miles up the Khyber Pass, and the enemy now held the Pass throughout its length. Wild's troops were very demoralized, and had a very large number in hospital when General Pollock arrived on February 5th. Captain Borton's diary gives the number as 1,700.[1] McCaskill's brigade arrived a day or two later, but owing to the state of Wild's brigade it was quite out of the question to think of an advance for the present. In addition to the sickness there was much disaffection among Wild's troops, who, as well as the Sikh auxiliaries, did their best to spread it among the native troops of the newly arrived brigade. Reinforcements had to be awaited.

At last, on March 31, 1842, the British camp was moved forward from Peshawar to Jamrud; but it was not till the morning of April 5th that Pollock advanced to force the mouth of the Pass. His whole force contained only one European infantry regiment (the 9th) and one British cavalry regiment (the 3rd Dragoons). The mouth of the Pass had been blocked by the enemy by the construction of a huge barricade of stones and branches, against which the artillery of those days was almost useless. Pollock had but one battery of horse artillery, one of field artillery, and two mountain guns.

The attack was divided into three columns—the centre led by the

[1] For the Afghan, Sikh, and Crimean campaigns we have had the great advantage of the admirable diary and private letters of the late Sir Arthur Borton, which were very kindly placed at our disposal by his son Colonel A. C. Borton. They are of the greatest interest, very full, written in careful and excellent English and full of comments on facts and outspoken criticism, intended of course, during his own time, only for the perusal of himself and his most intimate friends and relations.

grenadier company of the 9th, followed by parts of seven native battalions, the one British and one native cavalry regiment, the artillery, sappers, and baggage and treasure. This column was not to begin action, except as regards artillery fire, until the precipitous hills on either side had been cleared of the tribesmen, with whom they swarmed, and their summits crowned by the two flank columns. These columns were constituted as follows: on the right, two companies of the 9th, four of the 26th Native Infantry, and 400 friendly tribesmen were to lead under the command of Colonel Taylor of the 9th. Behind them were seven companies of the 60th Native Infantry, four of the 64th, some sappers, and

STORMING OF THE KHYBER PASS
A, B, C, D, Points referred to in Captain Borton's letter

another one and a half companies of the 9th. Major Davis of the 9th commanded this rear portion of the right column.

The left column, commanded by Major Huish of the 26th Native Infantry, was led by two companies of the 9th, followed by four companies of the 26th Native Infantry and 200 tribesmen. Behind them were seven companies of the 53rd Native Infantry and three companies of the 60th. The rear was brought up by four and a half companies of the 64th Native Infantry and one and a half of the 9th, all under Colonel Moseley of the 64th Native Infantry. The two flanking columns were therefore almost identical in composition; in each the 9th provided the two leading and one and a half rear companies.

When the heights had been crowned, the leading companies of the 9th, and the native regiment immediately behind them, were to come down again to enter the Pass, leaving the rest to hold the hills.

The attack began on the flanks at dawn, and the tribsmen facing the right and left British columns were surprised, for they expected the British to try and force the Pass only, leaving the enemy on the flanking hills to fire thence into their flanks. The tribesmen only realized the position at dawn when the British right and left columns were well started in their ascent of the hills. General Pollock's despatch describing the action gives the following account of it :

"Both columns, after considerable opposition, which they overcame in a most gallant style, succeeded in routing the enemy, and gaining possession of the crest of the hills on either side. While the flanking columns were in progress on the heights, I ordered Captain Alexander of the artillery to place the guns in position, and to throw shrapnels among the enemy when opportunity offered, which assisted much in their discomfiture. As Lt.-Colonel Taylor, from the opposition he had met with, and the extremely difficult nature of the ground, was some time in reaching the summit of the hill on the right, I detached a party (consisting of the grenadiers of the 9th Foot and six companies of the 33rd Native Infantry), under the command of Brigadier Wild, to assault it in front. It was, however, so extremely steep near the top that, notwithstanding the undaunted gallantry of the officers and men, they were unable to gain a footing on the summit, and I regret to say the enemy were enabled to throw stones with fatal effect upon some of the leading grenadiers of the 9th Foot. Finding the heights in our possession, I now advanced the main column to the mouth of the Pass, and commenced destroying the barrier, which the enemy had evacuated on perceiving their position was turned. A portion of the right and left columns being left to keep the heights, under the command of Lt.-Colonel Mosely and Major Anderson respectively, Major Huish and Lt.-Col. Taylor continued their advance to crown the hills in front and on each side, which were covered with the enemy, who appeared determined to contest every inch of ground; but nothing could resist the gallantry of our troops, who carried everything before them.

From Major-General McCaskill [Colonel of the 9th Foot], commanding the infantry division, who was on this occasion commanding the rear-guard, I received every assistance; as likewise from Brigadier-General Wild; to Lieutenant-Colonel Taylor my warmest acknowledgments are due for the spirit, coolness, and judgment with which he discharged the duties entrusted to him."

Some further details are given in the following extract from the Regimental Record of services :—

"The columns under the command of Lieutenant-Colonel Taylor for the capture of the heights on the right entrance of the Khyber Pass were formed at daybreak on the 5th April, 1842, in three divisions of four companies each protected on the right flank by a squadron of the 3rd Light Dragoons under Lieutenant Unett,[1] and in this order, with skirmishers and supports in front, advanced, driving a considerable body of the enemy up the hills, which were scaled and crowned in spite of a determined opposition. This effected, the troops moved to their left to clear the redoubts commanding the entrance to the Pass, which were abandoned on the approach of the British, the enemy suffering severely in their retreat. Lieutenant-Colonel Taylor finally succeeded in clearing off the enemy from their positions on the right of the road to Ali Masjid, although an obstinate resistance was offered at several points, especially over the bridge, where the enemy had concentrated in force. Having been reinforced by a detachment of the 33rd Native Infantry, Captain Lushington of the 9th Foot proceeded with it and the light company of the 9th Foot to the right to take the enemy's position in reverse, while Lieutenant-Colonel Taylor attacked in front. This had the desired effect of forcing their immediate retreat and clearing the bridge. No further opposition was offered by the

[1] Of course this means only as far forward as the foot of the steep ascent.

enemy, who retreated on Ali Masjid, while Lieutenant-Colonel Taylor pushed on and occupied the tower and mill within about a mile of that place."

Captain Borton's account of the attack on the right is well worth quoting in full. He writes in his diary :—

"The grey dawn saw us under arms some hundred yards in front of the site of our camp and opposite the several points of our intended attack. The right hill was to be stormed by Colonel Taylor, the left by Major Huish, while the formidable barricade erected across the mouth of the Pass was simultaneously swept by the fire of artillery.

"The attack on the right hill, the most difficult of ascent and most lofty of the two, was conducted in three columns—the centre under Taylor, the right under Gahan, 26th Native Infantry, and the left, with which was my company and half of Powell's, led by Major Anderson, 64th Native Infantry. As soon as it was day we advanced steadily over ground broken and intersected by deep ravines, each of which would have been a most formidable defence in the hands of an experienced enemy. The Khyberees evidently never contemplated our mode of attack or they would have occupied the heights in greater numbers. However, we found them in small, detached parties on the spur which projects from the foot of the mountain, beating their war-drums, screaming like fiends, and waving their long knives in the air. We soon drove them from their exposed situations, and they retired rapidly to the well-known rocks, from which they could deliver their fire in comparative security.

"The ascent was far more difficult than we had expected. When, at length, I did reach the top, and advancing seven or eight paces, found myself overlooking a deep ravine, down the sides of which the enemy were hurrying pell-mell, I was most agreeably surprised. Colour-Sergeant Whiteside and four men were killed and several wounded.

"In about twenty minutes, while watching the progress of

the fight, intelligence arrived that Gahan's party, which had reached the main summit after us, was hotly engaged and required to be reinforced. Anderson seemed disinclined to take this step, but sent me with my company to strengthen a party in possession of the highest pinnacle in our rear, which was the key of our position, but with express orders not to go beyond that point. I had not been here long before Sir Robert Shakespeare, who had ascended with Gahan's party, came to me to beg I would support Gahan, and was of course referred by me to Anderson.

"I, however, prepared to support them should they retreat. This they did almost immediately, with some precipitation. I was then thunderstruck by the sad news that my poor friend Cumming was shot dead, and that his men had not brought off the body.

"Anderson now appeared, and seeing that the enemy had in numbers taken possession of the point from which the retreating party had been driven, ordered me to drive them off. All the officers, some sepoys, and all the 9th on the spot rushed to the attack. The fire was very hot and balls passed on every side of me; a few men fixed bayonets and rushed the position. When ordered to retire, I sent the sepoys to the rear under their officer; then Powell with half the Europeans, with directions to support me in my retreat. One of my men fell and it was necessary to get him away before we retired."

After describing how Cumming's body had been thrown half naked on to an inaccessible ledge, he continues :—

"We suffered greatly during the heat of the day from want of water which, through difficulty of ascent and mismanagement, was not supplied.

"In the afternoon a reinforcement of *jezailchies* was sent to us and they went forward to provoke an engagement with the Afridis, from whose numbers they had themselves been recently recruited. They were driven back with three wounded, but brought in triumph a ghastly grinning head, for which their commander gave Rs. 20 as a reward. . . . Towards sunset, seeing that the rear of the baggage had at last entered the Pass, we descended to the Pass; but, before we had been able to procure water for the men, we were ordered to ascend and occupy during the night the next hill on our right."

Cumming's diary of course ceases abruptly before the storming of the Kyber, but attached to it is a full account of the operations in a letter from " Captain——" of the 9th to Cumming's father. From the similarity of much of it to Borton's account above quoted it is clear that " Captain——" was really Captain Borton, who we know was an intimate friend of Cumming. Of course it omits the painful account of the fate of Cumming's remains, but it contains a few further particulars as to the movements which should be mentioned. They were probably gleaned after the other account was written, and it also gives an explanatory sketch, such as Borton often added to his narratives. After describing the ascent to the crest, the letter says :—

" While this was doing, a most unsuccessful attack was made by the grenadiers[1] to turn the enemy at the shoulder overlooking the Pass, who were ordered by Pollock over an impracticable path at ' D,' where they became exposed to rocks which the enemy threw from above, killing Colour-Sergeant Whiteside and three privates, and wounding Captain Ogle and nine men ; whereas had he waited a little patiently the descent of our advancing party under Taylor, the enemy would have been taken in reverse without any loss. Taylor with his advancing party now descended the hill to dislodge the enemy from the next hill on the right of the gorge, and then, moving along the heights, to protect the head of the column in the Pass. A similar movement was made on the left, and Anderson's party, forming the right rear, had of course to occupy the main height ' A ' until the whole of the baggage and rear-guard had passed through the gorge. Cumming was bringing his company to ' A,' whence he could check any advance by the enemy, when he was ordered to ' B,' where his men were much exposed. Attacked in rear, he was ordered to retire and I [the writer of the letter] was

[1] Those of the 9th with the central column in the Pass.

sent forward to support him. As Cumming was retiring, he was shot through the head. Then another advance, ordered by Anderson, recaptured ' B.' After occupying it for a quarter of an hour the party retired, leaving one officer and three men wounded in the operation. Towards evening, as the enemy's numbers decreased the party descended and occupied the next hill over the gorge."

The left column seems to have had less difficulty, as the hill in front of it was not so steep as Colonel Taylor's, which was inaccessible in front and had to be turned by the right. On this day Lieutenant J. Slater Cumming was killed at the head of the 6th Company on the heights, and Captain Ogle was wounded. Besides these, in the 9th one colour-sergeant and six privates were killed, and one drummer and thirty-two privates were wounded.[1]

The centre column, thanks to the action on the flanks, was able to enter the Pass without being engaged, except the grenadiers sent to assist the right, and to camp two miles beyond the mouth. Ali Masjid was found to be evacuated by the enemy.

In the forcing of the mouth of the Khyber the 9th had greatly distinguished themselves, and it may well be doubted whether, without them the work would have been done at all; for, though the morale of the native troops rapidly improved with their success, it was certainly far from good before the attack. It had suffered from the repulse in January, and from the fear of what was before them in the difficult country defended by a fierce race. The Sikhs, who themselves had a wholesome dread of the Khyber, had been careful to impress a similar fear on the native troops.

The Sikhs had been left by Pollock to guard the road in his rear—a trust which they carried out by paying the Afridis to guarantee the Pass, whilst they went off home themselves.

From Ali Masjid to Landi Khana, Pollock's advance was unhampered except by the difficulty of marching the immense convoy of stores and ammunition which he was taking up to Jellalabad. Opposite Landi

---

[1] There is some confusion as to casualties in the several accounts. The figures here given are official and must be held to be the correct ones.

Khana was the fort of Lalpura in the occupation of a hostile chief. As there was no getting across the river there, Colonel Taylor was sent with a small force, including two companies of the 9th, to cross higher up. The crossing was effected with great difficulty, and the force came down the opposite bank, only to find the fort had been evacuated on their approach. There was no more serious opposition incurred short of Jellalabad.

At Jellalabad, where the 9th arrived on the 16th April, Pollock took over command of the garrison from Sale. The day previous to his arrival Sale had made a sortie and driven off his besiegers with heavy loss. Captain Borton relates how surprised the relieving force were to find the garrison of Jellalabad in quite good condition, the officers in smart uniforms, and very little sickness. They had expected to find a force in the last stages of exhaustion.

Meanwhile Lord Auckland had been succeeded as Governor-General by Lord Ellenborough, who, after first saying that we must "re-establish our military reputation by the infliction of some signal and decisive blow on the Afghans," veered round to a policy of withdrawal, as soon as it could be safely done, from the positions attained. Pollock actually received orders at the end of April to withdraw to Peshawar, subject to certain conditions.

On the very day of the forcing of the Khyber, Shah Sujah had been murdered in Kabul, and Fateh Jang, his successor, had been besieged in the Bala Hissar fort by Akbar Khan, who became the virtual ruler. Lord Ellenborough finally suggested to General Nott that he should retire to India via Kabul, and to Pollock that he should facilitate this roundabout retirement. That of course meant Pollock's advance to Kabul.

Pollock in this period had been wheeling the Shinwaris into line; but in that operation the 9th appear to have taken no part. On August 20th the advance on Kabul began from Jellalabad. Pollock intended to concentrate at Gandamak the whole of the 8,000 men whom he was taking with him to Kabul. He reached Gandamak with the advanced guard on August 23rd. Two miles farther on was the village of Mammu Khel, where the Afghan chiefs Haji Ali and Khairulla Khan had collected a force of tribesmen. The village lay on the flank of the Kabul road and it was necessary to clear it out. It was therefore decided to attack the position on the morning of the 24th in two columns, each headed by four companies of the 9th.

All went well at first: the enemy abandoned his position in front of Mammu Khel and the village of Kuchli Khel. Beyond that the fugitives were joined by those who had been driven in by the left column under General Tulloch, in which was the other wing of the 9th. Of what followed, the following extract from the report of General McCaskill (dated August 25, 1842) gives an account:

" He [the enemy] assumed a menacing attitude and occupied in force a range of heights and detached summits in the Soofaid Koh. The most salient of these was a spur of the mountain within long musket range of the buildings of Koochlee Khail. From this and from other eminences of the most precipitous character the Ooloose were dislodged with the utmost spirit and gallantry by the details under Lt.-Colonel Taylor, aided in the most effective manner by a party of Captain Broadfoot's sappers and miners. The enemy were reinforced from time to time and made many bold attacks, and kept up a sharp fire of *jezails* from the loftiest peaks of the mountain; but our troops, though so much pressed as to be compelled to recede from ground which they had gained in our direction, maintained an advanced position among the hills, until withdrawn by order of Major-General Pollock first into the plateau in front of the village of Koochlee Khail, which they burnt down, and then back upon the present site of encampment. In retiring over the plain between the principal villages the movement was covered by a squadron of the 5th and another of the 10th Light Cavalry, but the attempts of the Ooloose to annoy were timid and feeble in the extreme, and our troops did not sustain a single casualty from their efforts. Lt.-Colonel Taylor speaks in high terms of the support he received from Major Huish, commanding the 26th regiment of Native Infantry, who was wounded, and afterwards Captain Handscomb of the same corps, and from Captain Ogle commanding Her Majesty's 9th Foot. I beg to be permitted to bear my testimony to the merits of the Lt.-Colonel's own exertions on this occasion, as well to express my sense of the gallantry of all the troops engaged, and to acknowledge the able assistance which I received from — — — and Lt. Bethune H.M.'s 9th Foot (my Aide-de-Camp)."

The left column is stated earlier in the despatch, to have separated from the right after the first evacuation of the villages, and appears not to have been seriously engaged.

Captain Borton's diary, supplemented by his neat little sketch map, elucidates this despatch. He was himself with the left column. Of the enemy's position the following is in effect his description. From the "massif" of the Sufed Koh there extended nearly northwards a high rugged spur. From this again was thrown out what McCaskill calls the plateau, which was on a lower level and itself branched out into what Borton calls "feelers." The British approached these feelers, or we might call them "fingers," of which the plateau was the back of the hand, from the north through flooded rice fields, which made very heavy going. Borton speaks of three columns, but the two on the right were closely united. He himself was with the column which diverged leftwards on the fort of Mammu Khel towards the left margin of the plateau. The village was on the right margin.

The left column found the fort unoccupied and refreshed themselves liberally on the grapes in the gardens attached to it, whilst the right column, after taking the village, pushed on to another fort not far from the foot of the high, rocky spur and which Borton calls Khoode Khel. That they also took, and then pressed up the rocky spur itself, driving the tribesmen off it towards the valley on the right. There were some losses in this operation. On the spur, Borton thinks, the advance should have stopped; but Taylor thought otherwise, and began advancing to his right towards the valley. Engaging the enemy on the lower spurs leading down to this valley, Taylor soon found himself in difficulties against superior numbers.

Borton, now called up to relieve him, only arrived after he had retired to the plateau. For two hours after this the force was employed in keeping the enemy at a distance, whilst the sappers burnt the villages on the plateau and destroyed the vines and orchards by "ringing" the trees. This destruction Captain Borton deplores, and thinks perhaps unnecessary. It went to his heart to see the trees ruined for ever.

When the work of destruction was complete the troops withdrew to Mammu Khel, where, after destroying the fort, they remained for the night. The enemy admitted a loss of forty men, but this does not include about an equal number killed or wounded by the accidental explosion of a camel load of powder which the British had failed to remove from the right. In the scramble among the enemy for its possession it got ignited by a match, killing seven and burning thirty or forty more.

The loss of the 9th on this day was two privates killed, one officer (Captain R. S. Edwards) severely wounded, one colour-sergeant and seven men wounded. Three more men were killed, accidentally apparently, at Mammu Khel in the blowing up of the village strongholds.

The 9th remained here till August 30th, when they retired to Gandamak. It was not till September 7th that the whole of Pollock's force, marching in the lightest order possible, had closed up to Gandamak and was ready for the final advance on Kabul.

Sir Robert Sale with the first division moved out on the 7th; the second, under General McCaskill, on the 9th.

The 9th were in the 1st division, which, on September 8th, approached the hills commanding the road through the Jagdalak Pass to find them occupied by large numbers of Ghilzais. Pollock's report describes the enemy's position thus: "The hills they occupied formed an amphitheatre inclining towards the left of the road, on which the troops were halted whilst the guns opened, and the enemy were thus enabled, on this point, to fire into the column, a deep ravine preventing any contact with them."

For the fight which ensued we shall quote Captain Borton's diary. He writes:

"I can conceive few positions more formidable than that which the enemy had taken. On the crest of a lofty range to the left were situated a square fort and two extensive 'sungars' of rocks and bushes which literally bristled with armed men, while the right spur, thrown out from a still loftier height, was strengthened by a double and triple line of breastworks, all of which, as well as the 'sungar' on the top, were strongly occupied. The Colonel halted within range, as it proved (for poor Nugent was killed), of the enemy's 'jezails,'[1] and while the men loaded and preparations were made for attack, a few shrapnel were thrown with considerable effect into the works on the right and left. To the 9th was assigned the task of driving the enemy from their position on the left, while the 13th ascended the right hill.

"Away we went—pell mell under the hottest fire to which I have as yet been exposed.

"The hill was steep, but not otherwise difficult of ascent, and I reached the summit just in time to see Ogle (who had the start from the right) with three or four men peering into a 'sungar,' which, to my great surprise, we found empty. The rascals dared not await the rush but disappeared in all directions. When on the crest, we saw about 200 cavalry trotting along the hill. A squadron of dragoons found their way to the top, in answer to our cries, but it was too late. We chased them at the double for about a mile, but could only come within long shot of them. The cavalry withdrew and we occupied a commanding point to the left, where we kept the enemy in check during the remainder of the day, but not without several casualties. On the right, the 13th were successful in pushing the enemy from point to point and finally crowning the main height. Anxiously during the day did we look for the tail of the baggage and the arrival of the rear-guard; but the sun had set ere it reached the entrance to the pass.

"Ogle had descended with the mountain guns, leaving me to withdraw the remainder of my party at discretion. This I commenced doing as soon as I saw the rear sufficiently advanced, considering that they would make arrangements for covering their flanks as they moved forwards; when, however, I reached the crest overlooking the Pass I found that some stoppage had occurred and that, if I descended, their rear would be exposed to the enemy, who

[1] The Afghan "jezail" far outranged "Brown Bess" with which our men were armed.

pressed forward as soon as we began to withdraw. My present position was untenable; it was therefore necessary to send back Hook to re-occupy the commanding post we had just quitted, until we could descend with safety. This he did just before the enemy reached it, but was hotly opposed, reinforced by Powell, and at length, at a given signal, retired with one man severely wounded. Elmhirst and I then, crossing a deep ravine, pushed up the adjoining height (which we imagined that the rear had occupied, but which we found vacated) to cover their descent, and it was fortunate that we did so; for through the increasing gloom we could just perceive a small detached party, with which were Powell and Vigors, struggling down the side of the ravine with the wounded man, whom they had much difficulty in getting down, and some of the enemy pressing very close upon them; these we fired upon briskly and occupied their attention till we saw that the road was reached, and then, descending rapidly into the opposite ravine, we joined our forces below.

"The heights on both sides were now open to the enemy and they fired upon us from all sides, but it was too dark for any certain aim."

In this affair the 9th lost one sergeant and two men killed; one sergeant and sixteen men wounded.

The advance progressed without incident as far as Tezeen, where, on September 11th, the 1st division was joined by the 2nd. Pollock decided to halt on the 12th, a decision which seemed to Akbar Khan to denote hesitation, and induced him to move forward for a battle at Tezeen instead of at Khurd Kabul, where he had intended, if forced to it, to make his last stand. He was also called forward by his Ghilzai friends, and the fear that they might desert if he did not comply with their wishes no doubt influenced his decision. In the afternoon of the 12th the enemy began attacking the piquets on the British left. What happened may best be told in the words of Pollock's despatch :—

"I considered it necessary to send Lt.-Colonel Taylor with 250 men of H.M.'s 9th Foot to drive them back; some sharp fighting took place, and the enemy was driven up the neighbouring hills, from the crests of which they kept up a heavy fire. Lt.-Colonel Taylor, however, with a small party, crept up one end of the hill unperceived by the enemy, who were hotly engaged in their front, and lay concealed until joined by a few more of his men, when, rushing upon the flank of the astonished Afghans, he inflicted a severe lesson, pouring in a destructive fire upon them as they fled down the hill. A chieftain was found among the slain, who, it is supposed, was the brother of Khodabux Khan. The enemy remained inoffensive on our left flank in consequence of this well-planned and gallant affair of Lt.-Colonel Taylor's, and withdrew to the right where they commenced a furious attack."

Whilst Colonel Taylor was fighting as above, Captain Borton had been sent with his company on to an overlooking height, where they, with one company each of the 13th and 31st, three native infantry regiments, and some sappers, were under the command of Colonel Skinner of the 31st. Borton describes how he watched the rest of the 9th with Taylor in the valley below in their shirt-sleeves, towards sunset, steadily moving on the enemy's chief position under heavy flanking fire from an adjoining ravine. When they were nearly on the crest they lay down waiting for the men in rear to come up. The enemy were apparently unaware of their proximity when, at last, they fixed bayonets and charged, driving the enemy in confusion down the adjoining face. It was Elmhirst who cut down the chieftain, and many of the enemy were bayoneted here. The 9th's losses were three men killed and twelve wounded.

The night of the 12th-13th was disturbed by various small attacks. That night the British force camped in the Tezeen valley, encircled by lofty hills. From it leads the Pass of the same name, four miles in length and of great difficulty. Of it Pollock writes: "The Pass of Tezeen affords great advantages to an enemy occupying the heights, and on the present occasion Mahomed Akbar neglected nothing to render its natural fortifications as formidable as numbers could make it."

At the mouth of the Pass was left a rear-guard of 750 cavalry and 1,300 infantry, the latter including 143 men of the piquets of the 9th.

To clear the heights on either side of the Pass, the 13th were sent to the right, the 9th and 31st to the left. Of the action Pollock's despatch says :

"Our troops mounted the heights, and the Afghans, contrary to their general custom, advanced to meet them, and a desperate struggle ensued ; indeed, their defence was so obstinate that the British bayonet alone decided the contest. The light company of Her Majesty's 9th Foot, led by Captain Lushington, who, I regret to say, was wounded in the head, ascended the hills on the left of the pass under a heavy cross-fire and overthrew their opponents, leaving several horses and their riders, supposed to be chiefs, dead on the hill. The slaughter was considerable, and the fight continued during the greater part of the day, the enemy appearing resolved that we should not ascend the Haft Kotal. One spirit seemed to pervade all, and a determination to conquer overcame the obstinate resistance of the enemy, who were at length forced from their numerous and strong positions and our troops mounted the Haft Kotal, giving three cheers when they ascended the summit."

It should be explained that the Haft Kotal (Seven Hills) was the last stronghold beyond the Pass to which the enemy retired.

All that has been described above occurred in the main British column. We now return to Skinner's detachment on the right, with Borton's diary for our guide. Their mission was to capture some high peaks on their right, and to continue operating among the lower hills on the right flank of the advanced guard to the head of the Haft Kotal. The two higher peaks being captured without difficulty, the force moved down towards the lower hills. As they descended the enemy rallied and attacked in great force. Borton waited till they were close up before charging the Afghans, who fled down hill. In the pursuit Borton's men got separated by a considerable distance from their supports. They were counter-attacked by the enemy whilst in a poor position. Skinner was with them, and they were unable to get their supports up before they were compelled to fall back before superior forces. Borton says some of the 31st might have helped, but did not. Altogether, he describes the action as "a disgusting affair," in getting separated from the supports, and in the want of co-operation of the 31st. The 9th lost one sergeant and three men killed and four men wounded (two of them mortally). The bodies of the dead were mutilated by the enemy—a brutality which, to Borton's disgust, was repaid in the same way by the Gurkha sappers.

The rear-guard also had a good deal of fighting on this day, but there is nothing in it to be specially recorded, in so far as concerns the small detachment of the 9th. The total losses of the 9th on September 12th and 13th were two sergeants, one drummer, and eight men killed; Captain Lusington, one sergeant, and twenty-five men wounded.

Akbar Khan, who had been present in person, had now fled, and his followers being dispersed, the British advancing on Kabul, which was reached on the 15th, met with no further resistance. The fury of the troops was excited at Butkhak by the sight of the skeletons and other relics which marked the scene of the massacre of Elphinstone's army in the previous January.

From the point of view of regimental history, the general events of the occupation of Kabul, the arrival of Nott's force from Kandahar, the release of the prisoners, the retributive destruction, and political affairs may be disregarded.

It is otherwise with the military movements of the end of September and beginning of October. It appeared, about September 20th, that the Barukzais were again collecting in force in Kohistan, about Charekar, under Aminulla Khan, and it was decided to send General McCaskill of the 9th with a force, collected partly from Nott's and partly from Pollock's force, to disperse them. Here, again, we can follow Borton's excellent account of the fighting.

On September 28th the force was encamped about three miles from Istalif, and reconnaissances were sent out which were fired on by the enemy. Their retirement encouraged the enemy, who were already very confident, and had collected all their women and treasure in the town. Istalif is situated on two lofty spurs thrown out from the Hindu Kush range, which here runs north and south. The town is divided into three parts, the most important of which is to the north, separated from the minor section by the deep ravine between the two spurs. In this ravine is a watercourse. The entire front towards the plain on which the

British were encamped was covered, to a distance of a mile and a half, by thickly wooded gardens and vineyards. These were about half a mile deep from east to west.

As a result of the reconnaissance of the 28th, it was decided to attack on the enemy's left as the more accessible flank. As Borton, leading No. 7 company of the 9th, approached the foremost gardens, he was directed to open the ball with that company and one of the 26th Native Infantry, feeling the way for the other troops. He found the garden unoccupied, and once within it, found shelter from the fire of the town above. This movement protected the right flank of the other columns, which now moved leftwards against a garden and village strongly occupied by the enemy. These were stormed "in our usual manner."

" On went our gallant corps," writes Borton, " as ever in front, down the ravine and across the adjoining height. Again descending, the river was passed and our troops were in the city itself before another resolute stand was made against them."

We need not quote in full Borton's description of the panic in the place—the flight of the old men, the women, and the children, who had been so confidently kept there by the enemy, under the impression that the place was impregnable. Only in one case was a vigorous defence of a house made by a man of some consequence with a few followers. They killed and wounded several of our men before they were themselves destroyed. Among the British killed was Lieutenant Evans of the 41st, who had just remarked that he supposed he was going to escape unscathed, as he had already done in nine previous actions. There was a good deal of looting before the highest part of the town was reached, and the colonel of the 9th withdrew his men from temptation to a hill below and on the east, where they had already captured an enemy gun. Lieutenant Elmhirst and one or two men had first reached this trophy and turned it on the retreating enemy. " Our colours were then unfurled," says Borton, " and planted on each wheel in triumph."[1]

---

[1] Sergeant Banbury of the 9th was with Lieutenant Elmhirst on this occasion. His " statement of services," now in the possession of his son, Brigadier-General W. E. Banbury, C.M.G., shows that at Istalif he distinguished himself " by assisting

At the end of the day the 9th returned to camp, leaving General Stacy's brigade in charge of the town.

Another fuller account is given in Stacy's "Narrative of Services in Baloochistan and Afghanistan." It will be seen that it differs from Borton's mainly as to the capture of the gun, the award of which by Pollock to the 9th Stacy seems to resent. In substance it is as follows:—

The force was divided into two columns. The right under Brigadier General Tulloch comprised the 9th, commanded by Lieutenant-Colonel Taylor, the 26th Native Infantry, Captain Backhouse's mountain train, and Broadfoot's sappers. The left column, commanded by Brigadier-General Stacy, consisted of one wing of the 41st British Infantry, the 42nd and 43rd Native Infantry, two eighteen-pounder guns, and a horse battery. The rear-guard consisted of three squadrons of cavalry and the other wing of the 41st. Moving steadily across the enemy's front, which was in the gardens surrounding Istalif in a semicircle, the troops presently came within range of the enemy's "jezails." Two horse artillery guns then drove in the "Jezailchis," who retired on the village of Ismillah. Approaching the village the light companies were sent out to drive in the skirmishers. Then, as it was observed that there were several gaps in the enemy's defences, the word to advance was given, and the light companies of the 9th British and 26th Native Infantry dashed forward, followed by the rest of their regiments, entered the village first and drove the enemy towards the farther side, where they came under the fire of Stacy's column which had been delayed by having to make a detour.

This village being taken and set on fire, the troops brought up their left shoulders to advance on Old Istalif, which they had left a mile behind them. Pressing the defeated enemy before them, the right column entered the town of Istalif from the south-east corner in two divisions in parallel lines. The loss of Ismillah had created a panic

---

to capture a gun which the enemy were in the act of reloading and which was turned on them by Lieutenant Elmhirst." In consideration of his gallantry Sergeant Banbury was promoted, in 1851, to quartermaster of the 9th. Later, he became paymaster and captain in the 3/60th, from which he was transferred, with the rank of honorary major, to the 45th.

in Istalif, and the population were now seen hurrying up the precipitous pathways which led from the rear of the town towards Turkestan.

Meanwhile Stacy's column had again been delayed, disposing of a body of the enemy who might have attacked its left rear. Thus Tulloch's column was the first to enter Istalif, as it had been the first at Ismillah, and they now outflanked the enemy on his left in the gardens and orchards of Istalif. Attacked in front by the left column as it came up, the enemy was soon making the best of his way back into the town, losing heavily all the way. The firing had almost ceased when the town itself was entered; for the whole of the infantry was pressing upwards, without meeting serious resistance, towards the fort above it. About two-thirds of the way up, when the two columns met, a gun still manned by the enemy was seen on a lower spur. After a race between the light companies of the 9th and of the 43rd Native Infantry the prize fell to the former.

The enemy were now completely driven from Istalif, and the retirement of a few stragglers was expedited by the fire of the mountain train, dragged up to the heights above the town.

The losses on this occasion were much less than had been expected. The enemy were surprised by the attack on their left, when they expected it on their right, and had concentrated their defence there. This erroneous belief was induced by the direction of a reconnaissance on the previous evening.

The 9th had no one killed, and the wounded were Lieutenant Lister, one sergeant, and fifteen men.

Captain Smith of the 9th, General Tulloch's brigade-major, was specially commended by that officer in his report.

The regiment was back in Kabul on October 7th.

On October 12, 1842, the army, leaving behind it in Kabul another puppet ruler in the place of Fateh Jang, set out on its march back to India. The march was uneventful, in so far as the 9th are concerned, for they do not appear to have been involved in any of the very few and small attacks made by the tribesmen in the passes. The only approach to active work they had was when they were despatched, with the 26th Native Infantry, to attack the fort of Khuda Bakhsh Khan near Tezeen on October 13th. Finding that chief had decamped in haste, they burnt his fort and returned to the line of march.[1] Firozpur was reached on December 18th, where Lord Ellenborough celebrated the victorious but futile campaign with much feasting, reviewing, and self-glorification.

For this campaign Colonel McCaskill received a K.C.B. and the rank of Major-General; Lieutenant-Colonel Taylor a C.B.; Captains Ogle and Smith brevet majorities; and Captain Lushington the same brevet and a C.B.

---

[1] Amongst Sir Arthur Borton's papers is a table showing the casualties of the regiment in each action of the Afghan campaign which is here reproduced:

Action.	Killed.			Severely Wounded.			Slightly Wounded.		
	Offrs.	Sgts.	Ptes.	Offrs.	Sgts.	Ptes.	Offrs.	Sgts.	Ptes.
Khyber Pass	1	1	8	—	—	11	1	—	23
Mammu Khel	—	—	3	1	1	2	—	—	4
Jagdalak -	—	1	2	—	—	4	—	1	12
Tezeen Valley	—	1	3	—	—	8	—	—	4
Haft Kotal -	—	1	6	1	1	8	—	—	5
Istalif -	—	—	1	—	—	11	1	—	3
Total -	1	4	23	2	2	44	2	1	51

Total casualties—5 officers, 7 sergeants, 118 privates.

Total diminution of strength, from leaving Firozpur till return there, 107, or nearly 12¾ per cent.

CHAPTER XVIII

THE 1st BATTALION 1843–1853—FIRST SIKH WAR— SERVICE IN ENGLAND, IRELAND, AND MALTA

FROM Firozpur the regiment marched, on January 14, 1843, to Mubarikpur, arriving on the 31st and camping there till April 12th, when it was sent to Sabathu in the hills near Simla.

On December 7, 1844, Sir Thomas Arbuthnot was appointed colonel of the 9th in consequence of the death of Sir John Cameron in the previous month.

On March 8, 1844, the battalion moved to Kasauli, and remained there till November, 1845, when it left the hills for Umbala, which was reached on the 28th. After this revivifying period of over two years in hill stations it was now again to go on active service.

Ever since the death of Ranjit Singh in 1839 war with his State, or perhaps it should be said with his army, had been becoming more and more probable. The army, the Khalsa, which he had been able to control by his strong personality, had been trained and armed by his European officers, Allard, Ventura, Avitabile, and others, on the European model. In artillery particularly they were very strong, and it was calculated that, one way or another, the Sikh Kingdom owned some 250 to 350 serviceable guns, many of them of large calibre. The exact strength of the Khalsa in infantry and cavalry is not certain, but the regular troops alone counted 35,000 infantry and 15,000 cavalry.

In the weak or debauched hands of Ranjit Singh's successors and their ministers this army became the ruling power in the State, and it was strongly anti-British, partly from suspicion of British views of conquest, partly from contempt bred of the disaster in Afghanistan in

1841, and the withdrawal from Kabul in 1842, and partly from an entirely unfounded belief that they had materially helped to see the British through the difficulties of Pollock's advance. The Khalsa, with its European training and armament, supported by the most warlike races east of the Indus, was by far the most formidable enemy the British had yet encountered in India.

Preparations for the approaching war had been carried out to some extent, but they were always held back by the desire of the British authorities to avoid giving colour to the suspicion of aggressive designs. The movement of the 9th to Umbala was one of these preparations. The disposition of the British army towards the Sikh frontier on the Sutlej early in November, 1845, was 7,000 (only one European regiment) at Firozpur, 5,000 at Ludhiana, 10,000 at Umbala, Kasauli, and Sabathu, 9,000 at Meerut—in all about 31,000. By December 11th, the Governor-General, Sir Henry Hardinge, had directed the Commander-in-Chief (Sir Hugh Gough) to move up the troops from Meerut, Umbala, and other stations towards the Sutlej. Amongst them the 9th, under Lieutenant-Colonel Taylor, marched from Umbala for Firozpur on December 11, 1845.

On December 13th the Governor-General at Ludhiana received positive information that the Sikhs had crossed the Sutlej on the 11th and were concentrating in great force on its left bank. War was proclaimed by the Governor-General on December 13th.

Ludhiana was abandoned, except the fort, which could be defended by invalids and the less efficient men, and the remaining 5,000 men and twelve guns, with the Governor-General himself, moved to the great grain store at Busseean, where they joined up with the 7,500 men and thirty-six guns moving from Umbala on Firozpur. The march from Umbala to Moodkee, twenty miles short of Firozpur, over 150 miles of sandy roads, was very trying. The distance was covered in the remarkably short time of six days, and the troops began to reach Moodkee by noon on December 18th. Of the difficulties of the march Sir Hugh Gough's despatch of December 19th says: "Their [the troops] perpetual labour allowing them scarcely time to cook their food, even when they received it, and hardly an hour for repose, before they were called upon for renewed exertions." Anyone who knows India even in the cold weather will realize the wonderful marching powers exhibited by the European infantry in covering as they did twenty-six, thirty, ten, and twenty-one miles on four successive days. The last march was that to Moodkee.

Meanwhile the Sikhs, having crossed the Sutlej twelve miles below Firozpur, had made no attempt to attack Sir J. Littler there. He had successfully 'bluffed' them by offering battle with his small force of 7,000 men, of whom less than 1,000 were Europeans. They then occupied an entrenched camp at Ferozeshah, half-way to Moodkee, with over 30,000 men and 108 guns. Thence they were moving out a large force to meet the British advance from Busseean. The British troops, as they reached Moodkee, had already encountered and driven back what Gough calls the enemy's "feeling parties." This march had been specially trying, owing to the want of water on the road, and the troops were greatly exhausted when, about 3 p.m., the approach of the Sikh army was signalled. They had scarcely time to get under arms before they were engaged with a force estimated by Gough at 15,000 to 20,000 infantry, the same strength of cavalry, and forty guns,[1] which was found about two miles beyond Moodkee.

"The country," says Gough's despatch, "is a dead flat covered at short intervals with a low but, in some places, thick 'jhow'[2] jungle and dotted with sandy hillocks. The enemy screened their infantry and artillery behind this jungle and such undulations as the ground afforded; and whilst our twelve battalions formed from echelon of brigades into line, opened a very severe cannonade upon our advancing troops."

The cavalry and horse artillery had been pushed forward already against the enemy's cavalry threatening both British flanks, to cover the formation of the infantry, and the fire of these guns had obtained a mastery over those of the enemy.

The cavalry were now sent round both flanks of the enemy, and seem to have been remarkably successful in getting even into the enemy's

[1] The real strength was probably not more than 2,000 infantry, 10,000 cavalry and twenty-two guns against about 11,000 under Gough.
[2] Tamarisk.

rear and preventing him from using his superior strength to overlap the British flanks. The Sikh cavalry were unable to stand against them. The enemy's artillery was almost silenced for the time being by this attack and the British artillery fire. It was nearly dark when the infantry at last advanced to attack the Sikhs. Sir Harry Smith's division was formed on the right, Major-General Gilbert's (its European troops were not yet up) in the centre, and Sir John McCaskill's on the left. The last named included the 9th and 80th British Foot, with the 26th and 73rd Native Infantry. Gough's despatch continues:—

"When the infantry advanced to the attack, Brigadier Brooke rapidly pushed on his horse artillery close to the jungle and the cannonade was resumed on both sides. The infantry under Major-Generals Sir Harry Smith, Gilbert, and Sir John McCaskill attacked in echelon of lines the enemy's infantry, almost invisible amongst the wood and the approaching darkness of night. The opposition of the enemy was such as might have been expected from troops who had everything at stake, and who had long vaunted of being irresistible. Their ample and extended line, from their great superiority of numbers, far outflanked ours; but this was counteracted by the flank movements of our cavalry. The attack of the infantry now commenced, and the roll of fire from this powerful arm soon convinced the Sikh army that they had met with a foe they little expected; and their whole force was driven from position after position with great slaughter, and the loss of seventeen pieces of artillery, some of them of large calibre, our infantry using that never-failing weapon the bayonet wherever they stood. Night only saved them from worse disaster, for this stout conflict was maintained during an hour and a half of dim starlight, amidst a cloud of dust from the sandy plain, which yet more obscured every object."

This despatch of course does not deal with the 9th specially; but fortunately Major Borton wrote an account of this battle to his father in January, 1846, after he had been wounded at the battle of Ferozeshah. He describes the not unnaturally straggling condition in which the column had arrived, towards 3 p.m. on December 18th. He calculates the length of the march at twenty-eight miles, against the official twenty-one miles. Either was a very long day's work. He says that the straggling was so great that any attack by the enemy during the march must almost certainly have been fatal. The first orders on arrival were to be ready to move again at midnight, the enemy being supposed to be retreating.

Less than an hour after its arrival the 9th was ordered to stand to arms, shortly before 4 p.m., as the enemy was attacking. By the time the regiment was ready the battle was already raging, and half an hour's march brought the 9th under a very heavy fire. In the dust and smoke the enemy's position could not be clearly made out. At first the 9th was kept in reserve, but just before nightfall it was deployed to meet fresh advancing columns of the enemy. These were quickly driven back before nightfall brought the action to a close, "obliging us to rest satisfied with the field and most of their [the enemy's] guns." During the action Sir John McCaskill, in the centre of the rear of the British line, fell dead from his horse, his heart pierced by a grape shot. Borton says that the Sikh fire was generally high and particularly fatal to mounted officers.

When the moon rose it became possible to fetch in the dead and wounded.

In this battle the Sikhs were certainly very inferior in numbers of infantry, but their men were fresh and the British weary with their long march. The Sikh cavalry was greatly superior in numbers to the British, but inferior in quality. In artillery they had a marked superiority. They made the fatal mistake of attacking Gough with only a detachment, instead of using the bulk of their army against him, whilst containing Littler with a small force. They would have been still wiser to have overwhelmed Littler, as they might easily have done on the 12th, and so set their whole army free to deal with Gough on the 18th. It is not pleasant to think what might have happened had there been somewhat greater capacity in the Sikh higher command. There was none too much of it on the British side, for Gough was a hard-bitten old soldier whose ideas did not extend very far beyond a cavalry charge and an infantry attack with fixed bayonets.

The British losses, considering the forces engaged and the short duration of the action, were so heavy (872 killed and wounded of all ranks) as to indicate the brave resistance of the Sikhs. Amongst the killed were Sir Robert Sale, the hero of Jellalabad, and as already stated Sir John McCaskill, lieutenant-colonel of the 9th. Save for this loss the regiment suffered less than might have been expected. Two men were killed and Lieutenant Hanham, two sergeants, and forty-seven men wounded.

After bivouacking on the field for a few hours, and ascertaining that none of the enemy remained, the troops returned to their camp at Moodkee where, on the 19th and 20th, they were employed bringing in the wounded and the captured guns. They were now reinforced by the arrival of the 29th Foot, 1st Europeans, 11th and 41st Native Infantry, and a detachment of heavy guns.

It appeared clear that the Sikhs were aiming at the destruction of the relieving force rather than contemplating a serious attack on Firozpur. On the 21st Sir Hugh Gough, leaving the baggage, wounded, and captured guns in charge of two native infantry regiments at Moodkee, marched by his left at 4 a.m. Keeping three or four miles from the enemy at Firozeshah, he effected a junction with Sir John Littler, who had been warned to march out of Firozpur and meet him with as many of his troops as could be spared from the defence of that place. This reinforcement of 5,000 men, two cavalry regiments, and twenty-one field guns raised the main army to a strength of 16,700 men and sixty-nine guns.

The Sikh army on the left bank of the Sutlej, the strength of which had been over-estimated by Gough, numbered from 23,000 to 35,000 men, of whom 10,000 or 12,000 were cavalry, with from eighty to ninety guns. Tej Singh with another detachment was watching Firozpur, but was successfully evaded by Sir J. Littler.

The main body had entrenched itself, as Gough's despatch describes it, in " a parallelogram of about a mile in length and half a mile in breadth, including within its area the strong village of Ferozeshah, the shorter sides ooking towards the Sutlej and Moodkee, and the longer towards Firozpore and the open country."

The command of the army was a curious one, for Sir Henry Hardinge the governor-general, had volunteered, and his offer had been accepted, to serve as second in command under his own commander-in-chief. Hardinge, though he could not be a braver soldier than Gough, was decidedly his superior as a commander. It is hardly likely that such a situation as this will ever recur.

To Hardinge was assigned the command of the left wing, whilst

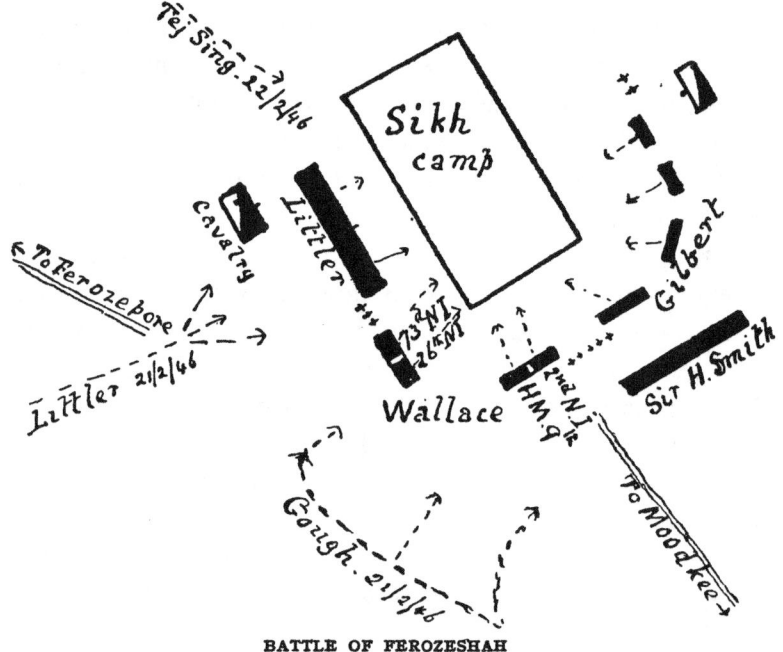

BATTLE OF FEROZESHAH

Gough, commanding in chief, gave his personal attention specially to the right. It was 1.30 p.m. when Sir John Littler joined up on the left, where his troops remained for the battle. In the centre was Wallace's[1] brigade with, counting from left to right, the 73rd and 26th Native Infantry, H.M.'s 9th Foot, and the 2nd Native Infantry. The bulk of the artillery was on Wallace's right under Brooke, and on the right wing was Gilbert's division with one troop of horse artillery. The cavalry was behind both flanks of Littler's division and the right of

[1] Wallace had succeeded Sir J. McCaskill, killed at Moodkee.

Gilbert's. The artillery was posted on the flanks and between the divisions, the bulk (thirty guns and howitzers), as already stated, being in the right centre.

It was 3.30 p.m. when the army was ready to attack. Littler's attack was to be directed against the long western face; Wallace was directed on the angle of the west and southern faces; Gilbert to extend the attack to the rest of the southern face and part of the eastern.

Littler's force was the first to be engaged, with only about an hour of daylight left. He had to deal with the pick of the Sikh army and a very heavy artillery fire. Arriving within 150 yards of the entrenchment he gave the order to charge. His men had almost reached the Sikhs when the British regiment on his right gave way, and retired before the devastating fire. Naturally his native regiments followed suit.

Now came the chance of Wallace's brigade, of the 9th and of their old comrades of the Afghan campaign, the 26th Native Infantry, who were on their immediate left. As the brigade advanced, the angle of the entrenchment came exactly between these two regiments, so that, whilst the 26th Native Infantry dealt with the southern end of the western face, the 9th attacked the western end of the southern face. Sir John Littler's despatch speaks of the 26th Native Infantry and the 9th being " drawn up in reserve " when his own division retired out of gunshot. A part of the 14th Native Infantry of Littler's division joined the two regiments in their attack, which was carried out with the utmost gallantry, the 9th and the 26th Native Infantry vieing with each other as old comrades. It was nearly dark when they went forward against the same awful artillery and infantry fire as had repulsed Littler's men. These fresh troops were, however, not to be denied, and carried the position with the bayonet, though not without terrible sacrifices.

Meanwhile Gilbert's division had, with heavy loss, carried the breastwork and guns opposite them, only to find themselves faced by the Sikh infantry and to suffer heavily from the explosion in their midst of one of the enemy's magazines. When darkness fell Gilbert had only succeeded in driving the Sikh infantry some 300 yards back from their guns. With Gilbert's left the 9th British and 26th Native Infantry, who had borne to their right in the attack, were intermingled. During the charge Major Barnwell with the Grenadiers and part of No. 1 Company got separated from the rest of the 9th and remained during the night in the centre of the Sikh camp with part of Sir Harry Smith's division. Sir Harry Smith's reserve had been brought up on Gilbert's right, in the hope of making an end of the affair. It had penetrated into the centre of the Sikh entrenchment where it halted till between 2 and 3 a.m., when it was driven out to the south-east. When they were gone, Gilbert's division, the 26th Native Infantry and the 9th alone remained in the parallelogram, for Littler's men had never been got forward again after their repulse, and were now in a village to the west.

Wallace had been killed, and the 9th and 26th Native Infantry were now practically part of Gilbert's division. Both the governor-general and the commander-in-chief were with Gilbert, all three striving to restore order and gather in stragglers.

Before daylight, just as the British troops were trying to snatch a few moments' sleep, the Sikhs began to fire upon them from a distance of 300 yards with heavy guns.

The enemy could still have hoped for reinforcement by Tej Singh with the 10,000 men with whom he was watching Firozpur. They could still have put up a good fight, if not have completed the victory which they had half-won. But ignorant and treacherous counsels prevailed, and when at daybreak the British again advanced they encountered no great opposition, even in ejecting the Sikhs from the village of Ferozeshah. What there was, was described by Sir Herbert Edwardes, who was himself present, as "little more than the passive resistance of the wreck of a great army."

When the entrenchment had been cleared and the British army, drawn up on the north-east front, was cheering the governor-general and the commander-in-chief, another storm threatened to break on them as Tej Singh advanced from the direction of Firozpur.

He began skirmishing and firing with artillery on the British left. The artillery fire received no reply, for, as Gough writes, "our artillery ammunition being completely exhausted in these protracted combats, we were unable to answer him with a single shot." There was still a chance of victory for the Sikhs, but Tej Singh failed to press home his attack after compelling the British, by a threat against Ferozeshah, to change front to the right. He suddenly ordered firing to cease and retired, followed by his force, on the Sutlej.

For details regarding the 9th we must again refer to Borton's long letter of January 11, 1846. In it he encloses a copy of his private report to Colonel Davis, temporarily commanding the brigade when it was written on December 25, 1845. Borton was temporarily commanding the 9th from the 21st to the 24th. The report states that on December 21st the junction with Sir J. Littler's force was effected about 3 p.m. some nine miles from Firozpur. A move was at once made to the right for the attack on the enemy's entrenched position. At this time Colonel Taylor of the 9th was commanding the brigade as a consequence of the death of Sir J. McCaskill at Moodkee. Colonel Barnwell commanded the 9th.

The 9th now deployed in a rather thick jungle, and halted till about 4 p.m., when it was ordered forward. Emerging in an open plain, it found itself within round-shot range of the enemy. Pushing on to within 800 yards of the entrenchments the men were ordered to lie down as the fire was very galling. During this period, Littler's force, engaged on the extreme left, had been repulsed and retreated across the front of the 9th, passing to the rear through the right of the brigade.

The enemy's fire increased before Taylor's brigade was ordered to advance again. When the 9th were within 400 yards of a powerful enemy battery they charged. In passing over this long space a break occurred in the centre of their line, and the grenadier company, with part of the right wing of the regiment, passed round the left of the enemy's battery, penetrating into the enemy's camp without much loss.

The left of the regiment, prevented by the smoke and dust from choosing its line, charged straight against the front of the battery. A terrible fire of grape and canister mowed it down. At this time Borton was wounded in the right arm, and carried back a short way by his horse. When he got back to the line he found the left wing retiring in some confusion caused by the alarming cry of "cavalry." Taylor, who had himself been with this wing had been killed after dismounting. Barnwell succeeded to the command of his brigade and Borton found himself in command of the regiment. He at once reorganized it and led it forward against the battery, which had now collapsed owing to the appearance of the right wing of the 9th in its rear. Captains Dunn and Field had been killed with Taylor.

As night fell Wallace, who had succeeded McCaskill in command of the division, brought the 9th over to the centre of the British position. When the regimental call was sounded there many men who had got separated in the action rejoined the colours, especially grenadiers who had followed Captain Daunt round the battery into the enemy's camp.

During the night which followed the men lay on their arms, suffering much from want of water and the severe cold; they were, too, generally under shell fire.

Towards daybreak the troops were again deployed and put in position. It was still early morning of December 22nd when the commander-in-chief ordered the regiment to attack the village of Ferozeshah, which, with many of their own guns, the enemy had recaptured in the night. "Advancing in beautiful style," the 9th stormed the village, bayoneting many Sikhs and again taking the guns. Thence they were presently withdrawn to the entrenched camp, where, on the 24th, the governor-general, riding through their line, called out Borton, shook hands with him, and "spoke in most flattering terms of the conduct of the regiment, saying that he had seen them fight day after day in the Peninsula. He had now again seen them fight two consecutive days, and was confident he could rely on their services if he required them on the morrow."

Here we part company, for the moment, with Borton, whose wound necessitated his absence from the field and his return on leave to England.

One more incident from his papers may be mentioned. There is a letter from Lieutenant Sivewright of the 9th to his mother, written after he was wounded in the leg at Ferozeshah, and before the subsequent amputation which caused his death. Lying out under fire during the night of the 21st-22nd, he heard close by the cries of some of our wounded who were being cut up by Sikh stragglers. A Sikh approached him intending, as he thought, to murder him. Sivewright levelled his pistol at him, but the Sikh had no evil intentions. He said the battle was a

SIR ARTHUR BORTON, G.C.B., G.C.M.G. 1814–93.
Commanded 1st Battalion, 1853–59. Colonel, 1889–93. Governor of Malta, 1878.
(*Ch. XVIII*)

question of fate, and eventually, becoming quite friendly, he carried the wounded officer into the British lines, and was with him till his death on the 28th. Sivewright was one of Borton's particular friends.

The victory of Ferozeshah was as hardly won as any battle in which the British army had been engaged. The trophies were seventy-two pieces of artillery, their losses 2,415 killed and wounded. What the enemy's losses may have been can never be known.

If the 9th had gained great glory by its conduct in this bloody battle, it had paid dearly for it in losses. The casualties were as follows:

Officers.—Lieutenant-Colonel Taylor, Captains Dunn and Field killed; Captain Borton, Lieutenants Taylor, Vigors, Sivewright, Cassidy, and Ensign Foster wounded.[1] Also Captain Havelock attached to the cavalry division as D.A.Q.M.G.

Other ranks.—One sergeant and 99 men killed; six sergeants, one drummer, and 162 men wounded.

Total killed and wounded of all ranks, 273.

Majors Davis and Barnwell respectively were promoted to the lieutenant-colonelcies vacant in consequence of the deaths of Sir J. McCaskill and Lieutenant-Colonel Taylor.

The victory was a Pyrrhic one, and, despite Gough's jubilant despatch, left the British as well as the native troops impressed by the valour and stubbornness of the foe. The Sikhs retired unmolested to a position on the right bank of the Sutlej, and were not hindered when presently they again crossed and entrenched a bridge-head on the left bank.

On January 17th Sir H. Smith was despatched to take Dharmkot, and in the course of his operations inflicted a severe defeat, at Aliwal, on Ranjur Singh on the 28th. In those operations the 9th was not engaged. It remained in the position taken up by the main army, facing the Sutlej from Ferozpur to Hariki.

On January 10th the 9th, now commanded by Lieutenant-Colonel Davis, had moved up from Arufki on the Sutlej for the purpose of

---

[1] Borton names Captain Gahan, as well as Lieutenant Sivewright, as having died as the result of an amputation. Perhaps Gahan was the officer of the 26th Native Infantry, who had been at the forcing of the Khyber in 1842.

watching the enemy's main position in the entrenched camp near Sobraon. This camp was a bridge-head on the left bank of the Sutlej, connected with the right bank by a bridge of boats. On February 1st the regiment was sent into the outpost line at Rodawala opposite the centre of the camp, about 2,500 yards south of it. The camp was surrounded by a semicircular rampart, and, owing to the bend of the river away from its centre, the whole included space was considerably larger than it would have been had the left bank formed a straight chord to the semicircle.

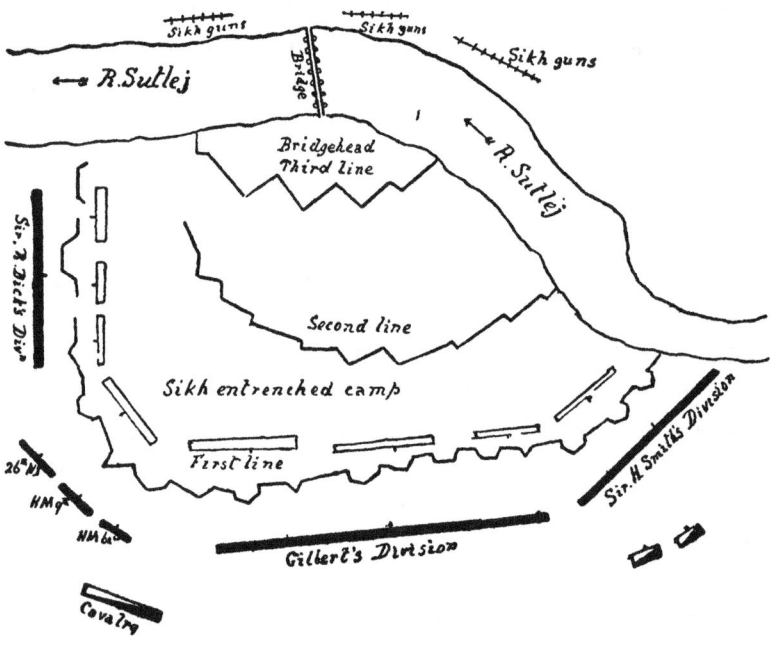

BATTLE OF SOBRAON

The fortifications were of uneven strength, not built with that regularity which would have been ensured by the working of a single engineer. The armament, too, varied. The weakest part was on the down-stream side on the Sikh right, where not only was there a want of continuity in the fortifications, but there was no heavy artillery in it, and it depended for its defence in this respect on one salient battery and some heavy guns beyond the river. Otherwise it had no artillery but 200

"Zumburaks."[1] There were gaps in the line, and the ramparts were generally of a slipshod construction. In the centre and left of the camp the works were better, and there were fifty-seven pieces of artillery on or behind them. There were three interior lines of breastworks concentric with the main enceinte. Under the circumstances Gough had decided that, when he felt strong enough to attack, he would do so chiefly against the Sikh right.

The strength of the army occupying this camp, under Tej Singh, was about 20,000 men, but there were 10,000 cavalry under Lal Singh higher up the river.

When Sir H. Smith had returned from Aliwal on February 8th and other reinforcements had come in, notably the siege-train on February 7th and 8th with reserve ammunition for a hundred guns, Gough felt strong enough, and prepared for the attack on the 10th.

That morning early the battering artillery was disposed at Rodawala and Chota Sobraon, opposite the centre and right of the Sikh works. The plan was to subject the camp to a heavy bombardment from these points, and then to send forward the infantry of the British left against the weaker works near the river, the attack of the centre and right being a feint. The guns were got into position unobserved in the fog of the early morning, and it was only at 7 a.m. that, as the fog lifted, they could open fire on the Sikhs, who, surprised by it, hurried to their posts. After two hours bombardment without any very great effect, the supply of heavy ammunition was running low and Gough decided to put in his infantry attack, as he was always only too ready to do.

The attack of the British left was led by General Dick's division, the 7th brigade leading, followed by the 6th. As reserve to these, on their right rear, followed the 26th Native Infantry, H.M. 9th, and H.M. 62nd, being the 5th brigade under the command of Brigadier the Honourable T. Ashburnham. To the right of these were Gilbert's and Smith's divisions, the latter with its right on the river. The cavalry was in reserve behind the left.

Sir Herbert Edwardes pronounced the left attack to be " beyond all comparison the finest attack of the campaign." Its vital importance

[1] Translated in Gough's despatch " camel-swivels."

was recognized promptly by the Sikhs, who, recognizing also that the attacks on their front and left were in the nature of feints, hurried up their best troops to meet it.

As Stacy's brigade, followed by Wilkinson's, both of Dick's division prepared to advance, the artillery galloped up on the flanks and delivered their fire from a range of 300 yards. The infantry, pushing steadily on without firing, charged with the bayonet. The outworks were carried and victory seemed at hand. But the Sikh reinforcements poured up and the flood was soon more than Stacy and Wilkinson could stem. Ashburnham's reserve, on their right rear, hurried into the desperate fight, with the 9th and the 26th Native Infantry. Even then the three brigades were in imminent danger of being swamped by the flood of Khalsa troops. With the utmost difficulty and the greatest gallantry they were clinging to the conquered entrenchments when the situation was saved by Gough's prompt action in ordering Gilbert and Sir H. Smith to convert their feints into a real attack. The reaction was at once felt on the British left, as the Sikhs, realizing the change, hurried back their troops from their right to meet the new danger on their centre and left.

The new enterprise of the British centre and right was a desperate one, for they had to attack those portions of the works which were really formidable, irrespective of their defenders, requiring a considerable effort to mount them, even if undefended. As has been already mentioned, they were defended by over fifty guns, backed always by the indomitable Sikh infantry. Nevertheless, though with a loss of between 1,100 and 1,200 men, the works were carried and the Sikh gunners bayoneted or cut down as they served their pieces to the very last moment, and finally defended themselves with their swords.

The British were now within the outer works on three sides, forcing back the enemy in a confused mass on the river, which, having risen in the night, was no longer fordable. The bridge broke down almost at once as the first bodies of fugitives crossed it. After that, as Gough's report says, " In their efforts to reach the right bank through the deepened water, they suffered from our Horse Artillery a terrible carnage."

In this hard-fought battle the total loss of the victors was 301 killed and 1,913 wounded. The 9th were fortunate in that they had only one officer, Lieutenant R. Daunt, slightly wounded. Twelve men were killed and six sergeants, one drummer, and twenty-four men wounded. Seven of the wounded men died of their wounds.

This time the victory was decisive, as it had certainly not been at Moodkee, or Ferozeshah, and two days later the British army was at Kasur, well beyond the river on the way to Lahore. The 9th marched from the battle-field on February 13th for Lahore, where they arrived on the 20th and camped on the plain of Mian Mir. Two days later, Lahore itself was occupied by a brigade of the victorious troops, on the complete surrender of the Sikh Government.

At Lahore, the 9th remained till March 23, 1846, when they were ordered to Meerut, arriving there on April 15th. On October 23rd they started on the long march to Dinapur, on the way home. Before marching the regiment had lost 175 men, who had volunteered for further service in India in other regiments. A second call for volunteers, at Allahabad on the way, resulted in the transfer of another 154 men. Reaching Dinapur, the 9th relieved the 39th, and in its turn was relieved, on December 30th, by the 98th. It then marched for Calcutta, where it embarked for England on March 13, 1847. It had served twelve Years in India—years during which it added to its battle honours " Cabool," " Moodkee," " Ferozeshah," and " Sobraon."

During its service in India from 1832 to 1847 the 9th had lost from deaths by wounds or disease twenty officers and 895 others.

It was now due for a few years of peace service, which can be very briefly recorded.

Landing at Chatham on July 10, 1847, it was transferred to Winchester, and during its stay there was formally authorized to bear on its colours and appointments the words " Moodkee," " Ferozeshah," and " Sobraon." Sir James Archibald Hope, K.C.B., succeeded to the colonelcy of the regiment, on February 18, 1848, on the transfer of Sir Thomas Arbuthnot to the 71st Highland Light Infantry.

The year 1848 was one of revolutionary disturbance throughout Europe, which found expression in England in the Chartist movement. Owing to disturbed conditions in the industrial districts of the North, the regiment was sent to Manchester, where it arrived on June 11th and occupied temporary barracks till July 22nd, when it marched to Liverpool. On the 29th it embarked for Dublin, where it was at first encamped in the Phœnix Park, till the atrociously wet weather compelled its transfer for a short time to the Richmond Barracks. On September 8th it marched for Newry, arriving there on the 11th, and detaching one company to Dundalk.

A new set of colours for the regiment had, apparently by a War Office muddle, been sent out to Calcutta just as the regiment was coming home, and consequently crossed it on the voyage, only getting back in March, 1848.

The new colours were presented on November 21st by Major-General Bainbrigge, who came over from Belfast to Newry for the purpose. In doing so he made a long address to the regiment, part of which is worth quoting as it gives a résumé of its history and achievements. He said:—

"In the name of Her Majesty Queen Victoria I now present you your new colours, to replace the old ones, endeared to you by many a hard-fought day; worn to tatters, covered with glory, handed down to the present generation unsullied and unstained. I call on you to guard these new colours with that loyalty and bravery which has always distinguished the regiment. You will rally round them in the moment of danger, remembering that the eyes of your Queen and of your country are on you, expecting that every man will do his duty. And what is that duty? It is nothing less than to offer your lives in defence of your Queen and your country. The most important badge in these colours is that of 'Britannia,' and which gives the name of the 'Britannia Regiment' to you. This badge, it appears by your records, was given to you for your distinguished gallantry at the battle of Almanza, in the War of Succession in Spain in 1707, on which occasion your regiment lost twenty-four officers and 300 men, out of 467, whom it took into the field. The regiment did not follow the example of other regiments, who laid down their arms the following day, but fought to the last, retiring from the field and covering the retreat of their general, the Earl of Galway, to Alcira, with three or four officers and about a hundred men under their commanding officer, Lieutenant-Colonel Steuart, showing an example that, though obliged to retire, there is to be 'No Surrender.' The regiment thus upheld the honour of Great Britain, and was rewarded by Queen Anne with the most honourable badge, to be worn not only on the colours, but also on your breastplates. This fact must inspire every individual with the highest sentiments of loyalty and bravery, and must excite you to acts of heroism. I see on these colours no less than nine names of victories gained in the Peninsula. These victories, gained over the invincible legions of Napoleon, the most warlike soldier of the world, are highly gratifying ; and in the battles in the Peninsula there were no defeats. The first on this list is that of Roleia, where the charm of invincibility was broken; here the 9th distinguished itself and gained great credit. At Corunna the 9th, forming part of Beresford's rear-guard, covered the embarkation—a high compliment to its discipline after the severe and harassing retreat. On that occasion they performed the mournful duty of digging the grave of their gallant and devoted chief, Sir John Moore, and, as the poet says,

> 'They buried him darkly at dead of night
> With his martial cloak around him.'

At Busaco the 9th Regiment came up most opportunely as the enemy had gained the crest of our position, charged him at the point of the bayonet down the hill, and the fate of the day in that part of the field was decided. Here their discipline was conspicuous in ceasing fire in the heat of action, at a moment when suddenly ordered to do so—a difficult thing to do when in the excitement of a battle. At Salamanca their discipline and steadiness were conspicuous. On that occasion they formed part of the right brigade, and for some time before the battle began that brigade was deployed into the line. They were at ordered arms, standing at ease. As files were knocked over, their comrades touched into the centre by the side step, as coolly as on parade ; Sir James Leith, who commanded the division, was riding at a walk backwards and forwards along their front A staff officer from the Duke rode up to him and delivered an order to advance and attack the enemy. He replied ' Thank you, sir, that is the best news I have heard to-day,' and turning to his men, took off his hat and waving it said, ' Now boys we'll at them.' The advance of that brigade in line was one of the finest things that was ever seen—up a rising ground and for nearly half a mile exposed to the enemy's fire. At St. Sebastian the regiment was again highly distinguished, and underwent very severe duty, displaying great bravery and perseverance in the trenches and in the storm. At the battle of the Nive, near the mayor's house, the enemy having got in rear of the regiment, Sir John Cameron faced his men about, charged the enemy in his rear, defeated them and took 160 prisoners. It is a singular fact that all the Peninsula badges (except that of Roleia) were gained under the immediate command of Sir John Cameron, the lieutenant-colonel of the regiment, who, though often wounded and suffering from ill health, was always found at the head of his regiment when fighting was going on. The services performed by this regiment in Afghanistan, in forcing the Khyber Pass, and the Tezeen valley, are of the highest order, and are known to be so by all who are informed of the fact ; but it is impossible here to enter into the details ; for their services the regiment obtained ' Cabool.' In this campaign the late General McCaskill and Lieutenant-Colonel Taylor, who were respectively the commanders of this regiment, were highly distinguished. The victories of Moodkee, Ferozeshah, and Sobraon, over the Sikhs, are highly glorious to the regiment, the Sikhs being the most warlike people in India, having been organized for a long period and instructed in European warfare by experienced French officers. At Moodkee we lamented the death of Sir John McCaskill. At Ferozeshah we lamented the death of the gallant and much-regretted Lieutenant-Colonel Taylor. At Sobraon your present gallant Lieutenant-Colonel Davis commanded the regiment and highly distinguished himself. It is very gratifying to me to see medals on the breasts of many officers and soldiers on parade, showing that they contributed to the glory of those days which will live for ever in our history. At Ferozeshah the Sikhs had above a hundred guns of the heaviest metal, which they served with great effect, repulsing our first attack; but the 9th here restored the day, bayoneting the Sikhs at their guns, driving their protecting infantry before them, and covering themselves with immortal glory. In this attack alone the regiment lost nine officers and 269 men killed or wounded. The gallant colonel being killed, the command of the regiment devolved on Major Borton, who was severely wounded and was rewarded for his gallant conduct on that occasion with the brevet rank of major. The discipline of this regiment has always been conspicuous. At Badajos, after the storming, they were placed in the town, the day after, to restore order and put a stop to further plunder, and of all the duties soldiers can be called upon to perform, this is the most arduous and painful, and it is what most tries discipline. Here many men were killed or wounded by friends, from straggling shots. In the retreat to Ciudad Rodrigo, when many regiments were disorganized, and a severe but well-merited general order was given out by the Duke, this regiment had still preserved its discipline, and had only two men absent, and consequently the 9th was exempted from that general order. In Canada, in 1815, when desertion was unfortunately very general from some of our best regiments, not a single man deserted from the 9th, and the Commander of the Forces, Sir George Murray, paid the regiment a high compliment on the occasion. On the arrival of the 9th from India your present lieutenant-colonel was asked if he was in want of any good non-commissioned officers; he answered 'No,' that he had a sufficiency of excellent non-commissioned officers. I am particularly gratified in finding so high a class of non-commissioned officers in this regiment, especially of colour-sergeants, whose duty it is to protect the colours in the moment of danger. Discipline is one of the highest requisites in the soldier; without it the bravest troops are no better than a rabble, and as the 9th has been noted for its discipline, I have every reason to think it will continue so."

The regiment was moved from Newry to Dublin in April, 1850, and in May to Athlone, in which neighbourhood it was split up into small detachments in the manner so familiar in 1919-21.

In March, 1851, it marched to Galway with three companies in outlying detachments. February, 1853, found its head-quarters at Clonmel, with five companies detached. In June Lieutenant-Colonel Borton took command of the battalion. In December, 1853, the whole battalion was assembled at Fermoy, preparatory to its transfer for the first time to Malta, which was reached on March 7 and 28, 1854.

CHAPTER XIX

THE FIRST BATTALION IN THE CRIMEAN WAR

DURING the regiment's service at Malta the Crimean War broke out, and, as it was destined to go there, its establishment was increased from ten companies to twelve. The total strength was twenty-two officers and 1,495 other ranks, figures which at once strike one as showing a very small staff of officers for so strong a battalion.

On January 6, 1855, the battalion was augmented to the strength of sixteen companies, of which eight were to be "service" and eight "depot." Of the sixty-eight officers, forty-three were for the "service" and twenty-five for the "depot" companies, and the total strength of the battalion, including officers, was fixed at 2,218. Three months later this establishment was altered from "one lieutenant-colonel and three majors" to "two lieutenant-colonels and two majors" and from "twenty-four lieutenants and sixteen ensigns" to "twenty-six lieutenants and fourteen Ensigns." From January 1, 1856, only one paymaster-sergeant was allowed, instead of two.

From November 10, 1856, the establishment was again reduced to twelve companies, with a total strength of 1,138.

From April 1, 1857, the strength was further reduced to 966 by the discharge of twelve sergeants, twelve corporals, and 148 privates. A letter of July 15, 1857, once more altered the number of corporals from thirty-six to forty-eight, and of privates from 804 to 792. The total sanctioned strength of the battalion after this last change was 978.

We have somewhat anticipated here in this matter of the varying establishment.

On March 28, 1854, England had declared war on Russia, and by the time the 9th embarked at Malta, on November 19, 1854, much had happened in the war in which the regiment had had no share. The invasion of the Crimea had begun in September, 1854, the battle of the Alma, fought on September 20th, had been followed by the first bombardment of Sebastopol on October 17th, the battle of Balaklava on October 25th, and Inkerman on November 5th.

It was not till November 27th that the 9th landed near Balaklava, now the advanced base of the British army besieging Sebastopol in alliance with the French and Turks. Its strength on embarkation was twenty officers and 544 other ranks. The great storm of November 14th had spread havoc in Balaklava, and the winter troubles of the ill-provided army had already begun. The story of the privations suffered by our unhappy men in the snow and mud of the Chersonese plateau has been too often told to bear repetition. When the 9th came on the scene there were already nearly 8,000 men in hospital, many of them doomed never to leave it alive. Cholera, brought with the army from Bulgaria, had ravaged the besieging armies. Clothing which had sufficed at the landing in September was utterly inadequate in November, and warmer clothing was still conspicuous by its absence. The trenches had been opened and were as full of mud and water as those in Flanders in the Great War of 1914-18. " Our men," Lord Raglan wrote, " are on duty five nights out of six, a large proportion of them constantly under fire." Twenty-one vessels laden with stores had been wrecked at Balaklava or in its neighbourhood ; everything was wanting—clothing food, fuel, shelter, medicines ; not only the little comforts which might have made life bearable in the trenches, but the barest necessities of existence.

This was the life to which the 9th on landing found themselves condemned. There was not even the excitement of battle, for the war of movement was ended for the present, and the time of assaults had not yet arrived.

The regiment was now commanded by Lieutenant-Colonel Borton, and we again have the advantage of his interesting letters.

On first landing, the 9th was encamped near Balaklava, and, seeing that it had not to carry its supplies over a long distance, it may be presumed it was not so badly off in that respect as when, a few days later, it was moved up to duty in the trenches.

A lurid light is thrown on the casual way in which men were sent out to the Crimea and treated there by a copy of a report amongst Borton's papers which says: " For some days after the 9th Regiment reached camp, the sick were exposed to the same privations as the healthy, lying in bell-tents on damp ground, without covering beyond that of a single blanket which was too often already wet. The weather was desperate and the duties in the trenches very severe. Cholera broke out on the third day, and in the absence of all necessary comforts, the mortality was of course very great, so that ninety deaths occurred amongst 450 men." To some queries put to the regiment the reply, dated April 17, 1855, says: " Of 540 men who landed on November 27th, 182 have died, 153 are sick absent, and thirty-eight sick present." It is also stated that twenty-nine men proposed as being unfit for active service had nevertheless been embarked. Of these,

17 died between December 5, 1854, and January 18, 1855.

10 were sick at Scutari,

1 was in the divisional hospital,

1 only was doing duty in camp.

The losses from disease began at once. Within a week of the landing fifty-seven deaths had occurred, by the end of 1854 the number reached a hundred.

A brief note in the diary, " January 6, 1855.—Tom Dent frozen to death last night," is pathetically eloquent. Walking back from Balaklava in a snow-storm, Captain Dent missed his way and sat down to rest with this fatal result.

On landing at Balaklava the regiment had been armed with Minié rifles in place of the old smooth-bore musket, and it was then attached to the 2nd brigade of the 3rd division.[1] The division was commanded by Sir R. England, the brigade by General Eyre, and the other regiments in it were the 18th, 28th, 38th, and 44th. The position of the brigade was on the extreme left of the English left attack adjoining the right

[1] See table in " Despatches and Papers issued by Horse Guards, 1857."

of the French left attack.[1] The English left attack was on the spur running towards the fortress and bounded on the right by the Woronzoff road and ravine, on the left by the Piquet House ravine, of which the upper right branch was known to our men as the " Valley of the Shadow of Death."

All through the winter of 1854–55, and the spring and early summer of the latter year, the regiment's duties were confined to supplying working parties and trench guards, and doing their best to keep a cheerful countenance in face of the most depressing and harassing conditions. Disease and exposure continued to take their toll, but from November 27, 1854, to June 10, 1885, the total casualties from enemy action are recorded as only two rank and file killed and ten wounded.

On June 15, 1855, Colonel Borton's diary says the men were busy getting armed with the Enfield in place of the Minié rifle, to go into action the very moment that they got a new weapon for the first time!

On the 18th June the regiment was at last to be engaged in active operations. On that day the French attacked towards the Malakoff on the right, the English right failed in the attack on the great Redan, and the left carried out a double attack on its front. The attack of the left brigade of Sir R. England's division is the one which concerns the 9th. General Eyre, commanding the brigade, reported on June 19th to his divisional general :—

" I moved off yesterday morning between 1 and 2 o'clock a.m. with my brigade, consisting of the 9th, 18th, 28th, 38th, and 44th regiments—total strength about 2,000 bayonets—and proceeded down the ravine on our left, by the French Piquet House, for the purpose of attacking the enemy's ambuscades, and of making a demonstration on that side.

" In attacking the first of these ambuscades we were anticipated by the French, who cleverly took them on their left flank as we advanced in front. Beyond this the French had no instructions

[1] It will be remembered that the two French attacks were respectively on the right and left flanks, whilst the English were the right and left centre. Of course, Sebastopol was never completely surrounded and was always open on the north side.

to co-operate with us; I therefore immediately pushed on an advanced guard under Major Fielden, 44th Regiment, composed of marksmen from each regiment, supporting it on the right by the

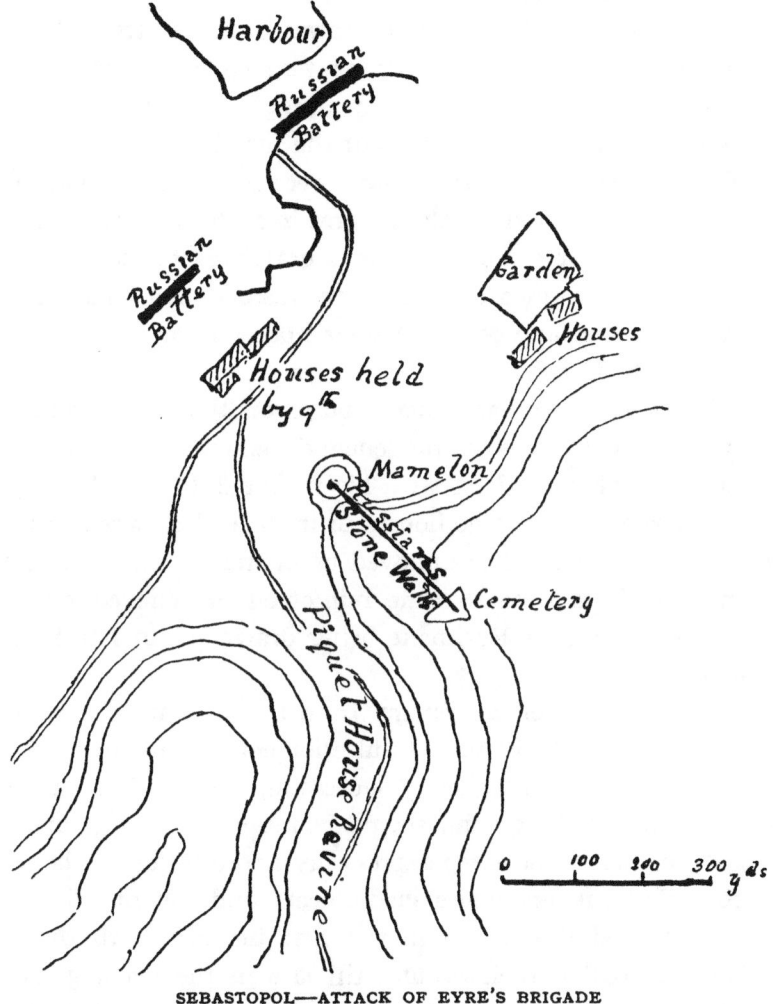

SEBASTOPOL—ATTACK OF EYRE'S BRIGADE

44th and 38th Regiments, and on the left by the 18th Regiment, keeping at first the 9th and 28th regiments in reserve.

"The enemy, whose strength I could not estimate, occupied a strong position; the right rested on a Mamelon, their left on a cemetery. These points were occupied by marksmen. The intervening ground was intersected and the road barricaded with stone walls, which our men were obliged to pull down, under fire, before they could advance.

"In rear of this position, towards the fortress, the enemy occupied several houses, and there were bodies of the enemy seen in rear, as reserves, but of what strength I could not say. This position, under fire of the guns of the fortress, was strong, and we could not expect to carry it and retain it without sustaining a considerable loss, and which, I regret to state, we have experienced both in officers and men; but it is gratifying to feel that they all most nobly performed their duty on this occasion. The 18th Regiment pushed on and occupied some houses immediately under the Garden-wall Battery.

"The 44th occupied some houses on the right, from whence they kept up a fire on the enemy's embrasures. Lieutenant-Colonel Lowth moved on with his regiment (the 38th), and after taking possession of some houses in front, endeavoured to turn the flank of a battery which annoyed us in front. These parties were afterwards from time to time reinforced or relieved by the 9th Regiment, the 28th Regiment being drawn up in line in rear to support the whole.

"Having driven the enemy from these points, I continued to occupy them, with the view to ulterior movements, in the event of the attack on the right being successful, and until it was decided what portion of the ground should be retained for siege operations.

"I cannot sufficiently express my appreciation of the conduct of the officers, non-commissioned officers, and men on this occasion. They attacked the enemy in the first instance with the utmost gallantry, holding their ground till late in the evening, although exposed all day to a concentrated fire from the guns of the fortress, in addition to which I believe the enemy brought up some field guns and kept continually firing shells. The losses occasioned were considerable, the total being thirty-one officers, forty-four sergeants, and 487 rank and file killed or wounded."

SIR HAMBLETON FRANCIS CUSTANCE, K.C.B., 1811–92.
Commanded West Norfolk Militia, 1854–81. Colonel, 1882–92. (*Ch. XIX*)

Eyre, being wounded, had to give over command of the brigade at 5 p.m. Later, as the ground was too advanced to be held, after the failure of the attack on the Redan, the troops were withdrawn unmolested by the enemy.

The report says later : " The conduct of all was so exemplary during this trying day that I can scarcely with justice particularize individuals. I beg however to thank the officers commanding corps for the assistance they afforded me, viz. Lieutenant-Colonel Borton commanding 9th Regiment, etc."

In a letter to his brother dated June 21, 1855,[1] Colonel Borton gives the following account of the action of his regiment on the 18th.

He begins by saying he thinks the whole attack of the 18th was a mistake. Nothing should have been attempted on our left until the French on the right were in possession of the Malakoff. As a matter of fact, the only success of the day was that of the brigade in which was the 9th. As for the assault on the Redan, he thinks Lord Raglan only allowed it because otherwise the French would have attributed their failure at the Malakoff to our slackness on their left. He continues :—

> "We [the 2nd Brigade] on the extreme left, far removed from the scene of assault, were early involved in the fight. Our brigadier, is, I suspect, greedy of distinction, being little inclined to err on the side of discretion. That he failed in judgment and allowed his troops to push on too far I cannot doubt, and hence our loss was far greater than it ought to have been. My regiment, much weakened by detached parties, was at first in reserve ; but it was not long before he paid me the doubtful compliment of cutting out for me a day's work which I am not likely to forget in a hurry. At about half-past five we were moved into the cemetery, which had already been taken, and which was the only point which should have been attempted until assured that the troops on our right

[1] A great part of this letter was published in the " Times " by the brother to whom it was addressed. Colonel Borton was deeply distressed at this, fearing that his outspoken criticisms might hurt the feelings of those regarding whom they were made. He intended that they should be kept for family consumption at that time.

were advancing. Beyond this, however, numbers flushed with success had advanced and taken possession of some houses immediately in front of a powerful battery and commanded on all sides by riflemen. This evidently vicious position they had for the most part been driven from; but, in his opinion, it was important that it should be maintained, and he ordered me to occupy it with my regiment.

"I had but time for one glance at the position, but that was quite sufficient to show me that it was a regular Balaklava charge[1] which was expected of us. However, there was nothing for it but to obey, so having whispered my view of affairs to Elmhirst, and told him the part I wished him to play, we sprang over the ridge and went at it. How I blessed my stars at having a good pair of legs to take me like the wind over the vines which entangled the path between me and a house on which I had fixed as my headquarters. Even Ferozeshah was a joke to it! Grape, canister, and round shot swept round one like hail, and for my encouragement, just as I reached the cover of the building, surprised to find myself with a whole skin, one of the latter crashed through the building as though it had been paper. Elmhirst had taken a line to my right and I was grateful to see that he also had reached the cover of some walls in safety; but, determined to join me, I almost immediately saw him spring from his lair and with uplifted sword call on his men to advance. Again the battery opened, and it was with most intent interest that I watched his charge down the hill. The vine holes—for they are partially sunk—made the footing very uncertain. He suddenly turned an awful somersault, and I thought it was all over with him as with many others. But no! Again he was on his legs. 'Forward men,' again reached the Russian battery and a few more strides placed him by my side. And didn't we then devoutly wish we were back again. However, there was nothing for it but to pack close, dodge the shots as best we might, and aggravate the enemy as little as possible. And there we spent

---

[1] "C'est magnifique, mais ce n'est pas la guerre" was a French general's characterization of the light cavalry charge at Balaklava.

fourteen weary hours, the enemy at one moment bringing down our houses with round shot, burying the wretched wounded beneath the ruins; then throwing shells amongst us which, owing to the softness of the ground, fortunately penetrated deep and in bursting only formed craters big enough for one's grave; and if a leg was injudiciously allowed to protrude beyond a certain limit it instantly furnished a target for a dozen rifle balls.

"Under these trying circumstances, it was most gratifying to find that my young soldiers, many of them having only landed the day before, behaved admirably. Indeed, to a family man who has got a sneaking kindness for his wife and bairns, it is amazing to see how recklessly some of them will expose life. When I wanted to send a report to the general I had no difficulty in finding volunteers to take it; the knowledge that they would get a drink of water was sufficient inducement, though certain to have some fifty rifle balls fired at them during their transit both ways. Many escaped through this ordeal almost miraculously, but one of my messengers came to grief. He was laden with commissions for water and reached the general in safety. At length he appeared, loaded with his precious freight, and broke covert, cheered on by the thirsty throng. As usual, he was twigged; in a moment a volley of balls cut up the dust around him, and, when within fifty yards or so of the goal, the poor fellow was winged and dropped heavily. For a time he was so still that we feared he had got his quietus; but shortly the vines began to move and he appeared dragging with him his wounded leg, two tins of the precious water, and with my note between his teeth like a good retriever. I found the gallant fellow's wound was slight, the ball having grazed his knee joint, and you may imagine my sorrow when part of the wall afterwards fell on him and hurt him a good deal. You will hardly credit that numbers begged of me immediately afterwards to go and bring in more water, which he left on the ground when he began to travel on all fours. A positive veto alone stopped them, for my homily to the text that water was not worth blood was not much thought of.

"This is a long tale, but fourteen hours might furnish many such anecdotes. To conclude my story: at nightfall, when the riflemen fired wide, we gradually got our wretched wounded to the rear; scorched and parched by a burning sun, my men filed off to the point we should, *me judice*, never have quitted, and at 10 p.m. choked with the dust of ages which had arisen from the ruins and bespattered us from head to foot with blood and brains, it was with a sense of no slight thankfulness that I again reached my hut."

The casualties on this day in the 9th were Captain F. Smith, killed; Lieutenant and Adjutant McQueen (slightly) and Lieutenant A. G. Douglas wounded; seven rank and file killed, and forty-five wounded. Private W. Cooke of the regiment picked up a live shell which had fallen close to a pit in which he and several others were standing and threw it clear to a distance, where it exploded harmlessly. This brave act saved the lives of himself and the others. He was for this act promoted to corporal on the field, and recommended for the French Legion of Honour. The reward strikes us as a beggarly one, considering that the V.C. was given to others for very similar acts, notably at the bombardment of Alexandria in 1882.

When the army was reorganized in August, 1855, into six divisions of two brigades each, the 9th was allotted to the 2nd brigade 1st division, and transferred to the right (British) attack which, from the closeness of the trenches to the Redan, was even more exposed than the left.

When the assault of September 8th was made the 9th were not called on to take any part, beyond standing in reserve with the rest of the 1st division. The French took the Malakoff, the English got into the Great Redan, but were driven out. A renewal of the assault on the Redan was rendered unnecessary by the evacuation of that work, and the rest of the south side of Sebastopol, by the Russians.

The regiment had to spend another winter in the Crimea, but, though there were hardships and another bad storm in December, 1855, to be borne, they were as nothing to those of the previous year. The 9th took part in the great review on February 25, 1856. It was not till

Brigadier General W. E. G. L. Bulwer, C.B.V.D. J.P.
Commanded
3rd Norfolk Rifle Volunteers – December 1878 – May 1883.
3rd Volunteer Batalion Norfolk Regt – May 1883 – April 1894.
Norfolk Volunteer Infantry Brigade – 1895 – 1897

May 1, 1856, that it finally left the Crimea, the conclusion of peace having been announced on April 2nd.

It is not for us to tell again the miserable story of mismanagement in the Crimea, which cost England far more lives than those attributable to the enemy's action. The general statistics for the 9th are given in a statement at the end of the volumns of "Despatches and Papers" issued by the War Office in 1857 as follows:—

	Officers.	N.C.O.'s and Men.
Strength on date of embarkation of headquarters. November 19th, 1854	20	549
Reinforcements up to 1st April, 1856	30	558
Decrease.	50	1107
Died in the East	3	137
Invalided home	18	153
Prisoners or deserters	—	1
	21	291
Strength on 1st April, 1856	31	725

The regimental records show the casualties in the Crimea between November 27, 1854, and April, 30, 1856, as follows:—

	Captains	Staff Officers.	Lieutenants.	Sergeants.	Drummers.	Other Ranks.
Died of disease	1	—	—	6	1	206
Died of wounds	1	—	—	—	—	6
Killed in action	1	—	—	—	—	14
Killed accidentally	1	1[1]	—	—	—	1
Wounded	1	—	2	5	—	78
Invalided	—	—	—	7	3	119

[1] This appears to be Surgeon H. le Blanc, of whose death Colonel Borton has left a note. On March 17, 1855, he left his tent, attracted by the firing in a sortie against the French trenches to the left. After visiting the trenches, he was returning, but being very short-sighted he lost his way and came upon a French sentry who, as le Blanc apparently did not answer his challenge, shot him dead.

Decorations bestowed by the Allies were distributed as follows:—

Legion of Honour	3	Sardinian Medal	3
Medjidich	10	French War Medal	7

The grant of the right to bear "Sevastopol" on the appointments and colours was made in due course.[1]

On April 28th the regiment was inspected by Lieutenant-General Lord Rokeby, who, in a divisional order of the 30th said: "The 9th Regiment having received orders to embark for Canada, the Lieutenant-General has great pleasure in expressing the approbation with which he regards its services whilst it formed part of the 1st division. The accuracy with which the 9th invariably observed the regulations of the service, and the efficiency it displayed in the performance of every duty fully sustain the reputation it had acquired in the 3rd Division during the early part of the campaign. The Lieutenant-General requests that Colonel Borton, C.B., the officers, non-commissioned officers, and rank and file will accept his thanks for the support they have afforded him in his command, and his best wishes for their future prosperity." Brigadier-General Ridley, in a brigade order, expressed an equally high opinion of the regiment's conduct.

Colonel Borton, for his services on June 18, 1855, had been given the C.B. and promoted colonel in the army.[2] Major Lister had been promoted to lieutenant-colonel, Captains Hawes and Browne to brevet-majors. The 5th Class of the Legion of Honour was gained by Captains Scott and Browne, Sergeant Ryder, and, as already mentioned, Corporal W. Cooke.

The strength of the regiment on embarkation for Canada was twenty-four officers and 667 other ranks. There were left behind in the Crimea, and at Smyrna, Malta, Scutari, and Sinope, eight officers and fifty-four other ranks.

---

[1] See Appendix IV.
[2] He received the Legion of Honour (5th class) in 1857.

CHAPTER XX

THE FIRST AND SECOND BATTALIONS, 1856–1881— IONIAN ISLANDS—JOWAKI CAMPAIGN— SECOND AFGHAN WAR

FROM Sebastopol the 1st Battalion went direct to Canada, arriving at Quebec on June 8, 1856, and proceeded to Kingston on the 12th. The voyage was made on H.M.S. "Resolute," from which ship Colonel Borton dates a private letter of the 7th May, 1856. In September, 1857, the battalion moved to Montreal, but the reduction of the forces in Canada entailed its sailing again for home on October 15th. Landing at Portsmouth on November 5, 1857, it was sent to Sunderland, where it remained till it was transferred, in September, 1858, to Aldershot. In October, 1859, it went to Shorncliffe, detaching two companies each to Woolwich and Chatham. These detached companies rejoined the head-quarters in the following January, and in February, 1860, the service companies, with twenty-two officers and 533 other ranks, embarked for the Ionian Islands, the depot companies remaining at Limerick.

THE THIRD RAISING OF THE 2ND BATTALION[1]

On July 24, 1857, when England was alarmed by the early events of the Indian Mutiny, orders were issued for the raising of a 2nd battalion of the 9th East Norfolk Regiment. Lieutenant-Colonel Charles Elmhirst of the 1st Battalion, then serving on the staff, was appointed to raise and

[1] This account of the earlier years of the 2nd Battalion after its raising in 1857 is mostly taken from the "Historical Records" compiled by Colonel C. H. Shepherd, D.S.O.

command the new battalion, and the following officers were nominated to it: Major Taylor from 1/9th; Major and Brevet-Lieutenant-Colonel Sankey, from the 47th Regiment; Captains Daunt and Nugent, from 1/9th; Captain Marston, from half-pay, late 51st Regiment; Captain McBarnett, from half-pay, late 79th Regiment; Captains McFarlane and O'Shea, from half-pay; Captain Cardew, from half-pay, late 19th Regiment; Captain Graham, from Lieutenant 67th Regiment; Lieutenants Grubbe, Agnew, Gipps, Bolton, Majors Bradshaw, Lynne, Coote, Perry—all from 1/9th; Lieutenant and Adjutant Wright; Quartermaster Arrowsmith, from half-pay, late 3rd Rifle Regiment, British Italian Legion. With this staff recruiting was commenced at Great Yarmouth in November, 1857, a number of non-commissioned officers having volunteered from the 1st battalion and other regiments.

By February, 1858, when the battalion moved to Bradford, its strength was twenty-two officers and 210 non-commissioned officers and men. At Bradford one hundred non-commissioned officers and men were received from the 1st battalion, and detachments were sent to Bury and Burnley. By June 25th, when the battalion went by train to Sheffield, the strength had risen to thirty-one officers and 609 non-commissioned offices and men, and when, on September 22nd, it entrained for Aldershot there were thirty-four officers and 812 non-commissioned officers and men.

The establishment for the battalion had been fixed in the order for raising it at eight companies with one Lieutenant-colonel (the colonel was counted with the 1st Battalion), two majors, eight captains, ten lieutenants, six ensigns, paymaster, adjutant, quartermaster, surgeon, assistant-surgeon, one sergeant-major, four staff-sergeants, one orderly-room clerk, twenty-four sergeants, one drum-major, sixteen drummers and fifers, thirty-two corporals, and 608 privates. Total 719, which was augmented from July 24th to 727 by the addition of eight colour sergeants.

On October 30, 1858, the 2nd battalion, now numbering thirty-three officers and 867 non-commissioned officers and men, left Aldershot by train for Portsmouth, where they embarked on H.M.S. "Himalaya" for Corfu, which they reached on November 12th. The depot companies

MAJOR-GENERAL CHARLES ELMHIRST, C.B.
Raised the 2nd Battalion for the third time, 1857–65. (*Ch. XX*)

had been sent to join those of the 1/9th, the Buffs, the 17th, and the 106th at Limerick, where they constituted a depot battalion.

Six of the seven Ionian Islands—Corfu, Cephalonia, Zante, Santa Maura, Ithaca, and Paxo—lie close to the west coast of Albania or Greece. Only Cerigo is off the south coast of Greece. They had been occupied by Great Britain since 1815, nominally as protector of the " United States of the Ionian Islands," constituted by the Treaty of Paris. Practically, the English Governor had for long been a much greater power than the Ionian Parliament. The time was approaching when, after much hesitation and opposition, even on the part of Mr. Gladstone, the islands were to be ceded to Greece under its new king, the brother of the princess who shortly afterwards became Princess of Wales. The two battalions of the 9th were to form part of the last garrison of the islands during their occupation by the British.

Of the various stations in these islands Corfu seems to have had most attractions, as there was a considerable society, and various amusements, such as yachting, and shooting on the adjoining mainland.

On December 30, 1858, Lieutenant-Colonel Bethune took over the command of the 1st Battalion from Colonel Borton, C.B. On March 3, 1859, its colours were presented to the 2nd battalion by Lady Buller, wife of Major-General Sir G. Buller, commanding the troops at Corfu, in the presence of the High Commissioner. She also addressed them.[1] The battalion remained at Corfu, only sending small detachments to Fano and Lazaretto, small islands forming dependencies of Corfu, and to Paxo, which, though a separate government, was only four miles long by two broad. On October 6, 1859, a larger detachment of three officers and one hundred men was sent to Santa Maura, a larger island.

In February, 1860, the 1st battalion arrived from England and the head-quarters of both remained at Corfu for the present, with companies detached to the other islands.

On August 1, 1860, a detachment of the 2nd battalion went to Ithaca, and in the middle of October four companies of the same battalion

[1] Her address is published in full in Colonel Shepherd's " Records."

were detached to Zante under Brevet-Lieutenant-Colonel Sankey. On October 30th the head-quarters of the 2nd battalion and six companies were transferred to Cephalonia, the largest in area of the islands, with a population of about equal to that of Corfu (approximately 73,000). Nevertheless, the station was less popular than the head-quarters of the Government at Corfu.

On December 4, 1861, the four companies of the 2nd battalion, which had been at Zante since October, 1860, returned to Corfu, whither they were followed, on December 21st and 23rd, by the head-quarters and six companies from Cephalonia.

In April, 1863, the head-quarters of the 1st battalion moved to Cephalonia.

In June, 1863, the 2nd battalion sent a detachment to Santa Maura, and on September 22nd another to Ithaca. The year 1864 saw the cession, with the full concurrence of the inhabitants, of the Ionian Islands to Greece, then ruled by King George I, formerly known as Prince William George of Glücksberg.

At the end of February, 1864, the 1st battalion lost four non-commissioned officers by the upsetting of a boat near Ithaca. The fortifications of Corfu were now being destroyed—a proceeding which was resented by the islanders, who had paid, sooner or later, a great deal for their construction. The destruction was necessary to calm the apprehensions of the Great Powers. At the same time the guns, over 400 in number, and stores were shipped to England. The 6th Foot were the first regiment to leave the islands. There remained the 4th Foot and the 2nd battalion of the 9th at Corfu, with the 1/9th in the other islands.

The 1st battalion left in May for Malta, where the head-quarters and the detached companies assembled, and sailed thence for Gibraltar.

It was on June 1, 1864, that the 4th and the 2nd battalion of the 9th left Corfu, the Governor, Sir Henry Storks, having sailed on May 31st. On the departure of the British Garrison, the following farewell address was presented by the Corfu Municipal Council. It is preserved, framed, in the mess of the 1st battalion :—

"To the English Garrison.

"Valiant Sons of England,

"By a generous decision of your august Queen, the wishes of this Grecian land have been granted, and you are about to leave this island, on which you have resided with us for half a century; and nobly have you behaved towards us.

"The Municipal Council of this island, under the influence of the unspeakable joy which it experiences in this memorable change in its destiny, at the moment of its entering a new career of national existence, cannot without emotion witness your departure and leave unexpressed the sentiments of sympathy that it entertains for the great nation to which you belong.

"As free citizens of a free nation you will not be indignant at the exuberant joy of a people passing from foreign protection to national liberty, nor will you consider it in any way connected with your departure, which affects us exceedingly, and causes us to express from our hearts the warmest wishes for your welfare, and for that of your illustrious country, to which we feel bound by gratitude and hopes.

"Farewell, brave sons of England, forget as we do whatever may tend to mar our mutual love; love us as we love you, and desire that we may imitate your national virtues.

"(Sd.) D. Courcoumeley (*Regent*).
S. A. Muistoxide.
G. Tombro.
A. Trifona.
M. Padovan.
A. Delviniotto.

D. A. Courcoumeley, *Secretary to the Municipal Council*."

"Corfu, 1st *June*, 1864."

Soon after leaving the Ionian Islands, as the two battalions parted company for a good many years, their history must be recorded separately.

THE 1ST BATTALION, 1864 TO 1881

Having reached Gibraltar in May, 1864, the 1st battalion remained there till August, 1865, when it was transferred to the Cape.

On the voyage out a man of the second half of the battalion died of cholera before arrival at Table Bay. There the disease again broke out on September 5th, and caused the deaths of nine men, one woman, and five children up to the 19th. The half battalion was sent for thirty days' quarantine at Saldanha Bay, returning to Capetown on November 11th.[1] It remained in Capetown till 1868, in January of which year it moved to King William's Town, but detached four companies to St. Helena. In June, 1869, it was ordered to embark at East London, but on arrival at that port the orders were cancelled and it returned to King William's Town in July, and stayed till July, 1870, when it was sent home to Dublin and the neighbourhood for fourteen months. September, 1871, saw it stationed at Cork, with numerous detachments in the surrounding country.

It was at the end of 1871 that Major-General Bates was appointed colonel of the 9th, in succession to General Sir James Archibald Hope, G.C.B., deceased. The latter had been colonel since February 18, 1848.

In July, 1872, the 1st battalion left Cork for the Channel Islands. The head-quarters and five companies were quartered in Guernsey, the other five companies in Alderney. After a year in these stations the battalion went, in August, 1873, for two years to Pembroke. On May 5 it had sent two companies to Yarmouth to form part of the 31st brigade depot. The rest were at the autumn manœuvres of July, 1873, on Dartmoor. They had landed at Devonport for that purpose. They reached Pembroke by sea on August 3rd.

[1] With reference to this there is a Saldanha Bay Fund in the 1st battalion. It is not known for certain what this fund is. It is said that some of the men were drowned in a shipwreck at Saldanha Bay and that the fund was started for the widows. On the other hand it is possible the intended beneficiaries may have been the families of the men who had died of cholera.

In July, 1875, the battalion went to Aldershot for a year; in July, 1876, to Colchester for another year; and in May, 1877, to Dublin. In April, 1878, its quarters were transferred from Dublin to Birr, whence it went in June to the Curragh for the summer, returning to Birr in September, and moving, in February, 1879, to Kinsale, where it had two companies on detachment. July, 1880, saw its transfer to Limerick till September, 1881, when it went to Templemore, whence it supplied detachments to the neighbouring country. The year was one when Ireland was more than ordinarily disturbed by Fenian plots. The battalion took its full share in the hard and unpleasant work of those troublous times, in guarding against threatened disturbances, protecting evicting parties, and the like. Such work weighs heavily on soldiers, who generally find it an uncongenial and thankless task.

THE 2ND BATTALION, 1864 TO 1881

During this period, whilst the 1st battalion was enjoying a peaceful existence, tempered only at times by the mild excitement of Irish alarums and excursions, the 2nd battalion was passing a less monotonous time, largely on foreign service.

We left it at Gibraltar in June, 1864. On September 1st, being under orders for China, its establishment was raised to three field officers, ten captains, twenty subalterns, fifty-four sergeants, forty corporals, and 730 privates. It transferred its unfit men to the 1st battalion, from which it received fit men to complete its strength.

On November 3, 1864, it sailed on H.M.S. "Tamar" for Hong Kong, where it arrived on February 7, 1865, and sent a detachment of two companies to Kowloon. Two other detachments were made, one of two officers and seventeen men sent to Canton, and one of one officer and three men to Foochow, both for the purpose of instructing Chinese troops in drill. The establishment was reduced by a hundred privates from April 1st.

At Hong Kong Lieutenant-Colonel T. E. Knox, from the depot battalion at Limerick, took over command of the 2nd battalion, on April 10, 1865, from Colonel Elmhirst, who had commanded it since its third formation in 1857. In July, 1865, there was so much sickness at Kowloon that the two companies there, as well as the head-quarters of the 2/10th, had to be withdrawn. Guards were supplied from Hong Kong.

At this time also the depot battalion at Limerick was transferred to Mullingar. In it were included the depot companies of both the 1st and 2nd battalions.

During 1865 the battalion had suffered very heavily from the unhealthy season. There had died, in the period February, 1865, to March, 1866, two officers, and fifty-three other ranks, besides six women and thirty-two children. There had been invalided home, in the same period, one officer and 150 other ranks, besides twenty-six women and thirty children. It was decided to send the battalion to recuperate in the healthier climate of Japan, and the left wing of nine officers and 286 men sailed from Hong Kong on March 30, 1866, for Yokohama. The right wing followed with the head-quarters on May 9th. Here they were joined by a small draft of Captain G. H. French, Ensign Shepherd, one schoolmaster, two sergeants, and thirty-four men from the depot battalion at Mullingar. A further draft of one lieutenant, four sergeants, and forty-four men arrived in March, 1867.

It is not necessary for us to attempt to explain fully the relations of the British and other European Governments to that of Japan, the real constitution of which was so little understood that the treaties for the opening of the Treaty Ports had been concluded with the Shogun, under the impression that he was, in theory as well as in fact, the supreme ruler. The existence of the Mikado seems to have been unknown to the negotiators of those treaties, and one of the first duties of Sir Harry Parkes as British minister was to obtain the formal ratification of the treaties. Nor did the foreign ministers fully understand the relations between the *de facto* ruler, the Shogun, and the feudal barons, the Daimios.

The storm was rapidly brewing which was to end in that revolution from which the Mikado emerged as the *de facto* as well as the *de jure* Emperor. It can easily be imagined that the position of the foreign ministers and their Legation guards was a very delicate one, and that undisciplined or overbearing troops might easily produce an explosion in a country which for centuries had displayed hostility to, and reluctance to enter into relations with, the " outer barbarian." In January, 1867, a new Shogun had been appointed—the last of the Shoguns—whose tenure of office was destined to be short.

In April, Sir Harry Parkes proceeded to Osaka, for the opening of which port negotiations were in progress, to visit the Shogun, whose conduct in the matter of the ratification of the treaties by the Emperor had been friendly. With him the British minister took, as escort, forty-four non-commissioned officers and men of the 2/9th, under the command of Captain Daunt and Lieutenant Bradshaw. On his return to Yokohama the minister expressed in very gratifying terms his appreciation of the exemplary conduct and smartness of the detachment.

The good conduct of a minister's guard seems a small matter to elicit such special commendation. But it must be remembered that dislike of the foreigner was still widespread in Japan, that it was liable to give rise to hostile demonstrations, should it be excited by any indiscretion on the part of officers or men, and that the best way to work for its suppression was by showing an excellent example of conduct. Moreover, Japan was a very different country in those days from what it is now, and it was desirable to call attention, by smartness on parade, to the efficiency of British troops. Later in the year, though the Shogun had resigned his office and favoured the sole government of the Emperor, trouble was brewing. On December 20th the 2nd battalion was again called on to send a detachment, of the same strength as before, with the minister, who, with the other foreign representatives, was proceeding to the formal opening of the ports of Osaka and Hiogo on January 1, 1868. They were with the minister at Osaka when the Daimios Satsuma, Tosa, and others, having seized the person of the Mikado at Kioto, announced his assumption of supreme authority and the abolition of the office of Shogun. The Shogun himself withdrew to Osaka, where he found the foreign representatives determined to observe strict neutrality in this domestic revolution. On his attempt to regain his position being disastrously defeated at Fushimi, he fled to Osaka, whence, after expressing his inability to protect the foreign missions, he fled again to Yedo.

Osaka, now in a state of anarchy, was no fit place for the foreign representatives, who withdrew to Kobe, the site selected for the settlement in connexion with the recently opened port of Hiogo. The guard of the 2/9th, commanded by Lieutenants Bradshaw and Bruce, arrived at Kobe, on February 3, 1868, with Sir Harry Parkes. Next day some 150 followers of the Daimio Bizen, an ally of Satsuma, well armed and having with them three field-pieces, entered Kobe. Two miles behind them was a larger body about 600 strong. These men were hostile to the foreigners, whom they looked upon, despite proclamations of neutrality, as friends of the Shogun. They ordered every one in the streets to fall on their knees, an order with which the Japanese complied, but which was naturally resented by Europeans. An Englishman narrowly escaped death, and a French marine and a United States sailor were wounded. This was in the main street of Kobe. Sir H. Parkes, with one of his escort, was inspecting the site of the new settlement and narrowly escaped the bullets, which were flying freely, before he could give the alarm. The detachment of the 9th turned out with great promptitude on the sounding of the " assembly " at the British Consulate. They marched about two miles before coming up with Bizen's people, who at once turned when they found they were pursued. The 9th, now joined by some French and American marines and the mounted escort, broke into skirmishing order and opened a brisk fire, under which their opponents soon broke up into small parties and fled for the hills behind Hiogo. In the pursuit the road was found covered with the baggage and very complete equipment of Bizen's men, who, in their flight, also abandoned their three field-pieces.

On March 23, 1868, Sir H. Parkes was with his escort at Kioto on his way to a formal audience of the Mikado when the procession was suddenly attacked by two Japanese running amok. The mounted escort, which was in advance, was thrown into confusion by the sudden attack, and no less than nine out of eleven of them were wounded by the two desperadoes. Sir Harry Parkes, who had a narrow escape, called out to cut down his assailant, who now came upon the guard of the 9th and was bayoneted, though not before he had severely wounded one of the men. It was believed more fanatics were lying in wait to renew the

CHINA, 1865.
Head-quarters, 2nd Battalion, Hong Kong.   Colonel T. E. Knox in Command.   (*Ch. XX*)

JAPAN, 1867.
Captain William Daunt drilling his Company before the native Court.   From a sketch by Captain C. J. Cramer-Roberts.

attack, but only two actually engaged in it. On March 31st, the detachment returned with the minister to Yokohama.

The rest of the regiment at Yokohama had enjoyed a quiet life, to the pleasures of which was added the hunting of a pack of beagles, with Captain Leighton as master. On April 14th the whole battalion sailed for England. When it left Yokohama it was still commanded by Colonel Knox.

The following extracts from letters from Sir H. Parkes to Colonel Knox, acknowledging the services of the battalion, are of interest. After the visit to the Shogun in April, 1867, he writes: " I have much pleasure in expressing my appreciation of the exemplary conduct of the detachment of Her Majesty's troops which accompanied me, by your direction, to Osaka . . . The efficiency and excellent order maintained among all the men throughout my stay at Osaka, which extended to six weeks, must have attracted much attention from the Japanese authorities and people, and you will share the gratification which I felt in observing how well the detachments, as the first body of British troops seen in that city, sustained the character of the army to which they belong. . . . I have therefore to beg that you will communicate to Captains Daunt and Aplin[1] and to Lieutenant Bradshaw, and to the non-commissioned officers and men composing this detachment, the high sense I entertain of the good services they have rendered on this occasion." He reported in the same sense to the Secretary of State, who expressed his satisfaction. In bidding farewell to the regiment, Sir H. Parkes wrote on April 11, 1868: " The security of Yokohama has been uninterruptedly maintained throughout that period. . . . It is due to the garrison to state that it furnished the most constant and the surest means of defence for this settlement. The worth of a regiment is not only proved by active duty in the field, and to state, as I can in this instance, that the garrison by its presence alone has proved a safeguard against aggression at a time when the country around Yokohama has been seriously disturbed by civil strife, is to bear high testimony to its efficiency and the value of its services. I am happy, however, to add that the 9th Regiment can claim the additional merit of having aided in promoting good feeling between

[1] Commanding mounted escort.

foreigners and the native population, which is as essential to the maintenance of friendly relations with this country as the exhibition of strength on the part of foreign powers."

When the battalion left Hong Kong the Major-General, in a farewell order of April 25th, desired " to express his great satisfaction at the appearance of the 2nd battalion of the 9th Regiment. The men were extremely clean, soldierlike, and steady under arms, and the movements were admirably executed. The report of the manner in which the regiment embarked at Yokohama reflects the greatest credit upon the old corps—every man in his place and steady; the rapidity with which the embarkation was effected was most remarkable."

On the long voyage round the Cape in H.M.S. "Tamar" the battalion touched at Hong Kong, Singapore, Mauritius, Capetown, St. Helena, St. Vincent, and Queenstown, reaching Kingstown on July 19th. Thence it proceeded, on the 22nd, to Richmond Barracks, Dublin, with a strength of 616 non-commissioned officers and men. The depot companies from Mullingar rejoined the rest of the battalion on the 28th. On arrival at Richmond Barracks the battalion was hospitably entertained by the 72nd Highlanders. On July 28th the establishment was reduced to 708 of all ranks.

On October 13, 1868, two companies were sent to Drogheda under Captain Perry, and on November 14th the remaining eight companies were sent for election duty at different times at Dundalk, Downpatrick, Monaghan, Carrickmacross, Trim, and Navan. Head-quarters at Dublin were represented only by the band and recruits. On November 29th there was polling at Drogheda, and the detachment there, with some of the 14th Hussars, had to escort unpopular voters from the railway to the polling booth. They were attacked by a mob; four officers and fourteen men were severely injured, and fifty rifles damaged by a continuous shower of sticks, stones, and bottles. Captain Daunt, commanding the escort, was knocked insensible at the bridge, and deposed, at the subsequent inquest, that on recovery he heard some shots, but he had given no order to fire. The infantry and cavalry charged the mob. The coroner's jury, at the inquest on a civilian killed, found a verdict of manslaughter against one of two privates of the 9th, alleged to have fired the fatal shot, but could not say which was the man. Eventually two privates were tried in Dublin for murder, but acquitted. On November 26th, 28th, and 29th, all the ten companies returned to Dublin. A few days later General McMurdo, on inspecting them, complimented the officers and men on their conduct at the recent elections.

On April 1, 1869, the establishment was reduced by forty privates.

On June 3rd the battalion with thirty-six officers and 579 other ranks embarked at Kingstown on the " Simoom " and reached Tilbury Fort on the 6th, whence they marched to Warley. On July 1st two companies, under Colonel Sankey, were detached to Woolwich, and thence, on October 26th, to Tilbury Fort. Four companies under Major Darling had been sent, on October 22nd, to the Isle of Grain. Only two were left at Warley. On June 21, 1870, the battalion marched to North Camp, Aldershot. On August 15, 1870, the establishment was augmented to one lieutenant-colonel, two majors, ten captains, fourteen subalterns, paymaster, adjutant, quartermaster, forty-nine sergeants, forty corporals, twenty-one drummers, and 660 privates, and on February 1, 1871, the number of privates was increased to 810.

The slowness of promotion in those days for officers unable to purchase their steps is illustrated by the fact that, on March 9, 1871, Lieutenant Wright, after holding it for fourteen years and eight months, gave over the adjutancy of the battalion to Lieutenant Clogstown. He had become Lieutenant in 1856.

On September 27, 1871, twelve officers and 373 other ranks were sent by rail to Chatham, and next day the head-quarters, with twenty-five officers and 558 other ranks, were railed to Shorncliffe.

On April 1, 1872, the number of lieutenants was raised to sixteen with forty-eight sergeants, forty corporals, eighteen drummers and 660 privates.

On December 31, 1872, Colonel Knox relinquished command of the 2nd battalion, and was succeeded by Brevet-Colonel H. J. Buchanan from the 1st battalion.

On May, 6, 1873, the depot companies of the battalion went to Great Yarmouth under Major Probart and joined the 31st brigade depot. On June 10th the left wing of the battalion marched to Dover under Major Daunt from Chatham and was quartered in Fort Burgoyne. On July 15th the head-quarters marched from Shorncliffe to the Citadel Barracks, Dover, and were quartered there till September, when both wings moved into the Shaft Barracks. On August 18, 1874, the battalion went by train to Cambridge Barracks, Portsmouth, whence, on October 23rd, it embarked on H.M.S. " Jumna " for Bombay, arrived there on November 26th, and next day went by rail to Deolali. Thence it went by train, in three detachments, to Mian Mir, and on December 19th started to march to Rawal Pindi, where it arrived on January 6, 1875. There it remained in garrison for nearly three years. During the hot weather of each year most of the regiment went into camp in the hills at Murree.

On November 5, 1877, the 2nd battalion started to march for Peshawar, whence, on December 2nd, fifteen officers and 559 other ranks proceeded to join, at Fort Mackeson, the field force, under the command of Brigadier-General Ross, C.B., acting against the Jowaki Afridis, who had long been committing outrages and giving trouble after the manner of their kind.

General Ross's column was just under 4,000 strong, consisting of parts of three British regiments (2/9th, 51st, and 4th Rifle Brigade), one horse, and one forty-pounder battery, one native cavalry regiment, four native infantry regiments and a detachment of sappers and miners.

The 2nd Brigade, in which was the 2/9th, was commanded by Colonel H. J. Buchanan of the 9th.

General Ross's column was to co-operate with that of Brigadier-General Keyes from the Kohat direction, which latter had been operating for some time.

Owing to floods, it was not till December 3rd that Ross's force was ready to start from Fort Mackeson.

In order to reach a position commanding the Jowaki villages in the Bori valley it was necessary to occupy a high ridge above the plain, to which access was obtainable by two passes—that of Kandao on the right and that of Shergasha on the left. The plan decided on was for Colonel Doran, with the 1st brigade, to move by Kandao, so as to turn the principal pass of Shergasha.

At dawn on December 4th Doran's column advanced, supported by the fire of the R.H.A. guns, and reached the top of the ridge without difficulty. The Shergasha Pass being thus turned, the enemy retired, partly into the Bori valley and partly along the ridge towards Khui. Meanwhile Colonel Buchanan had advanced, supported by his heavy guns, as soon as he saw Doran's men coming along the ridge from Kandao. Owing to the effective turning movement the top of the Shergasha Pass was reached without much difficulty, except from the nature of the ground. Both columns bivouacked on the ridge in considerable discomfort from the cold.

The enemy had occupied a small ridge in the Bori valley, from which Colonel Buchanan proposed to eject them next morning. He sent three companies of the 14th Native Infantry and two of the 9th British under command of Captain Maclean of the former regiment. The ridge proved steeper than was expected, but it was soon occupied by this column with the loss of only two sepoys wounded. During the next three days the troops were employed in destroying the villages in the Bori valley. On the first two days (December 6th and 7th) the enemy gave a good deal of trouble by occupying the rocky ridges above the villages, whence they maintained a brisk fire, followed, as the troops moved up, by showers of stones. In all cases, however, the process was the same, namely, a steady advance in skirmishing order by the infantry, covered by very accurate shell-fire from the R.H.A. on the commanding Shergasha ridge. In the three days the 9th lost only two men wounded; eight sepoys also were wounded. On the 8th the force was overtaken by a terrible storm, in which those on the Shergasha ridge spent a very miserable night.

The next objective of Ross's and Keyes's forces was to be a concentric advance on the Jowaki stronghold of Pastaoni.

From December 9th to 24th, Ross's force had been busy improving the communications in their neighbourhood; on the latter date orders were issued for a reconnaissance of the pass and the hills overlooking the Pastaoni valley. Two columns were used—the 1st brigade under Colonel Doran consisting of 150 bayonets of the 9th, a native infantry regiment, and two R.H.A. guns. Colonel Buchanan had in his column 120 bayonets from his own regiment, 300 each from the 14th and 20th

Native Infantry, and a mountain battery. His orders were to move towards the top of the Dand Sar but not to attack Pastaoni or go beyond the crest of the ridge, unless heavily attacked. Only a few shots were fired, and, after having gained the information required, the two columns returned to camp.

The advance on Pastaoni could not take place till December 31st, when the part of the 9th employed was again divided, one hundred bayonets with Colonel Doran and 300 with Colonel Buchanan. No other British regiment was employed.

Buchanan's column advanced over the same ground as that covered on the 25th, whilst Doran's was on his left, both moving on the pass leading to Pastaoni. The ground was extremely difficult, but the enemy offered practically no resistance till the skirmishers of Doran's column got within 500 or 600 yards of Pastaoni, when they were fired on by a small body of Afridis. These were soon driven off the rocky ridge above the village, without loss on the British side. Generals Ross and Keyes met that evening, but none of the latter's troops were at Pastaoni.

Ross's force remained at Pastaoni till January 2, 1878, when it returned to the Shergasha camp, after destroying the villages.

From January 2nd the troops were employed on various reconnaissances, in which there was no fighting, till the 15th, when it had been arranged for a combined advance to be made by Ross's and Keyes's forces against the Nara Khula defile, the last remaining Jowaki stronghold.

By 11 a.m. Ross's force, constituted the same as that of December 31st, was back at Pastaoni, having met with no opposition. At 1 p.m. Colonel Buchanan, with the 9th, the 14th Native Infantry, and the mountain battery, advanced by Walai to reconnoitre towards the Nara Khula defile. A few shots were fired, but the enemy were quickly dispersed by artillery fire, and the reconnaissance returned to Pastaoni, having accomplished its object.

On January 16th an advance was made by Walai and on the Torsappah range, but there was no fighting for the 9th, and practically none for anyone else.

On the 18th it was arranged that General Ross's force should abandon its communications with Shergasha, join Keyes's troops, and return to its camp below Shergasha via Kohat. The whole force united on that date, moved through the Nara Khula defile, and occupied Jamu. The command of the united forces now fell to General Keyes. Some surveying expeditions were made in the next day or two, but beyond the usual sniping there was no fighting. Throughout the expedition there was continual sniping at night from so-called friendly villages against which punitive action was forbidden by the political officers.

By the 24th General Ross's force was moving back by the Kohat Pass into the Peshawar valley, from which it had started. The 9th reached Peshawar again on January 26th, 1878. The last march of eighteen miles from Fort Mackeson was particularly trying in a downpour of rain. Terms were presently arranged by the Government with the Jowakis, with which we are not concerned. In the whole expedition the 9th only lost two men wounded. The hardships, however, had been great, and in this rocky country boots were quickly worn out and sometimes had to be bound with rags to keep them together.

On May 1st Colonel Buchanan was succeeded in the command of the battalion by Brevet-Lieutenant-Colonel Daunt.

On May 3rd the battalion was ordered to Hari Sing ka Burj, as part of a force to watch the Khyber Pass. Not only was trouble with Afghanistan brewing, but the Afridis in the Pass were giving trouble. At the end of May the battalion moved to Nowshera till the end of November, when, in consequence of the outbreak of war with Afghanistan it returned to Peshawar.

The only service performed by the 2nd battalion in the first part of the war was the escort of a convoy at the end of November, 1878. On the 29th of that month 200 men, under Major Ridsdale, Lieutenants Phillips, Cunliffe, and Vesey, were sent out to Jamrud.

Next day the convoy which they were sent to escort was attacked by tribesmen in the Khyber Pass. The attack was beaten off without difficulty, and the Pass cleared. On December 4th the detachment returned to Peshawar. Though the battalion does not appear in the statements of the Peshawar Valley Field Force, the officers and men engaged received for this service the grant of six months' " batta " and the Afghan medal. The battalion remained at Peshawar till May, 1879, when cholera broke out there, in consequence of which the head-quarters and four companies were sent to Nowshera, two companies remained at Peshawar, and two, which appear to have been infected, were sent into camp, whence they returned at the end of the month and joined the head-quarters at Nowshera. At the end of June the two companies at Peshawar rejoined the rest at Nowshera. The Peace of Gandamak was followed, in the beginning of September, 1879, by the murder of Sir Louis Cavagnari, the British Envoy, and his companions at Kabul, and it at once became apparent that a second campaign was inevitable.

On September 17th the 2nd battalion marched from Nowshera for Peshawar, under orders to hold itself in readiness for active service. On the 21st it marched out to Jamrud, but, cholera breaking out again that day, it returned to camp at Fort Bara, Peshawar. Six days later, being free of cholera, the battalion again moved forward, passing unmolested through the Khyber on September 28th and 29th, and arriving at Dakka on October 1st. There they were attached (with a strength of nineteen officers and 580 other ranks) to the 1st brigade of the 2nd division. The brigade was under the command of Brigadier-General C. J. Gough, V.C., C.B., and comprised, besides the 2/9th, the Guides cavalry, Guides infantry, 2nd and 4th Gurkhas, four mountain guns, a company of sappers and miners, and twenty men of the 10th Bengal Lancers.

The 1st division was commanded by Major-General Bright, who was in charge of the whole line of communications from the Indus to the front on the Khyber line. The portion assigned to Gough's brigade extended from Gandamak to Jagdalak, with a mobile column at Gandamak.

On October 2nd the brigade advanced as far as Busawal, where it was held up by difficulties of supply. By the 12th the Guides had occupied the fort at Jalalabad, the rest of the force having meanwhile reached Barikao.

On this day Gough received orders for the despatch of a flying column composed of the Guides, a wing of the 2/9th, and the mountain battery, all under the command of Colonel Jenkins, to march as quickly

KABUL, 1879.
The 2nd Battalion on Guard at the gate of the Bala Hissar. (*Ch. XX*)

as possible to Gandamak. The object was to overawe the Ghilzais, and to intercept fugitives of the Afghan regiments defeated at the battle of Chaharasia, fought by Sir F. Roberts, on October 5th, on his advance on Kabul.

Gough considered an advance to Gandamak (twenty-eight miles from Jalalabad) with so weak a column would be a dangerous division of his forces, and would leave him at Jalalabad with not enough to ensure safety. The flying column therefore only went as far as Fatehabad, about midway between Jalalabad and Gandamak. The wing of the 2/9th (300 rifles) was there on October 17th, with 480 rifles of the Guides infantry, 220 cavalry, and the mountain battery (four guns). The other wing was at Jalalabad. Sir F. Roberts meanwhile had occupied Kabul.

At Jalalabad there was another outbreak of cholera, which necessitated the wing of the 2/9th being sent into camp two miles from the rest.

About October 20th Gough, leaving a garrison at Jalalabad, rejoined Jenkins's column at Fatehabad, thus again uniting the two wings of the 2/9th. On October 23rd the brigade advanced to Fort Battye and occupied Gandamak with an advanced guard of the Guides and the mountain battery. Next day the whole brigade was at Gandamak.

The brigade was now to be employed as a movable column to advance by Jagdalak to meet a brigade being sent, early in November, by Sir F. Roberts from Kabul to meet it. On November 3rd the flying column started from Gandamak to join hands with General Macpherson's brigade from Kabul. It consisted of part of the 2/9th (450 strong), 300 native cavalry (Guides and 10th Bengal Lancers), 1,000 native infantry (Guides and 24th Punjab Infantry), one hundred sappers and miners, and eight guns (six mountain, two R.H.A.). On November 4th the advance continued, the Guides crowning the heights on either side, where necessary, and being relieved by the 2/9th and 24th Punjabis successively as they came up. Surkhab was reached that day after an uneventful march. On the 5th a very rough and difficult march took the column to Jagdalak. It was only disturbed by a few shots, the tribesmen who fired them retiring before the 24th Punjabis with the rear-guard. On the 6th the force moved, in two columns, by the two roads, one by the Jagdalak stream and the other, and better, above it.

The latter was taken by the 2/9th. The two converged six miles from Jagdalak. Three miles farther on General Macpherson was met at Kata Sang. His brigade encamped at the foot of the Lataband Pass, as the camping ground at Kata Sang was restricted.

The junction with the Kabul force having been effected, Gough took his brigade back to Gandamak, leaving a chain of posts to maintain the communication. In none of these was the 9th employed, and it reached Gandamak again on November 9th. On the 15th Sir F. Roberts assumed command of the whole Kabul Field Force from Kabul to Jamrud.

At Gandamak the winter had set in with great severity, and there was none too abundant a supply either of food or of warm clothing. The men were kept occupied with laying out their camp for the winter. On December 3rd one hundred men of the 2/9th formed part of the escort of the ex-Amir Yakub Khan for a short distance of his journey, as a state prisoner, to India.

By December 11th news was received of an impending attack by Azmatulla Khan on Jagdalak. The Guides, meanwhile, had been called up to Kabul, and it seemed likely that Gough's brigade would also be required. A considerable reinforcement was at once sent up from the rear to take his place, in that event, at Gandamak.

On the 14th Gough started for Jagdalak with the 9th, the 4th Gurkhas, and two squadrons of the 10th Bengal Lancers. Leaving half his force at Pezwan, he marched with the rest and two mountain guns to Jagdalak.[1] There he received telegraphic orders from Sir F.

---

[1] The following is from a diary kept by Captain (now General) Becher. The 9th were leading the infantry, when " just before reaching Jagdallak some sowars of the 10th B.L. who were passing reported that a party of theirs had just been fired into on the road and one man killed and another wounded. On reaching the fort on the Kotal we heard that our rearguard and baggage were attacked. The battalion was turned about in its fours and doubled down the hill. But before this was done the colours, carried by two subalterns, were ordered by the adjutant not to accompany the battalion to the expected fight, but to be taken into the fort. We afterwards heard that the recent decision at home that regimental colours were not to be taken on active service had that very morning reached our colonel. The colours of the 2/9th were thus the last British infantry colours to be under fire, for a few stray shots did come over the heads of the column before the colours left it."

Roberts to advance to Kabul. With his weak force the move seemed to Gough to be very dangerous, especially as Roberts was now shut up in Sherpur, unable to keep the field even with his 6,000 men.

The movement was held up for the moment. Gough's force at Jagdalak at this moment was as follows:—

> 2/9th - - - 487 men.
> 2nd and 4th Gurkhas, 507 ,,
> 10th Bengal Lancers, 220 ,,
> Two companies of sappers.
> Four mountain guns.

The 24th Punjab Infantry (one wing) with fifty lancers, two companies of sappers, and the other two guns of the mountain battery were at Pezwan.

On the 19th Colonel F. Norman left Pezwan for Jagdalak with a large convoy. As escort he had 670 men of the 24th Punjabis and 2nd Gurkhas, and the two mountain guns. To meet him Gough sent from Jagdalak a force under Major C. J. C. Roberts of the 2/9th, to assist him in disposing of the Ghilzais, who each day assembled and threatened the road below Jagdalak Kotal. Major Roberts found the Ghilzais posted as usual, and when he attacked they attempted to turn his flank. At this juncture Norman appearing on the scene, turned his two guns on to enfilade the whole of the enemy's line and drove them off with considerable loss. Major Roberts then covered the passage of the convoy, which reached Jagdalak safely. In this action the 9th had a sergeant and four men wounded, and Lieutenant Lombe was twice mentioned in despatches by General Gough. Another convoy with warm clothing came in safely next day.

Major Otway-Mayne says that on December 20th the camp was attacked all night, front and rear rank alternately lining the parapet and firing continuously. In the middle of this a native messenger crept up to the lines with a message from Sir F. Roberts in a cleft stick. He had a narrow escape and only avoided being shot by lying flat on the ground till he could make his mission known.

With Norman's reinforcements Gough now had 1,679 infantry, 242 cavalry, seventy-three sappers and six mountain guns. During the last day or two he had been held back by General Bright, who took a very serious view of the Ghilzai threat; but on December 20th he received definite orders from Sir F. Roberts to push on to Kabul at once.

On the 21st he started with his little force of seventeen officers and 483 men of the 2/9th, and one officer and forty-five men of the 72nd Highlanders, with 874 native infantry and sappers, and four guns.

Lataband post was reached on the 22nd, where the garrison (28th Punjab Infantry) was gathered in. On the 23rd it was found that the enemy had fortified the passage of the Logar river, but had abandoned the position. The cause of the abandonment was discovered that evening at Butkhak in the news of the heavy repulse, that morning, of the attack by the Afghans on Sherpur. Continuing its advance on the 24th, under considerable difficulties due to a heavy fall of snow in the night, Gough's brigade entered Sherpur without fighting, the Afghan forces having mostly dispersed in the night. There was deep snow everywhere. So great had been the cold that Major Otway-Mayne records having seen three " kahars " buried at Butkhak who had been frozen to death. Presents of warm mittens sent by Lady Borton were much appreciated. From Sherpur the battalion moved, on January 1st, 1880, to the Bala Hissar, and on March 31st the brigade was moved to the entrenched camp on the Siah Sang heights.

On April 16th the 2/9th formed part of the force under General J. Ross moving out to join hands with General Donald Stewart's army from Kandahar, which was expected shortly. Camping that night at Kala Kazi, to which place Sir F. Roberts had accompanied them, the force reached Maidan next day and halted till the 19th, on which day a foraging party, under Lieutenant W. G. Straghan of the 2/9th, found itself opposed to about 500 of the enemy. General Gough promptly came to the rescue with reinforcements, but it was too late in the day for any action. On the 21st Ross marched to Kala Durani, and on the 22nd to Sar-i-Top, where news was received, by heliograph, of Stewart's victory of Ahmad Khel.

On the 23rd Saidabad was reached. The hills in the neighbourhood were strongly held by the enemy, who retired on the approach of reconnoitring parties. They were back, however, next morning. On the 24th news was received of the approach of a large body of tribesmen from the north. On the 25th a large force of Ghilzais was discovered within two miles of the camp, and a force under Lieutenant-Colonel Rowcroft was sent against them. It included two companies (123 men) of the 2/9th under Captain C. M. Stockley, a wing of the 4th Gurkhas, one troop 3rd Bengal Cavalry, and two mountain guns. Another party under Major Combe, D.A.Q.M.G., was sent round by the Shekhabad road to attack the enemy's left as the frontal attack developed. It consisted of twenty-five sabres 3rd Punjab Cavalry, and three companies (168 rifles) of the 24th Punjab Infantry. Covered by the fire of the guns, Rowcroft's infantry quickly forced the Ghilzais from their position on the hills north-west of the British camp.

During this affair another Ghilzai force appeared on the left of Rowcroft's column. Gough now brought four companies of Gurkhas and two guns to disperse these, which was easily done by the guns. This body was then pursued by Rowcroft's men and suffered a heavy loss, including forty dead left on the field and a standard.

The Ghilzais were persistent and reappeared next day (26th), when Gough took a wing each of the 2/9th and 23rd Pioneers and two guns out against them. They were on a hill more than 2,000 feet above the camp when the guns opened on them at a range of 2,000 yards. Then Lieutenant-Colonel Daunt of the 9th, with two companies of his own regiment, and two of the 23rd Pioneers, advanced up the hill to the attack. The Ghilzais could not stand this and fled before the infantry reached the top. They were followed for some distance, but made no stand. The British had no casualties and the column returned to camp at 5.30 p.m. That was the end of trouble from these people. The whole of the operations of April 25th and 26th only cost the British one Gurkha killed, one man of the 9th, and three Gurkhas wounded.

On the 29th General Stewart came up and marched with Ross's force back to Argandeh, where he met and took over the chief command from Sir F. Roberts, when the force re-entered Kabul on May 2, 1880.

The next active work on which the 2/9th was employed was an

expedition to the Paghman valley. On June 14th General C. Gough moved out to Wazirabad with a brigade consisting of the 2/9th, 4th Gurkhas, 24th Punjabis, 3rd Bengal Cavalry, a company of Sappers, and a mountain battery. On the 18th the column was encamped near Kala Ghulam Haidar, at the foot of the Paghman range, and on the 20th there was news of a body of Ghazis in Maidan. A reconnoitring party of a squadron with two companies of the 2/9th and four of the 24th Punjab Infantry was sent out. It went as far as the Kotal-i-Safed Khak, and saw a considerable body of tribesmen, who retired firing a few harmless shots. On the 21st the brigade moved to a commanding ridge on the Paghman range, and was reinforced by the 3rd Punjab Cavalry. On the 24th it marched, in two columns, to Karez Mir, where it remained till July 12th, whence it reached Zimma on the 14th. On the 21st the 2/9th were replaced by the 67th and returned to Sherpur. The change was carried out for the benefit of the 67th who had been somewhat sickly in Sherpur.

About this time the negotiations for the installation of the new Amir Abdul Rahman were completed and orders issued for the evacuation of Kabul and northern Afghanistan. By August 10th, two companies of the 2/9th were already on their way to India, in advance of the other six, which were still at Kabul with General C. Gough's brigade, which, for the march, consisted of the 2/9th, 28th Punjab Infantry, and 45th Sikhs. Colonel Daunt was temporarily commanding the 3rd infantry brigade.

Gough's brigade was the last to leave Kabul, on August 11, 1880, and the 2/9th was the last regiment of that brigade. The brigade, throughout the march to Peshawar, acted as rear-guard. This duty, for a large force marching through a difficult country in hot weather, and encumbered by the large transport and numbers of followers of an Indian army, was very trying, and entailed halts at several places, which were anything but times of rest. Fighting there was none, and the march was generally uneventful. On September 8th Peshawar was again reached and Colonel Daunt returned to the command of the battalion.

At Peshawar there was another outbreak of cholera, entailing the battalion's going into camp and marching for Mian Mir, where it arrived on November 8th, having picked up its heavy baggage from the depot, which had been formed at Nowshera by Captain Cotton, apparently with the two companies sent in advance from Kabul.

After being present at Lord Ripon's durbar at Lahore, the battalion entrained on November 24th for Umbala, where it was encamped on the 25th.

CHAPTER XXI

THE MILITIA AND VOLUNTEER BATTALIONS TO 1881

IN 1881 the battalions, known officially since 1782 as the "9th or East Norfolk Regiment of Foot," received a purely territorial title as the "Norfolk Regiment." As the militia battalions were also, from this year, associated with them for the first time, this appears to be the place in which to give their history, as well as that of the volunteer battalions which were destined, in 1908, under the title of the Territorial battalions, to take their place also in the regiment.

A Constitutional Force had existed from time out of mind in one form or another; but it was not till 1662 that an "Act for ordering the forces in the several counties in the Kingdom," amended by another Act of 1663, at last organized the militia in a definite form, and abolished the old "trained bands," except in the City of London. The militia, in its then form, was called out in 1690, on the threat of a French invasion, and again during the Jacobite risings of 1715 and 1745. On the latter occasion the inefficiency of the force as a protection against invasion was realized, and the result, in 1757, was the passing of an elaborate Act for the regulation of the militia, the preamble to which reads thus: "Whereas a well ordered and well disciplined militia is essentially necessary to the safety, peace, and prosperity of this Kingdom."

Amongst other things, the Act prescribed the numbers to be raised by the various counties, and in this list the county of Norfolk is put down for 960. The Act was followed by an explanatory Act of 1758, and was put into force in 1759.

The force was still mostly in the hands of the lords lieutenant of

REVIEW OF NORFOLK VOLUNTEER CORPS, HOLKHAM, 1861. (*Ch. XXI*)

the counties, who were colonels of the local forces, and were very little under the control of the War Office.

Norfolk responded to the call by raising promptly the 1st Battalion Western Regiment of Norfolk Militia and the 2nd Battalion Eastern Regiment of Norfolk Militia. To these presently were allotted the numbers 39 and 40 in precedence. At first it had been proposed to have no fixed precedence list, but to allot seniority to the first arriving in camp or garrison. The list in which the numbers 39 and 40 appear was the result of drawing lots at St. James's Palace, in the presence of the King and the lords lieutenant of the counties assembled. As Norfolk had been the first county to raise its battalions it appears to have suffered an injustice in the ballot.

Service in the militia was strenuous in those days of constant wars and fears of invasion, and the force was continuously embodied for long periods at a time. From June, 1759, to December, 1762, both regiments were embodied on account of the Seven Years' War. Their next long embodiment was from 1778 to 1783, this time on account of the American and French wars. At the beginning of this period there was great enthusiasm amongst the principal inhabitants of Norfolk, as is evidenced by the "Norwich Mercury" of February 28, 1778, giving an account of a meeting held at the Maid's Head, Norwich, at which it was resolved that "in pursuance of the recommendations of H.M. Secretary of State, all possible assistance should be given towards recruiting the 9th Regiment of Foot, commanded by Lieutenant-General Earl Ligonier, until the same shall be completed, and that a bonus of three guineas, in addition to that allowed by His Majesty, be paid by this committee to every able-bodied man recruited and attested for the regiment." Subscriptions to the amount of £6,559 had already been received, and more were invited. An order of Lord Orford, then commanding the two militia battalions, is quoted by the same paper. It directs the assembly of both battalions for embodiment at Norwich on April 13th. A fine of £40 was notified as the penalty for failure to attend.

The Western battalion was reviewed on Mousehold Heath in the middle of May by General Pierson, who approved its appearance, and was afterwards entertained " in a very elegant manner " by Lord Orford at the Maid's Head.

From Norwich the Western battalion appears to have gone to Ipswich and neighbouring towns, where, at the beginning of February, 1780, we hear of the officers giving " a ball and a superb cold collation at Bamford's Assembly Rooms to the ladies of Ipswich and the vicinity." In August, 1780, the battalion was in camp at Tenpenny Common, where, as the " Mercury " was assured by a visitor, " the privates are so well satisfied and zealous in the service that, of eighty whose time expires shortly, few there are who have not expressed their intention of remaining in the corps as long as their services there are necessary." The regiment had been reviewed, on his way to Landguard, by Lord Townshend on August 15th.

In November, 1780, the Western battalion went into winter quarters at Hull. In May, 1782, it was at Swaffham and Dereham, *en route* for camp at Caister near Yarmouth. There it is stated that Lord Orford " is now erecting works for four heavy cannon between the camp and the sea, which, at a very moderate expense, will have superior advantage to the most scientific mounts thrown up by the professional men." The statement is indicative of the independence enjoyed by lords lieutenant in militia matters. It is permissible to doubt the correctness of the estimate of the value of these amateur works as compared with those erected by professional military engineers.

The regiment was reviewed by General Conway at Herringfleet in September, and " performed several manoeuvres much to the satisfaction of a large company." In the middle of November the camp at Caister broke up and the regiment passed through Norwich to winter quarters at Dereham, Swaffham, Lynn, Downham, etc.

At the end of March, 1783, both battalions were disembodied, the Western at Lynn, the Eastern at Wymondham.

Save for annual trainings the militia was not again embodied till 1793.

On March 31, 1792, Lord Orford gave place, as colonel, to the Hon. Horatio Walpole. The apprehension of war with France at the same time gave rise to the following notice : " Militia Insurance Officer for County of Norfolk and City of Norwich. The time of drawing for the Militia is nearly arrived and the price of substitutes extra high. The public are therefore respectfully informed that policies are issuing, at the shop of W. T. Robberd in the Market Place at Norwich, to insure, for the price of £10, for the purpose of procuring a substitute."

The militia was duly embodied on the outbreak of war with France in 1793. In May, 1794, the West Norfolk Militia was at Danbury in Essex. An advertisement for a deserter (one guinea reward for his apprehension) shows that the West Norfolk Militia had gone as far afield as Shorncliffe in October, 1796.

There had been a meeting at Norwich, in November, 1794, of the "Committee for Internal Defence and Security," at which it was resolved that "it may be expedient to add a certain number of volunteers to each of the companies of the militia," and the colonels were asked to submit a scheme. Whether this proposal was carried out is not clear.

Two more deserters from Shorncliffe were advertised for on December 3, 1796. This time two guineas each were offered, in addition to what was allowed by Act of Parliament. At this time the supplementary militia was started, and, on February 11, 1797, the first division of the Supplementary Norfolk Militia, numbering 365, was embodied. There were to be six divisions in all, parcelled out amongst different parts of the county. The 4th division, of 316 men, was assembled for training at Lynn.

On February 3, 1798, the 9th Regiment of Foot is recorded as marching into Bury St. Edmunds from Colchester, "for the purpose of recruiting its skeleton battalion."

In pursuance of the Act of Parliament, the skeleton regiments were now to begin recruiting from the supplementary militia, each regiment having a service district allotted to it. The bounty was to be eight guineas per man. Each regiment of supplementary militia was to be marched to its county town, and remain there till further orders. The supplementary militia was absorbed by the regular militia in the following year.

In 1802, after the Peace of Amiens, the militia were disembodied, only to be again embodied in 1803, after the renewal of the French war, and to be kept so till the first abdication of Napoleon in 1814. In February, 1804, a notice issued warning parishes which had made default in raising the number of men required for the militia and the army of reserve. An assessment of £10 for each man short was to be imposed on the defaulting area.

The two battalions were, as in the previous embodiment, sent to various parts of the coast. They were at Dungeness in September, 1805. The West Norfolk Militia was inspected at Canterbury on August 7, 1806, by the Duke of York, who seemed highly pleased with their appearance.

In 1809 an Act was passed prohibiting the enlistment of local militiamen in any other regiment of militia but that of their own county.

In August, 1809, the West Norfolk Militia was back at Norwich. In May, 1811, they were at Lynn, and in December at Woodbridge, whence they went to Harwich. By April, 1813, they were very far from their own county, at Berwick-on-Tweed, whence they went to Edinburgh Castle.

The local militia was called out occasionally for training. On January 22, 1814, it is recorded that the officers and staff of the 1st and 2nd Eastern and the 1st Western Regiment of Local Militia had made offers of extended service which, though graciously acknowledged by the Prince Regent, were not accepted.

The Western Norfolk Militia, being disembodied in 1814, were again embodied on the return of Napoleon from Elba. After Waterloo they volunteered for service in Ireland. They had made the same offer in 1798, when it was apparently not accepted. This time the offer was accepted, and the regiment was stationed at Clonmel and Templemore till April, 1816, when it was sent home and disembodied.

The history of the East Norfolk Regiment of Militia has been compiled in great detail by Sir Charles Harvey, to whose work[1] reference should be made by those who desire further information than our limits of space will allow us to give.

---

[1] "The History of the 4th Battalion Norfolk Regiment late East Norfolk Militia." Compiled by Colonel Sir Charles Harvey, Bart. 1899. Of course since the army reforms of 1908 the words "4th Battalion Norfolk Regiment" are no longer applicable.

COLONEL ROBERT THORNHAUGH GURDON (Lord Cranworth), V.D., 1829–1902.
Commanded 4th Norfolk Rifle Volunteers, 1873–82. Commanded 4th Volunteer Battalion
Norfolk Regiment, 1883–87. Colonel, 4th Volunteer Battalion Norfolk Regiment
1888–1902. (*Ch. XXI*)

On May 28, 1761, there is an order for the supply of colours to both regiments of Norfolk militia, through their colonel, Lord Orford.

In June, 1762, the East Norfolk Militia was sent from its headquarters at Yarmouth, where it was to leave " the necessary detachment," to Ipswich and Landguard Fort. In October they were ordered to Lyme Regis.[1]

During their next embodiment, in the period 1778-83, they were first sent to Colchester, Harwich, and Manningtree. They had several stations in Essex, and at Ipswich, in 1778. The year 1779 saw them near Yarmouth, at Cox Heath camp, whence they returned to Yarmouth. During 1780 they were mostly in their own county, except for a time at Tiptray camp near Colchester in the summer, whence they returned to Yarmouth. In 1781 they had a turn of work in support of the revenue officers. They went to Harwich, Ipswich, and other places in the neighbourhood, returning for the winter to Yarmouth. In 1782 their summer camp was at Warley in Essex, but the ensuing winter was spent in the neighbourhood of Dereham instead of Yarmouth. They were disembodied early in 1783.

During their next embodiment (1793-1802) they began by being sent to the Colchester neighbourhood, and on by Chelmsford to Chatham. In the summer of 1793 they were at Waterdown camp in Sussex, and various other places in that county. In 1795 they were at Gravesend, and in that year the practice of powdering the men's hair was abandoned, owing to the high price of flour, of which on the average the militiaman had to use one pound weekly to keep his head properly powdered. In April the regiment was ordered from Rochester to Hythe.

They were at Deal before being reviewed, on October 15th, by the Duke of York at Dover.

The year 1796 was the year of the supplementary militia, of which Norfolk had four regiments, as feeders to the regular militia. In August the numbers raised by ballot for the supplementary militia were 1,781 for the county of Norfolk, and 211 for the City of Norwich.

At the close of 1797 the East Norfolk Militia, after seventeen months at Chelmsford, went back to Norwich.

[1] Apparently Lynn was meant, not Lyme Regis in Dorset.

The Government, in February, 1798, was desperately anxious to get recruits for the regular army from the supplementary militia, as is evidenced by the following order addressed to the officer commanding the East Norfolk Militia: "You are to permit such a portion of the officers and non-commissioned officers under your command as you shall judge expedient to march to the places in the county of Norfolk in which you may think your influence most likely to promote the Inlistment of the Supplementary Militia into the 9th Regiment of Foot, at which place or places they may be allowed to remain until it shall be necessary for them to march so as to assemble at Norwich prior to the day which may be appointed for assembling the Supplementary Militia there." The order for embodying the supplementary militia, in part, is dated February 28, 1798. The embodied force was joined on to the regular militia.

In 1798 the East Norfolk, as well as the West Norfolk Militia, for the most part volunteered to serve in Ireland, but the offer was apparently not accepted.

In October, 1798, the East Norfolk Militia were at Ipswich, celebrating the Battle of the Nile and appearing in field days. It was in this year also that the supplementary militia, after a very short existence, was abolished, but allowed to enlist in the regular army for five years.

In February, 1800, the East Norfolk Militia was ordered to Yorkshire, to Pontefract, Doncaster, and Bawtrey. Thence they went, towards the end of the year, to Sheffield, to Newcastle-under-Lyme, and on to Stafford and Lichfield. In May, 1801, six companies were at Nottingham and two at Derby. Both divisions then moved to Manchester.

From Lancashire a long move was made, in September, 1801, to Chelmsford, where they were joined by a company of re-embodied militia from Lynn. In April, 1802, they were at Colchester, under orders for Yarmouth, where they were disembodied. In March, 1803, they were again embodied and sent to Beccles, Lowestoft, and other places in the neighbourhood, and thence on to Colchester, where they still were, as well as the West Norfolk Militia, in June, 1804. Next they went to Cox Heath camp.

It was probably in 1803 that there occurred the following quaint incident culled from the "Military Extracts" preserved at the Royal United Service Institution :—

"Major George Wyndham of the East Norfolk Militia, previous to their being reviewed by H.M. King George III, took considerable pains with his officers, all of whom were county gentlemen, to teach them to salute in a graceful manner. When they rehearsed their parts, on the morning of the inspection, he prided himself on the success of his efforts.

"At length His Majesty appeared on the parade ground, preceded by one of his Yeomen of the Guard (vulgarly yclept a Beefeater), and upon this official an unfortunate captain of a company threw away the major's carefully rehearsed salute, strutting past the King without making any return even to His Majesty's courteous salutation.

"On Major Wyndham remonstrating with his captain for the blunder, the latter replied, 'Fudge! Dost think I doesn't know the King? Why he had G.R. in large gold letters on his breast.'"

In 1805 as many as 31,000 men were drafted from the militia of England into the regular army, which necessitated recourse to the ballot to fill up the militia battalions. This heavy drafting was in consequence of the Act of 1805 allowing "a certain proportion of the Militia in Great Britain voluntarily to enlist with His Majesty's Regular Forces and Royal Marines." In the East Norfolk Militia the "certain proportion" amounted to 233 privates and eleven corporals out of a total sanctioned strength of 814 privates.

Substitutes for those drawn in the militia ballot became so expensive that in 1809 so much as £60 was paid for one, whilst others received as much as 4s. per diem, or a payment of so much per pound of the weight of their bodies.

In 1806 the battalion was at Hastings and Colchester. In 1808 the establishment of the battalion was fixed at 914, officers included, and they were stationed at Ipswich. In 1809 they were reviewed at Rushmere Heath, on their way to Chatham and Rochester. In 1810 they were at Sheerness and Chatham. In 1811 they were among the regiments which volunteered to extend their service to Ireland, and after marching to Bristol embarked, 700 strong, for Ireland, where they were quartered at Cahir. There they remained till May, 1812, when they moved to Mallow, only returning to Plymouth in June, 1813, and going to Honiton, where they were joined by recruits from Norwich. After a turn of service at Dartmouth, they returned to Yarmouth in June, 1814, where they were disembodied and not called out again, even for training, till 1820.

After 1815 there was a long period during which the militia received very little attention. In many years, sometimes five or six in succession, they were not even called up for annual training.

In 1820 a regimental order says: " The epaulettes, buttons, and other peculiar regimental ornaments of dress to be silver for the future, instead of gold as heretofore; old officers, however, previously appointed to commissions in the regiment are allowed to continue gold lace until called out in actual service."

In 1831 strict adherence to the King's dress regulations was enjoined, " and with black velvet and silver epaulettes and ornaments and the same buttons as the last uniform."

This brief sketch of the movements and employment of the two militia battalions is based on Sir Charles Harvey's history for the Eastern and on newspaper extracts, collected by Sir Kenneth Kemp, for the Western battalion. Space will not allow of fuller details in this history, but what has been said will suffice to show how important a part was played by the militia in the latter part of the eighteenth and the beginning of the nineteenth century, both as a home defence force when invasion was apprehended and as a source of supply for recruits for the regular army. It shows that being drawn in the ballot during the long terms of embodiment implied very much more than a mere sojourn for a short time in a training camp. It entailed long periods in camp or billets, often far away from the homes of officers and men, differing little, if at all, from the conditions of service at home in a regular regiment.

In May, 1854, colours were presented to the East Norfolk Militia by the Earl of Leicester (Lord Lieutenant) at Norwich, with the usual ceremonial and festivities. These colours, said to have been worked by Norfolk ladies, were still borne by the battalion in 1898.

NORWICH VOLUNTEER OFFICERS ON THE RIFLE RANGE,
MOUSEHOLD HEATH (1863).
From a painting presented by them to Captain H. S. Patteson. (*Ch. XXI*)

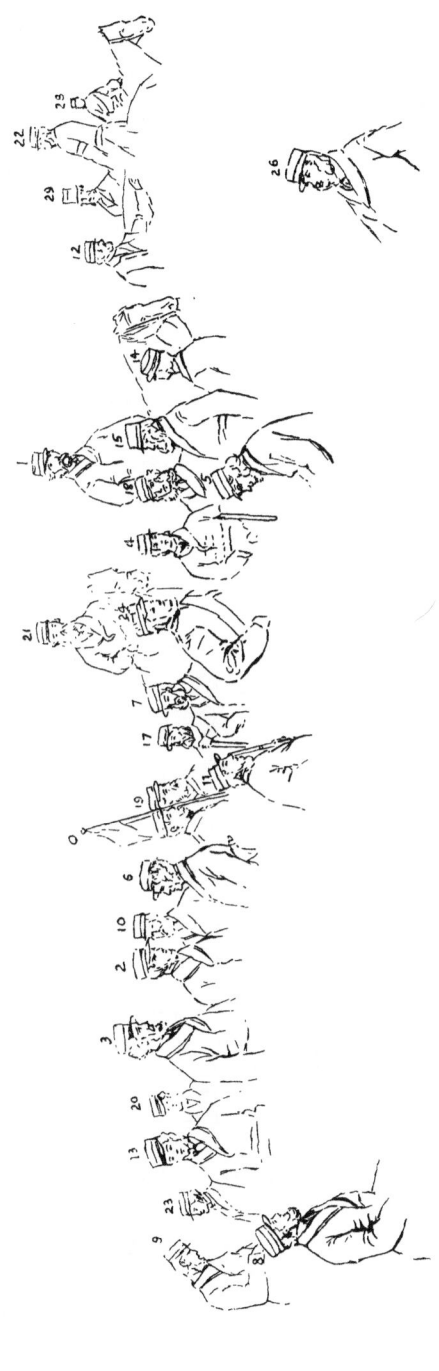

RIFFLE VOLUNTEERS—FIRST OR CITY OF NORWICH CORPS.

FROM THE PICTURE BY CLAUDE L. NURSEY. 1862

No1 Lt-Col Brett (Late Major of 17th Dragoons)	No8 Lieut Addison J Cresswell.	No 24 Captain Francis Hay Gurney (Inspector of Rifle Volunteers)
2 Captain Middleton.	9 Lieut Henry Morgan.	25 Cornet Fred Grimer
3 Captain Henry S Patterson	10 Lieut John Barwell.	23 Assistant-Surgeon W Drake.
4 Captain Charles Foster.	11 Lieut Fred T Keith	26 Ensign Donald Steward
5 Captain Simms Reeves.	12 Lieut John B Morgan.	27 Ensign James Dawbarn
6 Captain Edward Field	13 Lieut Charles Henry Gurney.	28 Aide-de-camp Sidney Brown
7 Captain John M Croker	14 Lieut Edward S Bignold	29 Robert Seaman Esq.
	15 Ensign Aug F C Bolingbroke	
	16 Ensign Alfred Master.	
	17 Ensign Beaumont W Jolly	
	18 Ensign John Goodwin.	
	19 Ensign S H Asker.	
	20 Ensign P E Hansell	
	O Colour Sergt Ferre	

On December 27, 1854, both battalions were called out for permanent service on account of the Crimean War.

In the spring of 1855 there was some excitement among the militia over the question of whether the Government was exceeding its powers. An Act of 1852 had limited the period of training to fifty-six days in the year, power to embody permanently being exercisable only when invasion was threatened. In 1854 power to embody during the war had been taken, but the recruits under the Act of 1852 objected to this as outside their terms of service. The end of it was that those who had joined before the Act of 1854 were released, and 200 of the West Norfolk Militia went home, thereby reducing the effective strength of the regiment to 460. As an inducement to them to rejoin under the new Act an additional bounty of £1, with a month's furlough on full pay, was offered and appears to have been successful. These changes were not encouraging to Colonel Custance and his officers, who had brought the regiment to a state of efficiency, when it was suddenly reduced, temporarily at any rate, by nearly one-third.

In June, 1855, the West Norfolk Militia was presented with colours by the Countess of Albemarle at Norwich. Lady Albemarle made a short speech to the officers and men, which was replied to by the Earl of Orford as colonel of the Norfolk Militia. The colours were then trooped and the regiment marched past and saluted. The event was celebrated by a dinner at St. Andrew's Hall in the evening.

The East Norfolk Militia was sent from Yarmouth to Colchester in January, 1856. They were quartered in huts at Colchester and their strength in February is recorded as 432 of all ranks. On April 23rd, they were reviewed, with other regiments, by Prince Albert at Wivenhoe Park. Early in June they were disembodied at Norwich.

The West Norfolk Militia went, early in July, 1855, to Aldershot, whence they went to Fermoy in Co. Cork. There they seem to have been popular, for, on their departure for Norwich in June, 1856, a deputation of the inhabitants presented a farewell address to the colonel, in which he was congratulated upon having the command of so highly respectable and well-disciplined a corps. At Norwich they were disembodied.

Sir Charles Harvey says that the East Norfolk Militia appears not to have been embodied in consequence of the Indian Mutiny. The West Norfolk Militia was embodied on November 10, 1857, at Norwich. On December 23, 1857, the head-quarters and three companies, under Lieutenant-Colonel Custance, went by rail to Chester, three companies commanded by Major Bedingfeld to Liverpool, and two companies under Captain Marsham to Stockport. The regiment was about 700 strong.

In April, 1858, the regiment returned to Norwich, and was disembodied shortly afterwards. After this there is nothing that need be noted till we come to the Cardwell reforms of 1881.

In 1881 occurred the first great change in the position of the militia. The old character of the militia battalions was radically changed, and the War Office took a much larger share in the administration, which had hitherto been almost entirely in the hands of the lords lieutenant. On April 16, 1881, were issued the orders for changes in the organization of the infantry of the line and the militia, to come into force on July 15, 1881. Each regiment of infantry of the line and militia was in future to be organized (for England, Scotland, and Wales) in four battalions, the 1st and 2nd being line battalions, the 3rd and 4th militia. As the Norfolk Regiment was already a double battalion regiment, there was no linking of another regular regiment. The West and East Norfolk Militia battalions became respectively the 3rd and 4th Battalions of the "Norfolk Regiment." The number "9th" disappeared as a regimental one, and was attached to the "Regimental District," which replaced the former "sub-district." The regiment was purely territorial, designated in accordance with the locality (Norfolk) with which it was connected.

All distinctions, mottoes, badges, and devices appearing hitherto in the Army List, or on the colours, as borne by either of the line battalions of a territorial regiment, were now to be borne by both.

The uniform of all battalions of a territorial regiment was to be the same, except that militia battalions were to wear the letter "M" on the shoulder strap.

The Volunteer Battalions

Another twenty-seven years were still to elapse before the Norfolk volunteer battalions were to be incorporated as the 4th, 5th, and 6th Territorial Battalions of the Norfolk Regiment, but this appears to be a suitable place in which to give a brief account of their formation and progress up to 1881. There has been placed at our disposal, for the purposes of this history, the manuscript history of the 4th Battalion Norfolk Regiment by the late Colonel J. R. Harvey, D.S.O., T.D. We will commence with a quotation from his preface:—

"An inquiry into the origin of the Volunteer is beset with considerable difficulty. It is necessary, on the one hand, to guard against the inclusion under the term Volunteer of such bodies of men as were from time to time raised for the purposes of defence, but who, being in receipt of pay and uniform, and subject, from the date of their enrolment, to military discipline, were indistinguishable from the regular militia. On the other hand, it must be borne in mind that all branches of the military service are connected by a common bond of affinity—the Militia with the standing army, of which it was once the backbone; the Volunteers with the Militia, on to which, at first, they were grafted, and so with the regular army and the old "Constitutional Force," which lay at the root of both.

"This affinity between the various branches of the service supplies the keynote to the development of the Volunteer; it does not lessen our difficulty, but it assists our purpose by demonstrating the futility of attempting to draw hard-and-fast lines. The Volunteer Force was not, any more than the Regular Army itself, the creation of a particular era of English history—some hitherto latent and unsuspected spirit of patriotism. The Volunteer, as the true type of the citizen-soldier, represents the outcome of the operation of those social laws and institutions whose aim has ever tended towards a fuller realization of the duties of the individual in his relation to the State."

Colonel Harvey, himself deeply interested in the 4th Battalion Norfolk Regiment, which he commanded in the war of 1914–18, when his health permitted, disclaims on its behalf any direct descent from the old volunteer corps of the later eighteenth and earlier nineteenth centuries.

From the close of the Napoleonic wars till the invasion of the Crimea the volunteer forces, as well as the militia, fell into abeyance. The nation went quietly to sleep as regards any necessity for a defensive force, other than the Navy. In 1847 the Duke of Wellington attempted, in a letter to Sir John Burgoyne, to wake the Government from its sleep, but it only stirred uneasily and was soon as fast asleep as ever. The march of events had more effect than the appeals of the old warrior of the days of Napoleon the Great. Soon there was on the throne of France Napoleon the Little, imbued with the traditions of his uncle, among which hostility to England had held the highest place. It is true that in the Crimea he was our ally, hoping to avenge on Russia some of the disasters of 1812 to 1815. Austria was the next to feel his vengeance in 1859. There remained Prussia and England, and on more than one occasion clouds arose indicating that England might be the next victim of the Napoleonic Vendetta. Then came the Indian Mutiny, the suppression of which necessitated the British Isles being left almost defenceless. At last the fears of the nation were aroused, and the pressure of public opinion forced the Government reluctantly to approve the raising of volunteer corps under the old Act of 1804. Even then it was made a condition that the corps themselves should bear all expenses, until they should be assembled for actual service. The first circular (of May 12, 1859) was followed a fortnight later by a somewhat stronger one, which is said to have been inspired by the Prince Consort. It advocated a system of drill and instruction interfering as little as possible with the ordinary avocations of the citizen-soldier, and directed to qualifying the volunteer force " to act efficiently as an auxiliary to the regular army and militia, the only character to which it should aspire."

It is remarked by Colonel Harvey that the volunteers of 1859 were more purely voluntary than those of 1804; for in 1859 the militia ballot was indefinitely suspended, and the ordinary citizen had nothing to make his service in any possible way compulsory. In 1804 the peasant class preponderated in the volunteers; in 1859 the conditions as to the corps paying their own expenses restricted the volunteers to the middle classes. In 1804 the service of volunteers was limited to the area of their military district; in 1859 there was no such limitation within the area of the British Isles.

Say what we may, it is certain that for many years after the revival of the volunteers in 1859 the corps met with scant encouragement from outside their own ranks, and had to contend against contempt and derision from the regular army, as well as from those less patriotic citizens who would not join them. To themselves is mainly due the credit for having lived this down, and at last come into their own in the terrible trials of the most awful war the world has so far known.

Eleven days after the circular of May 12, 1859, Norwich and the county of Norfolk were holding meetings for the raising of volunteer corps. Expenses were of course a great difficulty, and the cost of uniforms, to be borne by officers and men alike, had to be limited to £3 or £4. A tunic of grey cloth, braided with black mohair, buttoned down the centre, with a low upright collar, trousers of the same cloth, and a shako of hair cloth of the same grey were all that could be afforded. A black leather belt and ammunition pouches completed the get-up of the volunteer.

The first three companies were formed at once in the city of Norwich, with head-quarters in St. Catherine's Close. A fourth company was raised in November, 1859, and a fifth in January, 1860. Drills began at once under strict conditions, one of which was that a member absent for three drills, without sufficient excuse, could be, and actually often was, dismissed by the captain of his company. The Norwich companies were practically a battalion when the volunteers first appeared in the Army List early in 1860. It had five companies, all commanded by captains. Major Brett commanded the five. Eight other companies[1] appear under numbers four to eleven but only two of them (Yarmouth and King's Lynn) had captains, the rest being commanded by lieutenants. A rifle range for the Norwich volunteers was completed at Mousehold in 1860.

[1] Yarmouth, King's Lynn, Aylsham, Harleston, Diss, Loddon, Fakenham, Holkham.

A sixth company was added to the Norwich battalion in March, 1861, in the shape of the 1st Norfolk Mounted Rifle Volunteers.

In this year the Yarmouth corps was commanded by a major, and the other county companies were concentrated in the 1st Administrative Battalion under Lord Suffield, and the 2nd under Sir Thomas Beauchamp, Bart. The 2nd had its head-quarters at Norwich, and included the corps at Harleston, Diss, Loddon, Stalham, Blofield, Attleborough, Wymondham, and Thetford. It was presented with colours in 1863, the same as those of Colonel Robert Harvey's battalion of 1803.

It was not till 1877 that the old grey uniform was changed to scarlet for the 1st Norfolk Volunteers, or Administrative Battalion, and the change was made in the 4th so late as 1888. After 1876 the whole of the four Norfolk volunteer battalions became the Norfolk Volunteer Infantry Brigade under the command of the officer commanding the 9th Regimental District.

In 1861 the First Administrative Battalion consisted of the corps at Aylsham, Fakenham, Holkham, Reepham, Cromer, Dereham, and Holt. In October, 1862, was added the corps at North Walsham, and in July, 1863, those at King's Lynn, Swaffham, and Downham Market. A lieutenant-colonel was appointed to the battalion.

The head-quarters of the 1st Administrative Battalion were at Fakenham till July, 1862, then at Norwich, and from 1864 at Dereham.

In December, 1864, the Norfolk volunteers consisted of the 1st City of Norwich Corps, 2nd Great Yarmouth Corps, 1st Administrative Battalion, and 2nd Administrative Battalion. After some slight changes in 1865 the ten corps then constituting the 1st Administrative Battalion were, in June, 1872, formed into one corps and called the 3rd Battalion Norfolk Volunteers, consisting of ten companies and one sub-division.

Scarlet uniform had been assumed in 1877-78. In 1881 there were four battalions of Norfolk volunteers.

It may be mentioned here that during the reign of King Edward VII the 3rd Volunteer Battalion furnished all the guards that were required at Wolferton and Sandringham.

CHAPTER XXII

THE 1st BATTALION, 1881–1914, AND THE 2ND BATTALION, 1881–1900

THE 1st BATTALION FROM 1881 TO 1914

IN September, 1881, we left the 1st battalion at Templemore and in the neighbourhood.

In April, 1882, it left Ireland for Colchester, where it was stationed for two years. In July, 1884, it was moved to Gosport.

In December, 1885, with a strength of nineteen officers and 688 other ranks, it sailed for Gibraltar, where it remained till June, 1886, when it was sent to Aldershot.

The following extract from a minute by the Quartermaster-General in 1885 is of interest :—

"The Field Marshal Commander-in-Chief desires that an expression of His Royal Highness's gratification may be communicated to the 1st Norfolk Regiment as regards the high position taken by the battalion on the general list of efficiency for 1884, and the great improvement, from 42nd to 8th on the list, effected in the twelve months."

The year 1887 was the first Jubilee of Her Majesty Queen Victoria, and the battalion was specially selected to attend Her Majesty as Guard of Honour on that occasion. It was in the great review before Her Majesty on July 8th, at Aldershot, and its band played during her dinner at the Royal pavilion. On September 24th new colours were

384   HISTORY OF THE NORFOLK REGIMENT

presented to it at Aldershot by H.R.H. the Prince of Wales, afterwards King Edward VII, and Colonel-in-Chief of the Norfolk Regiment.

The following account of the presentation is given in the " Army and Navy Gazette " of October 1, 1887 :—

"Norfolk Regiment (9th). The Prince of Wales presented new colours to the 1st Battalion on Saturday to replace those which have been carried since 1848. . . . H.R.H. General Smith[1] and staff rode to Rushmoor Green, where the ceremony was to take place. and where Lt.-General Sir Archibald Alison and others were in waiting. Some time prior to this the battalion had marched on to the ground 600 strong. The old colours were placed on the left flank, one of them being but the shred of a flag. Colonel Massy was in command, and there was a large group of former or retired officers at the saluting point, including General Inglis, Major-Generals Daunt, Hawes, and Buchanan, Majors Farley, Terry, and Gully, Captains Dunn, Grubble, and Murray, Revd. J. Carrol, Brigade-Surgeon Jeffcoat, and Mr. E. H. C. Wellesley.[2] Sir Henry Bates, colonel of the regiment, was unable to be present. The proceedings began with the trooping of the old colours. The band marched up to the almost bare poles playing ' Rule Britannia ' and preceded the flags in their last progress along the line of the battalion ; there, the tour having been completed, the colours were borne away by the escort, the band playing ' Auld Lang Syne,' their ultimate destination being the Cathedral at Norwich, from which city many of the recruits are obtained.[3]

"The new colours were then brought from the rear, and having been uncased, were placed upon a pile made of the regimental drums,

[1] General Philip Smith, commanding 2nd Infantry Brigade.

[2] To these should be added Lieutenant-Colonel A. F. Bingham Wright, who was adjutant of the 2nd battalion from 1857 to 1872.

[3] This is an error. On November 12, 1887, the old colours were taken to Sandringham by Colonel Massy, Lieutenant and Adjutant Chater, Lieutenant Tonge and Colour-Sergeants Duke and Grant. There they were deposited, by special request of the Prince of Wales, in the chapel, after a service conducted by his chaplain in H.R.H's presence.

COLONEL JAMES DUFF, 1830–78.
Commanded 3rd Norfolk Rifle Volunteers, 1866–78. (*Ch. XXII*)

the Prince of Wales and Generals Alison and Smith, with the staff, riding forward for the presentation. Previous to this the Chaplain-General . . . conducted the usual religious service.

"Two of the subaltern officers—Lieuts. Tonge and Dods—having received the colours from the Prince of Wales, H.R.H. made a short address to the battalion, which had been wheeled up at the flanks to form three sides of a square, remarking that it had afforded him sincere gratification to present colours to a regiment which had always been distinguished for its faithful service and its good conduct. He claimed a kinship with the regiment from his connexion of twenty-five years with the county to which it belonged, and his wish was to see it continue to bear itself well in time of peace as it had always done in times of war. H.R.H. referred to some of the more remarkable incidents in the career of the Norfolk Regiment from its formation downwards, and said he was sure the battalion before him would always do its duty towards its sovereign and country and that in war the 1st Norfolk would always stand firm as a rock. Colonel Massy replied on behalf of the regiment, saying that he and his men accounted it a high honour to receive their new colours from the hands of the son of their Sovereign. The Norfolk Regiment had never turned its back upon an enemy except at the Nive, when it did so to capture a large number of prisoners."

After the ceremony the battalion marched past. The Prince then visited the barracks and lunched at the Officers' Mess before returning to London.

In December, 1887, the battalion was back again at Gibraltar, where it remained till February, 1889, when it embarked for India, arriving in Bombay on March 5th. Ten days later it was sent to Wellington in the Nilgherry Hills, detachments being sent to Calicut, Cannanore, and Malapuram.

In December, 1890, the battalion was transferred to Rangoon. At the end of 1892 a force of 200 rifles from the battalion was employed on operations in the Chin Hills under Brigadier-General Palmer.

The base of these operations was Fort White,[1] from which as a centre several punitive expeditions were sent out during the cold weather of 1892-93, their general objective being the destruction of offending Chin villages and of the crops in their neighbourhood. The columns sent out for this purpose were of varying strength, but, as a rule, a proportion of about two Indian infantry to one European was used. The several expeditions in which the Norfolk Regiment took part were the following, as described in the report of Captain Baker of the 1st Battalion Norfolk Regiment, who acted as intelligence officer:

"On November 10, 1892, a column of thirty-five rifles of the Norfolk Regiment and one hundred Indian infantry started to attack and destroy the village of Htanwe, about six miles north of Fort White. The village was destroyed and the crops burnt. A few harmless shots were fired by the Chins, two of whom were killed. Lieutenant Bellamy of the Norfolk Regiment took part in this expedition, which returned the same evening. On November 14th another column of one gun, seventy-five of the Norfolk Regiment and 185 native troops raided Pimpi, farther off in the same direction. Starting from Kennedy Peak on the 15th, over very bad country, Pimpi was reached on the 16th and found to be burning and cleared of all property. In the village fire was opened by the Chins from the surrounding spurs and continued the next day, without doing any damage. On the 18th the troops started back, still annoyed by fire, but the only casualty was one Gurkha wounded in the arm. A volley was fired into Kennedy Peak camp, again without damage. An ambush prepared by the Gurkhas, near the spur whence this volley came, succeeded in doing some damage to Chins returning to repeat the volley. Fort White was reached on the 20th."

The next two expeditions it is hardly worth while to describe in detail. The story was practically the same in both—a difficult march, with occasional shots or volleys from Chins which did little harm. Then the objective village was found to have been cleared; ambushes were set in places the Chins were likely to use for firing, and an unknown number of them were killed or wounded. The expeditions were:

[1] It will be seen later that the 2nd battalion had been engaged in earlier operations in these parts.

December 4, 1892—fifty Norfolk Regiment and one hundred others commanded by Captain Beale of the 1st Norfolk Regiment to Nashwin, south-west of Fort White; December 10, 1892—fifty Norfolk Regiment, 125 others; northwards. A more important expedition under Brigadier-General Palmer, C.B., started on January 3, 1893. The column comprised two guns, one hundred men of the Norfolk Regiment, and 380 native infantry and sappers.

This column remained out the whole of January. It crossed the Manipur River with difficulty by a raft, and from fixed points many small expeditions were sent out to harry the Chins, who were now beginning to feel that they would do well to keep in with the British. On three of these subsidiary expeditions Captain Beale of the 1st Norfolk Regiment was in command of fifteen to twenty-five of his own men, and from twenty-five to fifty Burma Rifles.

There were more expeditions to various villages on January 17th, February 8th, March 3rd and 12th, and April 7th and 8th, in all of which detachments of the Norfolk Regiment took part. The most important event was on January 19th, when some stockades flanking the line of march had to be cleared, but, as the only casualty was one sepoy wounded, this was not a very serious affair. Under the circumstances, it does not seem desirable to go into the somewhat complicated details of the few little fights that occurred.[1] What has been said of the earlier expeditions seems sufficiently to explain the nature of the work falling to the share of the Norfolk Regiment. Where small outlying posts occupying villages were left they were manned by native troops.

The really trying part of the operations, for British troops, was the marching, often by very bad paths through thick jungle and up and down precipitous hills.

During the seven months' service in the Chin Hills the casualties were three men wounded and seven died. Of the work of the detachment Captain E. R. J. Presgrave, commanding at Fort White, wrote on May 13, 1893: " The excellent work done by the army signallers (principally

[1] Full details are to be found in the report of Captain Baker, 1st Norfolk Regiment, Attaché, Intelligence Department, printed by the Government Press at Rangoon in June, 1893.

men of the Norfolk Regiment) has contributed in no small degree to the successful issue of the operations—posts being able to work at the shortest notice."

Brigadier-General Palmer on his way through Rangoon made a special point of calling on the commanding officer to express his extreme satisfaction with the way the men of the regiment worked, especially with regard to flanking parties and convoy duty, which was carried out among steep hills covered with dense jungle. " Latterly the men of the Norfolk Regiment were just as good at this work as the best Gurkhas."

During 1893, 200 men of the battalion were employed for seven days in putting down riots between Hindus and Mohammedans in Rangoon on the occasion of the Mohammedan festival of the Bakr Id.

In December of that year the battalion was transferred to Umbala.

In March, 1894, it went to Dagshai for the hot weather, returning to Umbala in October. In November it marched to Mian Mir to take part in the durbar held at Lahore by the Viceroy on the 30th.

In December it marched back to Umbala. In March, 1895, the battalion again went to Dagshai for the hot weather, returning to Umbala in November and proceeding, in January, 1896, to Allahabad, where Lieutenant-Colonel W. G. Straghan took over command from Lieutenant-Colonel D. K. Robertson on the latter's retirement. Colonel Straghan died in December on his way home on sick leave and was succeeded by Lieutenant-Colonel J. L. Govan.

In March, 1899, the battalion went to Colaba (Bombay), with detachments of one company each at Ahmedabad and Deesa. In 1900 Lieutenant-Colonel A. C. Becher succeeded to the command, Colonel Govan having died at Colaba on March 11th.

In July, 1899, Quartermaster-Sergeant Duke was presented with a medal for long service and good conduct. This is noteworthy as his father and grandfather had both earned the same distinction in the 9th Foot.

In June, twenty-four non-commissioned officers and men were sent as signallers to China with the expedition against the Boxers. They were attached to various units, some even to the American forces, and saw all the fighting there was. It seems unnecessary to follow in detail their movements. There were no casualties among them, though they did good service. A few were left behind to work the telegraph lines till these were taken over by the Chinese Government. The rest returned to the regiment. All of them received the medal for China 1900 with the clasp "Relief of Pekin."

Once more in March, 1901, the battalion was sent right across India to Dum Dum, whence it supplied a detachment to Barrackpore.

In March, 1902, it moved to Lebong,[1] but went on in October to Bareilly, and in November to Umbala, whence it took part in the manœuvres and durbar at Delhi in celebration of the succession of King Edward VII. It is stated that there "its yellow pugaries attracted much attention."

During 1902 a section of the battalion was trained at Fatehgarh at the Mounted Infantry School just started there.

On June 23, 1903, a telegram was received at Bareilly ordering one section of mounted infantry on service in Somaliland, with the force under Major-General Sir C. C. Egerton, which was proceeding to complete the hunt of the Mad Mullah which had been begun under Colonel Swayne and General Manning.

The section was sent as far as possible complete, and formed part of the 2nd Company British Mounted Infantry.

It is not proposed to follow in detail the movements of this section during the year of its employment in Somaliland. It made many trying marches and often had very uninteresting times in desert places. It was not engaged in the only serious fight there was in the expedition.

It lost none of its members, and in June, 1904, was sent back to England and attached to the 2nd battalion at Colchester. The General Service medal with clasp "Somaliland, 1902–1904" was awarded to Lieutenant Scobell and twenty-seven other ranks.

In December, 1903, Lieutenant Hadow, with a detachment of seventeen men and two maxim guns, was sent with the expedition from India to Lhasa. They were with Colonel Younghusband in camp during the winter at a height of 15,000 feet above the sea. They took part in the small action in April, 1904, and in the fight on the Karo-la under

[1] A small hill cantonment below Darjiling.

Colonel Brander. They took a hand later in the storming of the village of Palla, and when the fort at Gyantse was stormed the fire of the maxims on the breach helped to cover the stormers as they mounted it.

After that they advanced with the expedition to Lhasa. In November, 1904, they returned to India. They had no casualties. The medal for Tibet with the clasp " Gyantse " was awarded to all of the detachment, and Lieutenant Hadow was mentioned in despatches.

In September, 1904, the battalion embarked for South Africa and was sent to Tempe Barracks, Bloemfontein. In March of that year Lieutenant-Colonel W. G. Hamilton took over command from Colonel Becher; it passed to Lieutenant-Colonel G. Massy in the following year (1905).

On April 5, 1905, the facings of the regiment were, under the orders of the War Office, changed from white to yellow.

In 1905 and 1906 both the 1st and 2nd battalions were together at Bloemfontein. They had not served together since they were both in the Ionian Islands in 1864.

In January, 1907, the 1st battalion was sent home and reached Warley in February. On February 1, 1907, a notification appeared in the " London Gazette," as follows : " The King [Edward VII] has been graciously pleased to confer on the Norfolk Regiment the honour of becoming its Colonel-in-Chief." Looking to His Majesty's long and close association with Sandringham, the honour was a very appropriate one and served to bind the regiment still more closely to its territorial area. In 1909 the 1st battalion was detailed to furnish a detachment for duty at the Tower of London.

His Majesty, as Colonel-in-Chief of the Norfolk Regiment, arranged to present new colours to the 1st battalion in the grounds of Buckingham Palace on Friday, June 4, 1909 ; but the presentation was postponed till Saturday, the 5th, on account of the unfavourable weather, and, as the ground was still soft and wet on Saturday, His Majesty ultimately determined to make the presentation in the State Ball-room of the Palace.

The men were paraded at the Tower of London at a strength of about 480, exclusive of the band. They comprised half a battalion stationed at the Tower, three companies from Gravesend, and the head-quarters company from Warley. They marched to Wellington Barracks and left their arms there, as the ceremony was to be indoors. Thence they proceeded to the Palace, commanded by Lieutenant-Colonel Marriott, D.S.O.

The battalion was formed up on three sides of the ball-room, the band occupying the gallery. An altar of drums was arranged in the centre of the room, behind which Bishop Taylor Smith, Chaplain-General to the Forces, stood with his chaplains. The new colours were placed on the drums. At noon Their Majesties the King and Queen entered the ball-room, followed by their Royal Highnesses the Prince of Wales, Princess Victoria, and the Duke of Connaught.

The battalion was called to attention and gave a royal salute, whilst the band played the National Anthem. The old colours were borne into the room by the subalterns and their escort, and as they were marched to their position in rear of the battalion, the band played " Auld Lang Syne."

The Chaplain-General then read the Dedication Service, and after recital of the Lord's Prayer and a special prayer for the colours, pronounced the Benediction. Major G. Head, 2nd in command, with Captain C. E. Luard, D.S.O., now advanced to a position in front of the King and Queen and handed the colours to His Majesty, who stepped forward to receive them. The two lieutenants knelt to receive them at His Majesty's hands, Lieutenant J. Bagwell taking the King's colour and Lieutenant J. Longfield the regimental colour.

His Majesty then addressed the regiment as follows :—

" Colonel Marriott, officers, non-commissioned officers and men of the 1st Battalion of the Norfolk Regiment, I have not forgotten that twenty-two years ago, at Aldershot, I presented you with new colours. I did so on that occasion in order to identify myself with your regiment. I have lived now not far off half a century in the county of Norfolk, and as everything interests me so deeply in Norfolk, I was glad on that occasion, as I am on this, to associate myself with the regiment that bears the name of my county. I am sorry the elements do not permit of my presenting the colours to you out of doors, but the fact of my presenting them to you inside the Palace shows you the deep interest I take in to-day's ceremony. Your regiment has a long record of service. You first existed 220 years ago. During that period and up to the present time you have seen active service in every part of the globe and have greatly distinguished yourselves. I feel sure that in confiding these new colours to your care, you will always continue to uphold the dignity of your Sovereign and the welfare of your country. I have little fear that the great reputation which your regiment possesses will not be continued as long as it exists."

Colonel Marriott replied as follows :—

"May it please Your Majesty, on behalf of the 1st Battalion Norfolk Regiment I desire to return our heartfelt thanks for the great honour Your Majesty has conferred on the regiment in again presenting to this battalion its new colours, and for the gracious reference, Sir, you have made to its past history and traditions. It is a source of great pride and glory to us that Your Majesty is our Colonel-in-Chief, and whilst we guard these colours to-day entrusted to our care we assure Your Majesty of our constant loyalty and devotion."

A royal salute was then given, and as the new colours were borne to their allotted position His Majesty stood at the salute and the band played "Rule Britannia." The playing of the National Anthem brought the ceremony to a close.

Before leaving with the Queen, His Majesty directed that the commanding officer, the two subalterns, and the sergeant-major should be presented to him. He decorated Lieutenant-Colonel Marriott with the Fourth Class of the Victorian Order, Lieutenants Bagwell and Longfield with the Fifth Class, and presented Sergeant-Major Gleed with the medal of the Order. Amongst those specially invited to witness the ceremony were the wives of the officers and N.C.O.'s of the battalion.

On October 2nd a colour party consisting of Lieutenant-Colonel

COLONEL HENRY EDMUND BUXTON, V.D., 1846–1905.
Commanded 2nd Norfolk Rifle Volunteers, 1876–82. Commanded 2nd Volunteer Battalion Norfolk Regiment, 1882–97. Colonel, 1897–1905. (*Ch. XXII*)

Marriott, M.V.O., D.S.O., and Lieutenant and Adjutant Lancaster, with Colour-Sergeant Hall and sixteen men, took the old colours, which had been graciously accepted by His Majesty, to Sandringham, where they were lodged in the north-west part of the Church with suitable ceremony.

In November, 1909, the regiment was authorized to bear on its colours two somewhat ancient honours—" Havanna " and " Martinique, 1794." In the same year the following notification was received : " I am commanded by the Army Council to inform you that His Majesty has been graciously pleased to approve of the 9th Australian Infantry Regiment (Moreton's), Brisbane, to be shown in the War Office Army List as allied to the Norfolk Regiment."[1]

On November 19, 1909, a centenary memorial of Sir John Moore was unveiled by Miss Mary Carrick Moore at Shorncliffe, near the site of the general's residence in 1803-1804, when he commanded at the camp. To this ceremony Lieutenant-Colonel Marriott proceeded, taking with him the colours, with escort drums, and bugles of the 1st battalion, which had assisted at the burial of Sir John Moore at Corunna a little over a century before. After the unveiling there was a flourish by the drums and bugles and the latter sounded the " Last Post."

In December, 1909, the battalion moved to Malplaquet Barracks, Aldershot.

It was one of those lining the streets of London on the occasion of the funeral of King Edward VII on May 20, 1910, and performed the same service at the coronation of King George V on June 22, 1911. On December 2, 1910, also, King George was pleased to become colonel-in-chief of the regiment, as his father had been before him.

In 1912 when His Majesty visited Aldershot the 1st battalion furnished the Guard of Honour on his arrival.

It was commanded by Captain C. C. Wickham, D.S.O., with Lieutenant W. A. Balders as subaltern of the guard, and Lieutenant T. A. F. Foley carrying the King's colours.

On November 20th of the same year the 1st battalion went to

---

[1] After the conclusion of the Great War the Australian Army was renumbered in 1919, the 9th regiment becoming the 7th under the new arrangement. It is so shown in the Army List of 1921.

Palace Barracks, Holywood, near Belfast. On October 1st there came into force the new organization into four companies. A and B companies became the new A company, C and D became the new B, E and F became C, and G and H became D.

The battalion was still at Holywood when war with Germany was declared on August 4, 1914.

The 2nd Battalion from 1881 to 1900

We left the 2nd battalion at Umbala in December, 1881. Leaving Umbala on March 25, 1882, five companies marched to Sabathu for the hot weather, the other three going to Jutogh, near Simla, under Major Dickinson. On July 20th, a most unpleasant season for the transfer, the companies at Sabathu marched to Umbala, leaving sixty men behind. Two of the companies at Jutogh remained there and one was sent to Sabathu. On the 27th the five companies went by rail from Umbala to Morar, where they arrived next day. In October the detachments left at Jutogh and Sabathu rejoined the battalion, which received about the same time a draft from England under Major Seton and Lieutenant Seton. Another draft of 187 men with Major Allcard, Lieutenants Griffin, and Manners Smith arrived a year later on October 31, 1883.

On December 12, 1884, the battalion left Morar to march, four companies and head-quarters to Sitapur, and the other four, under Major Burton, to Benares.

On May 1, 1887, Lieutenant-Colonel C. S. Perry succeeded Colonel Roberts in command of the battalion. Colonel Roberts had succeeded Colonel Daunt on April 30, 1883.

In October, 1888, the battalion was ordered to Burma. The portion at Sitapur left that station on October 4th, was joined *en route* by the wing from Benares on the 28th, and on November 1st embarked at Calcutta on the I.M.S. "Canning" for Rangoon, where it arrived on the 6th. On November 17th, after a voyage up the Irawaddy by steamer and flats, it relieved the 2nd Battalion Royal Munster Fusiliers at Mandalay. There a mounted infantry company was formed under the command of Captain Lombe.

At the end of this year Sir George White was operating against the Chin Tribes with a force consisting of the 42nd and 44th Gurkhas, the 10th Madras Native Infantry, a company of Madras sappers, and a mountain battery. To reinforce him the 2nd battalion of the Norfolk Regiment sent, on December 28, 1888, A, C, and F companies, consisting of 200 non-commissioned officers and men under Major Shepherd, Captain Lombe, Lieutenants Luard and Brett, Second-Lieutenant Richardson with Surgeon-Captain le Quesne. On March 2, 1889, H company joined them, and on July 3rd E company followed.

The operations undertaken were generally of the usual harassing nature in the case of putting down the wild tribes of Upper Burma. There were constant raids by the dacoits on friendly villages, and for a considerable time Sir G. White was hampered by the orders of the Government of India, restricting his operations to a blockade, instead of the regular punitive expedition which he wished to undertake. On November 19, 1888, he had, at last, been given a free hand and collected his force as above described. The commander of the operating column was Brigadier-General Faunce, and the general line of his movement had been westwards from the Chindwin River towards the valley of the Manipur River. The Norfolk companies began to arrive in time to take a hand (with C company commanded by Captain A. H. Luard) in the capture of the village of Siyin (afterwards renamed Fort White), a little east of the Manipur River in the midst of the Chin Hills. There had already been several small affairs—attacks on parties constructing roads, slight resistance in some places where villages were destroyed, and the like. Two of these villages, Sagyilain and Tartan had been rebuilt by the Chins, and it was considered desirable to again destroy them. The troops had moved into Fort White on April 9th for the hot weather. On the 30th Major Shepherd, with one hundred rifles of the Norfolk Regiment, and one hundred of the 42nd Gurkhas, started for the rebuilt villages. Sagyilain was burnt with no resistance beyond some harmless long-range fire from the Chins. Tartan was a different matter. Against it Captain Otway Mayne took sixty-five of the Norfolk Regiment and sixty of the 42nd Gurkhas on May 4th. He found the enemy strongly entrenched in two stockades. They stood their ground against rifle fire, and a bayonet charge was required to dislodge them from the lower stockade. They had made a brave stand, as evidenced by the casualties on the British side. Of the Norfolk Regiment, Lieutenant Michel and two men were killed close up to the stockade, Captain Mayne and Surgeon-Captain le Quesne[1] were severely wounded, as also were nine Gurkhas. Of this affair Major Otway Mayne writes:—

> "Michel was killed about 10 to 15 yards away from me in a ravine close against a concealed stockade; in fact, I was going down to fetch him out when I got knocked over and le Quesne went down and bound him up and brought him out. Le Quesne was later tying up my right arm for me when a bullet passed between us and got him in the left arm. I was with young Michel when he died, about ten minutes later, having been shot high up in the femoral artery. On this occasion also Corporal Stephenson distinguished himself. He was killed and died at the same time as Michel from a spear wound in the throat."

After this heavy loss no attempt was made on the second stockade, though the men were eager to make it. A week later Brigadier-General Penn Symonds went against Tartan with 150 men, but found both stockades unoccupied and burnt them. This was the last operation of the expedition.

The hot weather of 1889 seriously tried the troops at Fort White, of whom thirty-one died and 177 were sent back sick to Mandalay. In the succeeding cold weather the detachments of the 2nd battalion rejoined head-quarters at Mandalay in small bodies, the last of which reached that station on December 3, 1889. For the attack on Tartan, Major Shepherd received the D.S.O., Corporal Harwood and Private Crampion the Distinguished Service Medal.

On April 30, 1890, Colonel C. S. Perry gave over command to Colonel G. S. Burton, one of the only two officers who were with the battalion

---

[1] Surgeon-Captain Le Quesne was awarded the Victoria Cross for conspicuous gallantry in dressing Lieutenant Michel's wound under fire.

throughout its service in India from 1874 to 1890. The other was Quartermaster Grehan.

The 2nd battalion left Mandalay on January 10, 1890, and embarked next day at Rangoon (where the 1st battalion had just arrived) on the I.M.S. "Canning" for Bombay, which was reached on the 24th. After a few days under canvas at Colaba, the battalion again embarked, on February 3rd, for England, reaching Portsmouth on March 5th and proceeding by rail to Colchester. There it was present at the Queen's birthday parade on May 23rd. The account of the battalion's appearance on this occasion is described by the "Colchester and Essex Mercury" in the following rather journalistic terms: "Next came the combined bands, brilliant in the sunlight with their varied instruments of music, their chequered uniforms, and heralding with a magnificent burst of 'Rule Britannia' the advent of the men of the Norfolk Regiment, who traversed the line of march in a manner that elicited praise, which was all the more hearty in view of the tattered colours, borne proudly aloft, telling eloquently of battles fought and victories won on many a hotly contested field; and also at sight of faces which bore signs of arduous service in Burma, from which they have lately returned."

From Colchester the battalion (then sixteen officers and 543 other ranks strong) went by rail to Warley on December 27, 1892. During this year new colours had been issued to the battalion by the Army Clothing Department.

This set of colours was dogged by misfortune. Of course they should have been presented. H.R.H. the Duke of Clarence, who was to have performed the ceremony, unfortunately died. H.R.H. Prince of Wales and the Duke of Cambridge were unable to find dates available. Then, whilst quartered at the Tower, the battalion was required to find the Queen's guard at St. James's Palace on July 10, 1893. The old colours had been completely worn out, so the new ones were carried. They got so completely soaked by heavy rain that it was no longer possible to have them presented.

On April 30, 1893, Lieutenant-Colonel C. R. Shepherd, D.S.O., succeeded to the command of the battalion on Colonel Burton's retirement on half-pay.

On April 28th B, C, D, E, and F companies were sent to the Tower of London, where they were stationed till September 16th, when they went to Pirbright Camp for musketry, and on completion of the course rejoined the rest of the battalion at Warley. During their stay at the Tower the five companies took part in the lining of the streets on May 19th when H.M. Queen Victoria opened the Imperial Institute. They were similarly employed on July 6th, on the occasion of the marriage of H.R.H. the Duke of York and Princess Victoria Mary of Teck, our present King and Queen.

In July the battalion furnished the Queen's guard, which was commanded by Captain Becher, with Lieutenants Bell and Carroll carrying the colours. It also furnished a guard of honour of one hundred men, under Captain Percy and Second-Lieutenant Steward, when H.M. the King of Denmark visited the city of London.

On September 7, 1893, the regiment lost its colonel, Sir Arthur Borton, G.C.B., G.C.M.G., who died in London and was buried at Hanton in Kent on the 9th. The coffin was borne to the grave by eight officers of the 2nd battalion. He was succeeded by Lieutenant-General (Honorary General) Charles Elmhirst, C.B., who died on December 14, 1893, and was in turn succeeded by Lieutenant-General (Honorary General) T. E. Knox, C.B.[1]

On April 27, 1894, six companies under Major Currie relieved the Scots Guards at the Tower, and on June 9th lined the streets from Mark Lane Station to the Mint for the opening of the Tower Bridge by H.R.H. the Prince of Wales.

In August these six companies went to Aldershot for musketry and were joined there by the rest of the battalion from Warley.

On May 2, 1896, Lieutenant Hare with thirty-one other ranks of

[1] Both Sir Arthur Borton and General Elmhirst were among the comparatively small number of the colonels of the regiment who, like Sir John Cameron, had been associated with it, and had led it as Lieutenant-Colonels, during the greater part of their military career. Sir Arthur Borton was with it in Afghanistan in 1842, in the Sikh war, and commanded it in the Crimea. General Elmhirst had been with it in the above-named campaigns and was second in command in the Crimea. When the 2nd battalion was raised for the third time, he was selected to raise it and command it as Lieutenant-Colonel for seven years.

the 2nd battalion embarked at Southampton as part of No. 6 Company Mounted Infantry for service in South Africa under the command of Lieutenant-Colonel E. A. H. Alderson.

The detachment was sent at first to Maritzburg in Natal, and only reached Salisbury, the capital of Mashonaland, on September 30, 1896. Hence it marched, with the rest of Colonel Alderson's force, to the Hartley Hills district to attack the stronghold known as Chena's Kraal, the head-quarters of Mashongombi, the rebel chief. The kraal was situated on a rocky hill constituting a formidable position, had it been defended by any but savages.

The Norfolk Mounted Infantry attacked the south side and came under quite a heavy fire, including some from the "Black Watch" (native contingent) firing at rebels from the opposite side. When the kopje was carried and the kraals on it were being searched out, one private was shot from a cave. He died of his wound. Otherwise there were no casualties amongst the Norfolk detachment, and there was no more fighting for them. They marched back to the coast at the end of November and went by sea to Maritzburg, where they, with the rest of the mounted infantry, were complimented on their conduct in the expedition by the Major-General commanding. They reached England on June 23, 1897.

In this year (1896) the 2nd battalion were highly successful in rifle shooting competitions. The Evelyn Wood Competition was won by H company, under Captain Ross. B company, under Lieutenant Wilson, carried off the third, and D company, under Lieutenant F. C. Lodge, the fifth prize in the same competition.

H company also won the Goldsmiths' and Silversmiths' Cup, and the Bowyer Cup. Altogether H company won money prizes to the value of £40 10s.

The Young Soldiers' Team of the battalion won the fourth prize of £4, and H company won £4 in the Inter-Company Volley Team Match.

On November 10, 1896, five companies, under the command of Major Phillips, left Aldershot for Ireland. On arrival at Queenstown next day two companies under Major Borton went to Fort Camden; the other three went to Spike Island under Captain Baker. The head-quarters of the battalion followed in January, 1897, leaving Aldershot on the 19th, under Colonel Shepherd. In bidding them adieu at the station, General Kelly Kenny, after expressing his regret at losing the " Holy Boys " from his brigade, said : " Smart in the field, champions on the range, well behaved in barracks and camp, twice the winners of the Evelyn Wood and other trophies, they leave behind them a record which will be long spoken of in the 3rd brigade."

After leaving Aldershot, head-quarters and three companies went to Kinsale.

On June 23rd, 1897, the mounted infantry section which had gone to South Africa in May, 1896, disembarked at Southampton and rejoined the regiment in Ireland. Lieutenant-Colonel L. H. Phillips took over the command from Brevet-Colonel Shepherd, D.S.O. (whose term of command had been extended by a year), on April 30, 1898. Towards the close of 1899 the 2nd battalion was brought over from Ireland to Aldershot preparatory to its employment in South Africa.

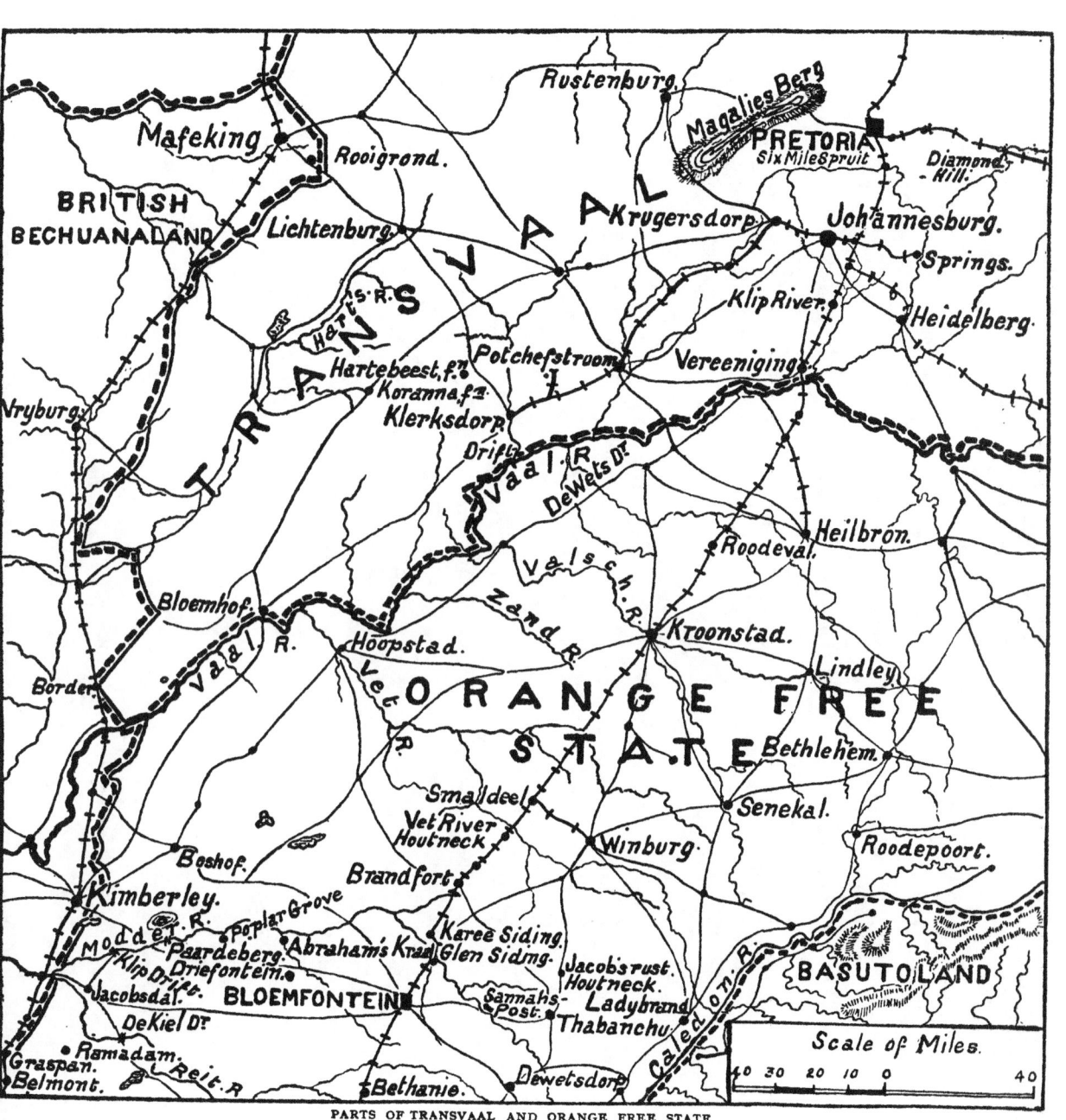

PARTS OF TRANSVAAL AND ORANGE FREE STATE

CHAPTER XXIII

THE 2ND BATTALION IN THE SOUTH AFRICAN WAR AND INDIA

THE battalion, completely mobilized at Aldershot, embarked at Southampton on January 4, 1900, on the "Assaye," with a strength of twenty-six officers, 984 other ranks, five horses, and one machine gun. Lieutenant-Colonel L. W. Phillips was in command with Major A. C. Becher as second in command. It disembarked at Cape Town on the 22nd of the same month, and was assigned to the 14th infantry brigade of the 7th division, the other troops in the brigade being the 2nd Lincoln Regiment, 1st King's Own Scottish Borderers, and the 2nd Hampshire Regiment, with a detachment of Army Service Corps, a bearer company, and field hospital. The mounted infantry company of the battalion was separated from it and formed one company of the 7th Mounted Infantry Corps along with companies from the Lincoln, King's Own Scottish Borderers, and Hampshire Regiments. The doings of the mounted infantry company will be dealt with in a separate section, after those of the rest of the battalion. It had already gone to South Africa when the battalion was mobilized.

The brigade was commanded by Major-General H. Chermside, and, with the 15th infantry brigade commanded by Major-General A. G. Wavell, and the divisional troops, made up the 7th infantry division commanded by Lieutenant-General C. Tucker. The military position in South Africa when the battalion landed at Cape Town may be briefly stated as follows:

Sir G. White was blockaded in Ladysmith, where Sir R. Buller was just making his unfortunate attempt to relieve him by the Upper Tugela, which ended at Spion Kop. In the western theatre General French was at Colesberg, opposed by Schoeman with 5,000 men, whilst Grobelaar had another 4,000 Boers about Stormberg. Cronje had some 8,000 at Scholtz Nek. Kimberley and Mafeking were invested respectively by 3,000 and 2,500 Boers. The general feeling on the British side, after the events of Ladysmith, Colenso, Magersfontein, and other actions, was one of depression, which had only been relieved by the confidence felt in the new Commander-in-Chief, Lord Roberts, who with his Chief of Staff, Lord Kitchener, had landed in South Africa on January 10th. Both names served to raise the spirits of the troops, and, combined with the large reinforcements from England, to inspire a hope that there would be no more of the disasters which had marked the first period of the war.

Lord Roberts's general plan was for an advance by one line only—that of the railway direct from Cape Town to Kimberley, and thence through the Orange Free State on its capital Bloemfontein. Only on this line was there a bridge over the Orange River still in British hands.

Cronje, hoping and expecting that the British would dash their heads against his entrenchments as they had at Magersfontein, was really to be turned by his left, and various movements were undertaken to alarm him for his right. They were completely successful in confirming him in his belief that the English could only make frontal attacks, that they could not leave the railway, and that their incapacity in marching unfitted them for turning movements on a large scale.

On February 8, 1900, the 6th division had been transported by rail to Modder River Camp, the 7th to Graspan and Enslin. Of the 9th division, as yet not completely organized, one brigade was at Modder Camp, the other was being formed at Graspan. The cavalry division, which, with the exception of one brigade of mounted infantry at Orange River Station, was at Modder River Camp, was not ready, as none of its brigade commanders had arrived. The 1st division was beyond the Riet River. The first objective was the relief of Kimberley and Mafeking, a result which could only be obtained by the removal of Cronje, who barred the way in his position at Magersfontein. Affairs at Kimberley having reached a stage which brooked no delay, the advance was ordered for February 11th, and the cavalry division was ordered to relieve Kimberley "at all costs," marching by Ramdam. To that place also the 7th division was ordered, its place at Graspan and Enslin being taken by the 6th. The 1st division, beyond the Riet below its junction with the Modder, would hold Cronje during the movement round his left.

On February 12th the 7th division again moved eastwards to support the cavalry division, which had been ordered to seize at least one crossing of the Riet River. They got across at Waterval and De Kiel's Drifts, having a brush with de Wet's and Andries Cronje's detachments of Boers. The 7th division followed first to Waterval Drift, and, without passing there, moved up the left bank of the Riet to De Kiel's Drift, where the outposts were taken over from the cavalry.

The great heat (it was still high summer in the southern hemisphere) and the want of water on the way had proved very trying to infantry who had but recently come off a long sea voyage, followed by a long train journey.

De Kiel's Drift was impracticable for wagons, and another drift a mile or two up the river was difficult, not from the small amount of water in the river, but from the nature of the approaches.

Lord Roberts's orders to General Tucker had been to push on from the Riet, so as to reach, if possible, the Modder in two marches. The distance was twenty-four miles.

There was so much uncertainty about water, and the men had been so much exhausted by their march from Ramdam, that Tucker was now ordered to halt on the Riet during February 13th. Even the cavalry only got off at 10.30 a.m. on the 13th.

Marching by night, the 7th division reached Wegdraai Drift, on the right bank of the Riet, at 2 a.m. on the 15th, and from there Jacobsdal was occupied by mounted infantry. The original intention of moving the 7th division straight across to the Modder had been abandoned.

General French, meanwhile, had got forward to the Modder, and on the 15th his place was taken by the 6th division, which had marched via Wegdraai on the 14th, and was replaced at the last-named place by the 7th division. Cronje's communications with Bloemfontein were now occupied by the British.

At 6 p.m. on February 15th French, who had pushed on from Klip Drift on the Modder, where he was relieved by the 6th division, entered Kimberley, one result of which was that Cronje, who had been little moved by the cutting of his communications with Bloemfontein, was thoroughly alarmed at seeing himself separated from his native Transvaal.

The 15th was an unfortunate day, for on it the "Supply Park," which had got across the Riet at Waterval Drift with great difficulty, was resting there under an insufficient escort when it was attacked by de Wet and A. Cronje from the east. The Boers were reinforced, and about 1.30 p.m. General Tucker was ordered back to its relief with the 14th brigade, in which was the 2nd battalion of the Norfolk Regiment. After a very trying march he reached the scene of the action about sunset with five companies of the 2nd Norfolk, seven of the 2nd Lincoln, and seven of the 2nd Hampshire Regiments. The Boers were now estimated at 1,500 men, and Tucker reported that, with troops tired as his were by their march, it would be unwise to attack without reinforcements. To send them would have dislocated Lord Roberts's plans for encircling Cronje, so Tucker received orders to be back at Wegdraai by daylight, abandoning the convoy. The order was received at 11 p.m., and it was not possible, if it was to be obeyed, to destroy the wagons and stores, most of which fell into the enemy's hands.

Cronje had at last started on his march up the Modder.

On February 16th the 14th brigade was with Tucker at Wegdraai, the 15th being at Jacobsdal, four miles off. The men were very tired after their march to Waterval Drift and back. The whole 7th division was ordered to concentrate at Jacobsdal early on the 17th. They were thus left behind during the pursuit of Cronje. Lord Roberts was detained at Jacobsdal on the 17th by indisposition.

On the 18th Lord Roberts telegraphed to Lord Kitchener that he was sending Chermside's (14th) brigade and the Guards at once, to reach Klip Drift early next morning. He also warned them, after the indecisive result of the fighting at Paardeberg, that they might have to push straight on there. Orders reached General Tucker at 4 p.m. on the 18th, directing him to send the 14th brigade at once to the front at Paardeberg, leaving the 15th at Jacobsdal.

The 14th brigade, starting at 9 p.m. the same night, had marched the sixteen miles to Klip Drift by 6 a.m. on the 19th. The 2nd Norfolk Regiment got their orders at 5 p.m. on the 18th and started, dinnerless, at 8 p.m. After three hours' rest the march was resumed, except by the naval guns and the transport. The guns were in action on Signal Hill, south-west of Cronje's position, by 3 p.m., and the infantry brigade was up at 6 p.m. The infantry had marched, on half-rations, just over thirty miles in twenty hours in intense heat and thick dust, with a very short supply of water, and with only the food the men carried. Considering

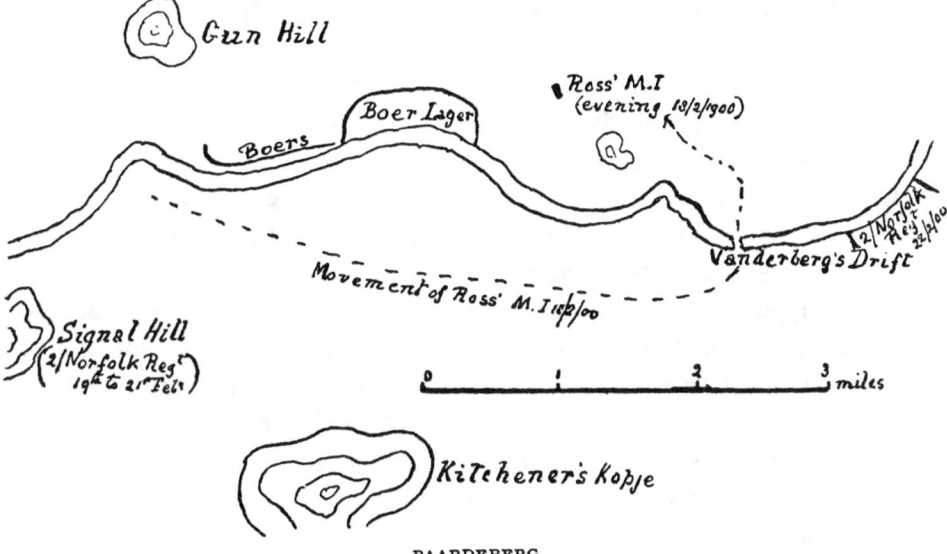

PAARDEBERG

how little opportunity of marching they had had since landing, the performance was highly creditable.

For various reasons, with which we are not concerned, Lord Roberts decided against another immediate assault after the failure of the 18th February.

In the evening of the 20th Chermside was ordered to continue the line of investment from the foot of Signal Hill to near Vanderberg Drift, above (east) of Cronje's position, using two of his four battalions. He took the Lincoln Regiment and King's Own Scottish Borderers, leaving the Norfolk and Hampshire Regiments where they were. During the night his column lost its way, and had to wait till morning to resume its march, which was only completed with a loss of thirty-eight casualties, due to his having got too near Cronje in the night. His two battalions took a hand in driving de Wet from Kitchener's Kopje.

During the night of the 21st–22nd, the Norfolk and Hampshire battalions were called up from Signal Hill to Vanderberg Drift, where they relieved the 18th brigade, which was sent to the west of Kitchener's Kopje as part of the line of defence against Boer attempts to relieve Cronje from outside. The 2nd Norfolk Regiment were in the river-bed facing downstream, and subject to continuous sniping, which caused several casualties.

The 14th brigade now formed part of the inner line of investment and was posted astride the Modder, east of Cronje's position. Arrangements were made for steady sapping towards the enemy's position. Of the 14th brigade the Norfolk and Lincoln Regiments were on the left bank of the Modder, the former in front, with brigade head-quarters between them and the Lincoln Regiment. The other regiments were on the opposite bank, and the 9th company Royal Engineers assisted in the digging of deep, narrow trenches, and fixing sites for them. By February 26th the front works on the left bank were forward to within 250 yards of the nearest Boer trenches. Though the casualties were not heavy during these days and nights, the work was very arduous and the troops suffered from want of sleep and food, it being only possible to bring up rations after dark. At times the covering parties were on half, and occasionally on only quarter, rations of biscuit. The weather, too, had broken, and, though the heat and dust were less trying, rain frequently flooded the trenches and made life in them very hard. The assault of the night of the 26th–27th, in which the 14th brigade had no share, ended in the unconditional surrender of Cronje at 6 a.m. on the 27th.

The losses of the 2nd battalion at Paardeberg were one officer killed and one wounded.[1] Two rank and file were killed and four wounded in sapping towards Cronje's lager.

On March 7th began the advance on Bloemfontein. On that day,

[1] 2nd Lieutenant Hylton-Jolliffe killed, Lieutenant Cramer Roberts wounded and captured. Neither of them was with the main body of the Regiment.

the 14th brigade, with the Guards on its right, remained halted from daybreak till 9.30 a.m. on the left bank of the Modder, a little east of Makauw's Drift. General Tucker and his men were equally eager to get forward into the fighting, which was in progress on their right front; but owing to the proximity of the river bank on their left, it was dangerous to do so till the 1st division beyond the river was in a position to cover their left. At 9.30 a.m. the 14th brigade moved slowly forward towards Table Mountain, south-eastwards, followed by the divisional artillery, which shelled the hill until it had to desist owing to the approach to it of Marter's mounted infantry. The hill was reported clear, and the 14th brigade moved cautiously on to Poplar Grove, which it reached at 3 p.m. During this day none of the infantry on the left (south) bank of the Modder were ever within rifle range of the enemy. That night the 7th division bivouacked on the south bank of the Modder beyond Poplar Grove, and remained there on March 8th, waiting for supplies. On the 10th news came in that the enemy were occupying Abraham's Kraal in uncertain strength.

The orders for March 10th prescribed an advance in three columns, of which the right consisted of the 7th division, with the 3rd cavalry brigade and Ridley's mounted infantry. This column marched at 5 a.m. to Petrusberg, where it halted for the night. It had no share in the action of Driefontein, which took place on its left on this day. On the 11th it marched without incident to Driekop, where it waited for the last convoy to come through Poplar Grove.

On March 13th, the day on which Lord Roberts entered Bloemfontein, Tucker's column moved forward to Panfontein, as water had run short at Driekop. On the 15th the convoy joined it, and on the 16th it was close to Bloemfontein. The strength of the 2nd Norfolk battalion on reaching Bloemfontein was sixteen officers, 763 other ranks, five horses, and one machine gun.

On March 19th the Boers had blown up the Modder bridge at Glen, fourteen miles north of Bloemfontein, before it could be reached by a company of the Coldstream Guards. There had been some skirmishes after that, and it appeared that the enemy were strong enough beyond the river to prevent the restoration of the bridge. Lord Roberts decided to drive them off and to occupy Karee Siding, a station on the railway north of Glen. On the 28th General Tucker received orders to drive the Boers from Karee Siding. He was to receive detailed plans from General French, who took with him what cavalry could now be mounted, only about 650, besides 880 mounted infantry, and four batteries Royal Horse Artillery. The 7th division had a strength of about 6,400, with two field batteries.

At Glen, French and Tucker settled their plan of attack. The Boers were astride the railway at Karee Siding. Their centre occupied the nek over which the railway passed. The position was naturally strong, but was not fortified. Their right was on Houdenbeck Hill, a kopje a mile and a half west of the station, whilst their left was on the hills east of it.

The plan was for French with the cavalry to pass round the Boer right and threaten their communications beyond Karee Siding, whilst Le Gallais, with the mounted infantry, was to act similarly against the Boer left. Whilst these movements against the enemy's flanks and rear were in progress Tucker's division would move north-westwards against Houdenbeck Hill in echelon, the 14th brigade leading.

By 10 a.m. on March 29th, French had taken Kalkfontein, southeast of Houdenbeck Hill and Le Gallais reported that his front was clear of the enemy.

Tucker now advanced with the 14th brigade, followed by the artillery and the 15th brigade, his right flank protected by mounted infantry. By noon French reported that he was round the enemy's right flank and that he was halting under cover of scouts to the east. Before Le Gallais 200 Boers with a gun were retreating northwards.

At this time the 14th brigade was approaching the low hills east of the railway, with the 15th on its left rear occupying the kopjes to the left of the line. About a quarter to one, when it was reported that there were no Boers on the kopjes south of Karee, fire was suddenly opened on the leading infantry of the 14th brigade from in front and on both flanks. The leading companies deployed and cleared the Boers off the nearer hills.

The British artillery then began firing on Houdenbeck Hill, at a

PRIVATE CHARLES CRAMPION, D.C.M.
Awarded the Distinguished Conduct Medal for gallantry in action at Tartan, Birmah, May 4, 1889. Also a clasp to this medal for the action at Karee Siding, South Africa, March 29, 1900, when he was wounded whilst helping a wounded comrade. (*Ch. XXII*)

range of 2,300 yards, from a point south-west of Karee Siding. Under cover of this the 14th brigade on the right, with the Norfolk Regiment leading on the right, pushed forward on a line of kopjes a mile and a half east of the station, the enemy falling back before them.

Here the Norfolk battalion halted, with the King's Own Scottish Borderers on their left, and were reinforced by the Hampshire Regiment, the Lincoln Regiment being in reserve with a section of field-guns, which were dragged up a steep height, whence they gave useful support to the brigade on their right. They were within short range of the Boers, who had entrenched themselves on the farther side of a ridge, the spurs of which they held with skirmishers.

By 2 p.m. the enemy had received considerable reinforcements, including guns, and a fire fight ensued, in which the heaviest loss fell on the King's Own Scottish Borderers. Presently the front line of the 15th brigade prolonged that of the 14th with two battalions, whilst the other two were held in reserve. The rest of the artillery had now moved nearer Karee Siding and was firing on the hill west of it, from which the South Wales Borderers on the left of the 14th brigade were receiving fire as well as from the front.

After 3 p.m. French again moved eastwards, threatening the communications of the enemy, who began to withdraw, enabling the 14th brigade to get forward again.

The Boer stronghold on Houdenbeck Hill was taken after a severe fight by the East Lancashire battalion of the 15th brigade, who, when they got to the top, found the enemy gone. This relieved the South Wales Borderers, enabled them to wheel to the right in support of the Norfolk Regiment and King's Own Scottish Borderers, and determined the retreat of the enemy. Pursuit as they fell back on Brandfort was impossible, as the cavalry horses were exhausted. The horse artillery had been checked by the fire of two heavy guns and their horses too were only able to proceed at a walking pace.

In this action the total loss on the British side was one officer (of the King's Own Scottish Borderers) killed and eleven wounded, eighteen other ranks killed, 155 wounded, and three missing. The King's Own Scottish Borderers alone lost one officer killed, five wounded, eleven other ranks killed and fifty-three wounded. The casualties in the Norfolk Regiment were Colour-Sergeant Hendry killed, Captains Luard and Peebles and seventeen other ranks wounded.

The troops bivouacked on the position taken. The 15th brigade remained there and the 14th was sent, later, to watch the Modder near Krantz Kraal above Glen. Half of the Norfolk Regiment was sent, under Major Becher, on April 4th, to garrison Glen. After the transfer of General Chermside to the command of the 3rd division, in place of General Gatacre, the brigade was commanded by Major-General J. J. Maxwell.

The advance from Bloemfontein to Pretoria, a distance of 300 miles, began on May 3, 1900, with an attack on the nearest of the Boer forces at Brandfort. The town of Brandfort was held by 450 Boers, whilst a larger force under de la Rey was on a line of kopjes two miles east of the railway. Two other groups, each of three kopjes, three miles south-west of Brandfort were hurriedly occupied as the British advanced.

Against these last-named groups of kopjes Hutton went with mounted infantry. Against Brandfort the 11th British infantry division advanced. Beyond this, westwards, was General Tucker with his 15th brigade, whilst the 14th was slightly north-east of the right flank of the 15th, together with Colonel Henry's mounted infantry and two Maxim guns. The attack of these two brigades was therefore a more or less converging one. The 15th brigade was opposed by the Wakkerstrom commando, but the resistance to Maxwell's 14th brigade, by the Ermelo Boers under Grobelaar, was more determined. All efforts to close with or outflank the enemy were evaded by him, and it was only at sunset that he finally retired on Winburg, carrying off the two guns he had with him. The brigade halted for the night at Modderfontein. Meanwhile the two groups of kopjes on the west had been taken after some resistance, and Brandfort had been occupied almost without opposition. The losses on this day were not heavy: in all six men killed and one officer and twenty-nine men wounded.

The 14th brigade was next engaged at the crossing of the Vet River at Coetzee's Drift on May 5th, but the passage was effected by Hutton on the British left, and the infantry on the right, though anticipating resistance, never came into action beyond receiving the fire of some Boer long-range guns east of the railway. The brigade bivouacked near the junction of the Vet with the Taaibosch Spruit, three miles east of the railway. Next morning it had to make the passage of both streams, a matter of some difficulty owing to the nature of the channels. There was no opposition, and Smaldeel was reached on the evening of the 6th, and the brigade halted there on May 7th and 8th. On the 9th it moved forward to Merriefontein, a little short of the Zand River, about ten miles east of the railway. The passage of the Zand at Junction Drift was already in the hands of Ian Hamilton's troops, who had come up from Winburg on the right of the 7th division.

On the 10th, for the passage of the Zand, Tucker's division was, in the absence of a drift in its own front, compelled to move towards Junction Drift. Near that another drift was discovered, and by 8.45 the 7th division was across, with Hamilton's division also north of the Zand on its right. For the attack on Doornkop on his left front Tucker used the 15th brigade, supported by the Hampshire Regiment and King's Own Scottish Borderers from the 14th, so that the 2nd Norfolk Regiment were not engaged on this day. They were only under some artillery and pom-pom fire. Owing to wastage from sickness their strength was now reduced to 660. The advance to Kroonstadt, which was occupied on May 12th, was uneventful for the Norfolk Regiment, as was the halt near there till the advance of the main column recommenced on May 22nd. At Kroonstadt the battalion was joined by 105 men of the Norfolk volunteers who had accomplished the remarkable feat of covering twenty-two miles in five hours of actual marching. On the 23rd the 7th division was at Roodewal on the railway, on the 24th at Nooitgedacht. It is unnecessary to follow in detail the movements across the Vaal, the occupation of Johannesburg and the advance on Pretoria as far as Six Mile Spruit, for during that period the Norfolk Regiment was with the main body, and was nowhere engaged. The 15th brigade was left behind to garrison Johannesburg. On the evening of June 3rd the 7th division was at Leeuwkop with the 11th division, some twelve miles south of Six Mile Spruit. The Boers were in position beyond the spruit south-west of Pretoria, on the foremost of two parallel ridges about two miles from the spruit. Lord Roberts's plan of attack was, as usual, a wide turning movement round the enemy's right by French and Ian Hamilton, combined with a frontal attack by the 7th and 11th divisions. As soon as the advance began on June 4th the Boers abandoned the southern ridge, leaving open the passage of the spruit, and took post on the farther side, with their left resting on Fort Schanzkop, the southern outlying fort of Pretoria.

The southern ridge was occupied by British mounted infantry about 10.30 a.m. Holding it dismounted in extended order, they awaited the arrival of the 7th and 11th divisions, which, after their thirteen mile march, crossed the spruit at noon. Advancing to the first ridge the 19th brigade of the 11th division stood on the left, with the 14th on its right. On the left Ian Hamilton had been called in from following the wide movement of French's cavalry. Tucker was about to attack the farther ridge when he received orders to await the arrival of Hamilton. About 3.30 p.m. the 19th brigade of Hamilton's force was on the left of the nearer ridge opposite the Boer right, with the 14th brigade on its right. Farther to the right the 11th and Guards brigades were moving against the left of the Boer position, which was being bombarded all along by a very superior artillery. Fort Schanzkop was soon found by artillery fire to be abandoned.

The 7th division, represented by the 14th brigade, had very little fighting, for the Boers gradually edged to their right along their ridge, and presently Hamilton decided to turn their right with de Lisle's mounted infantry, a movement which soon decided the Boers to abandon their position precipitately. The 14th and 19th brigades then advanced and occupied it. Major Becher's diary describes the action of the battalion on this day as "a long-range desultory fire fight across a valley between two rocky ridges three or four miles west of the town."

It had early become apparent that no serious attempt to defend the capital was contemplated. At 5 a.m. on June 5, 1900, Pretoria surrendered unconditionally.

The total loss in the action of the 4th was only twenty-seven killed and wounded, none of whom belonged to the Norfolk Regiment.

When Lord Roberts marched eastwards from Pretoria on June 7th the Norfolk Regiment was left, with the rest of the 14th brigade, to garrison the capital, whilst the other brigade (15th) of the 7th division performed the same duty in Johannesburg.

The battalion, with its head-quarters in the Pretoria Barracks, occupied the old Boer outlying forts with detachments.

In the middle of July the troops were rearranged and the garrison of Pretoria was formed of the 2nd Norfolk, 2nd Lincolnshire, 2nd Duke of Cornwall's Light Infantry, and 2nd Hampshire Regiments. The only incident during the regiment's occupation of Pretoria and the neighbourhood which calls for notice is the Boer attack on the outpost at Zuurfontein station, between Johannesburg and Pretoria, in the beginning of January, 1901. The post was garrisoned by a detachment of the Norfolk and some of the Lincolnshire Regiments. The Boers, guided by a Kafir through the only entrance in the wire entanglements round the station, captured an outpost and attacked the station for two hours, during which the rifle fire (there were no guns in action) was very heavy. Finally the enemy were beaten off with a loss of several killed and wounded. The Norfolk detachment lost two men killed and two wounded.

The period of regular warfare and anything approaching pitched battles closed with the dispersion of the Boer forces and the occupation of both capitals. Thereafter was the long period of guerilla warfare, against leaders like de Wet and de la Rey, which lasted into 1902.

Early in October, 1901, the 2nd Norfolk Regiment was at Rustenburg, eighty miles from Pretoria. They had been sent there in April by Lord Kitchener under Lieutenant-Colonel C. E. Borton, who in January 1901, had assumed command of the battalion in succession to Colonel Phillips, and was accompanied by a large convoy of one hundred ox wagons, a detachment of mounted infantry, and two field guns. The march from Pretoria to Rustenburg encountered no opposition beyond some sniping.

On arrival of the column at Rustenburg, the whole force there, under Colonel Doran, with the Argyll and Sutherland Highlanders and a field battery, returned to Pretoria, leaving Colonel Borton to hold the Rustenburg area with a force about half of that which it replaced. The area included Oliphant's Nek, Magato's Nek, and the straggling country town itself.

Colonel Borton's force had been there nearly six months on a very strenuous service, due to the necessity of adapting the outpost line to the reduced numbers available. The men never got more than two nights in bed consecutively; often they were up every other night. They only got convoys of food and letters three times in the period.

It was at the end of this time that General Kekewich's column was heavily attacked by de la Rey at Moedwil, and narrowly escaped destruction. At the time of that attack Colonel Borton had a strong detachment, under Captain Marriott, at Magato's Nek, within a few miles of Moedwil, and about six miles from Rustenburg. Most of Kekewich's Kafirs and loose horses fled during the attack to Magato's Nek, and thither also the wounded were sent on their way to Rustenburg, on which place Kekewich's column fell back to refit.

When this had been completed, the 2nd Norfolk Regiment took the place in Kekewich's column of the 1st Derbyshire Regiment, which had been badly knocked about at Moedwil and was now left to garrison Rustenburg.

On October 13th Kekewich took his column from Magato's Nek northwards to Bashoek on the Zeerust-Rustenburg road to await Lord Methuen, who was to join him in the pursuit of de la Rey. After getting in touch with Lord Methuen from Rietfontein Kekewich returned to Bashoek, Methuen again going westwards.

On October 28th Kekewich marched eastwards against hostile forces which he had heard of in the angle between the Eland and Crocodile Rivers. Before dawn the column was at Hartebeestspruit, where he found that the principal Boer force was at Beestekraal, twenty-five miles farther east. At 8 p.m. on the 29th he sent his mounted men to surprise Beestekraal and started off his infantry, including the Norfolk battalion, shortly afterwards. Before the infantry could arrive the mounted troops had disposed of the Boers, taking their farms and capturing seventy-eight prisoners. The whole force was back at Rustenburg on November 2nd.

On the 4th it again started to meet Lord Methuen. When the two forces met at Brakfontein on the 11th they found that the hunt for de la Rey was to be suspended whilst a movement was made against large bodies reported to be assembling in the Klerksdorp area. Kekewich accordingly moved southwards to Ventersdorp, where he arrived on the 15th, and on the 18th both his and Methuen's columns were in Klerksdorp.

On the 26th Methuen, with Kekewich's and Hickie's columns on his right, moved westwards through Hartebeestfontein. Kekewich also operated round that place, but could never get into touch with a considerable Boer force, the presence of which in the neighbourhood was indicated. The column returned to Klerksdorp on December 3rd with three prisoners and a quantity of booty. Lord Methuen, who had been more fortunate in another direction, returned to Klerksdorp next day. On December 11th both columns again moved westwards. Kekewich moved some distance away from Methuen's right, which he protected from 300 Boers from Witpoort under Vermaes. On the 13th there was a short fight with these which cost Kekewich's column two officers and eight men wounded. On the 15th Kekewich was at Rooipoort, whilst Methuen turned south after Potgieter's column, which doubled back northwards into the Makwasie Berg. Kekewich, though he did not receive Methuen's request to do so, moved on Palmietfontein and effectually, though without fighting, prevented the Boers from bolting from their covert in that direction. On the 20th both columns were back in Klerksdorp, the lion's share of the booty again falling to Methuen's column.

On December 27th Methuen and Kekewich again started for a foray towards the Makwasie Berg and Wolmaranstad. They found nothing in the former, and Lord Methuen went off westward towards Vryburg. Kekewich had failed to catch Potgieter as he broke northwards from the covert of the mountains, and, being out of touch with Methuen, he hunted small bands of Boers in his own neighbourhood. On January 2, 1902, he had a success against one lot, which was avenged by an ambush set for his scouts, in which he lost an officer and thirteen troopers. That day he was at Holfontein looking out for Methuen. Being now aware of the presence of Kemp and de la Rey not far north of him, he moved forward north-westwards. On January 4th, finding that de la Rey and Kemp were out of reach, he returned to Klerksdorp, which he reached on the 9th with twenty-six prisoners and 7,000 beasts. The difficulty in the Western Transvaal was to find any definite body of the enemy against which to operate.

After the return of Kekewich to Klerksdorp on January 9th his column was at Rietfontein, covering the construction of a blockhouse line. Up to the 29th it had taken twenty-eight prisoners in raids on small parties of Boers, the most important being at Brakpan on the 16th.

On February 1st the column was joined by that of Hickie from Tafel Kop and began moving northward, as the blockhouses were extended in the direction of Lichtenburg. De la Rey was reported to be at Roodepan, and other Boer camps were in that neighbourhood.

On February 4th a mounted force was sent after de la Rey, but found he was gone. However, it came upon Commandant Sarel Alberts, surprised his lager, and captured his force entire. The infantry at Leuwfontein had no part in this affair, beyond marching out westwards to cover the return of the mounted party.

Kekewich remained on the road to Lichtenburg till the blockhouses were completed on February 21st, when he was ordered back to Klerksdorp. On the 25th, at Hartebeestfontein, hearing of the loss of a convoy from Von Donop's column, he moved to Wolmaranstad, where he joined that officer, now in command of Methuen's column. The convoy had been captured, after a severe fight, by de la Rey, on its last march to Klerksdorp. De la Rey had disappeared as usual after his success.

Kekewich now had under him Hickie's column, of which the command had been handed over to Lieutenant-Colonel Grenfell. On the 28th Kekewich sent Grenfell with some 1,700 mounted men northwards to Rietfontein, and himself left on March 2nd with the infantry. On the 4th they were back in Klerksdorp.

Lord Methuen, who was at Vryburg, after handing over to Von Donop the actual command of his column, now requested Kekewich to send a force to meet him south of Lichtenburg on the 7th. He himself was bringing a column, hastily collected at Vryburg under Major Paris,

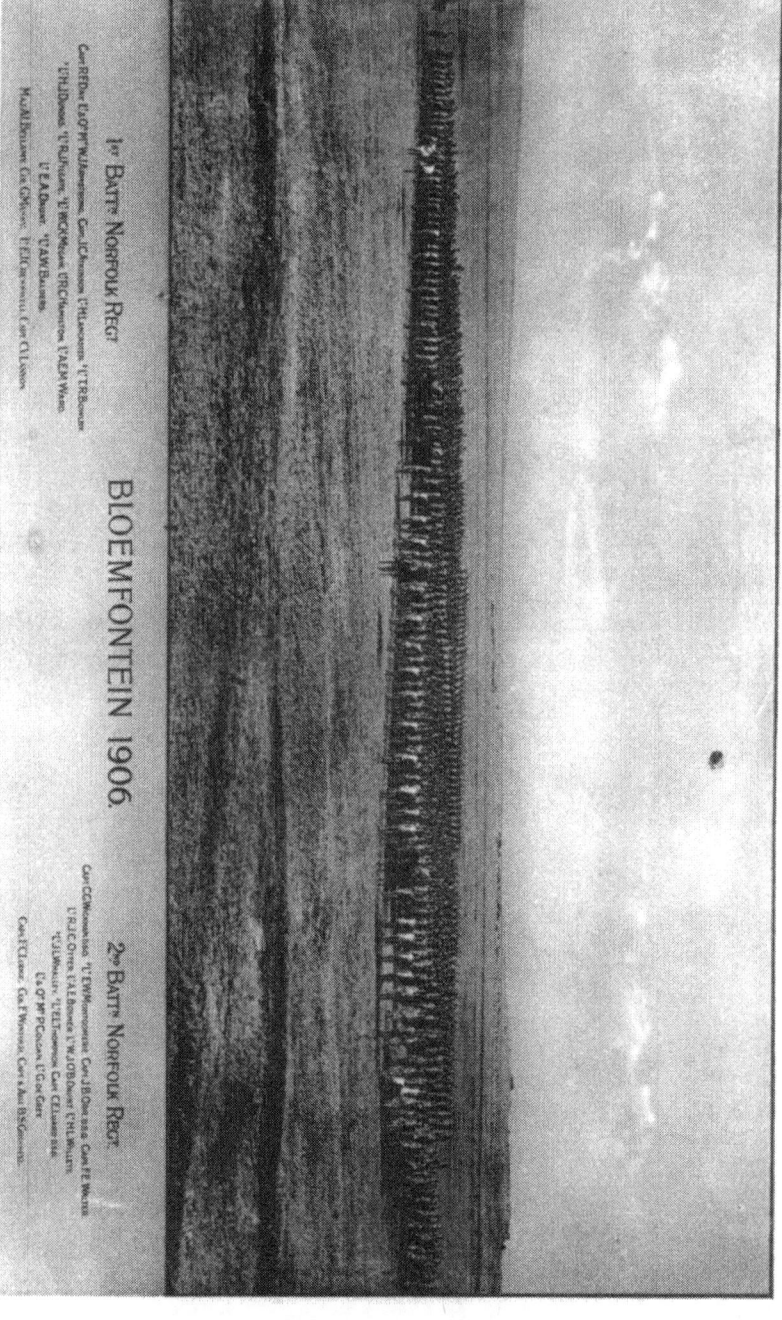

BLOEMFONTEIN, 1906. (Ch. XXIII)

and had ordered another under Colonel Rochfort to move northwards from the Vaal and drive De la Rey on to Kekewich and Paris about Rooirantjesfontein. To comply with Methuen's request, Kekewich sent Grenfell's force above mentioned. Grenfell duly arrived at Rooirantjesfontein on February 8th, but Methuen did not, for his column had been destroyed and himself wounded and taken by De la Rey at Tweebosch.

The disaster of Tweebosch severely shook the British position in the Western Transvaal, and Lord Kitchener's special attention was directed to reinforcing the troops there, and to the problem of finding De la Rey, with a force strong enough to beat him when found.

The main body of the 2nd Norfolk Regiment was sent to reinforce the garrison of Lichtenburg, but three companies of them were equally divided between the mobile columns of Von Donop and Grenfell, both being under the command of Kekewich. These columns were concentrated at Vaalbank, on the line of blockhouses connecting the Schoon Spruit with Lichtenburg, on March 22nd, and next evening started on a forty-mile march westwards in close order. There they faced about and extended north and south, so as to form a line with its left on the line of blockhouses, and its right at Geluk on the Little Harts River, where it touched the next force, Sir H. Rawlinson's, in the line of beaters of the country eastwards. The difficulties of this drive were very great, and the results were inconsiderable as regards captures of men. To Kekewich's columns fell only thirty-eight prisoners; but they also retook three field guns and two Vickers-Maxims lost at Tweebosch with Von Donop's convoy. Most units had some fighting with Boers slipping through the cordon, and all were fairly worn out when they again reached their starting point after an eighty-mile march. On March 29th Kekewich with his two columns, including the three companies of the 2nd Norfolk Regiment, fortified himself at Middelbult south of Lichtenburg, and on the 31st pushed out a night expedition towards Leeuwpan in search of De la Rey, who was reported to the westward. It found nothing, though there was some fighting on its left with parts of F. W. Kitchener's force, at Boschbult, where De la Rey was eventually repulsed. The Boer leader once more disappeared.

On April 8th Sir Ian Hamilton arrived at Middelbult to take command of the columns of Kekewich, F. W. Kitchener, and Sir H. Rawlinson operating in the Western Transvaal, and of a fourth column, under Colonel Thorneycroft, preparing to join him from Klerksdorp. He was now about to carry out a drive southwards, with his troops arranged in a semicircle on the Brakspruit. Kekewich, on the right of this advance, was entrenched on the night of April 10th at Rooiwal, near the mouth of the Brakspruit, with Rawlinson on his left about Boschpan, and F. W. Kitchener at Klipdrift to the south-east. Kekewich's column, on which an attack was anticipated, moved southwards on the 11th in battle formation, under orders to reconnoitre beyond the Harts River on his right. The columns on his left were closing in to his assistance.

As Von Donop, with Kekewich's mounted advanced guard, was moving westwards on the left bank of the Brakspruit, he encountered Kemp's Boers moving against Kekewich's right, which Kemp believed to be farther east than it really was. Kekewich over-night had really been farther east than was intended, and was now marching, with Von Donop on his right, and Grenfell on his left, to get to the left bank of the Harts River. At first Von Donop thought the Boers marching parallel to him were part of Rawlinson's force. It was not long after 7 a.m. when the mistake was discovered as the long Boer line of some 2,700 mounted riflemen advanced firing from the saddle and the British mounted men fell back on their supports. The Boer centre was now advancing in a close line against Grenfell's men, whose left they outflanked. As they appeared on the sky-line of the gentle slope leading down to the Brakspruit, Grenfell's troops were rapidly deployed, and Von Donop's also deployed, less rapidly, on their right. The Boer extreme left threatened to outflank even Von Donop's right. When Grenfell's deployment was complete the Boer line was within 600 yards, some 800 of them opposed to 1,500 rifles, besides six guns, all pouring a furious fire on the enemy as he moved forward riding knee to knee, and sometimes three or four deep. The British rifle fire was not so damaging as it might have been, for many of the troops were irregulars. We may safely assume that the better-trained fire of the Norfolk men contributed more than its share to the losses, which, at last, when the Boers' line was only 300 yards off, produced the psychological crisis when men begin to hesitate and an attack is on the point of breaking. A few came on, led by the gallant Potgieter, who fell dead within seventy yards of the British line. The moment for the counter-attack had come. Kekewich had only lost at this time seven killed and fifty-six wounded from the fire of the Boers from the saddle. His troops had displayed great coolness and steadiness, but the moment for counter-attack was missed and the Boers retired, leaving fifty dead and thirty badly wounded on the field.

Assistance from Rawlinson now came up and the Boers retired southwards, though a small force, which was disregarded, threatened Von Donop's right and rear.

By 9.30 a.m. Hamilton's troops were ready for the general pursuit, which he ordered. As they advanced, Kemp's force fled south and south-west. For Kekewich the pursuit ended at Nooitgedacht, where his now exhausted troops finished their day with the recapture of two field guns and a pom-pom taken by the Boers at Tweebosch.

The losses of the Norfolk battalion in this action of Rooival (or Rodeval) were Lieutenant P. Hamond (volunteer company) dangerously wounded and five men wounded, three of them severely.

Hamilton's command, having failed to round up the rest of Kemp's force, returned to Klerksdorp to refit and to prepare for the next drive, which began on April 25th, with the object of herding the scattered Boers into the angle between Vryburg and the western boundary of the Transvaal, where there were no natural or artificial obstacles to form the walls of the corral. The idea was to push farther west than the Boers expected, get to the west of them, and then, facing about and extending, to once more drive them on the blockhouses eastwards. On May 6th Kekewich was facing west at Rooirantjesfontein. By May 10th the whole British line was on the frontier between the Transvaal and British Bechuanaland, from which the Boers who had passed the frontier endeavoured to break back through Hamilton's line in the night. Their efforts were in vain, and next day nearly 400 surrendered.

Peace was now in the air and was signed on May 31st. The fighting for the 2nd Norfolk Regiment was over. If, in all these marches with Kekewich, the Norfolk men had had little actual fighting, they had

had extremely hard and responsible duties. When Kekewich's column was alone, composed as it was mainly of mounted and irregular troops, it depended for security in the shape of advanced, rear, and flank guards on its one regular battalion, the 2nd Norfolk, on the march. Marches were rapid, and every change of direction of the column necessarily entailed very heavy work on the flank guard on the outer side of the turn. At night, too, Kekewich had to depend on the Norfolk Regiment for his most important outposts. One great difficulty was the question of how to reinforce, or cover, an outpost suddenly attacked on the trackless veld, where generally there was no landmark to indicate the exact direction of an outpost. The plan resorted to, on the suggestion of Colonel Borton, was this: it was argued that the simplest plan of covering an outpost from the central camp was by rifle or machine-gun fire directed from the rear. With a parapet in front of the outpost, and nothing in rear to protect it from the fire of its friends, this was of course impracticable. The difficulty was got over by digging in with very little protection against the enemy in front, but a strong *parados* between the outpost and the camp. With this protection it was safe to fire over the heads of the outpost, which was saved from the danger of bullets from the rear by the bullet proof *parados*. The Boer was not the man to carry a trench by a charge, and the British troops, lying in a shallow saucer-like trench below the ground level, could well afford to dispense with a raised parapet in front in exchange for the added volume of fire from behind, rendered possible by the *parados*.

Testimony was borne to the efficiency of these arrangements by the Boer Commander Sellers, whom Colonel Borton met and conversed with after the peace. Asked why, on the many occasions on which he had been opposed to Kekewich, he had not attacked, he replied: "How could I? You were never out of our sight day or night for ten days [on a certain Trek], but you never gave one a chance; on the march you were surrounded by those d——d foothangers, who could not run away if we charged in, who would only lie down and shoot. Then every camp you vacated we visited and saw the fortifications you always dug to protect your outposts."

During the five and a half months the Norfolk Regiment was with

General Kekewich, it was the only infantry battalion still on trek with mounted troops. All the others were either in country towns like Rustenburg or else in blockhouses.

The Mounted Infantry Company

We must now trace the doings of the Mounted Infantry Company of the Norfolk Regiment. The trained mounted infantry had left Fermoy under Lieutenant J. B. Orr before the battalion was mobilized. On the voyage out H company, under Captain C. Ross, was earmarked for mounted infantry, and apparently was amalgamated with the men who had gone in advance. The whole (numbering four officers and 164 other ranks) was commanded by Captain (now Major-General) C. Ross. That officer has furnished an amusing account of the general ignorance, at first, of horse management among officers and men. One volunteer's qualification consisted in his having been a bus conductor who had been accustomed to harnessing and unharnessing the horses. The best man at horse management was handicapped by a weight of nineteen stone, which no mounted infantry pony could possibly carry. He had to be detailed to the remount department.

Sore backs were common among the Argentine ponies, which, with many difficulties, were at last got into order when they were made over to the company at Orange River. Before Paardeberg was reached thirty per cent of the ponies were suffering from sore backs or wrung withers. The men, too, had a good deal to learn in the way of riding. Nevertheless, the company soon gained a golden reputation.

The company was attached to the 7th Battalion Mounted Infantry in the force under the command of Colonel Bainbridge. We shall endeavour as far as possible to disentangle the doings of the Norfolk company from those of the rest of the 7th Mounted Infantry; but, as in the days when grenadier battalions were formed from the grenadier companies of many regiments, it is not always possible to distinguish one company from the whole battalion. Thanks to the courtesy of General Ross we are able to do a good deal more in this direction than was possible with the grenadier companies of older wars.

The strength of the 7th mounted infantry battalion when first organized was 450. In Lord Roberts's advance against Cronje they were attached to the force under Colonel Hannay. They should have joined French's force at Ramdam on February 9, 1900, but owing to bad staff work at head-quarters they only reached Ramah at 7 a.m. on the 10th, where they halted for the day. Thence Colonel de Lisle was sent with 1,300 men towards Wolvekraal. As de Lisle found the enemy too strong there, he was reinforced next morning by the 2nd and 7th Mounted Infantry and Kitchener's Horse. Hannay, agreeing that the Boers in the hills were still too strong to be attacked, ordered a retirement, but not before some of his men had come in contact with the Boers and suffered some loss. The convoy which they were protecting had meanwhile passed.

The next affair in which the 7th Mounted Infantry were engaged was de Wet's attack on the "supply park" at Waterval on February 15th. As soon as the news of the attack on the convoy was received the 7th Mounted Infantry, under Colonel Bainbridge, was ordered back, and arrived about noon. As attempts were made to move the convoy the Boers fired heavily on it with guns and rifles. Colonel Bainbridge now endeavoured to turn the Boer right, hoping to be able to clear them out entirely when infantry reinforcements came up. The infantry on arrival, after 2 p.m., were too exhausted by their march to do anything, and the mounted infantry, having arrived within 600 yards of the enemy, were driven back in some confusion.

In the end Roberts decided to abandon the convoy and the 7th Mounted Infantry had no more fighting here. They went to Wegdraai on the 16th. That night at 11 p.m. they marched with the Highland brigade for Klip Kraal Drift, which they reached on the 17th. There had been an action there on the previous day.

On the 18th most of the 7th Mounted Infantry were on the left of Kitchener's attack on Paardeberg; but the Norfolk company was separated early from the other three, and eventually found itself in the right attack, on the upstream side of the Boer lager. We can therefore disregard the action of the other three companies.

Before the 7th Mounted Infantry received its orders for the day the Norfolk company was detached as escort to a battery. On joining the battery, the services of the company as escort were found not to be required, and Captain Ross, not knowing what had become of the rest of the battalion, judged that the east flank was the more important and moved in that direction. Presently he met Lord Kitchener, who directed him to cross the drift about three miles upstream and attack the Boer lager by the north bank as quickly as possible.

Near the drift Colonel Hannay was met and ordered the company to clear two kopjes on the south bank just beyond the drift. When that had been done, about 1 p.m., the company was sent, dismounted, to the north bank and ordered to attack a small white house on the north bank two or three miles west of where it then was. Captain Ross had about twenty of his own men and a dozen of another mounted infantry unit. The rest of his company were crossing with Lieutenant Cramer Roberts,[1] one of his subalterns.

Captain Ross's detachment had arrived within 1,000 yards of the white house in extended order (eight paces) and been fired on. They were moving parallel to the river when Cramer Roberts's portion joined their left, between it and the river. Across its front was a narrow valley, apparently open to enfilade fire from the left bank. As Ross was swinging his right round to turn the head of it, heavy rifle fire passed over his head directed at something behind him. The target was Hannay, charging with thirty or forty mounted infantry and some led ponies, who galloped through and passed the valley under heavy enfilading fire. They disappeared beyond the farther bank, and appear to have galloped into a wire fence, where Hannay was killed. Ross following, over a bare slope heavily enfiladed, collected his men under the only shelter, a small knoll on the hill short of the white house. There he extended, facing south, with the white house 700 or 800 yards on his right. It appears that most of the rest of the company were unable to cross the valley, and in trying to do so Lieutenant Cramer Roberts was wounded. The main attack was by both banks of the Modder from the east, and most of the Norfolk company becoming involved in it, retreated

[1] This officer was afterwards taken prisoner by the Turks at Kut in 1916 and recently died, partly it is believed in consequence of ill-treatment whilst in captivity.

when it was repulsed. Meanwhile Captain Ross with twenty or thirty men lay on the crest of the ridge, looking down an open slope towards the river, with British shells exploding 200 to 500 yards in front of him, and British rifle fire from the south bank striking within fifty yards.

After dark, hearing that Cramer Roberts was wounded, Ross went and found him, with half a dozen other wounded men, behind the knoll. He then returned to the drift and fetched some ammunition, but no food. The night was spent at the knoll, and in the morning Ross was ordered back to the drift. As some of the wounded were too bad to be moved, all were left, with Cramer Roberts and a white flag (a white sweater). They were gathered in by the Boers, who treated them with the greatest kindness. Ross then recrossed at the drift and returned to Paardeberg Drift, where the ponies were found. Only Ross and Cramer Roberts had been with the mounted infantry on this day. The other two officers, Lieutenants Hylton-Jolliffe and Wickham, had been taken as gallopers, and on that duty Hylton-Jolliffe was killed. The company had been hurried into action in driblets as it got across the river, and got mixed up with other mounted infantry units. The men only rejoined their own company by degrees during the next two or three days.[1]

After Paardeberg the Norfolk company continued with the 7th Mounted Infantry to Bloemfontein, where we lose the guidance of Captain Ross, who was no longer with it. There is unfortunately no record enabling us to trace the doings of the Norfolk company, as distinguished from the rest of the 7th Mounted Infantry, and it is not considered desirable to follow in detail the actions of the latter as a regiment. It was with Ian Hamilton's Winburg column at the end of April, and was under fire at Koranna Spruit, and again at the crossing of the Zand River on May 19th. It had little fighting in the rest of the advance to Pretoria, and at Diamond Hill on June 11th and 12th it only played a watching part.

At the end of June it was with Sir Archibald Hunter at Heidelberg and Frankfort, mainly employed on guarding and escorting supplies.

---

[1] The above account of Paardeberg is almost verbatim that kindly furnished by Major-General C. Ross, C.B., D.S.O.

After that it was engaged in Bruce Hamilton's operations about Spitzkranz, which ended in the surrender of Prinzloo's force.

In October and November, 1900, came the operations in the Free State, including the affair at Bothaville when Colonel Le Gallais, after surprising the Boer lager, was killed. The 7th Mounted Infantry were then with Le Gallais's reserve, which was hurried up to his support.

In the early part of 1901 the 7th Mounted Infantry, including the Norfolk company, were in Pilcher's column during Knox's operations to prevent de Wet's projected attack on Cape Colony. There was much hard marching and shortage of food, but no fighting for the 7th Mounted Infantry. In the end de Wet succeeded in evading Knox's column.

After this there were various operations, drives, and clearing of the enemy in areas surrounding fixed points. In none of these is it possible to identify the precise part played by the Norfolk company, as distinguished from the rest of the 7th Mounted Infantry. It is therefore beyond our province to describe them in detail.

The last operations in which the 7th Mounted Infantry were employed consisted in the protection, in March and April, 1902, of the constabulary posts in the north-west of the Free State against de Wet.

The casualties of the 2nd Norfolk Regiment during the South African war were as follows :—

	Killed or Died of Wounds.	Died of Disease.	Wounded.	Captured by Enemy.	Missing	Total.
Officers	4	—	5	2	—	11
N.C.O.'s and men	11	55	39	15	2	122

One more man died of disease with the Natal force. It is not known under what circumstances he was there. These losses appear to include those of the mounted infantry company.

The officers killed or died of wounds were : Lieutenant R. H. Buxton,

Lieutenant Oliver and 2nd Lieutenant A. L. Grove of the 2nd Battalion, and Lieutenant J. C. Hylton-Jolliffe of the 3rd.

The Militia Battalions.

The 3rd battalion was embodied on January 26, 1900, and remained so till April 11, 1902. It was actively employed in South Africa, as will now be narrated.

After the initial disasters of the war, when Lord Roberts had gone out to take the chief command, Lord Lansdowne telegraphed to him, on January 9, 1900, that seven militia battalions, from those who had volunteered for service overseas, would be sent for lines of communication duty. To this Lord Roberts replied, on the 12th, that he would require another eight militia battalions for the same purpose, and would be glad even of thirteen. That was a time when, under the pressure of public opinion in England, all his demands were complied with, and by April 2, 1900, thirty-six militia battalions, all of course with their own consent, had left England, thirty of them for South Africa.

By the time Lord Roberts was ready to start operations he had nineteen militia battalions distributed on his lines of communication in Cape Colony. When he started from Bloemfontein for Pretoria he had twenty-three battalions to hold the three railways leading northwards through Cape Colony. The Norfolk battalions had been amongst the majority who had, as soon as they were asked, volunteered for foreign service.

The 3rd battalion embarked on February 25, 1900, with twenty-two officers and 503 other ranks. After a short stay near Cape Town they were sent on by sea to East London, where they disembarked on March 21st. By April 4th the battalion was concentrated at Bethulie Bridge, whence they proceeded to Springfontein and Edenburg in the Orange Free State, dropping on the way detachments to guard various bridges and culverts on the main line from Capetown to Bloemfontein.

On July 13, 1900, the head-quarters of the battalion moved to the railway crossing at Kafir River, midway between Edenburg and Bloemfontein, guarding the railway with detachments in blockhouses at various points of a section fifty miles in length between those two places. Colonel Custance, the officer commanding the battalion, was given the command of the whole section.

The guard of this section was anything but a sinecure, for Kaffir River was a favourite spot for crossing the railway by enemy despatch riders, and the blockhouses were frequently attacked. On this section the battalion remained for exactly twelve months, when it was sent south to Norval's Pont, the place where the railway crosses the Orange River, the frontier between Cape Colony and the Free State. From there they occupied blockhouses for a distance of twelve miles south and eighteen miles north of the Orange River. Here, too, they were exposed to frequent attacks, but elaborate defences, in the shape of barbed wire and trenches parallel to the line, combined with excellent telephonic communication between the posts, enabled them to render the railway a barrier almost unpassable by the Boers.

The work in small detachments was extremely trying to the men, though their actual casualties (eleven men killed or died of disease) were not heavy. One of their officers (Lieutenant Hylton-Jolliffe) was killed, but he was not with the battalion. He lost his life whilst acting as galloper at Paardeberg. The battalion remained in this position till nearly the end of the war in 1902, when it embarked for England and was disembodied.

The honours awarded to individuals were: C.B., Colonel Custance; D.S.O., Major Beale, Captains Bagge, and Harbord; D.C.M., Sergeant-Major Tunnell, Quartermaster-Sergeant Quantrell, and Sergeant Vincent. The medals given to all who served in South Africa were the Queen's South Africa medal, with clasps "Cape Colony" and "Orange Free State," and the King's South Africa medal, with clasps "1901—1902." The battalion was authorized to bear on its colours and appointments the words "South Africa 1900–1902."

Colonel Kerrison, who commanded the 4th battalion, has supplied some notes on it during the South African War from which the following are extracted:—

On May 1, 1900 the battalion was mobilized and collected at Norwich, whence it was sent to Colchester and accommodated in huts with three other militia battalions; Major Dods, an old Norfolk regular officer was adjutant and Captain Grehan quartermaster.

Soon after it arrived all the details of the 1st, 2nd and 3rd battalions were attached, and amongst them was the 1st battalion band.

The battalion volunteered for service abroad but the offer was not accepted. On October 16th the men were accommodated in new barracks which had just been completed as far as the men's quarters were concerned, but as the quarters for the officers were not finished they were put into the Cavalry Barracks.

Early in 1901 the battalion was again asked to volunteer for service abroad, which they did, but were only sent, on April 29th, to Guernsey, where they were quartered in the Citadel.

Whilst at Colchester the inauguration of the Australian Commonwealth was carried out and picked men were sent from every arm of the service and from different regiments. Forty men of the 4th Norfolk Regiment were sent to represent the militia.

On July 16, 1901, the battalion was sent back to England and disembodied. Soon after the embodiment a company of mounted rifles was formed and sent out to South Africa and gained considerable credit, one of the junior officers, Lieutenant Hamond, being given the D.S.O., and as he subsequently joined the regulars he was then the youngest officer in the army with that distinction.

After the battalion was disembodied some of the officers were kept on to serve with the details of the Lincoln Regiment, who were sent to Guernsey to take the place of the 4th Norfolk Regiment.

In 1902 the battalion was not called out for training, but in 1903 it was at Colchester for its month's training.

In 1904 the battalion was encamped on Mousehold for training.

THE VOLUNTEER BATTALIONS

At the commencement of the war, when serious trouble was not anticipated, the Government refused many offers from volunteer battalions and others. By the beginning of 1900 their views had changed with the course of events, and in his telegram of January 9th, Lord

Lansdowne told Lord Roberts that he was accepting the offers of service by volunteers at the rate of one company for each battalion at the front.

Volunteers for service in South Africa were invited from the four Norfolk volunteer battalions, a call which was freely responded to, not only by offers of suitable officers and men, but also in the subscription of funds to provide them on service with luxuries not supplied by Government.

At a meeting of the commanding officers of the four battalions at Norwich arrangements were elaborated for uniforms and equipment for the men selected, and officers and men for two companies were selected as follows :—

1st Volunteer Service Company :
  Captain G. F. Archdale, 3rd Volunteer Battalion.
  Lieutenant B. H. L. Prior, 1st   do.
  Lieutenant H. L. Willett, 4th   do.
  And 115 other ranks.

2nd Volunteer Service Company :
  Captain A. W. M. Atthill, 2nd Volunteer Battalion.
  Lieutenant W. J. Barton, 3rd   do.
  Lieutenant J. E. Hotson, 4th   do.
  And 115 other ranks.

Captain Archdale being unfortunately incapacitated by illness, Captain W. Diver of the 2nd battalion took his place in command of the First Service Company.

The original idea was that the volunteer company for each battalion was to form a 9th company, replacing the mounted infantry company taken from it.

The First Service Company embarked for South Africa on the " Doune Castle " in February, 1900 ; the second was despatched by the " Kildonan Castle " on March 16th.

On arrival the companies were attached to the 2nd battalion, and the history of that battalion's doings in South Africa equally describes those of the two volunteer service companies, which formed an inseparable part of it. A third detachment of sixty men went out in March, 1902, and returned in August.

For the services in the campaign of these two companies, representing the four battalions of Norfolk volunteers, the latter were authorized to bear on their appointments and colours the inscription " South Africa 1900-1902," and those serving in the two companies of course received the same medals as the officers and men of the 2nd battalion.

In April, 1901, the reinforcements sent out to South Africa and the general position of affairs enabled Lord Kitchener to dispense with a number of the volunteer companies who had so nobly come forward for service abroad. Amongst the twenty-three companies sent home was the First Volunteer Service Company of the Norfolk Regiment, which sailed on April 22, 1901, from Cape Town.

On their arrival at Norwich on May 16th they had a splendid reception from a dense crowd as they marched to the Market Place. There they were addressed in complimentary terms by the Mayor, Mr. J. J. Dawson Paul, and silver medals were presented by the Mayoress. After this ceremony the company, under the command of Captain Diver, was entertained at dinner by the Mayor at the Agricultural Hall.

The second company remained with the battalion in the operations under Kekewich and only sailed from Cape Town on May 7, 1902. At Norwich, on May 27th, they were received with the same honours as the first company and were entertained at dinner at the Maid's Head by the Sheriff of Norwich, Colonel H. T. S. Patteson.

The third detachment and one hundred reservists returning in August, 1902, met with a similar reception.

The 2nd battalion on its return reached Colchester on February 10, 1903. Next day its colours were returned to it and war medals were presented by General Gatacre. On the 16th, on the invitation of the Mayor of Norwich, Lieutenant-Colonel J. R. Harvey, D.S.O., the battalion went by train to Norwich under the command of Lieutenant-Colonel C. E. Borton, C.B. After marching through the city, welcomed by a great crowd, it was entertained to dinner at St. Andrew's Hall at the expense of the citizens. The address of the Mayor was responded to by Colonel Borton, and after dinner the regiment, except about 150 men going on furlough, were seen off by their hosts on their return journey to Colchester, where they were to reorganize.

Later, on April 9th, at Colchester, Colonel Harvey presented to the regiment a handsome gold cup in commemoration of their recent visit to Norwich and of their service in South Africa. The cup was subscribed for by the inhabitants of Norwich and the county of Norfolk.

On November 17th, 1904, a memorial to the Norfolk men who died in the war was unveiled on Castle Meadow, Norwich. It consists of a bronze figure of Peace, nine feet high, standing on a granite pedestal thirty feet high. On it some 300 names are inscribed, including Norfolk men of other corps as well as those of the Norfolk Regiment. It was unveiled by General Wynne. Two windows in the Cathedral were also put up in memory of officers and men of the Norfolk Regiment, with tablets bearing their names.

In 1904 Lieutenant-Colonel Wintour, C.B., took over command from Colonel C. E. Borton, who had held it since March, 1901. After spending three years at Colchester the 2nd battalion was sent back to South Africa in 1905, and was, as already mentioned, stationed at Bloemfontein along with the 1st battalion. There, in 1906, there was erected in the old cemetery a monument to the memory of the officers, non-commissioned officers, and men who fell in the South African War.

From Bloemfontein the 2nd battalion was transferred, in October, 1908, to Gibraltar, and thence, in February, 1911, it embarked for Bombay to be stationed at Belgaum.

Colonel A. H. Luard, who commanded the battalion at this time, writes that, to his personal knowledge, during the twelve months after its landing in India, there were only four cases of drunkenness, though it was not a "teetotal" corps. The canteen books showed an average daily consumption of less than one pint of beer per man. There was no crime, and only one court martial for a civil, not a military, offence.

On November 25, 1911, it returned to Bombay temporarily for the visit of Their Majesties King George V (colonel-in-chief of the regiment) and Queen Mary. It furnished the guard of honour, which remained in Bombay during the whole of the Royal visit. After taking part in the lining of the streets on December 3rd and 4th, the battalion returned to Belgaum on the 6th. It was, however, represented at the Delhi durbar by a colour party consisting of Lieutenant-Colonel A. H. Luard,

D.S.O., 2nd Lieutenants H. E. Hall and R. T. Frere, and three other ranks.

At Belgaum the battalion remained till the 3rd November, 1914, when it embarked, under the command of Lieutenant-Colonel E. C. Peebles, D.S.O., for the Persian Gulf to play its part in the Great War of 1914-18. Colonel Peebles had succeeded Colonel Luard in command on September 1, 1912.

The 4th, 5th and 6th Battalions 1909-1914

In 1908 Mr. Haldane's reorganization of the forces of the United Kingdom created a great change in the positions of the then existing militia and volunteers.

The militia, as such, ceased to be raised. The greater number of the existing battalions were converted into special reserve battalions, and the remainder were disbanded. In the Norfolk Regiment the establishment of the Depot was merged in that of the 3rd battalion, which replaced the two former battalions of militia, and, having accepted liability to serve in any part of the world, became part of the first line of Army Reserve. The colours of the 3rd battalion thus constituted bore the same distinctions as those of the 1st and 2nd, the three thus becoming most closely associated. The functions of the 3rd battalion as special reserve in time of war involved mobilization along with the regular reserve, and the supply of drafts to the regular battalions at the front. These functions also entailed on officers and men a training of several months at the commencement of their military career, and in each subsequent year a shorter period of training as a battalion.

Under the new organization the volunteers also disappeared under their old title, and became the territorial battalions of the regiments to which they were attached. They became the second line of the army with the following duties in war:—

(1) To supply garrisons for fortresses and stations at home.
(2) To act as a defensive force against invasion.
(3) By voluntary agreement only, to supply units for the expansion of the expeditionary forces.

The territorial force being organized on a divisional basis like the expeditionary force, it became necessary to raise new corps in some places and to reduce, or redistribute, them in others. Norfolk was called upon to contribute its quota to the East Anglian Division in the shape of two eight-company battalions, each of 1,009 officers and men. As there were four battalions of Norfolk volunteers it became necessary to amalgamate them into two only. This was done by uniting the 1st and 4th volunteer battalions and the 2nd and 3rd into two battalions, which became respectively the 4th and 5th (territorial) Battalions of the Norfolk Regiment.

There was, in addition to these, a 6th (territorial) battalion (cyclists) which requires to be dealt with specially. The following account of it is derived mainly from notes furnished by Colonel Prior, to whom it is greatly indebted for its organization and development.

During the command of Colonel Dawson, from 1891 to 1895, a cyclist company of the 1st volunteer battalion was organized. The example was followed by the other three battalions. From 1900 all four battalions had cyclist companies, and in the Norfolk Volunteer Infantry Brigade, these four companies were formed into a composite battalion at the annual training, and received special training beyond what had hitherto been usual. For this most of the credit is due to the enthusiasm of Lieutenant-Colonel W. H. Besant, then Brigade-Major. Mr. Haldane, in his reforms of 1908, had recognized the value of cyclists in any scheme of defence in a close country like England, and decided to form eleven cyclist battalions, a number which was afterwards increased. Of the original eleven battalions, the 6th Norfolk battalion was one.

As a nucleus it took over from the four disbanded volunteer battalions, four officers and 176 non-commissioned officers and men. The officers were Major B. H. L. Prior of the 1st volunteer battalion, Captains F. S. Ayre of the 3rd, W. E. Salter of the 4th, and Lieutenant S. K. Woodger of the 2nd.

The establishment of the new battalion was fixed at twenty-one officers (including a regular army adjutant) and 480 other ranks, divided into eight companies, each of two officers and fifty-four other ranks, battalion head-quarters, machine-gun section, motor cyclists, and signallers. This establishment varied from time to time, and in the war of 1914–18 was largely increased.

The first commanding officer was Lieutenant-Colonel Prior. At first there were many difficulties. Companies were formed at Norwich, Yarmouth, Lynn, Thetford, Fakenham, and Ditchingham; but till the end of 1908 a regular adjutant and permanent staff instructors had not been appointed. After this there was rapid progress. A drill hall and head-quarters were provided at Norwich by the County Association, and the battalion acquired a very high reputation for efficiency and enthusiasm in the six years preceding the outbreak of the Great War. The general idea of the defence scheme, in so far as it concerned cyclist battalions, was to line the whole eastern and southern coasts with observation posts of cyclists, with supports and a battalion reserve farther inland. In this way it was hoped to get early information of any hostile landing, and to facilitate the concentration on threatened points of the supports and reserves. At first the coast assigned to the 6th Norfolk extended from the Wash to Southwold; but on the formation of the 6th Suffolk Cyclist Battalion the sphere of the Norfolk battalion was restricted to the coast of its own county.

Space will not permit of our transcribing the whole of Colonel Prior's enthusiastic account of the system of training of his battalion. It extended to lengths in the direction of staff rides, machine-gun training and other matters which could only be possible with officers and men alike keen and intelligent. As a final proof of their enthusiasm it may be mentioned that, when their annual training ended in 1914, the battalion resolved to continue their training, so as to be ready for mobilization if and when it was ordered.

The Norfolk Regiment as reorganized in 1908, therefore, consisted, up to the commencement of the Great War of 1914–18, of the following units:—

    1st Battalion,
    2nd Battalion,
    3rd (Special Reserve) Battalion,
    4th (Territorial) Battalion,
    5th (Territorial) Battalion,
    6th (Territorial) Battalion (cyclists).

In October, 1909, King Edward VII reviewed, at Norwich, the whole territorial force of Norfolk and presented colours to the 4th, 5th, and 6th battalions of the Norfolk Regiment. On the regimental colours appeared the battle honour " South Africa, 1900-1902."

The first combined manœuvres of the three territorial battalions were carried out near Sheringham at the end of July, 1910, followed by a twenty-seven-mile march into Norwich, which, especially considering that the men had started work at 7 a.m. was a remarkably fine performance.

In August, 1911, the East Anglian Territorial Division was, for the first time, encamped together near Thetford. They were some 8,000 strong, under the command of Major-General the Hon. J. H. Byng.

The last annual camping, before mobilization for the war of 1914-18, was in Holkham Park, where the Norfolk and Suffolk brigade, about 2,000 strong, under Colonel R. Bayard, D.S.O., was inspected and reviewed by the Earl of Leicester, Lord-Lieutenant of Norfolk. The men had hardly returned to their homes when the mobilization order of July 29, 1914, was issued. As above mentioned, the 6th Norfolk battalion remained on duty till the mobilization.

INDEX

VOL. I

Abercromby, Sir R., 137, 139, 144–146, 148
Afghanistan, 1st Afghan War, 288–309; 2nd Afghan War, 359–366
Albemarle, Countess of, 377
Albemarle, Earl of, 69–79
Alcantara, siege of, 50
Alcira, defence of, 54
Almanza, battle of, 52–54
Arbuthnot, Sir Thomas, 310, 326
"Ariadne," wreck of, 39, 151
Army of Occupation in France, 280, 281
Athlone, Earl of. *See* Ginkel
Athlone, siege of, 24–26
Aughrim, battle of, 26–29
Australia, mission to, 428
Australian 9th Infantry allied to Norfolk Regt., 393

Badajoz, 226, 227
Bainbrigge, General, 327–329
Ballymore, capture of, 22
Barba del Puerco, action at, 223
Barbados, 103, 106, 282
Barham Downs, camp at, 138
Barrosa, battle of, 214–216
Barry, Lieut., 6
Bates, Sir H., Colonel of Regiment, 348
Bayonne, 271; sortie from, 278
Becher, Lt.-Col., 362n., 388, 401, 410, 412
Belleisle, expedition to, 65–68
Bemmis Heights, battle of, 92–94
Bertie, Lt.-General, 136
Berwick, Duke of, 12, 13, 22, 48–54
Bidassoa, passage of (Croix des Bouquets), 265–269
Bloemfontein, 390, 407, 431
Bonaparte, Joseph, 238, 239, 241, 243, 247, 250
Borton, Lt.-Col. C. E., 413–420, 430
Borton, Sir A., 289, 290, 292, 293, 299–306, 313, 319, 320–339, 342, 398
Boyne, battle of, 15–20
Brandfort, action, 410

Brest, expedition to, 34–36
Britannia badge, 62, 136, 153
Browne's battalion at Barrosa, 214–216
Brownrigg, Sir R., Colonel of Regiment, 150, 154, 284, 286
Buchanan, Lt.-Col., 355–359
Burgos, 240; retreat from, 241–244
Burgoyne, General, 85–100
Burton, Lt.-Col., 397
Busaco, battle of, 200–210

Cadiz, 36, 213, 216
Cameron, Sir John, 154, 168, 193, 194, 199, 237, 244, 246, 248, 254–276, 282, 283, 284, 286, 310
Campbell, Colin (Lord Clyde), 155, 168n, 216, 244, 246, 254–256, 268
Campbell, Col. James, 106, 109–112
Canada, 83–85, 279, 280, 343
Cape of Good Hope, 348
Castello de Vide, 48, 49
Casualties of 9th Foot: Irish War, 15, 20, 23, 29; Brest, 35; Almanza, 54; Belleisle, 68; Havana, 77, 78; Saratoga campaign, 90, 91, 93; West Indies, 1794–6, 104, 111, 112, 117, 123, 124, 126, 129; North Holland, 145; Roliça, 162; Corunna retreat, 185; Busaco, 259; Barrosa, 216; Fuentes de Oñoro, 223; Salamanca, 237; Burgos, 240; Villa Muriel, 242; Osma, 246; Vittoria, 250; San Sebastian, 255, 256, 258, 264; Croix des Bouquets, 268; Nive, 272, 276, 277; 1st Afghan War, 296, 300–302, 305, 308, 309; Sikh War, 315, 321; India (1832–1847), 325; Crimea, 339–341; Jowaki expedition, 359; 2nd Afghan War, 363; Chin Hills, 387–396; South African War, 406, 409, 413, 419, 425–427
Cathcart, Lord, Colonel of Regiment, 60
Channel Islands, service in, 132, 348
Charles, Archduke, 41, 51
Cherbourg, 36

Chin Hills, operations, 1892, 385–388 (1st Battalion); 1888, 395–396 (2nd Battalion)
Clausel (French General), 234, 236, 238, 240, 250
Colours and Battle Honours, 62, 63; saved at Saratoga, 99, 100; saved in wreck of "Ariadne," 151, 152; 284, 325–329, 341, 362, 377, (Militia), 383, 384, 390–393, 397, 435 (Territorial Battalions)
Convention Troops (Saratoga), 98–100
Cornwall, Col. H., 1, 2, 7
Corunna, retreat to, 174–181; battle of, 183, 184; evacuation, 185
Crampion, Private, D.S.M., 396
Crawfurd, Lt.-Col., 264
Crimean War, 331–342
Croix des Bouquets. See Bidassoa
Cumming, Lt. J. S., 286, 287, 294, 296
Cunningham, Col. John, 7, 10, 11
Custance, Col., 377, 378

Daunt, Lt.-Col., 320, 351, 353–355, 359, 365
Davis, Lt.-Col., 290, 321
De Bernière, Lt.-Col., 135, 136, 152
Delaborde, French General at Roliça, 158–162
Dieppe, expedition against, 36
Douro, passage of, 195, 196
Drogheda, 14, 15
Duke, Quartermaster-Sergeant, 388
Dundalk, 13

East Norfolk Regiment—title, 63, 100
Echlin, Captain, 12, 13
Edward VII, King, 384, 390–393, 435
Elmhirst, Colonel, 302, 306, 337, 343, 349, 398
Establishment, 2, 3, 4, 5, 6, 7, 32, 33, 40, 42, 46, 58, 59, 60, 61, 64, 65, 80, 81–83, 133, 134, 136, 153, 154, 213, 281, 282, 331, 344, 349, 355
Eyre, General—Attack at Sebastopol, 335–339

Farlow, Captain, 15, 20, 22
Ferozeshah, battle of, 315–321
Ferrol, expedition of 1800, 147, 148
Fisher, Col. Gerrit, 125, 136, 138, 148
Flanders, campaign of, 1702–1704, 41–46
Florida, 79–81
Fort Anne, action at, 89–90
Fuentes de Oñoro, battle of, 220–223

Galway, capture of, 29
Galway, Earl of. See Ruvigny
Gamarra, Mayor, bridge of (Vittoria), 249–250

George V, King, 393, 398
Gibraltar, 61, 197, 213, 217, 348, 383, 431
Ginkel (Earl Athlone), 21, 22, 23, 26, 28, 29, 42
Gloucester, 1, 4, 63
Gomm, Lt.-Col., 120n
Gomm, Sir W., 120n, 138, 139, 141–145, 147–149, 151–163, 171, 185, 208, 212, 224–226, 229, 240, 243, 244, 248, 258, 259, 264, 268
Graham, Sir T. (Lord Lynedoch), 213–216, 245, 248, 249, 251, 253, 256, 263
Grenada, revolt of, 126–131
Grenadier and light companies, 4, 5, 22, 30, 67, 68, 76, 77, 86, 103, 104, 106, 109–115, 118, 120, 121, 122, 140, 142, 156
Grey, Sir C., 104–122
Guadeloupe, 116–122

Hadow, Lieut., 389, 390
Hale, Sergeant (diary quoted), 155n, 161, 166, 171, 174, 181, 183, 190, 200–209, 223, 226, 239, 242, 244, 246–249, 264, 269, 271
Hamilton, Lt.-Col. W. G., 390
Harbord's troop, 14
Hare, Lieut., 398
Hargrave, Col., 61
Harvey, Sir C., 372, 378
Harvey, Lt.-Col. J. R., 379
Havana, siege, 69–79
Hay, Brigadier, 234, 246, 248–250, 262, 273
Hay, Leith, 234
Helder (North Holland), expedition of 1799, 136–147
Hill, Lt.-Col., at Fort Anne, 89–90; keeps colours at Saratoga, 99
Hill, Sir R., 157, 160
Hong-Kong, 349
Hope, Sir John, 269, 271
Hope, Sir James Archibald, 326, 348
Hounslow, camp at, 4, 5
Hunter, Peter, Col., 150, 153n
Hussey, Lt.-Col., 33, 34, 48, 49

Inch (Londonderry), 11, 12
India, 286–326, 356–367, 385–390, 394–397, 431, 432
Ionian Islands, 343–347
Ireland, quarters in, 32, 39, 58, 61, 81–83, 101, 150, 156, 285, 326–330, 348, 349, 354, 355, 399, 400
Irish War (1689–91), 8–13
Istalif action, 305–308

Jagdalak Pass, 300–302, 363, 366
James II, King, 1, 4, 7, 9, 11, 13, 14, 15–20, 41

Japan, 350-354
Jowaki expedition, 356-359
Junot (French General), 157, 163-168

Kane, Brigadier-General R., 60
Karee Siding, 408, 409
Kekewich, General, 414-421
Khyber Pass, 289-296
Kirk, Major-General Percy, 10, 11, 13, 21
Knox, Col. T. E., 349-355

Lacy, Major, 5, 6, 8
Lamb, Sergeant, diary of, 83
Le Fleming papers, 12n
Leith, Sir J., 199-207-226, 234, 235, 258, 265
Le Quesne, Surgeon, V.C., 395, 396
Liège, storming of, 44
Ligonier, Earl, 81, 99
Limerick, 20; 1st siege, 21-23; 2nd siege, 29-31
Lisbon, 47
Londonderry (siege), 9, 10, 11, 12, 13
Luard, Lt.-Col. A. H., 431
Lundy, Col. R., 9, 10

McCaskill, Sir J., 286, 288, 289, 292, 298, 300, 305, 309, 314
Madrid, 51, 239
Mammu Khel action, 298-300
Manners, Col., 136, 138, 139, 146, 148
Marlborough, Duke of, 34, 42, 43, 44, 45
Marmont, Marshal, 224, 227-238
Marriott, Lt.-Col., 391, 392, 414
Martinique, 104-113
Mashonaland, 398, 399
Massena, Marshal, 199, 200, 201, 218-223
Massy, Col., 384, 390
Medows, General, takes company of 9th to India, 99
Militia, 134, 135, 138, 154, 186, 278; early history, 368; West Norfolk, 369-372, 377; East Norfolk, 369, 370, 373-377; in South Africa, 426-428
Minorca, 60
Molle, Lt.-Col., 152, 162
Monmouth's rebellion, 1
Moodkee, battle of, 312-315
Moore, Sir J., 169-184; death and burial, 184, 185; memorial of, 393
Morgan, Sir J., 2
Mounted Infantry at Havana, 72; Somaliland, 389; Mashonaland, 399; South African War, 421-425
Murray, Sir G., address in Canada, 288

Nicholas, Col. O., 7
Nive, battle of the, 270-277
Nivelle, passage of, 269, 270

Orange, Prince of. *See* William III, King
Orford, Earl of, 369, 373, 377
Osma, action near, 246
Oswald, Brig.-General, 248, 258, 265
Otway, Col. James, 60
Otway-Mayne, Major, 364, 396

Paardeberg, 405, 406, 422, 423
Palamos, 37
Peebles, Lt.-Col. E. C., 432
Perry, Lt.-Col., 396
Phillips, Lt.-Col. L. H., 400, 401, 413
Powlett, Col. Sir C., 61
Precedence of British Regiments, 58
Pretoria, 410-413
Prior, Lt.-Col. B. H. L., 433, 434
Purcell, Lt.-Col. James, 2, 6, 7, 8

Rangoon, 385-388
Reade, Brig.-General G., 61
Rey (French General), 251, 256, 258, 263, 264
Richards, Col. S., 10, 11
Roliça, battle of, 158-163
Rooival action, 419
Ross, Major-General C., 421-424
Ruvigny (Earl of Galway), 28, 49, 50-54

St. Croix (French General), 66-68
St. Kitts, 103
St. Lucia, 113-115, 119, 123-126
St. Ruth (French General), 23, 25, 26-28
Salamanca, 169, 170, 228, 229; battle, 231-237
Saldanha Bay, 348
San Bartolomeo Convent, storming of, 253-255
San Sebastian, siege of, 251-264
Saratoga, campaign, 85-97
Sarsfield, 22
Saye and Sele, Lord, 100
Schomberg, Count, 13, 14, 16, 17
Schomberg, Count Mainhard (Duke of Leinster), 17, 48, 49
Shales, Commissionary-General, 14
Shepherd, Lt.-Col., 396, 397, 400
Shooting prizes gained, 399
Signallers in China, 388, 389
Sikh War, 310-326
Sobraon, battle of, 322-325
Solms, Count, 20, 33
Somaliland, 389
Souham (French General), 241-243
Soult, Marshal, 172-174, 177-185, 192-197, 241, 242, 270, 272, 273, 277, 278
South Africa, 390, 400-431
South African War, 401-431
Spanish Succession, War of the, 41, 47-56
Stacy, Brig.-General, 307, 308
Story, Rev. G. W., 14, 29

Steuart, General W., Colonel of Regiment, 2, 11, 12, 13, 15, 22, 23, 24, 28, 32, 33, 36, 37, 59, 60
Steuart, Lt.-Col. W. (junior), 54
Stuart, Lt.-Col. John, 152, 156
Suttie, Captain, 72, 152, 156

Talmash, General, 28, 31, 34, 36
Tarifa, 213, 217
Tarragona, 217
Taylor, Col., 284, 288–296, 298, 302, 303, 319
Territorial battalions, 432–435
Tezeen Pass, action in, 302–305
Three Rivers, action at, 84
Tibet, expedition, 389, 390
Ticonderoga, 87, 88
Title of Regiment, 1, 63, 100, 368
Tobago, 103, 104, 282, 283
Torres Vedras, lines of, 210–212, 218

Uniform, 62, 63 ; 379 (Militia) ; 381, 382 (Volunteer) ; 390

Vaughan, Sir J., 123, 126
Victoria, Queen, 398

Villa Muriel, action of, 241, 242
Vimeiro, battle of, 163–168
Vittoria, advance to, 245–246 ; battle of, 247–250
Volunteers, 379–382, 411, 428–430

Walcheren expedition, 186–190
Waldegrave, Hon. J., 61
Wellesley, Sir A. *See* Wellington
Wellington, Duke of, 156–158, 163–166, 169, 192–212, 218–247, 248, 250, 251, 261, 269
Weser expedition of 1805, 150–152
West Indies, 103–131, 282, 283
West Norfolk Regiment, 101*n*
Whitmore, Colonel of Regiment, 77, 81
William III, King, 7, 9, 11, 15–20, 39, 40, 41, 42
Wintour, Lt.-Col., 431
Worcestershire Regiment (29th Foot), 160–162

Yorke, Sir Joseph, 64

Zuurfontein action, 413

NOTES

It is suggested that all Battalions, the Depôt, and individual possessors of this book should here note errors or omissions, and any material bearing on these records which had not come to hand before publication. Also other matter for future record.

If, in course of time, a third volume should be contemplated such notes would greatly simplify the work of writing future history.

Errors or omissions in these volumes could be noted in an Appendix of the 3rd Volume without disturbing the present edition.

W.H.B.

www.ingramcontent.com/pod-product-compliance
Lightning Source LLC
Chambersburg PA
CBHW060416300426
44111CB00018B/2866